# BECOMING THE BUDDHA

BUDDHISMS:

A PRINCETON UNIVERSITY PRESS SERIES

EDITED BY STEPHEN F. TEISER

*A list of titles in this series appears at the back of the book*

# BECOMING THE BUDDHA

## THE RITUAL OF IMAGE CONSECRATION IN THAILAND

*Donald K. Swearer*

PRINCETON UNIVERSITY PRESS

PRINCETON AND OXFORD

PUBLISHED BY PRINCETON UNIVERSITY, 41 WILLIAM STREET,
PRINCETON, NEW JERSEY 08540
IN THE UNITED KINGDOM: PRINCETON UNIVERSITY PRESS,
3 MARKET PLACE, WOODSTOCK, OXFORDSHIRE 0X20 1SY


LIBRARY OF CONGRESS CATALOGING-IN-PUBLICATION DATA

SWEARER, DONALD K., 1934–
BECOMING THE BUDDHA : THE RITUAL OF IMAGE CONSECRATION IN
THAILAND / DONALD K. SWEARER.
P. CM. —(BUDDHISMS)
INCLUDES BIBLIOGRAPHICAL REFERENCES AND INDEX.
ISBN: 0-691-11435-8
1. ABHISEKA (BUDDHIST RITE) 2. BUDDHISM—THAILAND—RITUALS. 3. THERAVADA
BUDDHISM—RITUALS—HISTORY. I. TITLE. II. SERIES.
BQ4990.T4S98 2004
294.3'438—DC21 2003048222
BRITISH LIBRARY CATALOGING-IN-PUBLICATION DATA IS AVAILABLE
THIS BOOK HAS BEEN COMPOSED IN SABON
PRINTED ON ACID-FREE PAPER. ∞
www.pupress.princeton.edu
PRINTED IN THE UNITED STATES OF AMERICA
1 3 5 7 9 10 8 6 4 2

*To Family Both Absent and Present*

MY PARENTS, ELOISE AND EDWARD, AND

BROTHERS, BILL AND HOWARD

AND TO NANCY, SUSAN, AND STEPHEN

SOME BEING devoutly disposed, will make the image of this God at their own charge. For the making whereof they must bountifully reward the Founder. Before the eyes are made it is not accounted a God, but a lump of ordinary metal, and thrown about the shop with no more regard than anything else. But when the eyes are to be made, the artificer is to have a good gratification, besides the first agreed upon reward. The eyes being formed, *it is thenceforward a God.* And then, being brought with honour from the workman's shop, it is dedicated by solemnities and sacrifices, and carried with great state into its shrine or little house, which is before built and prepared for it.

—Robert Knox, *An Historical Relation of Ceylon*

# CONTENTS

*List of Illustrations* xiii

*Preface* xv

*Note and Abbreviations* xvii

PART I

INTRODUCTION 3

CHAPTER 1. BUDDHA AND BUDDHA IMAGE 9
The Power of Images 10
The Buddha Image in Northern Thailand 12
Scriptural Accounts of the First Buddha Image 14
The Buddha Image: An Art Historical Perspective 24

CHAPTER 2. MEETING THE BUDDHA: TEMPLE, IMAGE, AND RELIC 31
*Wat,* Reliquary, and Buddha Image 31
Reliquary and Image: Correlative Signs of the Buddha's Presence 35
Buddha Image and *Wat:* Nature and Function 40
Consecration and Renewal 42

CHAPTER 3. CONSTRUCTING A BUDDHA IMAGE 46
Bronze Image Manufacture in Northern Thailand 46
Texts 50
*Tamrā Kān Kosāng Phraphuttharūp* (Manual for Making a Buddha Image) 50
*Ānisong Kān Kosāng Phraphuttharūp* (The Meritorious Blessing for Making Buddha Images) 60
*Yan Phraphuttharūp* (Buddha Image *Yantra*) 63
Analysis 68

PART II

CHAPTER 4. THE RITUAL: OPENING THE EYES OF THE BUDDHA 77
The Setting 79
The *Bodhimaṇḍa* 79
Offerings to the *Guru* 83
The Ritual Process 86
Preliminaries 86
*Paritta* and Image Consecration 88
Texts 90

*Buddhajayamaṅgala Aṭṭhagāthā* (The Auspicious Victory) 90
*Dasa Pāramī* (The Ten Perfections) 91
*Sukho Buddho* (Happiness Is the Buddha) 92
*Jinapañjara Gāthā* (The Victor's Cage) 92
*Paritta* and *Abhiseka* 93
Opening the Eyes of the Buddha 94
Sermons: Ordaining the Buddha 96
The Performative Power of Meditation and Holy Monks 99
The Third Watch of the Night 102
Texts 107
*Maṅgala Udāna Gāthā* (Stanzas of Auspicious Joy) 107
*Yo Kho Ānanda* (O Ānanda) 107
*Buddhānussati* (Remembering the Buddha) 107
Making the Buddha Present 108
Appendix 4.1 *Paritta* and *Suat Mon* 115
Appendix 4.2 Monastic Biographies: Luang Pū Lā, Luang Pū Wāen, Khrūbā Phrohm 118

CHAPTER 5. INSTRUCTING THE IMAGE 122
Introduction and Analysis 122
Texts 129
*Pathom Somphōt* (The Buddha's Supreme Enlightenment) 129
*Ānisong Pathom Somphōt* (The Meritorious Blessing for Copying or Listening to the *Pathom Somphōt*) 137
*Sitthāt Ōk Buat* (Siddhattha's Renunciation) 138

CHAPTER 6. EMPOWERING THE IMAGE 152
Introduction and Analysis 152
Texts 156
*Buddha Abhiseka* (Consecrating the Buddha) 156
*Suat Bōek Phranet* (Opening the Eyes of the Buddha) 164

## PART III

CHAPTER 7. THE BODY OF THE BUDDHA: POPULAR BUDDHISM AND BUDDHOLOGICAL THEORY 175
Buddhas: Past, Present, and Future 176
Buddha-body and Dhamma-body 184
Buddha Images, Kings, and Power 192
Texts 197
*Tamnān Kā Phū'ak* (The Chronicle of the White Crow) 197
*Tamnān Phra Silā* (The Chronicle of the Stone Buddha Image) 205

CHAPTER 8. CONSECRATION TRADITIONS IN OTHER BUDDHIST CULTURES: REASSESSING THE *BUDDHĀBHISEKA* 211
Auspicious Eyes: Enlivening the Image 212
Dhammicization: Image and Reality 218
Transformation: *Sādhana* 222
Syncretization: Buddha, Gods, and Ancestral Spirits 224
Conclusion: Stories and Saints, Icons and Images 230
Appendix 8.1 Hindu or Buddhist? 232

EPILOGUE: IF YOU MEET THE BUDDHA, KILL HIM! 235
P. A. Payutto (Phra Dhammapiṭaka) 238
*Sacred Objects, Efficacious Deities, and Miracles* 239
Buddhadāsa Bhikkhu 242
Who Sees Me Sees the *Dhamma* 243
Everyday Language/*Dhamma* Language 244
Phra Bodhirak and Santi Asok 246

*NOTES* 249

*GLOSSARY OF SELECTED PĀLI AND THAI TERMS* 299

*SELECTED BIBLIOGRAPHY* 303

*INDEX* 321

# LIST OF ILLUSTRATIONS


| | | |
|---|---|---|
| Frontis. | Candle-illuminated Buddha image consecration ritual | |
| 1. | Image of Khrūbā Phrohm | 10 |
| 2. | Mural of Sujātā offering milk rice to the Buddha | 32 |
| 3. | Diagram of Wat Haripuñjaya | 34 |
| 4. | Chedī. Wat Phrathāt Doi Suthep | 39 |
| 5. | Carving a wax Buddha image mold | 48 |
| 6. | *Yantra* plaques | 51 |
| 7.a. | Buddha image *yantras,* northern Thai script | 65 |
| 7.b. | Buddha image *yantras,* roman script | 66 |
| 8. | Covering the eyes of a Buddha image | 78 |
| 9. | *Bodhimaṇḍa* | 80 |
| 10. | *Maṇḍala* design over *bodhimaṇḍa* | 82 |
| 11. | Offerings to the *guru (khan wai khrū)* | 84 |
| 12. | Monks chanting the *suat bōek* | 95 |
| 13. | Preaching a sermon | 97 |
| 14. | Laymen meditating | 100 |
| 15. | Luang Pū Lā receiving a *dāna* offering | 101 |
| 16. | *Māe Chī* preparing milk rice | 103 |
| 17. | Forty-nine bowls of milk rice offered to Buddha images | 103 |
| 18. | Newly consecrated Buddha images | 105 |
| 19. | The *abhiseka* of Buddha images | 105 |
| 20. | Luang Pū Lā blessing congregants and images | 106 |
| 21. | Water pouring ritual *(truat nām)* | 106 |

# PREFACE

I FIRST ATTENDED a Buddha image consecration ceremony *(buddhābhiseka)* in 1977. My teacher of northern Thai, the late Āchān Singkha Wannasai, the doyen of northern Thai language and literature, was the lay ritual leader *(āchān wat)* for the event and suggested that I accompany him. Much of what I have learned about northern Thai Buddhism I owe to Āchān Singkha. I acknowledge my debt to his guidance and, in particular, for introducing me to the ceremony. My brief exposure to the ritual convinced me of its importance and inherent interest for an understanding of northern Thai Buddhism.

It was not until 1986 that I began specific research on the *buddhābhiseka* ceremony. During that year I studied two of the texts associated with the ritual in collaboration with Āchān Manī Phayomyong and Āchān Sommai Premchit, now emeritus professors in the Chiang Mai University faculties of education and social sciences, respectively. I also accompanied Āchān Manī to an image consecration ceremony at Wat Mū'ang Man in Chiang Mai, where he presented gifts *(waen thān)* to the monks on behalf of the assembled laity. His knowledge of northern Thai Buddhist traditions has been an especially important resource for this study, and he was my principal informant on the reading of *Sitthāt Ōk Buat* (Siddhattha's Renunciation) included in this work.

My research continued during my 1989–90 sabbatical leave in Chiang Mai with a subsequent visit in 1994, collaborating principally with Āchān Sommai, Āchān Manī, the late Āchān Bumphen Rawin, then chair of the Department of Thai Language and Literature at Chiang Mai University, and Phaitun Dokbuakaew of the archive division of the university's Social Research Institute. I read the *Tamnān Kā Phū'ak* (The Chronicle of the White Crow) and the *Pathom Somphōt* (The Buddha's First Enlightenment) with Phaitun. Āchān Sommai's expertise in Pāli, northern Thai, and Lao as well as his general knowledge of Thai Buddhism has made his assistance invaluable. Although I am responsible for the descriptive and analytical sections of this book, I am grateful for Āchān Sommai's assistance on Pāli text translation, especially the *Suat Bōek Phranet* (The Eye-Opening Sutta), our collaboration on the *Buddha Abhiseka,* and his comments on other texts included in the volume.

In 1989–90 I observed four northern image consecration ceremonies, two in Chiang Mai, one in Lamphūn, and one in Chiang Rai, as well as one central Thai ritual performed in Phuket. Phra Khrū Prachak of Wat Sāen Fāng, Chiang Mai, officiated at four of the ceremonies and willingly shared his knowledge of the *buddhābhiseka* ritual. During a visit to Myanmar and Laos in 1990, my conversations about the ceremony with scholars and monks in both countries were useful for comparison purposes.

Over the several years of this project I have consulted numerous scholars in England, Europe, the United States, and Sri Lanka, in particular, Yael Bentor, Anne Blackburn, Helen Bondi, Heinz Braun, Bryon Earhart, Louis Gabaude, Robert Gimello, Lilian Handlin, Norvin Hein, Charles Hallisey, Steven Hopkins, Mei-huang Lee, Donald S. Lopez Jr., Hwang-soo Kim, Punchi Megaskumbhara, Udaya Meddegama, Robert Sharf, H. Daniel Smith, Peter Skilling, and Kevin Trainor. I am especially indebted to Thanissaro Bhikkhu (Geoffrey DeGraff), Frank E. Reynolds, and John S. Strong for their careful reading of the entire manuscript and their extensive critical suggestions and recommendations. Finally, I wish to thank the students in my fall 2000 Harvard Divinity School seminar, "The Buddha in Image, Myth, and Ritual," for moving this project toward completion.

For their support of my research in northern Thailand I wish to thank Swarthmore College and Eugene M. Lang, the Council for the International Exchange of Scholars (Fulbright Program), the John Simon Guggenheim Foundation, and the National Endowment for the Humanities.

For her careful editing of each draft and preparing the index I am grateful to Nancy Chester Swearer. For the many kindnesses and generous help received from friends and colleagues who supported and expedited my work in Thailand, Myanmar, and Laos I acknowledge with thanks, in particular John and Martha Butt in Chiang Mai, Ratana Tungsavadi in Bangkok, and Robert Schmidt in Myanmar.

# NOTE AND ABBREVIATIONS

Transliteration of Pāli follows standard convention; transliteration of Thai follows ALA-LC romanization with the following exceptions: ch instead of čh (e.g., *chao* not *čhao*); e instead of ē (e.g., *phranet* not *phranēt*); o instead of ǫ (e.g., *mon* not *mǫn*). In some cases place or proper nouns follow standard usage. Pāli terms are sometimes transcribed in Pāli, for example, *devatā, cetiya,* and others in Thai, for example, *thewadā, chedī,* depending on the context.

| | |
|---|---|
| A | *Aṅguttara Nikāya* |
| AA | *Aṅguttara-Aṭṭhakathā* |
| BA | *Buddha Abhiseka* |
| BEFEO | *Bulletin de l'École française d'Extrême-Orient* |
| Bv | *Buddhavaṃsa* |
| BvA | *Buddhavaṃsa-Aṭṭhakathā* |
| Cp | *Cariyapiṭaka* |
| D | *Dīgha Nikāya* |
| DhA | *Dhammapada-Aṭṭhakathā* |
| EFEO | *École française d'Extrême-Orient* |
| It | *Itivuttaka* |
| Ja | *Jātaka* |
| JA | *Jātaka-Aṭṭhakathā* |
| Jinak | *Jinakālamālīpakaraṇaṃ* |
| KBV | *Kosala-Bimba-Vaṇṇanā* |
| Mhv | *Mahāvaṃsa* |
| M | *Majjhima Nikāya* |
| MLV | *Mālālaṅkāravatthu* |
| Ja-nidāna | *Nidānakathā* |
| Paṭis | *Paṭisambhidāmagga* |
| PS | *Paṭhama Sambodhi* (Thai, *Pathom Somphōt*) |
| PSL | *Pathom Somphōt Lānnā* |
| PST | *Pathom Somphōt Thet (desanā)* |
| S | *Saṃyutta Nikāya* |
| SB | *Sitthāt Ōk Buat* |
| TKP | *Tamnān Kā Phū'ak* |
| TPS | *Tamnān Phra Silā* |
| ThagA | *Theragāthā-Aṭṭhakathā* |
| SBN | *Suat Bōek Phranet* |
| Vism | *Visuddhimagga* |

## DATES

B.C.E = Before Common Era
C.E. = Common Era
C.S. = Culasakarāja
B.E. = Buddhist Era

# PART I

Candle-illuminated Buddha image consecration ritual.
Wat Mū'ang Man, Chiang Mai, Thailand.

# INTRODUCTION

THE GREAT WORLD RELIGIONS focus on one or more central figures who may be divine, human, or some combination thereof. What would Buddhism be without the Buddha Gotama, Islam without Muhammad, Christianity without Jesus the Christ? It is unimaginable. Myth and ritual, creed and philosophy derive from or point toward these extraordinary and often supermundane figures. This study explores a specific dimension of this central feature of the world's great religions using as its referent the Theravāda Buddhist tradition as it developed in the Chiang Mai valley of northern Thailand. Specifically, it examines the Buddha image consecration ceremony and its Buddhological significance within popular northern Thai religious thought and practice.

In the *Mahāparinibbāna Sutta,* the Buddha explains to his beloved disciple, Ānanda, that after the Blessed One's death the *dhamma* and *vinaya* will be his disciples' teacher (D II.154). This passage is frequently cited out of context to support several doctrines considered to be quintessentially Theravādin, in particular, that the Buddha was an enlightened being but not to be revered as divine; that he was to be respected as a teacher of the *dhamma* but was not to be become an object of attachment. In this study the lessons derived from popular Buddhist thought and practice in northern Thailand appear to be diametrically opposed to such views. The Buddha that emerges through the medium of the image becomes a grantor of boons, and the Buddha's teaching about nonattachment falls victim to an obsessive preoccupation with sacred objects revered for their protective potency and economic value.

Are we, then, witness to two oppositional forms of Buddhism—an "original" monastic worldview of high moral philosophy and spiritual practice versus a thoroughly compromised, if not debased, tradition of magical expectation? Such a dichotomy is the projection of the logical mind uncomfortable with the incongruities within religious thought and practice, and the creation of Buddhist apologists whose relatively narrow view of a nontheistic, rationalistic Buddhism appeals to the modern mind. But the lived tradition of Buddhism, like all classical religions, is not so tidy. It teems with paradox, myth, legend, and symbol not so easily rationalized into a logical system. The seeming oppositions and paradoxes found in the Buddha image consecration ceremony reflect a dialectic at the very core of Buddhism between the ideal of an ultimate personal transformation and the need to address the entire range of life experiences bracketed by birth and death. This dialectic is reflected in distinctions that permeate the tradition between the mundane (*lokiya*) and transmundane (*lokuttara*), and applies to the person of the Buddha himself: human and supernatural, teacher of the *dhamma,* miracle worker, grantor of boons. Indeed, the *Mahāparinibbāna Sutta* incorporates these several views of the Buddha in a single text and exhorts the Buddha's followers not only to honor the *dhamma* but to venerate the Buddha's bodily remains (*sarīradhātu*).

This study of the Buddha image consecration ceremony in northern Thailand brings together a wide range of meanings of the person of the Buddha both explicit and implicit in this richly complex ritual. On one level the ceremony provides a fascinating arena for a study of the relationship between myth and ritual. The distinctive texts chanted and preached during the nightlong proceedings represent various episodes in the mythic, legendary life of the Buddha. The meaning of the Buddha story is enhanced as episodes of the sacred biography are correlated with successive phases of the image consecration ritual.

On another level this study explores Theravāda Buddhology within the context of popular practice by examining the content of particular texts chanted and preached during the ceremony. The integration of text and context provides a more nuanced picture of the Buddha at the center of a living Buddhist tradition. At the same time, the texts and the ritual that define the contemporary northern Thai Buddhist ceremony invite comparison with other Buddhist traditions past and present. Cross-cultural comparisons among Buddhist and Hindu/Brahmanical traditions further illuminate the Buddhological significance of the northern Thai ceremony while challenging certain textbook distinctions between Theravāda/Hīnayāna, Mahāyāna, and Vajrayāna views of the nature of the Buddha.

The texts chanted and/or preached in the ritual have connections to Pāli canonical and extracanonical Buddha biographical material. For example, the *Paṭhama Sambodhi* (The Buddha's Supreme Enlightenment) has a much longer literary form in both its Pāli and northern Thai versions. But within the context of the Buddha image consecration ceremony the text is adapted to its use and function rather than as a written text or a literary document per se. Just as the story of the Buddha "takes place" within a given physical, religious, and social context, so also the sacred biography "takes form" in an image of the founder.

Through the image, the life of the Buddha assumes a present reality not simply as a reminder of a sacred story but as a physical representative of the story's protagonist. The inseparable connection between the image and the sacred biography within the context of the ritual suggests that the historical development of the Buddha image and the Buddha story may have been closely connected from the very beginning. No attempt will be made to prove such an assertion, but this study suggests this possibility. One of the major functions of the Buddha image consecration ceremony is to instruct the image in the life story of the person the image represents. If both Buddha biographies and Buddha images developed around the first century C.E., then it may be reasonable to see in their joint emergence not only the motive force for Buddhist devotional sentiment, but the raison d'être for a ritual with the performative power to create a living representation of the *tathāgata*. The consecration ceremony, however altered over time and space, has fused the person and story of the Buddha with the image of the Blessed One in, as some would claim, a most miraculous way.

The consecration ceremony contextualizes and contemporizes the life story of the Buddha. The Blessed One comes to life as do other characters in the story such as the mythic Māra and the female devotee, Sujātā. By contemporizing a mythic time, the image consecration ritual connects the Buddha with other ritualized heroes past and present: with the pious Phra Mālai and the noble Prince Vessantara, whose lives are often celebrated concurrently with the consecration of a Buddha image; a young man being ordained into the monkhood, whose begging bowl is filled with small Buddha images and amulets; or, the senior monk elevated in ecclesiastical rank, whose consecration ceremony and that of a Buddha image coincide.

The Buddha also lives in the form of particular Buddha images that have their own sacred stories (*tamnān*). Some of these images, such as the Emerald Buddha in Bangkok, have a special relationship with kings. Others, like the Lion Buddha image of Chiang Mai processed through the city streets to bring rain during the annual New Year celebration, have a power derived from an association with nature as well as royalty. The Buddha also lives through his images and ceremonies that empower/consecrate him as the redeemer of macrocosmic time—those Buddhas of the past eons, Dipaṅkara, Kassapa; of the present age, Gotama Buddha; and of the future, Metteyya—and of personal or microcosmic time, the birthday Buddha images of the days of the week. In these ways the Buddha image contextualizes and contemporizes the person of the Buddha.

The consecration ceremony establishes a common thread of meaning inherent in most Buddhist rituals by connecting the founder with past and present, the dead and the living. Two designations given to the ritual illustrate this generalized significance: "eye opening" (*bōek phranet*) and "consecration" (*abhiseka*). To open the eyes of a Buddha image is to enliven it, to bring it to life, to make it present, to instill it with power. Within the context of Buddhist ritual and ceremonial practice, to *abhiseka* means to consecrate by pouring water or lustrating. At the deepest level, *abhiseka* not only makes sacred in the sense of purifying, but it also recreates and makes new as symbolized by the life-giving force of water. To *abhiseka,* then, is to focus and disseminate power, the power of the sacred, the holy, the divine, indeed, the power of life. An abhiseked image or an amulet of the Buddha, a royal personage, or a holy monk possesses such power. Yet, *abhiseka* permeates all aspects of life, as does water itself—a teenager reverently pouring water over the hands of parents, relatives, and teachers at Thai New Year; a monk sprinkling a water blessing on assembled congregants with a grass whisk; a lay practitioner anointing a *cetiya* enshrining sacred relics at a monastery's annual celebration. Beyond the image or the ritual, then, *abhiseka* conveys an attitude toward life that conjoins a belief in the magical power or potent efficacy of particular objects, such as Buddha images, amulets, and relics, with a more profound sense of the sacred that unites and makes meaningful a world often experienced as threatening and chaotic.

Most Buddhist rituals in Theravāda Buddhist Asia begin with taking refuge in the Buddha. Modern critics and reformers of Theravāda Buddhism in Thailand, such as Buddhadāsa Bhikkhu, Phra Dhammapiṭaka, and the Santi Asok movement with whom I conclude this study, argue that "taking refuge" does not mean relying on the Buddha in the sense that a Christian might rely on God's grace or a Hindu might appeal to the intervention of Viṣṇu or Śiva. Although Christian and Hindu theological presuppositions differ radically from normative or orthodox Theravāda Buddhology, the Buddha that emerges from this study reveals a tremendously complex set of meanings embedded in the simple affirmation, "I take refuge in the Buddha" (*buddhaṃ saranaṃ gacchāmi*).

I have organized this study into three parts. The first, chapters 1–3, is an extended prolegomena to the Buddha image consecration ritual. It includes a discussion of the Buddha image from literary and historical standpoints—the story of making the first image and art historical debates about the appearance of Buddha images (chapter 1); a description of the temple-monastery (*wat*), the most common physical and ritual setting for larger than life-size freestanding images of the Buddha with special attention to the relationship between reliquary and image (chapter 2); and an analysis of the construction of the image itself (chapter 3). The second part begins with an extended ethnography of the *buddhābhiseka* ritual as performed in northern Thailand, supplemented by an analysis of the hermeneutic of presence in recent Buddhological studies (chapter 4). The two subsequent chapters develop this descriptive analysis of the ritual in terms of its two most prominent components—programming the image with the story of the Buddha, in particular, the night of the Blessed One's enlightenment which the ritual reenacts (chapter 5); and the ritual empowerment of the image, in which the supernal qualities of the Buddha are infused into the image (chapter 6). The final part brings two different interpretative perspectives to bear on the meaning of the *buddhābhiseka* ritual and the Buddha image: chapter 7 analyzes the *buddhābhiseka* for its rich Buddhological potential; chapter 8 examines thematic commonalities among consecration rituals in several Buddhist traditions and the most distinctive features of the northern Thai *buddhābhiseka* that emerge from this study. Since the very existence as well as the nature and meaning of material reminders of the Buddha have been much contested, I conclude with a brief consideration of contemporary Thai Buddhist aniconic dissenters.

*Becoming the Buddha* focuses on a particular ritual in northern Thai Buddhism. Because the ritual connects with many other elements in the teachings and practice of Buddhism, the study has broader implications for our understanding of Buddhism and of other religious systems as well. One of these implications is the complex, multivalent set of meanings ascribed to the absent founder of a religious tradition and its saints made present in material signs.

# 1

# BUDDHA AND BUDDHA IMAGE

THE GREEKS INVENTED the myth of Narcissus to illustrate the folly of self-love. However, this moral lesson obscures an equally important truth presumed by the story—the power of an image. We, the readers, often overlook or disregard this truth. If the hearer or reader identifies with Narcissus, the moral of the story is lost. We understand the moral tragedy of mistaken self-love because we have privileged access to Narcissus's assumption that his reflected image is a person. But if we put ourselves in Narcissus's place, the point of the story shifts from mistaken self-love to the putative reality of an image: the image perceived by Narcissus is not a mere reflection or a symbol but Narcissus himself.

The nature of the relationship between image and reality—or, more precisely, between material objects such as icons, images, and relics and the holy persons or the divine beings they represent—has been continually at the heart of religious controversy. Consider the priestly critique of Ba'al image worship in the Hebrew scriptures, the iconoclastic controversy that divided Christendom in the ninth century, or Orthodox Islam's abhorrence of any image that might compromise Allah's sovereign, transcendent perfection. Even Hinduism and other polytheistic traditions cannot agree on iconographic representation of the divine being, and the proposition that early Buddhism was aniconic as a reflection of its nontheistic nature is being challenged as a construction of late-nineteenth/early-twentieth-century scholarship that obscured an earlier Buddhist iconic tradition.

What has been a defining theme in the history of religious doctrine and practice has become a subject of considerable current scholarly interest. Studies by art historians and historians of religions, in particular, have ranged from broadly comparative interpretations of material representations as subjects of power to culture-specific descriptions of particular images and rituals of image consecration. This study of the Buddha image consecration ritual in northern Thailand addresses a fundamental set of polarities in the history of religious thought and practice between image and reality, presence and absence, mundane and transmundane within the historical context of Buddhism, its cultural environment of northern Thailand, and the context of contemporary scholarship.

## The Power of Images

In 1973 I visited a monastery in northern Thailand, Wat Phraphuttha-bāttākphā (The Place Where the Buddha Dried His Robes and Left a Footprint), located in Lamphūn Province about 40 kilometers southwest of Chiang Mai, Thailand's second largest city. The highly revered abbot of this monastery was well known for his strict adherence to the *vinaya* and his accomplishments in meditation.[1] The monks began their daily regimen with meditation at 4:00 A.M. and closed the day with a final evening meditation following the communal chanting ceremony. An aura of tranquil equanimity characterized the abbot's demeanor, habits, and actions, lending credibility to testimonials of his extraordinary spiritual attainments.

In 1994 I returned to Wat Phraphutthabāttākphā, six years after the abbot's death and cremation on January 30, 1988. Although he was deceased, his presence was still palpably felt. In the preaching hall, life-size bronze statues of the abbot flank the central Buddha image and his large color portrait hangs on the wall. Here, too, are found bronze images of the abbot and his offering bowl to receive donations. At the entrance to the preaching hall one can buy color pictures of the abbot, medallions embossed with his image, his biography, books of his teachings, as well

1. Image and portrait of Khrūbā Phrohm. Wat Phraphutthabāttākphā, Pāsāng, Thailand.

as audiotapes of his *dhamma* talks that are broadcast over loudspeaker for all to hear. A newly constructed *chedī*[2] enshrining the abbot's bodily ashes overlooks the monastery grounds from the vantage point of a small hill that dominates the area. In these ways the abbot is represented by the four classifications of relics associated with the Buddha and Buddhist saints: bodily artifacts, and artifacts of use, remembrance, and teaching.

My experience at Wat Phraphutthabāttākphā in 1994 was distinctive but hardly unique. Even though the meaning and function of images and other material representations of persons revered as holy or divine are historically and culturally specific, they also share commonalities with the nature and use of such material representations found in other religious and cultural traditions. Two are especially pertinent.[3]

*Representation and resemblance.* My visits to Wat Phraphutthabāttākphā recall King Pasenadi's experience related in the *Kosala-Bimba-Vaṇṇanā* (KBV), a thirteenth-century text compiled in Sri Lanka, written to explain the occasion for the construction of the first Buddha image. When the abbot was alive, I went to the monastery for *darśan,* to meet the abbot and to be in his presence in much the same way that King Pasenadi journeyed with his entourage to see the Buddha. Even though the abbot had been deceased for six years, at the time of my second visit he was not absent. He was present through a variety of material representations, first and foremost his image. As I entered the monastery I joined dozens of devotees who placed flowers, incense, and candles before his lifelike statue. We sat in quiet contemplation for some time, gazing on the image, before climbing the hill crowned by the *chedī* that contained his bodily ashes, circumambulating the saint's holy relics, and meditating before a Buddha image in a small chapel located nearby.

The aura of the abbot permeates the entire *wat* compound. Many pilgrims and devotees who knew the abbot when he was living remember his presence. However, the aura of his presence depends not only on memory but also on various material reminders, especially the abbot's image: "The aura of the living presence can never be wholly dispelled in the case of the resembling image."[4] A figure resembling human form enables the "reconstitution of life"; it makes "the absent present and the dead alive."[5] For King Pasenadi the resembling image that engendered his devotion acted as the ritual surrogate of the Buddha. Similarly, metonymically the verisimilitude between the statue and the abbot of the *wat* coalesces signified and sign. The image's resemblance to the person of the abbot, confirmed in memory by those who knew him and by photograph for those who did not, enhances the representational power of the image: "what is represented becomes fully present, indeed representation is subsumed by presence."[6] A religious image or photograph is not merely a copy of original; it is in ontological communion with the original.[7] Cognitively, aura or presence may be expressed in ontological terms, but at the affective level it is simply felt. It is an emotional as well as a cognitive experience. It is felt in our hearts and sinews as well as grasped by our minds.[8]

*Efficaciousness.* Belief in the effectiveness of religious images results from the affective cognition of the ontological communion between sign and signified. This efficaciousness or power may be indicated by supernatural stories of origin or miraculous feats attributed to the image.[9] Efficaciousness also derives from rituals of consecration and empowerment, the focus of this study. In addition, the effectiveness of an image derives from an identification between the beholder and the reality the image re-presents, coupled with the belief that contemplation of the image can lead to personal transformation.[10] Efficaciousness, therefore, is a quality understood to be not only inherent or sui generis to the image, but also dependent on the relationship between the beholder and the object of contemplation. By immersing oneself in the image, the beholder awakens to an intractable reality beyond the "civilized code of perfect illusions."[11]

## The Buddha Image in Northern Thailand

Observers of Thai Buddhism are inevitably impressed by the ubiquitousness of the Buddha image. Thirty-five years ago Luang Boribal Buribhand observed, "Perhaps more than any other country in the world, Thailand is the land of Buddha images"; and in her recent study of Thai Buddha images Dorothy Fickle remarks, "A visitor to a Buddhist country such as Thailand is soon overwhelmed by the number and variety of images of the Buddha encountered throughout the nation."[12] With few exceptions every monastery (Thai, *wat* )[13] displays images in its principal buildings, inside niches of large *chedī*s, or placed under *bodhi* trees. Most homes and businesses display a *pūjā* shelf or altar for Buddha images; amulet and image vendors hawk their wares on street corners, and popular religious magazines headline stories of their miraculous powers.

Buddha images and amulets pervade popular Thai religious culture, but imaging the Buddha is not a modern phenomenon. There never was a time when the Buddha was not imag(in)ed in story, myth, symbol, or a material form. Freestanding Buddha images that begin to appear in India by the first century of our era should not be understood as evidence of the sudden emergence of a popular Buddha cult. Rather, these statues reflect a complex, ongoing interaction of philosophical and historical factors that shaped Buddhist devotion from the very beginning. The still widely held view that the devotional piety of Indian peasants degraded the ethical rationalism of an "original" Buddhism does not stand up to historical scrutiny or the logic of religious piety.[14]

Many Western scholars and modern Buddhist apologists have depicted the Buddha as a spiritual virtuoso defined primarily by his enlightenment and downplay his supernatural powers and miraculous feats. In their view, the Buddha of myth and legend—the object of cult veneration—emerged several hundred years after his death in response to the growing popularity of Buddhism during the Mauryan period.[15] According to this two-level model, the early Buddhist tradition replicated the renunciant path of the founder. Like the Buddha, the earliest followers were *nibbāna*-seekers. Inspired by the spirituality of monks, lay supporters generously provided for their material needs in order to free them from such mundane tasks. This view claims that as Buddhism spread throughout Indian society after the third century B.C.E., its nibbānic values inevitably became compromised and the singular character of the early *saṅgha* was inexorably changed, indeed, sullied. From this point on—so goes the argument—the Buddhist tradition has been a dual system for two types of people: those who pursue the ideal goal of *nibbāna,* and those for whom religious observance serves a more pragmatic function of worldly well-being. This same dualistic or two-tier model has also been applied to a historically simplistic distinction between an early Hīnayāna phase of Buddhist sectarianism doctrinally incompatible with iconographic depiction of the Buddha and the development of Mahāyāna Buddhism doctrinally predisposed to imaging the Buddha.[16]

Buddhist texts and archaeological evidence clearly indicate that the Buddha's contemporaries and early generations of followers perceived the Blessed One in several different ways. From the very beginning the meaning of "Buddha" was multivocal, not univocal. To argue that the cult of the person of the Buddha emerged only centuries after his *parinibbāna* primarily to meet the needs of popular lay devotion ignores the fact that from the outset renunciant movements such as early Buddhism reflected the diverse social environments from which they arose. Furthermore, the view that constructs the Buddha solely in terms of his *nibbāna* fails to acknowledge that the subculture of religious mendicancy including early Buddhism also supported cults of particular ascetics, yogis, and miracle-performing mendicants.[17] It seems plausible, then, to postulate that modern Thai devotion paid to the "Lord Buddha" (Thai, *phraphutthachao*) is but a later, particularized cultural expression deriving from one of the sundry early constructions of the Buddha.

Theravāda—the tradition that formulated its definitive institutional traditions in Sri Lanka, including exegetical norms and liturgical forms, and began its ascendancy in mainland Southeast Asia after the eleventh century B.C.E.—has always celebrated the historical Buddha, Siddhattha

Gotama, the sage of the Sakya clan. By critical scholarly standards, however, the historical Buddha of Theravāda is also the Buddha of myth and legend, not solely the renunciant whose awakening to the truth (*saccadhamma*) of the origin and cessation of suffering (*dukkha*) and of the interdependent co-arising nature of reality (*paṭicca samuppāda*) inspired a new religio-philosophical tradition. The Pāli canon of the Theravāda tradition, its normative Pāli commentaries, and rich vernacular traditions depict the Buddha as an extraordinary "teacher of gods and human beings." Stories abound regarding the miraculous nature of his birth, his supernormal powers, and the spectacular and miraculous displays of Buddha relics. The Buddha celebrated throughout Buddhist Southeast Asia combines various personae. The central plot—the story of the conqueror (*jina*) of suffering and rebirth (*saṃsāra*) who becomes the teacher of the *dhamma*—spawned a profusion of diverse subplots over time and place. My focus will be on one of the contexts in which this multifaceted story takes place, namely, the Buddha image consecration ritual (Pāli, *buddhābhiseka;* Thai, *phutthāphisek*) in northern Thailand.

This study of the ritual begins with the image itself, the debates about its origins, and the place the image holds in Buddhist belief and practice. While the primary referent is the northern Thai Buddhist tradition, this study presumes a broader pan-Buddhist framework as well as an even more far-reaching comparative perspective on the nature and role of images, icons, and signs of sacred power as cultural expressions of religious worldviews.

## Scriptural Accounts of the First Buddha Image

> Can a gift be given to both Orders with the Buddha in front (of them) after the Tathāgata has attained (final) nirvana? It can. How? An image (of the Buddha) containing relics should be put on a seat facing the two Orders, and a stand put there, and when the offering of water . . . and the rest have been made, everything is first to be offered to the Teacher.
>
> (Ps. V.73)[18]

This passage from the commentary on the *Majjhima Nikāya* is part of a wide range of Buddhist scriptures that refer to both the existence and construction of Buddha images. Among them is an important account of how the first Buddha image came to be made. Although there is no corroborating historical evidence to confirm this account, the legend of the first Buddha image has more than mere etiological value. Above all, the story and the rationale for making the statue provide insight into the nature and function of Buddha images. Therefore, although the story of the genesis of the Buddha image is a legendary account, what it reveals about how early devotees of the Buddha perceived the image contributes to an understanding of why anthropomorphized forms of the Buddha appeared.

The foremost example of the genesis of the first Buddha image, the story of the sandalwood statue, appears in Buddhist texts written at different times in several Asian countries. The pervasiveness of the story indicates that early in the history of the development of Buddhism it came to represent a normative, widely accepted pan-Buddhist explanation of the nature, origin, and function of the Buddha image that incorporated local variations of time, place, and vested sectarian interests. Because this study focuses on Buddha image consecrations in the Theravāda tradition, I have chosen the version of the legend as recounted in the *Kosala-Bimba-Vaṇṇanā* (The Laudatory Account of the Kosala Image), a thirteenth-/fourteenth-century Pāli text from Sri Lanka. It also appears in the *Vaṭṭaṅgulirāja Jātaka,* a collection of Pāli *jātaka*s composed in Chiang Mai, north Thailand, during the same period.[19]

The occasion for creating the sandalwood image is the Buddha's temporary absence from the Jetavana Monastery. King Pasenadi of Kosala comes to pay the Buddha a visit only to find him away on a journey and his dwelling empty (*vihāraṃ suññaṃ*). When the Buddha returns the following day, the king tells him of his disappointment. "So," the king said, "for the benefit of the whole world (*sabbalokahitatthāya*) I would like to have an image made in the likeness of the Tathāgata (*tathāgatasadisaṃ paṭimaṃ*)."[20] The Buddha accedes to the king's request, adding that whoever builds an image of whatever size and material accrues a great, immeasurable, incalculable benefit (*appameyyaṃ asamkheyyaṃ mahānisaṃsan*). Returning to his residence, King Pasenadi orders a Buddha image made of sandalwood displaying the thirty-two marks of a *mahāpurisa* (great person) inlaid with gold and clothed in yellow robes. After its completion he invites the Buddha to see the image, which was placed in a bejeweled shrine. As the Buddha enters the shrine, the statue arises to greet the Fully Enlightened One who, upon "seeing the statue's appearance, says, 'Reverend sir, after me you will illumine my teaching. For the sake of the teaching, endure five thousand years.'"[21] All present, humans and gods, the earth and Mount Meru, pay obeisance to the Buddha image. The king then invites the Buddha to sit in the shrine beside the statue as the Blessed One who together with the *saṅgha* are given food donations. After a seven-day *dāna* the Buddha then expounds on the meritorious benefit of making Buddha images and of copying texts. Over half of the KBV describes these rewards: avoiding rebirth in the Buddhist hells; being reborn in aristocratic, wealthy families; and the eventual attainment of enlightenment.

For this study, the most relevant aspects of the story to be examined are the connection between kingship and the Buddha image; the polarity of absence and presence; the relationship between the Buddha image and the *dhamma;* the significance of the Buddha image for the survival of the tradition (*sāsana*); the role played by vision, that is, the mutual gaze between the image and the Buddha; the fluidity of the distinction between a sentient being and a nonsentient object; and the function of the image with regard to seminal concepts in the belief system of popular Buddhism, especially those of rebirth and meritorious benefit or advantage (*ānisaṃsa*).

The interrelationship between kingship and Buddhahood in Buddhism is complex and long-standing. The legends of the Buddha's birth and early life up to the renunciation of his royal status interweave these two ideals. The ten perfections (generosity, virtuous conduct, restraint, wisdom, endeavor, tolerance, truthfulness, resolution, lovingkindness, equanimity) embodied in the Theravāda understanding of the *bodhisatta* path are similar to the ten royal virtues that define the righteous Buddhist monarch. Popular notions of Buddhist kingship in Southeast Asia, especially Myanmar (Burma), integrate the concepts of *bodhisatta* or future Buddhahood with that of the world ruler (*cakkavattin*). Although both the world ruler and the Buddha are "wheel turners," the Buddha turns the wheel of the *dhamma* epitomized by his first public teaching (*Dhammacakkappavattana Sutta*), rather than the wheel of worldly power.

That in the KBV the king of Kosala initiates the construction of the sandalwood image comes as no surprise. Because of their wealth and status kings were the natural patrons of the construction of Buddha images, *thūpa*s, *cetiya*s, and monasteries. Moreover, from the beginning of the Buddhist tradition, kingship was uniquely connected with material signs of the Buddha, symbols such as the *bodhi* tree and footprint, but especially relics and images. The Indian Buddhist practice of enshrining Buddha relics in *thūpa*s may derive from a custom associated with the interment of the remains of chieftains.[22] Moreover, some scholars hold that fashioning anthropomorphic forms of the Buddha may have developed from the custom of imaging rulers.[23]

In the *Aśokāvadāna* the account of King Asoka associates the king specifically with the relics of the Buddha and his image.[24] Both Pāli and vernacular Buddhist chronicles from Sri Lanka and mainland Southeast Asia further perpetuate the relationship between kingship and material signs of the Buddha.[25] The importance of Buddha relics and images to the work of kings reflects a political hegemony based on ritual rather than military or political power.[26] Robert L. Brown argues that the Thai custom of swearing allegiance to the king by the country's ministers in front of the Emerald Buddha image should be interpreted not simply in the

Weberian terms of political legitimation but as representing the belief shared by both kings and the general populace that the image is an object with a sui generis power: "That these objects are images of the Buddha is important, but their power to influence the people and the state stems most fundamentally from their ability to function as *objects* of power, rather than as portraits or symbols of the Buddha."[27]

The KBV makes it quite clear that the monastery empty of the Buddha's presence was the immediate cause for the construction of the image. Three basic reasons are given. The first concerns ritual as a necessary expression of religious sentiment. The people experience mental anguish (*domanassa*) when they cannot see the Buddha.[28] This feeling is not solely a personal reaction to not being in the physical presence of the Buddha; the Blessed One's absence deprives Pasenadi and his entourage the opportunity to offer the teacher garlands and perfumes. Without the presence of the Buddha in some form, ritual as an expression and enactment of religious sentiment cannot take place (*apūjetvā*). When religious sentiment is stifled, the shared preparations and activities associated with ritual performance are frustrated and the opportunity for merit making lost. But, with the Buddha present as the recipient or object of the ritual act, both personal and communal satisfaction (*somanassa*) is achieved. Ritual at all levels depends upon the presence of the Buddha, in person, imaged, or represented by a material sign.

Second, the image discloses the Buddha's teaching (*dhamma*). Upon seeing the image the *tathāgata* says, "Reverend sir, after me you will illumine my Teaching."[29] The claim in the KBV corroborates the famous saying in the *Saṃyutta Nikāya* (III.120): "Whoever sees me (the Buddha) sees the Dhamma; whoever sees the Dhamma sees me (the Buddha)." The form or the image (*rūpakāya*) functions as a sign of the 84,000 teachings of the Buddha (*dhammakāya*).[30] The Buddha image and the *dhamma* are as cohesively conjoined as the Buddha and the *dhamma*. In northern Thailand during the construction of the Buddha image and later at its consecration, the *dhamma* is ritually infused into the image.

Third, the image ensures the continuation of the tradition, a claim that in this instance logically refers to the *saṅgha* as the historical institution that emulates and represents the Buddha and teaches the *dhamma*. When King Pasenadi and his entourage fail to see the Buddha, the monastery is considered to be totally empty; only its form remains. The Buddha must be *seen*, that is, he must be present for the ritual to be efficacious, for the *dhamma* to flourish, and for the *saṅgha* to prosper. The king of Kosala, therefore, is justifiably distraught when he visits the Buddha only to find him absent.

Perhaps the most puzzling episode in the KBV is the interchange between the Buddha and the sandalwood image. What does it reveal about the nature of the Buddha image? When the nonsentient image sees the sentient Fully Enlightened One, it rises to greet him. When the Buddha, in turn, sees the image, he speaks to the statue as though it were a sentient being. The conversation presupposes an act of mutual seeing or recognition. Furthermore, that the image (*paṭimā*) looks like the *tathāgata* transforms the mutual gaze into a mirror-like self-reflexive recognition. The Buddha sees himself in the image and, likewise, the image sees itself in the Buddha. That the image looks like the *tathāgata* seems not to denote a physical resemblance but a mutual, self-reflexive act—the statue sees itself in the Buddha and the Buddha, in turn, recognizes his Buddha-self in the statue. In this way the sandalwood image represents or mirrors the Buddha. The image does not physically resemble the Blessed One nor does the statue's apparent "aliveness" mean that it *becomes* the Buddha in a physical sense. Rather, the power through or by which the image represents the Buddha is the power born from this act of mutual recognition; the Buddha recognizes the image as the Buddha.[31] The statue is more than a mere reminder. It represents the living presence of the *tathāgata* much as a mirror represents the reality it reflects. When King Pasenadi's entourage presents offerings to the sandalwood image they do so not because the image bears a photographic likeness to the Buddha but because they recognize themselves to be in the very presence of the Buddha.[32] When King Pasenadi offers food to the Buddha, the teacher is seated in the shrine beside the sandalwood image as though the image were the Buddha's twin.[33] Human twins, though separate persons, are alike. Similarly, the Buddha and the image differ but they share the same *tathāgata* genus.

In his study of the Amida Buddha Triad at Zenkōji in Nagano City, Japan, Donald McCallum refers to the image as an "icon."[34] He chooses this term because even though *icon* generally refers to a pictorial representation, he finds the term *image* to be so neutral that it fails to connote the "sacred and mysterious qualities" of the Zenkōji Amida image.[35] McCallum proposes three possible interpretations of the Zenkōji icon and the cult of Buddha images in Japanese Buddhist devotional practice: the icon as a representation or likeness of the image; as a symbol of the deity; and as the deity itself. The first refers to an idealized anthropomorphic representation that "gives the worshiper some sort of direct access to the Buddha whose appearance is depicted"; the second believes the Buddha to be so transcendent that an icon can serve only as a symbolic substitute to provide a stimulus for spiritual progress; the third assumes the first, directly contradicts the second, and "insists the object of worship is alive."[36] Regarding the Zenkōji icon McCallum concludes, "The desire to worship a living icon, very deeply rooted in human psychology, is expressed in an especially direct manner in the cult of the Zenkōji Amida."[37]

Following McCallum's analysis of the Zenkōji Amida Triad, the image in the KBV may be regarded as a living icon that provides direct access to the Buddha whose appearance is depicted. From a Peircean perspective the image combines the traits of icon and index.[38] As icon it refers to the object it denotes by virtue of its own character. That is to say, it shares characteristics with that for which it is a sign as, for example, when *x* is taken as a sample of a certain kind of cloth, *y*, by virtue of similarities.[39] For Charles Morris, an iconic sign denotes an object having certain properties it possesses itself but in degrees.[40] In the fullest degree, which would fit the Amida Triad and the image in the KBV, the iconic sign-vehicle has all the properties of what it denotes. An index refers to the object that it denotes by virtue of being profoundly affected by it. In Kevin Trainor's view, an indexical sign has both a locative and a material connection with the object to which it refers.[41] In the case of the KBV the image mirrors, represents, or is a specific instantiation of Buddha-ness in a particular time and place.[42]

From the very outset, the building of a Buddha image was considered to be beneficial (*hita*) and meritorious (*ānisaṃsa*). The emphasis that the text places on the meritorious reward or benefit from constructing a Buddha image, having one constructed, copying a text, or having one copied suggests that the KBV should be classified as an *ānisaṃsa* (Thai, *ānisong*) text. This would explain the text's overriding concern with the benefit resulting from such pious acts in terms of rebirth states and conditions. Furthermore, to classify the text as *ānisaṃsa* relegates its etiological purpose of justifying or legitimating the building of Buddha images to a place of secondary importance. From this perspective, instead of legitimating their construction the legend serves the hortatory function of promoting a long-standing tradition of the manufacture of Buddha images. The basic purpose of the story, then, is to demonstrate that constructing Buddha images results in incalculable meritorious benefits. The inclusion of delineated rewards for copying texts as well as constructing Buddha images supports this interpretation of classifying the KBV as a *ānisaṃsa* text. It is possible, of course, that the *ānisaṃsa* was a later addition to an etiological tale for which there is literary evidence from Faxian's (Fa-hsien) diary written in the early 400s C.E.

In the *Vaṭṭaṅgulirāja Jātaka,* the legend of King Pasenadi and the construction of the sandalwood image appears as the frame story of the present. In the story of the past, the Buddha narrates an incident from one of his previous lives as King Vattaṅguli where, as a consequence of having repaired the broken finger of a Buddha image when he was a merchant in Aggavatī, he was able to defeat an army merely by lifting and bending his finger. This *jātaka* structure provides the opportunity to further accentuate the *ānisaṃsa* nature of the story, for the numerous benefits that accrue from making Buddha images are recounted in both the story of the past and the story of the present. These benefits include being handsome and sweet-smelling, achieving a heavenly rebirth or powerful kingship, and ultimately Buddhahood itself. Thus, although in mythic time King Vattaṅguli is the future Buddha, in the narrative time of the *jātaka* the instrumental cause of his achievement of Buddhahood is the merit he earned from constructing a Buddha image. "O venerable image," says the king, "by the merit thus obtained, in the future I shall become the Buddha, the omniscient victor in this world."[43]

Thanissaro Bhikkhu proposes that the depiction of the Buddha as a field of merit (*buddhakhetta*) became a dominant theme in the Pāli *apadāna,* the thirteenth book in the *Khuddaka Nikāya* ("group of small texts"), which coincides with the rise of the veneration of images and relics.[44] He contends that the construction of the Buddha as a mainstay/protector (*nātha*) and *buddhakhetta* represents a tension in the tradition between the Buddha's own example and teaching that progress on the path requires individual effort ("be an island unto one's self"), and the apadānic view where progress shifts from individual effort to *pāsāda* or faith in the Buddha as protector. The Buddha provides the opportunity for devotees to make merit by performing all kinds of services (*adhikāra*) for him, including material gifts, showing respect through word or gesture, or singing his praises.[45] The Buddha's field of merit is operative not only while the Buddha is alive, but also through his continued post-*nibbāna* presence in his relics and images. In this sense both relics and images are indexical signs because they represent the Buddha's actual, material presence, and it is this indexicality that makes the image or relic essential to merit-making activities. "The relic or image has to be there for the merit to be generated. A relic accomplishes this by actual physical connection to the Buddha. . . . It was either part of the Buddha's body or the Buddha's body came into physical contact with it."[46] Because an image lacks this historical connection it must be "charged" with the Buddha's presence and this is accomplished by enclosing a relic in the image or through the consecration ceremony that infuses Buddha-ness into it.

Other versions of the building of the sandalwood image appear in legends similar to the stories from the Pāli tradition. The Chinese pilgrims, Faxian in the fifth century and Xuanzang (Hsüan-tsang) in the seventh century record the story of King Pasenadi's Buddha image. These accounts contain two significant variations. Faxian records that the Buddha's absence was occasioned by his ninety-day stay in Tāvatiṃsa (Sanskrit, Trayastriṃśa) Heaven to preach the *dhamma* to his mother, not because the *tathāgata* was away on a journey.[47] In Xuanzang's diary Pasenadi constructs an image upon learning that King Udayana of Kosambī, a monarch who figures prominently in Mahāyāna accounts, had commissioned a statue of the Buddha.

The primary Mahāyāna variant is King Udayana's Kosambī image of the Buddha, for which there is a considerable literature.[48] An early version of the story of the Udayana sandalwood image is found in "Sermons in Ascending Numerical Categories" (*Taishō Daizōkyō* II, No. 28).[49] Here, as in the KBV, the immediate cause prompting the construction of an image is the Buddha's absence. In accordance with Xuanzang's account, the Buddha is not simply away on a journey but is in Tāvatiṃsa Heaven preaching to his mother and the *devatā*. In this version, King Pasenadi of Kosala is accompanied by King Udayana of Vatsa, better known by its capital, Kosambī. The main protagonist is King Udayana, not King Pasenadi, whose feelings of distress prompt the building of the sandalwood image. In an apparent act of one-upmanship, King Pasenadi builds a golden image of equal size: "These two were the first two images of the Tathāgata to be made in Jambudvīpa."[50] When he descends from Tāvatiṃsa Heaven, the Buddha tells Udayana that the royal monarch will be rewarded with health and strength and will be reborn as a *lokapāla* (world-guardian).

The sermon is a late-fourth-century translation from the Sarvāstivāda *Ekottarāgama* compiled by the Tocharian monk, Dharmānanda, and, in all likelihood, composed under the influence of the school of Kosambī.[51] This version of the story naturally emphasizes the role of King Udayana as a way of enhancing the growing importance of Kosambī as a Buddhist center beginning in the second century B.C.E.[52] In a contemporaneous text, the "Sūtra of the Sea of Mystic Ecstasy," translated by Buddhabhadra between 398 and 421 C.E., there is no mention of King Pasenadi. King Udayana commissions an image cast in gold that is taken on the back of an elephant to the staircase just as the Buddha is descending from Tāvatiṃsa Heaven.[53] There the image dismounts and walks in the air to greet the Buddha while flower petals drop from the image's feet and rays of light radiate from its body. The *tathāgata* pays respects to the image and prophesies that it will ensure the well-being of the *saṅgha*. The 100,000 Buddhas who accompany Sakyamuni's descent add: "After the Buddha's Nirvāṇa, anyone who makes and installs an image, and worships the same with banners, flowers, and incense, will in the time to come assuredly attain the pure mystic ecstasy of contemplating the Buddha."[54]

Other versions of the Udayana image reinforce the story's basic themes. The "Scripture on the Production of Buddha Images" (*Zuo fo xingxiang jing*), a Chinese text from the end of the Han dynasty (25–220 C.E.), closely resembles the structure of the KBV. Like the KBV, the "Scripture on the Production of Buddha Images" begins with the occasion of the building of a Buddha image.[55] King Udayana pays his respects to the Buddha when the Blessed One visits Kosambī. The king's heart "leapt with joy" upon seeing the Buddha, and after venerating the "teacher of all in heaven and on earth" he declares his intention of producing an image of the Buddha for later generations to worship, remarking, "I never weary for a moment of gazing on the Buddha. . . . I dread no longer being able to look upon the Buddha after the Buddha is gone."[56] Like the KBV the largest portion of the text enumerates the multifold future blessings that result from producing Buddha images, including being reborn without defilements, rebirth in heavenly realms, and the attainment of *nibbāna,* all of which gives the text the cast of a blessing scripture (*ānisaṃsa*).[57]

In an episode from the now lost "Record of the Buddha's Journey in India," collected by the fifth-century Chinese pilgrim, Faxian and preserved by the Japanese monk Chōnen (tenth century), King Udayana orders a sandalwood image constructed and installed in the Jetavana *vihāra* in Sāvatthi (Sanskrit, Śrāvastī). In this version the nonsentient image also pays respects to the Buddha upon his return from Tāvatiṃsa Heaven and the *tathāgata* prophesies that the image will produce great benefit for the people of the eastern Xia.[58] But in his diary Faxian does not mention King Udayana although he does refer to a cult at Jetavana of a sandalwood image commissioned by King Pasenadi. Xuanzang records seeing several highly revered sandalwood Buddhas: one in a large *vihāra* at Kosambī commissioned by King Udayana and associated with the propagation of the *sāsana*; another at Jetavana in Sāvatthi ordered by King Pasenadi following King Udayana's commission of the sandalwood image; and a third image at Han-mo in Khotan that was reputed to be the original Udayana statue.[59] In Xuanzang's account of the Udayana Kosambī image he records the following: the image radiates divine light; copies or likenesses of the image were made; the artist who constructed the image observed the Buddha's bodily marks in Tāvatiṃsa Heaven; and the sandalwood image rises and greets the Buddha upon his return.[60] The power of the mutual gaze between image and devotee appears in every account.

While variations of the story of the sandalwood image enjoy a wide provenance, other texts justify or explain the production of Buddha images without making specific reference to the sandalwood image.[61] In a *jātaka* tale that appears at the end of the *Dao-xing bo-re jing* written by Lokakṣema in 179 C.E., the wise *bodhisattva,* Dharmodgata, explains to Sadāprarudita the nature of the body of the Buddha and the rationale for making an image of it:[62]

> The Buddha's body is like the images which men make after the Nirvāṇa of the Buddha. When they see these images, there is not one of them who does not bow down and make an offering. . . .
>
> If there is a man who has seen the Buddha in person, then after Nirvāṇa he will remember the Buddha and for this reason make an image because he

wants men in this world to revere the Buddha and receive the merit of the Buddha. . . .

The constitution [construction?] of the perfect Buddha's body is thus, you do not use one thing or even two but rather tens of thousands of things. . . . If men constantly see the Buddha performing meritorious deeds, then they too will constitute a perfect Buddha body.[63]

Some of the themes found in the construction of the sandalwood image appear in these passages: the building of the image is linked to the Buddha's absence, in this instance, his *parinibbāna;* people joyfully respond to the image with respectful gestures that include prostrations and offerings as one would act toward the living Buddha; worshiping the image accrues merit; and seeing the image that represents the Buddha's accumulated meritorious deeds produces an empathetic response in the viewer.

The conjunction of resemblance and remembrance is also found in the *Dao-xing bo-re jing.* The text links them with reverence or worship, and merit. Remembrance of the living Buddha is what engenders resemblance. Memory, like a mirror, reflects the living presence of the Buddha much as in the KBV the image mirrors the Buddha. In the words of the text, "If there is a man who has seen the Buddha in person, then after Nirvāṇa he will remember the Buddha and for this reason make an image, because he wants men in this world to revere the Buddha and receive the merit of the Buddha." Through memory one re-presents the living Buddha not simply for personal, imaginative reflection but rather, to create an image of that very likeness as the subject of veneration and the guarantor of blessing.

As stated in the KBV and other texts, it is the image as the very presence of the Buddha that makes rituals efficacious and meritorious. Other material representations of the Blessed One function in a similar way. These include bodily relics and material signs of the Buddha such as the perfumed chamber (*gandhakuṭī*) and portraits of the Blessed One. Abundant literary and archaeological evidence exists for an early cult of the Buddha's bodily relics. According to the *Mahāparinibbāna Sutta,* the distribution, enshrinement, and veneration of the Buddha's remains occurred immediately after his cremation. Kevin Trainor finds support in the closing verse of chapter 30 of the *Mahāvaṃsa* (Mhv) for the view that the Buddha's relics are a functional equivalent of his living presence:[64] "A wise person, confidence adorned, who has venerated the living Sugata/Most-venerable, Best of Worlds, Darkness-free/and venerated his relics, broken up out of concern for human welfare,/realizing, 'That merit is the same,' surely that one venerates the Sage's relic just as the Sugata alive." And similarly, in the *Vaka Jātaka* King Bimbisāra says to the Buddha:

> When you are gone, O Blessed One, I shall be unable to do you honor. I shall be unable to make the customary offerings to you and it will grieve me. Give me a lock of your hair, give me the parings of your fingernails, I shall place them in a temple in the midst of my palace. *Thus I shall retain something that is part of you and each day I shall decorate the temple* (caitya) *with fresh garlands and I shall burn rare incense.*[65]

The current scholarly debate over whether the cult of Buddha relics included both monastic and lay support is of less relevance to this study than the strong evidence that both images and relics were believed to represent the living presence of the Buddha, and that this presence was crucial to devotional rituals and the ideology of merit making that accompanied it.[66]

Both relic and image represent the living presence of the Buddha; both are fields of merit and objects of devotional veneration; both are indexical signs of the image's iconic nature that carries with it the power of *darśan.* All accounts of the sandalwood image highlight a feature distinctive to the image as cult object, namely, the power of mutual gaze. In the KBV, the mutual gaze not only infuses the image with the living presence of the Buddha, it is essential to the efficaciousness of the devotional act itself. Beholding the likeness of the Buddha, especially his face and eyes, evokes an overwhelming sense of presence. Buddhist *avadāna* texts record stories of the procession and enshrinement of likenesses of the Buddha that elicit extraordinary emotions. In the *Bodhisattva Avadāna Kalpalatā* the Buddha sends a portrait of himself to Princess Muktālatā of Sri Lanka: "when the princess placed the portrait on a golden throne, the people became lost in contemplative union with the effigy and the princess on contemplating the sacred portrait of the conqueror abjured all desires for an endless period of time."[67] Similarly, in the *Divyāvadāna* when Upagupta beholds the likeness of the Buddha created by Māra, he is elevated to a state of ecstatic delight (*prāmodayaṃ utpannaṃ*).[68] In these Sanskrit *avadāna* accounts of seeing the likeness of the Buddha, O. C. Gangoly finds echoes of Dhaniyā Gopa's exclamation recorded in the Pāli *Sutta Nipāta* (i.2.31), "We go for refuge to the one with eyes (*cakkhunā*)."[69] Even though this connection may seem far-fetched, one could consider the *Sutta Nipāta* passage as referring to taking refuge in the Buddha whose living presence is perceived in the ritual act of the mutual gaze of image and devotee.

## The Buddha Image: An Art Historical Perspective

The issue of the origin of the Buddha image elicits heated debate among art historians. For this study the most relevant aspects of the debate center on the historical-contextual questions regarding the nature and meaning of the Buddha image. They revolve around four distinct but related issues: the geographic-cultural locus of the first Buddha image; the approximate time the Buddha was depicted figuratively; whether figurative depiction of the Buddha emerged only subsequent to an aniconic phase, a development possibly linked to the Mahāyāna conception of the *bodhisattva* or abstract Buddhological theory; and the relationship between the emergence of Buddha images and popular piety, especially pilgrimage to sacred sites. [70]

Although no consensus has been reached on these issues, current opinion favors the following views: figurative representations of the Buddha, including Buddha images, occurred early in the tradition; Buddha images should be considered within at least two artistic, religio-cultural contexts, namely, Indian figurative representations contemporaneous with early Buddhism and other material representations of the Buddha, especially relics; instead of a simplistic two-tier aniconic/iconic scheme of development, the appearance of figurative depictions of the Buddha in relief and in the round reflect historical factors such as sectarianism, philosophical disputes, the institutionalization of a devotional cult, and economic rivalry among Buddhist centers competing for pilgrims, devotees, and patrons.

The debate on the geographic-cultural locus of the production of the first Buddha images originated in 1927 with A. K. Coomaraswamy's essay "The Origin of the Buddha Image,"[71] which challenged Alfred Foucher's influential article, "L'Origine grecque de l'image du Bouddha."[72] Coomaraswamy disputed Foucher's contention that the earliest Buddha images were made in Gandhāra under Greek influence. In agreement with Victor Goloubew's 1924 review of Foucher's book, Coomaraswamy asserts that Indian artists in Mathurā created the first human representations of the Buddha, images that were modeled on precedent figures of *yakkha*s, who represented fertility and prosperity.[73] Coomaraswamy's position that Mathurā images were produced independent of Greek influence, preceded or were contemporaneous with Gandhāra images, and were modeled on earlier images of *yakkha*s is now widely accepted, even though this view has been refined and qualified, and the overall historical precedence of Mathurā Buddha images continues to elicit debate.

Coomaraswamy's counter to Foucher's notion that the first Buddha images were borrowed from Greek prototypes was based in part on three assumptions regarding Indian religious culture: "original" Buddhism (and Jainism) was a monastic religion lacking elements of worship, devotion, and cult; the emergence of realistic images of divine or superordinate beings was a pan-India phenomenon (i.e., Brahmanism, Buddhism, Jainism) associated with the development of popular devotional beliefs (*bhakti*) and rituals (*pūjā*); the prototypes for devotional images in Buddhism, Jainism, and Brahmanism were cults of kings and "the worship of Yakṣas and Nāgas as tutelary divinities or *genii loci,* and of feminine divinities, powers of fertility."[74] For Coomaraswamy the *bhāgavata* cults of the *yakkhas* and *nāgas* must have developed gradually into *bhāgavata* cults of Viṣṇu and the Buddha. To support his view he cites Upāli's reference in the *Majjhima Nikāya* to the Buddha as "incomparable, worthy of offerings, a person beyond comparison, a Yakkha," and the Buddha's assurance in the same collection "that even those who have not yet entered the Paths are sure of heaven if they have love and faith toward me."[75]

In challenging Foucher's thesis, Coomaraswamy cites artifact remains as evidence for the Indian origin of Buddha images. He points out that such evidence proves that images of deities and human beings in relief and in the round existed in India by the third or second century B.C.E., and that *bodhisattas* were represented in the Sāñcī and Bhārhut bas-reliefs as were figures of a meditating *yogi* and a teacher. Coomaraswamy suggests that imaging the Buddha, who was an ascetical, meditative adept as well as a teacher and a *bodhisatta,* would be a logical extension of tendencies in the religious culture of pre-Buddhist India. Here he refers to figures of the Buddha in a meditation pose on coins of Maues (ca. 100 B.C.E.) and Kadphises I (ca. 40–78 C.E.). Coomaraswamy summarizes his evidence with the following statement: "practically every element essential to the iconography of Buddha and Bodhisattva figures appears in early Indian art before the Buddha figure of Gandhāra or Mathurā is known."[76]

Regarding the date of the first Buddha images, Coomaraswamy is relatively cautious. On the basis of the evidence at his disposal he concludes that Buddha images came into general use before the beginning of the reign of King Kaniṣka in the middle of the first century C.E., that Mathurā was a significant Buddhist center prior to the reign of Kaniṣka, and that Mathurā images were at least contemporaneous with and probably prior to Gandhāra Buddha images. "All that we can assert with confidence," he says, "is that the earliest Buddha types in each are in the local style; and that later on, though some mutual influence was felt, the outstanding character of the development is one stylistic Indianization in Gandhāra, and one of adherence to the Mathurā type in the Ganges valley."[77] Coomaraswamy affirmed without qualification, however, that the classic Gupta-style Buddha image derived not from Hellenistic but from Kuṣāṇa types.

Coomaraswamy's evidence for Indian rather than Greek influence for the origin of Buddha images suggests that their production may have occurred considerably earlier than the first century C.E. John Huntington among Indian art historians today believes that anthropomorphic depictions of the Buddha may have appeared within one generation subsequent to the Buddha's *parinibbāna*.[78] He claims both literary and archaeological evidence as support for the view of the production of early Buddha images for the purpose of gaining merit associated with seeing the Buddha (*buddhadarśanapunyā*): "The phenomenon seems to have been unquestioned and to have been a completely natural and spontaneous reaction to the situation of allowing persons who had not been able to gain merit by seeing the Buddha in person either while he was absent during his lifetime or, because of his death and cremation, after his lifetime, to do so by seeing an image of him."[79]

Huntington cites as evidence references to the construction of images in several Buddhist texts. He divides these into Buddha image narratives prior to and after the *parinibbāna* of the Buddha. A story from Tāranātha's *History of Buddhism in India* and the *Biography of Dharmasvāmi* stands out because it refers to sites and postures of images Huntington considers "elemental," that is, precedent to later image traditions associated with centers of Buddha image production, such as Mathurā and Gandhāra.[80] Although the two narratives vary in some details, Huntington summarizes the basic story as follows: an elderly Māradhi woman (about 120 years old in Tāranātha's account), who became a lay follower of the Buddha toward the end of the Buddha's lifetime, had three sons who after their conversion to the *sāsana* wanted to build shrines to honor the teacher. The two eldest sons build *vihāra*s at Vārāṇasī and Rājagaha and the third son constructs the perfumed chamber (*gandhakuṭī*) of Vajrāsana at Bodhgayā into which the Mahābodhi image was installed. In both versions of the story the old mother, who was personally acquainted with the Buddha, is the only one who can confirm that the image was made in the likeness of the Buddha.

Huntington argues on the following grounds that the story suggests an early origin of the Buddha image: the three sites mentioned are associated with the seminal but nonmiraculous events in the life of the historical Buddha, namely his birth, enlightenment, and first teaching, unlike the miracle sites of Śrāvastī and Sāṅkāśya, the site of the Buddha's descent from Tāvatiṃsa Heaven that had become popular by the time of Asoka; the account of the woman's viewing of the image refers to the convention of making images in the four postures—sitting, standing, lying, and walking; the details of the episode of the woman's viewing of the image and her comparison with the living Buddha has "a strong air of validity."[81] Huntington concludes that the accounts by Tāranātha and Dharmasvāmi support the position that the Mahābodhi image in the *gandhakuṭī* was "probably made within the lifetime of a single individual after the *nirvāṇa* of the Buddha and second, the strong suggestion that a developed image tradition existed that included four different postures of the Buddha."[82] In his view this legend provides clear evidence for a complex tradition of imagery near 400 B.C.E. Huntington elicits additional support for his view of the early origin of the Buddha image in the work of Lewis Lancaster, who claims that at least by the first century B.C.E. there was a *well-established* tradition for making Buddha images because of the belief that seeing a Buddha image produced merit (*buddhadarśanapunyā*).[83]

Huntington cites textual and archaeological evidence that challenges the view that Buddha images appeared only after a clearly defined pre-iconic phase. He contends that sculpted images grew out of popular piety: the need to gain merit by seeing the Buddha; the desire to view the Buddha after his *parinibbāna*; and the force of the Buddha's personality ("If only . . . [the people] could capture the presence of his being that had convinced them of his truths, might it not somehow remind them of his way and encourage them along the path just as he had done?")[84]—and links the emergence of images and Buddhist devotionalism (*bhakti*) with the gradual development of the Buddhist cenobium.

Huntington challenges the inherited tradition of a pre-iconic early Buddhism, but he does not entirely escape another construction of early Buddhism called into question by Gregory Schopen and others that defines early Indian Buddhism primarily from the perspective of the monastic *saṅgha* as a group of spiritual virtuosi. Huntington appears to consider the earliest phase of the Buddhist tradition to be one of wandering *nibbāna*-seekers who were inspired by the personal example of the Buddha to follow his path; and although monks and nuns may have sponsored the construction of Buddha images, the impetus for Buddhist devotionalism came primarily from lay piety, namely, offering an image as a meritorious act. When considering the origin of Buddha images, Huntington rejects the dualism of aniconism versus iconism, but he appears to retain the distinction between the historical-rational and the mythical-miraculous. This leads him to evaluate narratives of the construction of shrines and images at Vārāṇasī, the site of the first discourse, and Bodhgayā, the site of the Buddha's enlightenment, as early whereas, by contrast, stories connected with Śrāvastī and Sāṅkāśya are later because they are associated with mythic and miraculous events.

Huntington's position may be historically accurate—that the sites associated with the Buddha's birth, enlightenment, first teaching, and death were the loci of early shrines to the Buddha—but his use of the history/myth distinction as a criterion for evaluating whether the appearance of Buddha images is early or late beclouds the issue regarding the basic meaning of the image as the Buddha's surrogate, as a replacement for the Blessed One, whatever the setting. Surely, from the outset the Buddha was venerated as a powerful holy man capable of miraculous feats, not just after Buddhism expanded, became institutionally complex, developed devotional rituals, and embellished stories about the Buddha into a mythology. It may be relevant to observe that even today Buddhist devotees venerate monks whose charisma radiates from exceptional spiritual achievement not only for their wisdom and understanding, but also for their protective powers that are associated with their bodily persons. The faithful seek them out for *darśan* in much the same way that King Pasenadi and his entourage in the KBV sought out the Buddha, and they venerate their relics and icons after their deaths. By being the Buddha's surrogate or twin, the image enables the devotee to obtain the dual benefit of seeing the Buddha—that is, being in the Buddha's presence with the multiple meanings that signifies—and honoring him through meritorious gifts.

The aniconic/iconic debate among art historians continues unabated between Susan L. Huntington and Vidya Dehejia.[85] The crux of their disagreement hinges primarily, although not exclusively, on the interpretation of the bas-reliefs at early Buddhist pilgrimage sites, in particular, Bhārhut. Based on her analysis of archaeological, inscriptional, and literary evidence, Huntington argues that the scenes were intended to be representations of sites of public devotion to the Buddha, namely, pilgrimage, circumambulation, and presentation of offerings, not actual scenes from the Buddha's life. This reading obviates the necessity of theorizing that the iconography of an empty throne, a wheel of the law, or a *bodhi* tree and the corresponding absence of an anthropomorphic representation of the Blessed One was necessitated by early Hīnayāna Buddhology. In her view, the discovery of early pre-Kuṣāṇa Buddha images coupled with a "scene-site" rather than a "scene-Buddha story" reading of early bas-reliefs undermines the misguided aniconic/iconic dualistic theory enunciated by Foucher and perpetuated by art historians until today.

Dehejia challenges what she considers to be the narrowness of Huntington's view and proposes a multivalent reading of early Buddhist iconographic depictions that she regards as three kinds of emblems: representations of the person of the Buddha in a narrative art primarily concerned with the biography of the Buddha; represenions of sacred locations or *tīrtha*s and the devotions performed there; and as attributes of faith, for example, the tree may recall the Buddha's enlightenment, the pillar his teachings, and so on.[86]

In a lengthy rebuttal, Huntington counters what she sees as Dehejia's misinterpretation of her position and Dehejia's resuscitation of the aniconic view.[87] Despite the differences in their positions, however, both scholars agree that the pilgrimage sites inclusive of their iconography represent the living presence of the Buddha.[88] Where they disagree is whether or not the scenes depicted are inherently multivalent, namely, that narrative presentation simultaneously depicts a historical event associated with the life of the Buddha *and* a holy pilgrimage site. For this study, however, the agreement regarding *presence* is what is most pertinent.[89]

In interpreting early Buddhist iconography from the vantage point of pilgrimage Susan Huntington notes that Buddhist texts associate three kinds of relics with pilgrimage: bodily relics, relics of use, and relics of remembrance that include Buddha images.[90] Although this formal classification of relics developed relatively late, it is reasonable to assume that it represents a long-standing precedent. The association of relics in this broad sense with devotion to the Buddha, in particular, pilgrimage, suggests that both the nature and the function of the Buddha's representational signs, including his image, are grounded in making the Buddha present. Like King Pasenadi in the KBV, one visits a pilgrimage site to be in the very presence of the Buddha, make ritual offerings to the Blessed One, and in doing so make merit.

The purpose of this chapter has not been to establish definitive parameters for the historical appearance of the first Buddha images, although recent scholarly opinion does support a time closer to the *parinibbāna* of the Buddha than that held by an earlier generation of art historians and Buddhologists. Through an examination of scriptural accounts and art historical evidence, my purpose has been to lay the foundation for considering why and how the first Buddha images came into being in order to better understand the nature of the image and its relationship to the person of the Buddha.

# 2

# MEETING THE BUDDHA: TEMPLE, IMAGE, AND RELIC

> Ritual is first and foremost, a mode of paying attention. . . . The temple serves as a focusing lens, establishing the possibility of significance by directing attention, by requiring the perception of difference. Within the temple the ordinary becomes significant, becomes "sacred."[1]

IN THAILAND AND OTHER BUDDHIST CULTURES, images of the Buddha in the round are found in many settings ranging from colossal statues situated on hilltops to small images placed in home shrines. The most common locations for life-size or larger statues lie within the precincts of a *wat* (temple-monastery).[2] Although individual or family devotions may take place before a home altar, and a hilltop Buddha statue might be a pilgrimage destination, most communal Buddhist devotional activities are conducted in an image hall within the *wat* compound. At the *wat* devotees encounter the Buddha in many forms: his image, mural depictions of the *bodhisatta*'s life story, Buddha relics enshrined in a *cetiya* (Thai, *chedī*), or other material signs such as a footprint or *bodhi* tree. The *wat,* which houses the major symbols of devotional practice, is the physical locus for various religious activities and the principal context in which belief in the Triple Gem is ritually enacted. Before turning to a more detailed study of the construction of the Buddha image and the ritual of image consecration, the physical context of the *wat* in which Buddha images reside and where rituals are conducted merits consideration.

## *Wat,* Reliquary, and Buddha Image

*Wat*s in Thailand vary greatly in size and complexity.[3] Rural *wat*s in poor villages may contain only a few modest buildings while those in larger, more prosperous settings may be quite magnificent, especially those designated as one of the country's more than 150 royal *wat*s.[4] Even forest monasteries at some remove from towns or villages can be either a collection of humble monks' dwellings built near a small cave sanctuary or physically well-endowed compounds that stand in stark contrast to their natural setting. Humble or grand, most *wat*s have an image hall that functions as the center for public meetings, ceremonies, and rituals.

Although Thai monastery-temples are diverse, they share similarities that reflect traditions developed in India and Sri Lanka.[5] For example, the classic Theravāda distinction between town monasteries and forest monasteries still formally pertains, even if in practice the lines are often blurred. More germane for this study is the functional distinction between that part of the monastery devoted to public rites and ceremonies called "the Buddha's place" (*buddhavāsa;* Thai, *phutthawāt*) and that reserved primarily for monastic purposes such as dormitories and the *uposatha* hall (Thai, *bōt*), where ordinations and the fortnightly recitation of the disciplinary rules (*paṭimokkha*) are held.[6] This part of the *wat* is called the "monk's place" (*saṅghavāsa;* Thai, *saṅghawāt*), a distinction that reflects both the historical development of the Buddhist monastery and practical differentiations in use.

In modern Thailand *wat* compounds may or may not be clearly delineated into *phutthawāt* and *saṅghawāt* areas. Many small village temple-monasteries may have an image hall (*vihāra;* Thai, *wihān*), a few wooden dwellings for monks (*kuṭi*), an open pavilion (*sālā*), a *chedī, bodhi* tree,

2. Buddha image with mural of Sujātā offering milk rice to the Buddha seated under the *Ajapāla* tree. Wat Phrathāt Doi Suthep.

footprint, and other material signs of the Buddha located in a manner dictated more by practical rather than symbolic considerations. Older, more established *wats* may clearly demarcate areas, as seen at Wat Phrathāt Doi Suthep, Chiang Mai's major pilgrimage site on Suthep Mountain. After a 12 kilometer drive or an arduous climb, the *wat* is reached by a steep flight of 185 steps protected on both sides by a *nāga* balastrade. Monks' residences and other *saṅghawāt* buildings are located on the first level at the top of the staircase. The *chedī*-reliquary at the center of the *phutthawāt* rises from an elevated platform surrounded by an iron fence with Buddha altars located at the four cardinal directions. The *phutthawāt* compound is encircled by a cloistered wall and four chapels. The cloister walls are covered with murals of the Buddha's life story before which Buddha images sit at regular intervals.

Pilgrims ascend to the uppermost platform and circumambulate the *chedī* three times holding flowers, incense, and candles, afterward placing them before the large Buddha image in the main chapel. They stand reverently before the *chedī* believed to contain the Buddha relic brought by the renowned monk, Sumana Thera, to Chiang Mai in the fourteenth century. With folded hands raised to their foreheads they repeat the following Pāli *gāthā:*

> I pay homage continuously to the divine lord of men and gods and worship the golden *cetiya* and the most worthy hair and forehead relic that it enshrines.

Before leaving, devotees may visit the Buddha altars and chant additional Pāli *gāthā* asking for wisdom, knowledge of the *tipiṭaka,* protection from punishment in hell, or ordination into the monastic order.

Wat Phrathāt Haripuñjaya, the largest monastery-temple in Lamphūn Province located 30 kilometers south of Chiang Mai, traces its origins to the mid-eleventh century. According to the northern Thai chronicles, it was constructed by Ādittarāt (Pāli, Ādittarāja), ruler of the pre-Tai, Mon-Lawa kingdom of Haripuñjaya.[7] Schematically Wat Haripuñjaya represents two concentric squares surrounding a *chedī*-reliquary at the axial center. Both squares are encircled by high walls. The inner square demarcates the *phutthawāt* and the outer one, divided into four units, constitutes the *saṅghawāt.* It includes dormitories for monks and novices, classroom buildings, and the *ubōsot* or *bōt* (Pāli, *uposathāgāra*), the hall where monastic business (*saṅghakamma*) is conducted. The *bōt* represents the heart of the *saṅghawāt.* It is the only building consecrated by sacred boundary stones (*sīmā*), and, as the location of the fortnightly recitation of the monks' rules (*paṭimokkha*), the *bōt* symbolizes the discipline (*vinaya*) that defines monastic life. At the end of the rains retreat and at Āsāḷhā Pūja that celebrates the Buddha's preaching of the

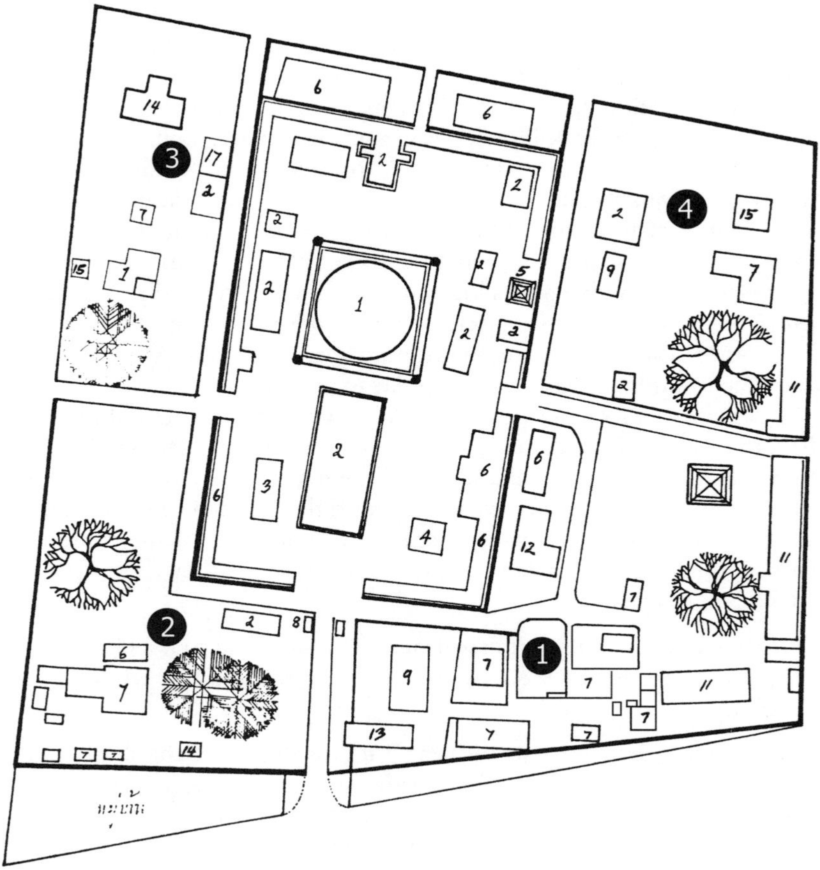

3. Diagram of Wat Haripuñjaya, Lamphūn, Thailand.

Bold numerals 1–4 designate the four divisions of the Saṅghavāsa encompassing the Buddhavāsa. Other structures include the following:

1. Relic *cetiya*
2. Vihāra
3. Library
4. Bell Tower
5. *Cetiya*
6. Open veranda
7. Monks' quarters
8. Guardian lions
9. Ordination hall
10. Museum
11. School buildings
12. Office of the school principal
13. Pond
14. Drum
15. Kitchen

*Dhammacakkappavattana Sutta,* all fully ordained monks in the district of Lamphūn gather for a joint recitation of the *paṭimokkha.*

The *phutthawāt* constitutes both the structural and functional center of Wat Haripuñjaya with the *chedī*-reliquary as its focal point. As a reliquary (*sarīradhātucetiya*), the *chedī* locates the Buddha at a particular place while simultaneously symbolizing the axial center of the Buddhist cosmos and its archetypal levels—the realms of desire, form, and beyond form. Hence, the *chedī* integrates both Buddhological and cosmological meanings, instantiating the presence of the Buddha at Wat Haripuñjaya while serving as an index of the universal *tathāgata* of cosmic time.

## Reliquary and Image: Correlative Signs of the Buddha's Presence

> A stupa, as a man-made object, is created at a precise point in time, in an exact place, and by people with specific intentions.[8]

> The power of the relic . . . to create places of powerful religious significance, constitutes one of the distinctive functions of the relic cult in the Buddhist tradition.[9]

In Thai *wat*s a mutually symbiotic relationship pertains between reliquary and image, although the close association between *stūpa* enshrined relics and temple images is not unique to Thailand. Precedence for such practice is found in India and Sri Lanka, and comparable patterns exist in other Theravāda countries. Furthermore, the custom of enclosing Buddha images in *chedī*s and placing relics in Buddha images has been widely practiced in Buddhist Asia. Thailand, in particular, is noted for the central importance of the Buddha image and the location of the Buddha image hall in close proximity to the *chedī.* Monastic architecture from the early Tai kingdoms of Sukhōthai, Chiang Saen, Haripuñjaya (Lamphūn), and Chiang Mai provides ample evidence that both image and *chedī* have been equally important signs of the Buddha's presence and twin foci of devotional practice.[10] The primary significance of the *chedī* or *stūpa* has been a matter of scholarly debate, however.

An earlier generation of scholars emphasized the cosmological and cosmogonic symbolism of the *stūpa,* and in doing so deemphasized specific place-based meanings.[11] The archetypal microcosmic/macrocosmic significance of the *stūpa* is highlighted in Paul Mus's monumental study of Borobudur and A. M. Hocart's interpretation of the Sinhalese *dāgoba.*[12] John Irwin develops the cosmological symbolism of the *stūpa* in a cosmogonic direction, observing that the Buddhist *stūpa* has roots in ancient

Vedic creation mythology associated with Indra.[13] Recent interpretations of the *stūpa* have qualified this emphasis on the cosmological and cosmogonic aspects of these structures as undervaluing the *stūpa* as a memorial mound on the grounds that the inference is not supported by historical evidence and that it ignores more recognizable Buddhist doctrinal meanings. Gérard Fussman suggests that Irwin's cosmogonic interpretation is historically problematic: "Irwin's interest in the *stūpa* seems to stem from the idea that the *stūpa* embodies much older concepts, that it is evidence for a lost neolithic ideology which prevailed the world over; and that whether the Buddhists, or the Buddhist elite, was aware of it or not does not matter."[14] Fussman argues that, first and foremost, the Buddhist *stūpa* was intended as a memorial mound similar to a cenotaph built in honor of a king: "When seeing it people remember the Buddha and his teaching, which induces in them a good thought (*kuśala-citta*), which produces good *karma (puṇya)*."[15] Fussman further contends that as a symbol of the *parinibbāna*-gone Buddha, the *stūpa* was initially intended to represent the Buddha's body, albeit his *dhamma* body. It naturally follows that later the Buddha's bodily relics would be associated with the *stūpa,* although Fussman finds no evidence of a relic cult prior to the second century B.C.E., a view challenged by Kevin Trainor and others. Trainor cites recent archaeological evidence at Vaiśālī that dates the core of the ancient *stūpa* discovered there to the beginning of the fifth century B.C.E., which seems to corroborate the tradition preserved in the *Mahāparinibbāna Sutta* that Vaiśālī received a portion of the Buddha's relics after his *parinibbāna.*[16]

Fussman suggests two different sources for the cosmological significance of the *stūpa*. It might have been transposed from cosmically designed *maṇḍala*s used by monk-meditators and transferred to the *stūpa,* or *stūpa*s were conceived as axial world mountains when associated with the king as world ruler (*cakkavattin*) and magical protector of the state.[17] In either case, cosmological significations ascribed to the *stūpa* should be taken as a second order of interpretation. As a reliquary, the *stūpa*'s primary purpose is to make the absent Buddha present.

Peter Harvey agrees with Fussman that the Vedic, cosmogonic symbolism Irwin sees in the *stūpa* has less legitimacy than more proximate Buddhist doctrinal meanings.[18] The Buddhist *stūpa* should be considered primarily as a reminder of the Buddha, as a reliquary with overlapping layers of symbolic meaning. He justifies this view on the grounds that in several Buddhist texts the dome of the *stūpa* is referred to as a *kumbha* (pot), and that in both Sanskrit and Pāli versions of the *Mahāparinibbāna Sutta* the Buddha's relics were collected in a *kumbha*. Harvey observes that the *stūpa* dome is a container of the Buddha's relics with miraculous powers attributed to them, and that equal merit is ascribed to devotion to the Buddha's relics as to the Buddha when he was alive.[19] In addition to being a container for Buddha relics and their power, the *stūpa* symbolizes the enlightened mind of a Buddha rising above the world of gods and humans: "the unshakeable nature of the mind full of Dhamma . . . On top of the *stūpa* is a top enclosure . . . complete with honorific parasol-discs, equivalent to a Bodhi tree, symbol of a Buddha's enlightenment and his enlightened mind."[20] Thus, for Harvey, the *stūpa* as a focus of Buddhist devotion represents the body of the Buddha in the form of physical relics and, even more important, the Buddha in the form of his *dhammakāya*.[21]

Kevin Trainor's reading of the cult of corporeal relics of the Buddha in the Sinhalese chronicles (*vaṃsa*) also challenges the ahistorical, axial, cosmological, symbolic interpretations set forth by Irwin, Mus, and Adrian Snodgrass from the perspective of "the localization of authoritative presence."[22] In contrast to Harvey, however, for Trainor Buddha relics should be seen in terms of royal and renunciant paradigms of power. As *mahāpurisa* (great person), the Buddha possesses a body purified by the ascetical practices of the renunciant, and yet exercises "unlimited political power over various ranks of gods and lesser spirits that embody the cosmos."[23] The Sinhalese *stūpa* incorporates the power of renunciant and king to create particular centers of sacrality that define the relic cult in Sri Lanka and the Buddhist tradition more broadly. The monastery is one of those centers, a location in which—as Senake Bandaranayake has demonstrated in his study of Sinhalese monastic architecture at Anurādhapura—a close relationship pertained between the *stūpa*-reliquary and the image hall.[24]

Additional support for the localization of authoritative presence is found in Hiram Woodward's study of the Thai *chedī* as icon and symbol. He contends that within the context of Thai monastic architecture the Buddhist idiom of the *stūpa* as memorial mound, reliquary, and symbol of the *dhamma* takes precedence over cosmological and cosmogonic theories.[25] Of more direct relevance to this study, however, is Woodward's emphasis on the symbiotic relationship between the *chedī* and the Buddha image. He observes that in the context of the Thai temple-monastery compound, the *chedī* should be seen not in isolation, but in terms of its physical relationship to other structures in the *wat* compound, especially the Buddha image and the Buddha image hall. The *chedī* should be understood as a constitutent element of the monastic complex, "a segment, generally, of a straight line upon which the *chedī* is merely a point, the other main point being the Buddha image in the image hall."[26] In the symbiotic relationship between *chedī* and image hall we have two correlative forms of the Buddha's presence.

Woodward analyzes the close interrelationship between Buddha image and Buddha relic in architectural, formal, and historical terms.

Architecturally, *chedī* and image hall within the Thai Buddhist *wat* share an axial proximity. An even more immediate, formal proximity pertains when Buddha images are placed on raised platforms at the cardinal directions directly abutting a *chedī*. Buddha images may also be located in cloisters surrounding a *chedī* or in niches built directly into the *chedī*, or images, especially damaged ones, may be encased inside a *chedī*.[27] From a historical perspective, as Kevin Trainor has demonstrated in the case of Sri Lanka, the *buddha-sāsana* was transmitted by relics as well as Buddha images, and both are evidence of royal support of particular sectarian traditions. In Thailand notable examples of the role of images in the transmission of Buddhism are the Emerald Buddha and Stone Buddha images discussed in chapter 7. Of equal significance are the Buddha relics associated with the rulers of Chiang Mai, especially King Kū'nā (r. 1355–85).[28]

In the fourteenth century, the Thai monk, Sumana Thera, brought a relic from the kingdom of Sukhōthai to Chiang Mai.[29] Earlier the Thera had traveled from Sukhōthai to Lower Burma to be reordained by Udumbara Mahāsāmi into a Sinhala order of forest-dwelling monks. At the request of King Kū'nā Sumana established this forest lineage (*araññavāsa*) in Chiang Mai, bringing with him a highly revered Buddha relic. According to the northern Thai chronicle (Thai, *tamnān*) tradition, upon Sumana's arrival in Chiang Mai, the relic miraculously divided in half, one relic enshrined by Kū'nā at Wat Suan Dok (Flower Garden Monastery) and the other at Wat Phrathāt Doi Suthep on nearby Suthep Mountain. Sumana Thera transmits and legitimates the Sinhala forest tradition to Chiang Mai through its teachings and also through the agency of a powerful relic. The relic that miraculously divides into two parts becomes both the cultic center of the royal monastery-temple where the cremated remains of the Chiang Mai princely family are enshrined and the protector of the Chiang Mai valley from the *chedī*'s vantage point atop Suthep Mountain. Sumana installs in Chiang Mai both the *dhamma* and the protective power of the Buddha represented by the relic.

While bodily relics represent the Buddha because of a "historical connection through space and time" and Buddha images "gain their authority by their capacity to represent the Buddha visually," both can be classified as indexical; moreover, in the Theravāda tradition they share a common classification as a memorial (*cetiya*) to the Buddha even though differences arose over the practice of relic veneration and the appropriateness of one type of memorial over another.[30] In a fundamental sense both relic and image denote the Buddha as a real, living presence, albeit in different ways. The *stūpa* and the image both instantiate the *tathāgata* present throughout time and space, thereby enabling devotees to meet the Blessed One within the sacred precincts of the northern Thai *wat*. Temple image and enshrined relic are correlative forms of the Buddha's real presence.

4. Chedī. Wat Phrathāt Doi Suthep, Chiang Mai, Thailand.

## Buddha Image and *Wat:* Nature and Function

The Thai *wat* is admired as a magnificent architectural monument and revered as a symbolically significant sacred space. But it is more than buildings or symbol; it is the religious, cultural, and social center of the community. In a broad, cultural sense the *wat* both expresses and defines the centrality of Buddhism for Thai identity. The *chedī* and the image form the foci for understanding the living presence of the Buddha. On one level this reality is simply a matter of belief, an a priori assumption about the nature of things.[31] On another level, this belief is continually reinforced and reenacted through the wide range of *wat* activities. The *wat* is a sacred space not only for its physical attributes but, even more so, for what takes place there. Among its many functions, the *wat* is a continual reminder of the Buddha and his teachings.

Within the setting of the *phutthawāt,* pictorial narrative conjoins with image and relic to represent the person of the Buddha and his story. Wat Phrathāt Doi Suthep and Wat Haripuñjaya are notable venues for depicting the life of the Buddha.[32] At the former, scenes from the life story of the Buddha from his birth to the distribution of his relics cover the inner wall of the cloister surrounding the *chedī.* Both the inner and outer walls of the main image hall at Wat Haripuñjaya are adorned with signature episodes from the Buddha's life story together with representative scenes from the ten *bodhisatta* rebirths of the Buddha prior to his appearance as Prince Siddhattha. At both *wat*s the scenes from the Buddha's life story provide a narrative setting for the image. Visually, the story of the Buddha from his past lives, his awakening, *parinibbāna,* and beyond lead the devotee to the central image, the very person of the Blessed One. Narrative and image merge to make the *wihān* a sacred space where all can enter into the Buddha's presence.

That the Buddha image in the northern Thai context represents its original prototype is made evident in the account of the Lion Buddha image (*Phra Buddha Sihing*) in the *Jinakālamālīpakaraṇaṃ* (Jinak) (The Sheaf of Garlands of the Epochs of the Conqueror), an early-sixteenth-century Pāli chronicle written in Chiang Mai by the monk Ratanapañña. The Jinak claims that this famed northern Thai image was made 700 years after the *parinibbāna* of the Buddha at the request of the king of the Sinhalese:

> [The king] wishing to see the form of the Buddha (*sīhaḷarājā Buddharūpaṃ passitukāmo*) went to the monastery and asked the leading Elder of the Order, "It is said that our Buddha visited this island of Lanka three times during his lifetime. Is there anyone who has seen him?" At that instant by the power of the destruction of the cankers (*khīṇāsavaṃ ānubhāvena*), the

> king of the Nāgas, appearing before him in the guise of a youth, created a likeness of the Buddha (*buddhavesaṃ*) in order to dispel the doubt of the king of the Sīhaḷas. For seven days and nights the king paid homage to the image of the Buddha (*buddharūpaṃ pūjesi*). The king then had master sculptors summoned before him and having had an image of the first Buddha (*buddhapaṭima*) made of beeswax similar to that created by the king of the Nāgas and having had the outer mold carefully finished, had an alloy consisting of molten tin, gold, and silver poured within. When the rest of the work such as filing and rubbing was finished it was dazzling and resplendent like the living Buddha (*jīvamāna-buddho*) himself.[33]

As in the KBV, the image's likeness to the Buddha is associated with the Buddha's living presence revealed when he visited Sri Lanka. The archetypal image in this account was fashioned by an extraordinary artisan qualified by his supernatural powers as a *nāga* king and his transcendence of the four defilements (*kāmāsava, bhava-, diṭṭha-, avijja-*). The power of this image derives from the fact that it is the actual form (*rūpa*) of the Buddha and also by the exceptional nature of its maker. In actualizing the Buddha's presence—that is, by serving as the Buddha's representative, double, or surrogate—the image enables worship (*pūjā*) to occur. Copies of the Lion Buddha image are then made according to the lost wax method, a process still followed in northern Thailand. Although additional statues are fabricated by human artisans, they, too, are "like the living Buddha himself" because they represent the original prototype.[34]

In northern Thai *wat*s the main image hall is both the central space for devotional and ritual activities and the residence or dwelling place of the Buddha in much the same way that the *gandhakuṭī* (perfumed chamber) was the Buddha's residence in early Indian monasteries.[35] At Wat Haripuñjaya an immense Buddha image dominates the hall. Congregational events that take place in the *wihān* include the morning and evening monastic chanting ceremonies, weekly sabbath services during the rains retreat (*vassa;* Thai, *phansā*), and all major festivals. The image that presides over these events does more than evoke the Buddha's person and his life story taught in sermons and portrayed in murals; it is the central locus of a sacred space where devotees recall (*buddhānussati*) the Buddha and by that recalling enter into his very presence. *Anussati* implies more than ephemeral images of a remembered person or event. *Buddhānussati* conveys the sense of being in the actual presence of the Buddha and being so deeply moved by the power of this experience that one "sees the *dhamma,*" namely, the true likeness of the Buddha.

Wat Haripuñjaya's main Buddha image represents the powerful qualities that led to the *tathāgata*'s victorious awakening symbolized by his conquest of Māra (*māravijāya*). While monks recite the *paritta* ("protection") (Thai, *suat mon*), which is at the core of all ceremonies, they hold in their hands a white cord (Thai, *sāi siñcana*/*paritta* cord) that connects the main Buddha image to alms bowls filled with water set before them. The didactic function of the Pāli chant takes second place to the ritual transference of the power stored in the image, through the agency of the chant and the medium of water, to the assembled congregation. As the *gāthā* recited at the conclusion of merit-making rituals (Thai, *phithī tham bun*) makes plainly evident, the meritorious power generated by the ceremony extends even beyond those who are physically present to all sentient beings living or deceased:

> May all creatures without number share in the merit that I now make and other merit that I have made, whether they are persons that I have not seen or persons indifferent to me, or those hostile to me, namely all creatures born in the three worlds with the four kinds of birth, with the five aggregates or one or four who move about in the world or out of the world or are fixed in the world.
>
> In sharing this merit of mine with all creatures, may all those who know of this rejoice. As for the creatures who do not know of this offering of merit by me may the *devatā* tell them. In their rejoicing for the merit that I have offered may all creatures escape the consequences of evil and have continual peace and attain *nibbāna*. May the good hopes of all creatures be fulfilled.[36]

The Buddha image serves as a visual reference for temple rituals but, beyond that, the efficacy of the ritual depends upon the Buddha being present at *that* time and in *that* place (i.e., as indexical icon). It is this presence that the Buddha image consecration ritual actualizes.

## Consecration and Renewal

As is true for Buddha images and enshrined relics, the *wat* itself becomes sacred through rituals of consecration. In northern Thailand the rites for dedicating and consecrating new buildings within the monastery precincts are grand merit-making occasions (*poy luang, ngan chalong*) that may last for several days.[37] Protective rituals that inaugurate these events include offerings to the guardian deities of the four quarters, the zenith and nadir, and to the saintly Phra Upagutta, who is invoked to protect the sacred precincts.[38] The festivities include processions with devotees carrying elaborate floats filled with donations for the *wat*. The climax of the *poy luang* includes two activities: the actual consecration of the newly constructed structure such as a *bōt, wihān,* or *chedī,* and the dedication of donations to the *wat*. The first act ritually sanctifies the various structures of the *wat;* the second provides an opportunity for the laity to benefit from the auspicious merit generated by the occasion.[39]

I have established that formally the most sacred building in the *wat* is the *bōt.* It is protected by nine boundary stones (*sīmā*), one buried in the ground at the building's center and eight located at the major and minor directions around the perimeter.[40] Legally, the king of Thailand, representing the government, grants the *saṅgha* permission to consecrate a piece of land by *sīmā,* that once consecrated land should not be used for any other purpose.

The consecration ceremony, called "planting the boundary stone" (Thai, *plūk sīmā*) or "burying the symbol" (Thai, *fang lūk nimit*), begins with a chant to purify the plot of ground. The monks invited for the occasion stand in the middle of the *bōt* and perform four Pāli chants to remove the potency of previous boundary stones (Thai, *suat thon*), before consecrating the new boundary markers first as the "place not without three robes" (*ticivarāvippāvāsa*) and then as "the place of the association of equals" (*samānasanāvāsa*), saying, "O *bhante,* may the Sangha hear me. The Sangha now consecrates the *sīmā* which the Sangha has set aside as a place where the *bhikkhu*s may keep the *uposatha* in equality, making it an area not without the three robes, a place set apart from houses and door yards."[41]

Four monks then leave the *bōt* and engage in a question-and-answer chant before each *sīmā* stone, beginning at the east and then moving in a clockwise direction to the seven other boundary stones. One of the four monks asks, "What is the symbol of the east?" The other monks answer on behalf of the earth and the *saṅgha*: "The stone is the symbol." This formula is repeated twice before each stone is buried. The four monks then reenter the *bōt* and declare that the *sīmā* markers have been properly installed. A ninth stone is lowered into the ground in the middle of the *bōt* with all members of the *saṅgha* present. Unlike the perimeter boundary stones that are designated simply as *baddha-sīmā* (boundary stones), the ninth stone is called the *buddha-sīmā,* suggesting that this stone implants the presence of the Buddha in the center of the most sacred *saṅghawāt* structure. The sacrality of the consecrated *bōt* is reinforced during ordination rituals. As a prelude to the ordination ceremony the ordinand circumambulates the *bōt* three times, stopping before the most venerated marker in the middle of the east side. After prostrating three times before the marker, he then rises and enters the hall to be ordained and begin a life in the lineage of the Lord Buddha.[42]

The consecration of a *chedī* and a *wihān* takes place within the context of a *poy luang* celebration, the extent and complexity of which depends on the wealth of the sponsors and the prominence of the *wat.* As with the dedication of the *bōt,* the consecration of the *chedī* and *wihān* focuses on a ritual act distinctive to each structure but with greater cosmological and apotropaic significance. The ceremony consecrating a *wihān* reaches its climax when a tiered umbrella (Thai, *chat*) is installed at the center of the ridge pole and a *cho fā* (sky tassel) is affixed to the roof gable.[43] During a ceremony I witnessed in 1989 at Wat Pa Sao, Bān Pa Sao, Lamphūn Province, northern Thailand, the *chat* and *cho fā* were raised into place by ropes and pulleys. The laity in attendance jointly pulled on the ropes while holding a *sāi siñcana* (*paritta* cord) as the monks invited for the occasion chanted *paritta* (Thai, *suat mon*).

If the sacred structures within a *wat* compound are damaged and rebuilt, they will be reconsecrated. Following an earthquake that damaged the *chedī* at Wat Phrathāt Doi Suthep in 1988, a ceremony to reconsecrate the refurbished structure took place in November 1989. The host of the event was the governor of Chiang Mai Province, with most of the cost borne by a Chiang Mai business leader.

This ceremony began with an evening of *paritta* chanting by a group of distinguished monks. In addition to the standard repertoire of *suat mon* texts and others distinctive to the northern Thai *paritta* tradition, the monks recited the *Buddha Abhiseka* (Consecrating the Buddha), a chant essential to the Buddha image consecration ritual. The following morning elaborate propitiatory offerings were given to a pantheon of protective gods and spirits (Thai, *phithī sangwœy thewadā):* traditional Brahmanical deities such as Indra and Viṣṇu; the spirits of the kings and princes of Chiang Mai; the protective guardian deities of Suthep Mountain and the spirits of the sages associated with it, especially Vāsudeva, after whom the mountain is named; the spirit of the famed monk, Khrūbā Sīwichāi, who revived Buddhism in the Chiang Mai area in the 1930s; and the guardian deity situated atop of the *chedī* itself. The ceremony was led by a lay ritual expert noted for his performative expertise. Following the propitiatory offerings to the *thewadā,* the lotus petal crown of the *chedī* dome was filled with precious jewels, reputed to include 5,000 diamonds and valuable Buddha relics in the form of amulets and small images. Afterward the spire, capped by a gilded umbrella, was set in place to the chanting of the assembled monks and the cries of *Sādhu, Sādhu* by the cheering crowds gathered for the event.

The *wihān* and *chedī* share common elements. The most distinctive architectural feature of the *wihān* is its multilevel roof, often tripartite, representing the three levels (*bhūmi*) of the Buddhist cosmos embodied in the architectonic form of the *chedī.* The *wihān,* like the *chedī,* is crowned by an umbrella with its symbolic axial and royal potency. The *nāga* motif undulating down the edge of the roof from the ridge pole symbolizes protective power reminiscent of Mucalinda's role in the legend of the Buddha's enlightenment. The ritual consecration of *chedī* and *wihān* constitutes them as a sacred space suitable for the surrogate presence of the Buddha.

*Chedī, wihān,* and *bōt* instantiate the Buddha in a particular place; they locate the eonic *tathāgata* within the cultural space and historical time of northern Thailand. These structures serve as locales wherein the Buddha is encountered whenever monks recite the *paṭimokkha* and devotees meditate quietly before a Buddha image or present offerings of flowers and incense at the *chedī.* At major monastery-temples, this presence is dramatically renewed by the community of monks and laity, men and women at Visākha Pūjā, the annual celebration of the Buddha's birth, enlightenment, and death and during the circumambulation and lustration of the *chedī* at the *wat*'s annual anniversary festival. This study locates the Buddha image consecration ritual where it belongs contextually—within the institutional and ceremonial tradition of northern Thai Buddhism.

# 3

# CONSTRUCTING A BUDDHA IMAGE

I BEGAN THIS STUDY of the *buddhābhiseka* in northern Thailand by first considering the nature and meaning of the Buddha image and the physical context in which the consecration ritual is conducted and larger than life-size images are emplaced. Before turning to a description and analysis of the Buddha consecration ritual, it will be relevant to examine the traditional image-manufacturing procedure and the portrayal of image construction in premodern northern Thai texts. This chapter on the making of Buddha images includes a description of the manufacture of bronze images in northern Thailand; translations of three texts related to the construction of a Buddha image (*Tamrā Kān Kosāng Phraphutthārūp* [Manual for Making a Buddha Image], *Ānisong Kān Kosāng Phraphuttharūp* [The Meritorious Blessing for Making a Buddha Image], and *Yan Phraphuttharūp* [Buddha Image *Yantra*]),[1] and concludes with an analysis of how these texts enlarge our understanding of the Buddha image.

## Bronze Image Manufacture in Northern Thailand

In contemporary Thailand, anthropomorphic figures of Sakyamuni Buddha appear in many sizes, forms, and compositions. The most prevalent are glossy mass-produced pictures, temple murals, embossed amulets on neck chains, small freestanding images for home shrines, and larger than life-size images found in *wat*s. Although freestanding images may be fashioned from wood, glass, stone, or other materials, most temple and shrine images are bronze or bronze alloys. Traditionally, artisans in Chiang Mai who specialized exclusively in the manufacture of bronze images were commissioned to cast an image for donation to a *wat* as the centerpiece of a major merit-making festival (*poy luang*). A few families living near the southern perimeter of the old Chiang Mai city wall continue to make bronze images in the manner of earlier generations.[2] Donors may commission the casting of an image, but more frequently they simply purchase a bronze factory-made image sold at stores specializing in religious paraphernalia.

Among the Chiang Mai artisans, Duangchan Chantharat has been honored for perpetuating the northern Thai cultural art form of bronze image casting. He was born in 2480 B.E./1937 C.E. and lives south of the old city wall in the area between the Suan Prung and Chiang Mai gates once known as the village of Chāng Lo (literally, the "village of molten metal casters"). Image casting began here over 150 years ago but the tradition has gradually waned as less time-consuming, more commercially profitable types of bronze manufacture have developed. Only four families maintain this tradition and three of them are from the Kaewduangsaeng clan. Duangchan is the last surviving family member of the Chantharat clan of bronze image artisans.

Duangchan began working under his father's tutelage at the age of seventeen, with previous training as a wood carver and a silversmith, two other traditional crafts located in the same general area of Chiang Mai. His skill as a craftsperson was much admired, especially the quality of his molds and the beauty of his Buddha and deity images. Duangchan has refused to capitulate to modern mechanized bronze casting methods, preferring to use the traditional techniques of his forebearers. In 1987 he was nationally recognized when a member of the royal family commissioned several Buddha images for presentation at merit-making ceremonies under royal patronage.

The manufacture of bronze Buddha images in the Chiang Mai region still follows the centuries-old lost wax method.[3] Because every large image is cast in its own mold, each image is unique. The process involves twelve steps: (1) clay is kneaded together with paddy chaff and sawdust; (2) the pedestal of the Buddha image mold is formed and sun dried until hard; (3) the body excluding the head is completed, sun dried, and smoothed; (4) the head is made separately because the work is delicate and to ensure a good fit with the torso; (5) once the core figure has hardened, the mold is covered with several layers of beeswax mixed with tree resin, and then carefully carved according to a predetermined model; (6) the carved wax mold is coated with two layers of clay overlaid with metal mesh followed by a third layer of clay with sufficient drying time between each layer; (7) the entire piece, which now resembles a misshapen mound, is then tilted at an angle over a wood fire, allowing the wax to melt and drain away through holes at the bottom; (8) the clay mold is baked in an oven for about twelve hours in order to harden it sufficiently to withstand the heat of the molten bronze; (9) the molten bronze or bronze alloy is poured first into the head[4] and then into the remainder of the image through openings in the base; (10) after the metal has cooled for a day the outer layer is removed; (11) holes, cracks, and other imperfections are repaired with melted bronze followed by sanding and buffing; (12) the image receives a final polishing. From start to finish the process of manufacturing a large image may require several months.[5]

The artisan does not create an image solely of his own inspiration but follows a design dictated by an iconographic tradition such as the

5. Insorn Kaewduangsaeng carving a wax Buddha image mold.
Chiang Mai, Thailand.

distinctive northern Thai Lion Lord style. Because a new mold is made for each image, some minor variations may be introduced inadvertently. The beauty of a particular image depends not only upon the image maker's skill in capturing the essence of a particular style, but also upon the vagaries of chance. It is claimed that the skill of the image maker reflects an inner quality indicative of the mental traits associated with meditation, especially concentration and equanimity. The Chiang Mai image maker I observed was, indeed, extraordinarily focused when engaged in the exacting process of carving the wax mold.

Consecration ceremonies generally do not occur at the place of manufacture, although a lay ritual practitioner (*āchān wat*) may conduct a simple ceremony before an image is moved in order to ensure safe transport. A completed temple-size image may be purchased by a shop or delivered to a *wat* by a donor to be consecrated when it is installed. The image maker I observed in Chiang Mai annually invites monks to his home to chant *paritta* in order to guarantee the success of his business, with no specific link to the blessing or consecration of the images themselves. However, Brahmanical-type rituals invoking the spirit of the artisan's teacher and various deities may be held in conjunction with the manufacture of images.

Most bronze or bronze alloy temple-size Buddha images are made at an artisan's workshop, but they can be cast at the *wat* where they are to be installed. Alexander B. Griswold describes an event that occurred at a central Thai *wat* in which the construction and consecration of the image were integrated.[6] Even though the object being donated was a large temple bell, the process for making a Buddha image is nearly identical. The mold, having been made earlier at the workshop, was transported to the *wat,* where it was placed on a brick fire box built for the occasion located in middle of the monastery compound. Four square brick hearths for melting the various metals—copper, tin, lead, bronze, brass, silver ornaments, coins—donated by the villagers surrounded the fire box. After several days of festivities and merit-making activities, the holy object was cast on the final evening. As monks chanted and meditated in the *wihān* throughout the night, the mold over the fire box was heated to melt and expel the wax. Pious laypeople tended the smelting fires, adding gold rings and other valuable ornaments as an act of merit. Shortly before dawn the chief artisan, dressed in a clean white costume signifying the Brahmanical nature of the rite, paid respects to the spirits of his teachers and asked for their aid in casting the holy object. Afterward, holding lighted incense sticks, he knelt before a table on which were arranged both vegetable and meat offerings to Brahmā, Viṣṇu, the *devatā,* and the guardian spirits of the *wat.* The monks then filed out of the *wihān* holding the *abhiseka* cord (*sāi siñcana*) attached to the main Buddha image. While seated in a circle around the monastery courtyard, they resumed chanting as the abbot sprinkled holy water (*nām mon*) on the mold and the workmen pouring the molten bronze. The workmen carefully used tongs to lift the crucibles full of molten bronze alloy from their hearths and carried them to the fire box, where the molten metal was poured into the mold. Small Buddha images were made with the excess bronze alloy, each one touched by the abbot holding the sacred *sāi siñcana* cord.[7]

In northern Thailand image pourings held at *wat*s are unusual, although in recent years they have occurred more frequently, possibly because their relative rarity produces generous contributions to a monastery. On February 26, 2002, the date coinciding with the celebration of Māgha Pūjā, I attended an image-pouring ceremony at Wat Māe Takhrai, a rural monastery in the Sankampaeng District of Chiang Mai Province, with hundreds in attendance. The ceremony began at 8:00 A.M. with offerings to the guardians of the four quarters and ten directions. Subsequent morning events included a ritual invoking the Hindu gods, the guardians of the place, and the spirits of the rulers of Chiang Mai (*phithī sangwoey devatā*), and a life-extension rite (*phithī sū'pchātā*) to ensure the success of the image pouring. After the monks invited for the occasion were given their noon meal the two main events of the afternoon took place. At the astrologically auspicious time, calculated to be 3:39 P.M., molten bronze was poured into several small and one temple-size Buddha image molds set up within a sacred space (*rājawat*) demarcated by a bamboo fence outside the main image hall. The image pouring was conducted by artisans who had changed into white, Brahmanical costumes from the work clothes worn during their morning labors tending hot charcoal fires to melt small sheets of bronze inscribed with astrologically auspicious *yantra*s donated by the faithful. To coincide with the image-pouring ceremony presided over by a senior monk, an image consecration ritual was being conducted inside the image hall. Hundreds of new, home altar size images were placed on a raised platform in the central nave of the hall still under construction. Seventy-two monks from Chiang Mai and other northern Thai cities chanted consecration recitations while government leaders and other dignitaries were invited to light a series of auspicious candles and to present gifts to the monks. The event was held in honor of Thailand's Queen Sirikit's seventy-second birthday in 2547 B.E./2004 C.E., when the main image hall will be dedicated and the eyes of the temple Buddha image made will be opened.

## Texts

### Tamrā Kān Kosāng Phraphuttharūp[8]
### *(Manual for Making a Buddha Image)*

#### Introduction

The following translation from an anthology associated with making Buddha images and related rituals describes traditions of Buddha image construction and the consecration of Buddha images, *chedī*s, and *wihān* that may date from the fifteenth and sixteenth centuries, the golden age of northern Thai culture.[9] There are striking parallels between the contemporary ceremonies consecrating a *wihān,*a *chedī,* and a Buddha image with the instructions found in this text. The recitation of protective chants (*paritta*) is central to these rituals. The invitation to Phra Upagutta that concludes this anthology places this type of dedicatory ritual within the tradition of *poy luang* ceremonies. Particularly noteworthy is the parallelism between the construction of a *chedī*-reliquary and a brick-stucco Buddha image as they share a similar symbolic structure and, as noted in chapter 2, are correlative instantiations of the Buddha's presence within the context of the Thai *wat.*

#### The Appropriate Day for Constructing a Buddha Image

Here I will describe the technique for building a new image, a *chedī* and a *wihān.* [If it is built] on the first day of the waxing moon it will meet with success; if on the second day a thief will create mischief; if on the third day the slaves of the temple and of the Buddha image will prosper;[10] if on the fourth day the slaves of the Buddha image will suffer; if on the fifth day lightning will strike; if on the sixth day the people will fight one another with swords and spears; if on the seventh day the people will make offerings (*pūjā*); if on the eighth day they will have troubled hearts; if on the ninth day the enemy will disturb the *sāsana*; if on the tenth day the people will be joyful; if on the eleventh day the slaves of the Buddha image will experience problems; if on the twelfth day people will have troubled hearts; if on the thirteenth day they will have peace of mind; if on the fourteenth day the people will live to an old age; and if on the fifteenth day the slaves of the Buddha image will suffer loss and soon die.[11]

### The Technique for Making a Buddha Image or a *Chedī*

To construct a new Buddha image or a *chedī* select six smooth, good-quality clay tiles; polish and paint them with lacquer; then gild them with gold leaf. Attach a silver plate to one tile and on it inscribe the following *yantra* (Thai, *yan*), "*amhehi*" [for our sake]. Attach copper plates to the other five. On one of them inscribe the first *gāthā* (Thai, *kāthā*)[12] of the *yantra,* "*pajjota*" [illuminating]; on the second, the second *gāthā*; on the third, the third *gāthā;* and on the fourth, the fourth *gāthā*. Then bake

6. *Yantra* plaques for the consecration of a *chedī* or brick and stucco Buddha.

the four tiles. On the fifth inscribe the *yantra, "sugato sukhaṭhānaṃ"* [the Buddhas of noble birth].

Having completed the inscriptions, arrange a large offering tray in accordance with traditional procedures. Repeat the "*namo tassa*" [Homage to the Buddha, *dhamma, saṅgha*] three times, and then recite, "The Buddha has appeared in the world, the *dhamma* has appeared in the world, the *saṅgha* has appeared in the world" (*buddho uppanno loke, dhammo . . . , saṅgho . . .* ). Then, put the tile to which the silver plate is attached at the center of the *chedī* [or the image] while chanting, "The virtue of the Buddha, the virtue of the *dhamma,* the virtue of the *saṅgha*" (*buddhaguṇaṃ, dhamma-, saṅgha-*),[13] and, "I pay homage to the Buddha, the *dhamma,* the *saṅgha*" (*namo buddhāya, -dhammāya, -saṅghāya*). Afterward put the tile with the *gāthā, "pajjota"* [illuminating], on the east side, saying, "*namo buddhassa, . . . dhammassa, . . . saṅghassa,*"[14] "I find my support in the Buddha, the *dhamma,* and the *saṅgha*" (*buddhaparāyaṇo, dhamma-, saṅgha-*). Put the tile with the second *gāthā, "bhojiyo"* [nourisher], on the west side, saying, "The [power of the] Buddha, the *dhamma,* and the *saṅgha* are limitless" (*appamāṇo buddho, . . . dhammo, . . . , saṅgho*)[15] and "The Buddha is my protector, the *dhamma* is my protector, the *saṅgha* is my protector" (*buddho me nātho, dhammo, . . . saṅgho . . .* ). Then take the tile to which the third *gāthā, "namāmi tiratanaṃ varaṃ"* [I bow before the noble Triple Gem], is attached, and place it to the north, saying, "I take refuge in the Buddha" (*buddhaṃ saraṇaṃ gacchāmi*) and so on until the third time "[I take refuge] in the *saṅgha.*" Take the tile with the fifth *gāthā, "yo dhiro muni no"* [He who is learned, our sage], and place it to the south.[16]

[When all the tiles are properly placed in the image or the *chedī*], if one wants to make a reliquary casket for interring precious and valuable objects, one should make a container for that purpose. Chanting, "He [the Blessed One] has virtues like the following . . . (*itipi so*); [the *dhamma*] was well proclaimed [by the Blessed One] . . . *(svākkhāto . . . );* [the *saṅgha*] is well disciplined (*supaṭipanno*)."[17] Use the tile with the *yantra, sugato,* for the reliquary cover. Put the *yantra* in the midst of the sacred objects. Then lay bricks in accordance with the architectural form up to the place where the relics (*dhātu*) are to be enshrined in the casket at the heart of the *chedī* [or image]. These include abbreviated stanzas of the 84,000 teachings of the Buddha and numerous precious objects of gold, silver, and other costly things. Secure the cover of the reliquary and then put it on a tray with puffed rice, flowers, and incense.

Perform the auspicious consecration ritual by chanting, "*suvannakāro . . . ; namo tassa . . . ; namo me*[18] *. . . ; sukhito . . . .* until *mettasuttaṃ.*"[19] Chant three times [see above for the translation of the following Pāli terms] *"buddho uppanno loke; dhammo . . . ; saṅgho . . ."*; chant three times *"buddhaguṇaṃ, dhamma-, saṅgha-; namobuddhāya, . . . dhammāya, . . . saṅghāya, namo buddhassa, . . . dhammassa, . . . saṅghassa; buddhaparāyaṇo, dhamma . . . , saṅgha . . . ;"*[20] chant three times *"appamāṇo buddho, -dhammo, -saṅgho"*; chant three times *"buddho me nātho, dhammo, . . . saṅgho. . . ."*[21] Then chant the three refuges beginning with *"buddhaṃ"* until *"tatiyampi"* and ending with *"saṅghaṃ."* Then continue chanting *"itipiso . . . , svākkhāto . . . , supaṭipaṇṇo . . . ,"* followed by [these recitations]: *"sabbe buddhā balappatā, mahākaruṇiko, sakkatva, natthi me, hiriottappa,*[22] *santipakkhā, bahum,*[23] *jayapañjara,*[24] *uṇhassavijaya,*[25] *sukho,*[26] *arogyā paramālabhā santuṭṭhi."*[27]

Take the object that has been made as the heart[28] of the image and after putting it in the opening previously prepared, close the opening. Continue the construction until it is finished. While chanting put the main offering tray in the proper place. Having completed the installation of the sacred objects, turn over the offering tray. If the rite is done in this manner, the monastery, its lay devotees, and the surrounding areas will thrive and prosper. The explanation of the construction of the *chedī* and the Buddha image is finished.[29]

## The Ceremony Regarding the Buddha Image Consecration

To consecrate a new or a repaired Buddha image, whether large or small, in order to guarantee power, prestige, and prosperity, bathe the entire image with sacred turmeric water and anoint it with sandalwood paste. Then write on a palm leaf and repeat three times, *"avijjāpaccayā . . . pe . . . anekajāti . . . yadā have"* [a reference to the Buddha's awakening to the cause of suffering]. Roll it up and put it on the lap of the image or on its chest. Afterward, take a *bodhi* tree of suitable size, put it in a pot filled with earth and sand; take eight handfuls of green *kusha* grass [*Imperata cylindrica*] and spread them at the base of the *bodhi* tree behind the image. Arrange four white jars at the four corners and fill them with water. Encircle the Buddha image and the *kusha* grass three times with cotton cord [Thai, *sāi siñcana*/water lustration cord]. Having done this, then prepare the main offering tray consisting of 10,000 cowrie shells, 10,000 areca [betel] nuts, two pairs of large candles, eight pairs of small candles, eight strands of dried areca nuts, eight cones of betel leaves, one piece of red and another of white cloth, 12 kilograms of unhusked rice, 1 kilogram of milled rice, a hand of bananas, one bunch of coconuts, four mats, four fans, four serving spoons.[30]

Construct the Buddha image according to the size and weight determined by the prescribed plan and apply gold and silver to the appropriate features. Put the image in the place stipulated by the monastery and the devotees who sponsored the building of the image. Having done this, take three mirrors and attach candles to them. Place one mirror in front of the image with the others to the left and the right. Invite the monks to sit together and chant, *"namo me,"* followed by the *Mahāsamaya Sutta* in its entirety[31] and the [following recitations] *"bāhuṃ, jayapañjara, sambuddhagāthā, yadā have,"* and then chant the eye-opening stanza, *"eso no satthā . . .* [This is our teacher . . . ] *. . . . khayaṃ ajjhagāti* [he has come to the end (of craving)]," finishing it in the first watch of the night; chant the *"atha kho bhagavā tassa yeva rattiya majjhime yame . . . khayaṃ ajjhagāti"* [Then the Blessed One in the second watch of the night . . . came to the end of craving], finishing it in the second watch of the night; end with, *"atha kho bhagavā pacchimaṃ yāmaṃ . . . tasmāhaṃ uppako jinoti,"* completing it [the stanzas of the Buddha's conquest of rebirth] in the third watch of the night. As the sun rises, remove the white cloth head covering and the beeswax from the eyes of the image. Light nine candles and chant the following, *"avijjāya . . . pe anekajāti; . . . yadā have."* Afterward chant the *Dhammacakkappavattana Sutta,* the *Maṅgala Sutta* beginning with the *"evam me"* until *"mahāmaṅgala suttaṃ"* and ending with *"sukho; . . . ārogyā . . . paramaṃ sukhaṃ."*[32] Then strike a gong to signal the end of the ritual. Conclude the ceremony by making an offering of forty-nine lumps of rice and place them before the image. If the ceremony is performed according to the above instructions, the Buddha image will be resplendent with immense power (*teja*) for the benefit and the well-being of the devotees and the monastery.

### The Proper Proportions of the Parts of a Buddha Image

If one wants to construct a Buddha image equal in size to the Buddha himself, measure from knee to knee when seated in a cross-legged position; divide this distance into four lengths—one part equals the distance from the base of the spine to the navel, a second from the navel to the chest, a third from the chest to the chin, and a fourth from the chin to the hairline. The upper arm from the armpit to the elbow equals the length of the face; the length from the elbow to the wrist also equals that of the face, as does the distance from the wrist to the end of the fingers; the length of the fingers is half the length of the face; the length of one finger joint equals one-third of one side of the face; the palm of the hand equals the width of one side of the face; the width of the forehead is half the length of the face; the size of the thighs and the calves is equal to the length of the face; the sole of the foot is equal to the length of the face; the toe is equal to one-third of the length of the face; one toe joint is equal to half of the length of the toe; from the breast to the top of the shoulder equals the length of the face; the width of the shoulder is double the length of the face; the distance between the nipples equals three-fourths of the length of the face; one-third is the length of the mouth and the distance between the eye and the forehead; the pupil of the eye is rounded like the hoof of a bull; the eyeball is made to shine like a clove of garlic; the eyebrow is curved like Indra's bow; the ears are as long as the face; the top of the ear is level with the eyebrow. The image reflects three different faces: Thai, Khom [Khmer], and a robber [king].[33] The Thai face is similar to that of the king of kings. The blend of these three, which characterizes the Buddha image, is called the *rājasiṅha* (the Lord Lion).

## The *Dhammakāya*[34]

[The following are the correlations between the body of the Buddha (*rūpa*) and the *dhamma*. The assimilation of the two is the *dhammakāya*.]

*Sabbaññutāñāṇa pavara sīsaṃ* = Head (supreme omniscience)

*Nibbānārammaṇa pavara virājita tejaṃ* = Aura of Flame (which illumines the noble objective of *nibbāna*)

*Ahaṃ sugato homi, ahaṃ avero homi, ahaṃ abyāpajjo homi, ahaṃ anīgho homi, ahaṃ sukhi attanaṃ pariharāmi* = Body (I am the Sugato; I bear no ill will; I do no one injury; I have no hatred; I maintain myself in happiness)

*Catutthajjhāna*[35] *pavara nalāṭam* = Noble Forehead (fourth meditation state)

*Vajirasamma patiñāṇa pavara uṇṇalomaṃ* = Noble Forehead Mark (diamond-like foreknowledge)

*Nīla kasiṇa sobhātika ñāṇa pavara bhamu yugalaṃ* = A Pair of Noble Eyebrows (blue meditation object knowledge)

*Dibbacakkhu paññācakkhu buddhacakkhu dhammacakkhu pakkha pavara cakkhudvayaṃ* = Two Noble Feather-Shaped Eyes (divine eye, wisdom eye, Buddha eye, *dhamma* eye)[36]

*Dibbasota ñāṇa pavara sotaddhvayam* = Two Noble Ears (divine ear knowledge)

*Gotarabhū ñāṇa pavara uttaranāsaṃ* = Noble Aquiline Nose (the wisdom of the lineage of the *ariya*)

*Anuttara vimokkhādhigama ñāṇa pavara kaṇṇaddvayaṃ* = Two Noble Ear Lobes (knowledge of supreme liberation)

*Lokiyalokuttaṃ ñāṇa pavara oṭṭhaddvayaṃ* = Two Noble Lips (knowledge of the mundane and transmundane)

*Sattatiṁsa bodhipakkhiya ñāṇa pavara subhadantā* = Two Noble Sets of Teeth (knowedge of the thirty-seven factors of enlightenment)

*Catumagga ñāṇa pavara catudāṭhā* = Four Noble Eyeteeth (knowledge of the four paths) [*sotāpatti-, sakadāgāmi-, anāgāmi-, arahatta-*][37]

*Catusacca ñāṇa pavara jivhā* = Noble Tongue (knowledge of the four noble truths)

*Appaṭihata ñāṇa pavara hanukaṃ* = Noble Jaw (unlimited knowledge)
*Anuttaravimokkhādhigamana ñāṇa pavara kaṇṭhaṃ* = Noble Neck (knowledge of the realization of supreme liberation)
*Tilakkhaṇa ñāṇa pavara gīvāvirājitaṃ* = Noble Throat (knowledge of the three characteristics of existence)
*Catuvesārajja ñāṇa pavara bāhuddvayaṃ* = Two Noble Arms (knowledge of the four self-assurances)
*Dasānussati ñāṇa pavara vaṭṭaṅgulisobhā* = Well-Rounded Noble Fingers (knowledge of the ten recollections)
*Sattabojjhaṅga ñāṇa pavara pīṇauratalaṃ* = Full Noble Chest (knowledge of the seven factors of enlightenment)
*Āsayānusaya ñāṇa pavara thanayugalaṃ* = Pair of Noble Breasts (knowledge of the dispositions)
*Dasabala ñāṇa pavara janghādvayaṃ* = Two Noble Calves (knowledge of the ten powers)
*Catuiddhipāda ñāṇa pavara pādadvayaṃ* = Two Noble Feet (knowledge of the four bases of mystic power)
*Sīlasamādhipaññā ñāṇa pavara saṅghāṭī* = The Noble Saṅghāṭī Robe (knowledge of moral virtue, concentration, and wisdom)
*Hiriottappa ñāṇa pavara paṅsukūlapaṭisevana cīvaraṃ* = The Noble Burial Ground Robe (knowledge, shame, and fear)
*Aṭṭhaṅgikamagga ñāṇa pavara antaravāsaka* = The Noble Outer Robe (knowledge of the eightfold path)
*Catusatipaṭṭhana ñāṇa pavara kāyabandhanaṃ* = The Noble Waistband (knowledge of the four foundations of mindfulness)

Taken together these characteristics of the Buddha are called the *Dhammakāya*. If one constructs a Buddha image and chants as written in this text, *it will be the same as though the Buddha himself was present* [italics mine]. The monastery will prosper and will be firm in the faith.

### The Method for Making a Wooden Image

Now we shall relate the method for building a Buddha image for our well-being, happiness, prosperity, good fortune, and social status. Anyone who wishes to obtain the above benefits—rulers, laypeople and monks, men and women—should prepare offering trays with puffed rice and flowers. Present them to the *devatā* who protect the *dua pong* tree [*Ficus hispida*], asking for permission to carve a Buddha image from it. Then cut down the tree and allow it to dry. Afterward, carve out the Buddha image and inscribe the horoscope of the sponsor on a silver plate. Then install into the image the *gāthā* which represents the Buddha by chanting three times, "*Buddho bodheyya mutto moceyyaṃ tiṇṇo tāreyyaṃ*" [Having attained Buddhahood, I shall enable others to attain it; having myself gained release, I shall enable others to attain release; having crossed over, I shall enable others to cross over]. After that, inscribe the *buddhamaṅgala-gāthā* around the horoscope and repeat it three times. Finally, inscribe around the horoscope the following *gāthā,* which will make the mind firm and stable, "*Satimā satinimittaṃ anubanditvā satimā minanaṃ daḷhaṃ yatha thambhe daḷhaṃ cittaṃ mama*" [With mindfulness follow the object of the mind; with mindfulness measure firmly; like a stable post let my mind be fixed], and repeat this three times. Having done this, put the dried fruit of the *dua pong* tree on the seat of the image; roll up the silver plate on which the horoscope has been inscribed and put it inside the chest of the image; decorate around the image with all the offerings necessary to consecrate the image. Make an aura for the top of the head from the wood of a mango tree; a base for the image from the wood of a jackfruit tree; the right arm from the wood of a jujube tree; the left arm from the wood of the jambolan tree. The silver plate on which the *gāthā* is inscribed should weigh one baht [15 grams]. Then lacquer the image and repeat the following *gāthā,* ". . . *Yo sannisinno*" [ . . . who is well seated]. After the image has been relacquered and polished, gild it with gold leaf. On the birthday of the builder of the image invite five monks—even more would be better. Respectfully present to the image offering trays with incense, candles, puffed rice, and flowers. Invite the monks to chant the *maṅgala* for opening the eyes of the image; afterward, take the image and put it on the home altar as the Buddha of the head of the family, so that everything will be successful in the present and this meritorious act will lead to rebirth in heaven and *nibbāna* in the future.

### The Ceremony for Placing the Umbrella on the Top of the *Chedī*

If an umbrella is to be installed on a new *chedī,* prepare a large offering tray as described previously. Then make a figure of a *devaputta* (deity) or a *haṃsa* (swan), and attach a rope for hoisting it. At an auspicious time invite four monks with auspicious names to sit at the four corners around the umbrella. They should then simultaneously chant the consecration verse three times, "homage to the Blessed One; the Buddha, the *dhamma,* and the *saṅgha* which have appeared in the world; to the virtue of the Buddha, *dhamma,* and *saṅgha.*" Then chant "*namo buddhāya*" three times followed by, "homage to the Buddha, *dhamma,* and *saṅgha.*" Afterward, continue with, "I find my support in the Buddha, the *dhamma,* and the *saṅgha,*" followed by "the Buddha, *dhamma,* and *saṅgha* are my protectors." Repeat three times, "I take refuge in the Buddha, the *dhamma,* and the *saṅgha.*" And then chant the "*itipi so* . . . , *svākkhāto* . . . , *supaṭi-*

*panno . . .*" three times each, followed by "*sabbe buddhā balappattā*" [the powers of all the Buddhas], and end with the "*bhavatu sabbamaṅgalaṃ.*"[38] Take the multitier umbrella and its fittings and install them one after the other, chanting continuously until the pinnacle is reached. Throughout, the monks at the base of the *chedī* should chant the *maṅgala* simultaneously with the monks at the top. Having done this, sprinkle the umbrella with sacred turmeric water from top to bottom. Take the sacred cord, tie it to the green *kusha* grass, and encircle the *chedī.* Then prepare four white clay urns filled with water; cover them with white cloth and banana leaves. After that, put them at the four corners of the *chedī;* light the wicks of four large candles on the four urns. In the evening invite the monks to chant the *maṅgala* and the eye-opening stanzas as described earlier. Here ends the description of the installation of the umbrella on top of the *chedī*-reliquary.

## The Ceremony for the Raising of the *Cho Fā*

Now I will describe the installation of the *cho fā* and *pān lom*[39] on top of the *uposatha* (Thai, *bōt*) hall and the *wihān* for our well-being and prosperity and the elimination of danger and worry. Take the *cho fā* and the ridge pole decorations and put them together in a suitable place. Then prepare a large offering tray in accordance with the instructions; fill a silver bowl and other containers with sacred turmeric water and sandalwood perfumes and place them in the middle of a congregation of monks (*saṅgha*). At the same time prepare an offering for the *saṅgha* in accordance with one's means. Chant the *maṅgala* [the *paritta* that follow] according to the tradition: "*sakkatvā . . . vupasamentu te,*" "*n̥atthi me,*" "*hiriottappasampannā,*" "*santipakkhā,*" "*jayapañjara,*" "*bāhuṃ,*" "*uṇhassavijayo . . . uṇhassavijayo nitthito,*" and finally chant "*sukho . . . ārogyā.*" Then take sacred turmeric water and sprinkle it over the *cho fā,* the ridge pole decorations, and the *pān lom.* Having done this, install them in their respective places [on the ridge pole of the *wihān*]. Upon completing the installation, turn over the offering tray. If the ritual is performed in this manner, the monastery, its lay devotees, and the surrounding areas will thrive and prosper. Here ends the explanation of the installation of the *cho fā,* the ridge pole decorations, and the *pān lom.*

## The Ceremony and Incantation to Invite the Presence of Upagutta

Ceremonies for constructing or casting a Buddha image, building a *chedī* to enshrine a relic, and occasions such as consecrating a Buddha image, the donation of a Buddha image, a *kuṭi, wihān,* and *bōt* to a monastery, and the ceremonies of *parivāsakamma* [disciplinary acts] and *sīlasod-*

*hanakamma* [acts of the purification of the precepts] should be preceded by a ritual invoking the presence of Phra Upagutta.[40] Invite Phra Mahā Upagutta to prevent the evil power of Māra from endangering our religion and the donations we have made. Only Phra Mahā Upagutta can defeat Māra, because the Buddha predicted that he would protect the *sāsana* for 5,000 years. Build a shrine not too far and not too near; prepare an offering tray of puffed rice, flowers, eight pairs of candles, a tray of areca nuts, a clay pot filled with water, a set of monk's robes and bowl, an iron walking stick, a fan, and a tray of fruit.[41] Prepare a seat for Phra Mahā Upagutta in the shrine, invite him to remain there, and ask for his blessing in the following manner:

"I worship the *saṅgha,* pure, noble, worthy of offerings; of subdued faculties, having destroyed all faults, full of innumerable virtues and free of intoxicants. In the midst of the southern ocean is a kingdom three *yojana* high where Upagutta resides. Let us worship this Upagutta Mahāthera.

"Phra Mahā Upagutta Thera, the supreme *arahanta,* who resides in the middle of the sea in a copper palace three *yojana* high, attained *nibbāna.* I respectfully worship Phra Mahā Upagutta, the supreme *arahanta.* O Phra Mahā Upagutta Thera, the supreme one, filled with auspicious qualities, the *arahant* full of magical power, whom the Buddha predicted would protect the *sāsana* for 5,000 years and save those who make merit by his power, please defeat and drive Māra away. Now all of us, monks and laypeople in Jambudīpa, following the traditions laid down by the Buddha, perform these meritorious acts in all villages and towns for the maintenance of the *tathāgata*'s *sāsana* for 5,000 years; all of us, young and old, male and female, who support the Buddha's *sāsana* in Chiang Mai and in every monastery are filled with faith and confidence in the meritorious acts of Phra Upagutta.

"This great occasion filled with faith and promise was sponsored by ( . . . ), an observant follower of the Buddha's religion at *wat.* . . . The abbot, named . . . of *wat* . . . initiated by . . . led the ceremony, be it a *parivāsakamma* or *sīlasodhanakamma.* When these occasions occur as in this year of . . . , in the morning all the monks should recall the *arahant,* Upagutta, endowed with wisdom, moral virtue, compassion, purity, and supernatural power. Therefore, we erect this shrine (*maṇḍapaprasāda*), where we install Upagutta's seat (*āsana*), appropriately decorated as his residence. All the devotees place offerings consisting of the following customary requisites: three yellow robes, an alms bowl, a pot of water, a tray of betel nuts, and an iron walking stick in order to invite the miraculous *arahant* to come to help. Now all of us bring offering trays filled with flowers, puffed rice, and candles in order to invite the *arahant,* Upagutta, who is filled with purity. May you be compassionate toward the Buddha's religion and all of us, monks and laity; may you accept our invitation and come to protect all of us from all accidents and harm that will cause trouble; may all such events be dispelled; may the supreme *arahant* come to protect us from Māra, the enemy, who will attempt to disturb us by bringing fierce heat, strong winds, conflagrations, and dangerous animals. These catastrophes will result in fear, sickness, wounds and injuries, quarrels, altercations, and fires that will level homes to the ground. All are caused by Māra, the enemy. May the supreme *arahant* come to protect us from all such misfortunes:

"We offer this incense, flowers, and puffed rice to the elder Upagutta. May he accept them with compassion toward us. The *sambuddha* has proclaimed that the elder Upagutta will vanquish Māra and his retinue. With his great power Upagutta will dispel future calamities. In the name of Upagutta, by the majesty of Buddha, by the majesty of the *dhamma,* the majesty of the *saṅgha,* all calamities are entirely [dispelled]." Repeat three times.

## Ānisong Kān Kosāng Phraphuttharūp[42]
## (*The Meritorious Blessing for Making Buddha Images*)

### Introduction

*Ānisaṃsa* (Thai, *ānisong*), or blessing texts, rival *jātaka* and *tamnān* as a literary genre associated with the ritual traditions of popular Buddhism. In northern Thailand they are often attached as a coda that affirms the meritorious blessing of copying, reading, or listening to the text in question. Or, as in the case of *The Meritorious Blessing for Making Buddha Images, ānisong* may appear independently, usually to be recited at the occasion dictated by its subject matter. In this case, I assume that *The Meritorious Blessing for Making Buddha Images* was to be recited on behalf of a donor at the time of the consecration of the image because merit making (Thai, *tham bun*) is central to the *buddhābhiseka* and other Buddhist rituals. Even though the principal sponsor of the ceremony receives special blessings, this occasion provides the opportunity for all participants to make merit. For this reason it is classified as a *poy luang,* or grand merit-making celebration.

*Namo tassatthu. Evaṃ me sutaṃ [ekaṃ] samayaṃ bhagavā Sāvatthiyaṃ viharati Jetavane Anāthapiṇḍikassa ārāme.* O brethen! Once upon a time the Blessed One dwelt in Anāthapiṇḍika's monastery in the city of Vesali. At the time he wandered from village to village and from town to town in order to preach the *dhamma* to the gods and human beings.

The Blessed One went to a village of wealthy potters. He entered the village and sat with the community of monks at the base of a nearby *nigrodha* tree. On that occasion the people living in that village, upon hearing that the Blessed One was seated at the base of the *nigrodha* tree, brought him offerings of incense, candles, perfumes, and flowers. They presented their offerings, paid their respects to him, and sat down nearby at a suitable place.

After taking their places, the potters invited the Blessed One with the following words: "O Blessed One! We ask you and the community of monks to dwell in this place for the happiness of us all." The Blessed One accepted the invitation by keeping silent. The potters, knowing that by his silence the Blessed One accepted their invitation, built a large pavilion (*mahāmaṇḍapa*) around the *nigrodha* tree, decorated it with banners, incense, candles, perfumes, flowers, and so on, covered the floor with mats and carpets, and set out water for drinking and washing for the community of monks headed by the Buddha. The potters, wishing to listen to the *dhamma*, requested him to preach. The Blessed One then preached [a sermon] about the incomparable blessing derived from the construction of a Buddha image. As they listened the potters were filled with joy. Afterward they took their leave.

The following day the potters reassembled, decorated the *maṇḍapa*, and made approximately 3,300,000 small Buddha images using the same clay from which they made pots. They put the images in the kiln in front of the Buddha and asked his permission to fire them in order to be hard and durable. The Buddha granted his permission. Having fired and gilded the images, the potters put them on a large altar protected by a white umbrella. Afterward, they worshiped the images with offerings of flowers, incense, candles, and perfumes. Later, they invited others to prepare perfumes and various food offerings saying, "O brethren! We shall now consecrate the images. Please join us in making merit in accord with your own faith." Having issued this invitation, they brought the Buddha images to the place where the Blessed One resided and gave extensive offerings to the community of monks. The Buddha accepted the offerings of the potters and preached the following sermon about the meritorious blessing for making the Buddha images:

"Those who have had a Buddha image made in order to promote the religion of the *tathāgata* and for the benefit of human and celestial beings will receive great rewards. They will be reborn for several lifetimes as a king of kings (*cakkavatti-rāja*), a conqueror of the four continents, as rulers of both large and small cities, as persons of great wealth (*mahāseṭṭhī*), as Brahmans who have mastered the three Vedas, as Indra, as the head of all female celestial beings (*devakaññā*), and also as Brahmā, the highest of all the Brahmās.

"O *bhikkhus*! In addition, the laity who build an image of the *tathāgata* will not experience any suffering, nor will they be reborn in any family of low class such as a hunter of birds or animals. Rather, they will be reborn into a wealthy and noble family with male and female servants, elephants, horses, cows, water buffalo, and workers, as a consequence of making an image of the *tathāgata*.

"O *bhikkhus*! After I have passed away, the village of the potters will become a city called Kumbhanagara, where my religion will be established and flourish for 5,000 years. O *bhikkhus*! This is the meritorious blessing for making a Buddha image from potters' clay. In those days the community of monks living in Kumbhanagara will engage in intensive study and meditation; moreover, the potters of Kumbhanagara will have great faith in the Buddha's religion."

The Blessed One preached the meritorious blessing for building a Buddha image and then uttered the following stanzas: "*Yo koci dāyako karoti Buddha-bimbaṃ pattena vā so anubhavati phalānisaṃsāni pañcakappāni iti* . . . O *bhikkhus*! Whoever is full of faith and makes an image of the *tathāgata* from a leaf will receive meritorious blessings for five eons; those full of faith in the Triple Gem who make an image of the *tathāgata* by painting it on cloth, will receive meritorious blessings for ten eons; those who make an image of the *tathāgata* from clay will receive meritorious blessings for fifteen eons; those who build an image of the *tathāgata* from wood will receive meritorious blessings for twenty eons; those who build an image of the *tathāgata* from horn or tusk will receive meritorious blessings for twenty-five eons; those who build an image of the *tathāgata* from bricks will receive meritorious blessings for thirty eons; those who build an image of the *tathāgata* from stone will receive meritorious rewards for thirty-five eons; those who build an image of the *tathāgata* from lead or tin will receive meritorious blessings for forty eons; those who build an image of the *tathāgata* from brass, copper, or iron will receive meritorious blessings for forty-five eons; those who build an image of the *tathāgata* from silver will receive meritorious blessings for fifty eons; those who build an image of the *tathāgata* from the pollen of flowers will receive meritorious blessings for fifty-five eons; those who build an image of the *tathāgata* from gold will receive meritorious blessings for sixty eons; those who build an image of the *tathāgata* from precious gems will receive meritorious blessings for sixty-five eons; those who build an image of the *tathāgata* from a sandalwood or *bodhi* tree will receive meritorious blessings for seventy eons or will receive meritorious blessings forever."[43]

Because the potters built the Buddha images from clay, the Enlightened One preached the sermon on the meritorious blessings of building a Buddha image. But, O monks, the meritorious blessing of building a Buddha image from the various materials enumerated above is of less value than what one has in the mind. As the Buddha himself taught in the *Dhammapada, "Manopubbaṅgamā dhammā, manoseṭṭhā manomayā"* [All the dhammas are preceded by the mind, grounded in the mind, made by the mind]. This refers to three kinds of *dhamma* without form, that is, *vedanā, saññā,* and *saṅkhāra.* The meaning is as follows: the first is the mind that enjoys five sensual pleasures; the second is the mind that perceives meritorious and demeritorious *kamma,* which is benevolent and malevolent; and the third is the mind that investigates all kinds of evil and goodness. These three types of *dhamma* have no bodily form. For this reason, the Buddha preached, *"Manopubbaṅgamā . . ."* meaning that of all *dhamma*s the mind is first and foremost.

At another time Phra Mahādevamālai[44] preached to the poor man who presented him with eight lotus buds as follows: *"Yo hīnaṃ vā paṇītaṃ vā pasanna mānaso dānaṃ deti, tassa icchā samijjhanti."* This means, "O laymen, he who gives a *dāna* gift whether of low or high quality with true faith and intention, all his wishes will come true."

Therefore, whenever Brahmans and monks, men and women give *dāna,* keep the precepts, listen to the *dhamma,* practice *mettā-bhāvanā,* they should eliminate all defilements in their heart such as greed, hatred, and delusion which will interfere with merit making. At the end of the Buddha's sermon, many people achieved the fruit of being a stream-enterer (*sotāpattiphala*).

## Yan Phraphuttharūp[45]
## (*Buddha Image* Yantra)

### Introduction

*Yantra*s play an extraordinarily important role in northern Thai culture even though they are most often associated with Hinduism, Tantra, or esoteric forms of Buddhism.[46] Protective *yantra*s are as pervasive in northern Thai Buddhist practice as is the chanting of protective *sutta*s (Thai, *suat mon kāthā*).[47] Chanting the *paritta* in Thai Buddhist parlance is called "chanting the *mantra,*" and this act links the aural and visual dimensions of various protective and empowering rites. For example, when a new house or business is consecrated monks chant protection *sutta*s and draw a *yantra* (Thai, *tham yan*) in a prominent place, usually over the front door. Tai ethnic groups in northern Thailand and the Shan States often wear protection *yantra*s on their persons: as inscriptions on amulets worn around the neck, as bodily tattoos that may cover much of the upper torso, or as *yantra* inscribed undershirts. Protective *yantra* banners are sold at all famous *wat*s, especially pilgrimage sites with reliquary *chedīs*. The *Manual for Making a Buddha Image* provides evidence that *yantras* were incorporated into the construction of Buddha images. The text from which the following *yantra* diagram was copied stipulates that eleven *yantra* diagrams are to be inscribed on strips of silver or gold and placed on various parts of the image: the heart, the right and left legs, the front and back of the torso, and so on.

*Yantras* are made in a variety of shapes, although the most common are either round or square with a specific number of "eyes" (Thai, *dā*) or connected squares in which the syllables of a *gāthā* are written. While some *yantra* chessboard grids can be read sequentially from left to right, line by line (see *yantra* 1), most are the "skip" (Thai, *taen*) variety (*yantras* 2 through 11 below). Meaning cannot be derived from skip *yantras* simply by reading the letters sequentially in any direction. Skip *yantras* resemble a picture puzzle in which individual pieces must be correctly placed if the picture is to be revealed, or a game of anagrams with individual letters that must be placed in a specific sequence to spell a word. The form of the *yantra* suggests that it encapsulates meaning on both esoteric and exoteric levels—meaning that is both hidden and manifest—much like the image itself represents reality in both a particular form (*rūpakāya*) and beyond form (*arūpa* or *dhammakāya*). An elderly monk informed me that a *yantra* maker perceives the arrangement of the letters during meditation; however, the publication of *yantra* books demonstrates that *yantra* formats are routinized.[48] Insom Chaiyachomphū observes that the *yantra* maker must both memorize the *gāthā* to be inscribed and the maze-like grid on which he writes the syllables.[49]

The following text includes eleven *yantra* acrostic grids followed by their decoding and translation into Pāli and English. Each box contains a Pāli letter written in Tai Yuan script. The first grid is read sequentially from left to right, line by line. Grids 2 through 7 and 8 through 11 are the skip type. Meaning can only be derived by combining the letters in the proper combination to make words. The key to the thirty-two-eye grid is indicated on the transliterated *yantra* diagram.

1. *om he he tiṭṭha bandha bandha*
   *dhāreyya dhāreyya nirudheyya nirudheyya*
   *devadaṭṭa devadaṭṭa*
   *uṇṇāmaṇī sijjhanti*
   *siddhi svāha*

This *gāthā* is confusing due possibly to scribal errors, although repeated words suggest it was intended as a *dhāraṇī*. It appears to refer to the conquest of the evil Devadatta, who tried unsuccessfully to kill the Buddha and create dissension in the *saṅgha,* and to the Buddha's victorious enlightenment. The two forces, destruction and creation, comple-

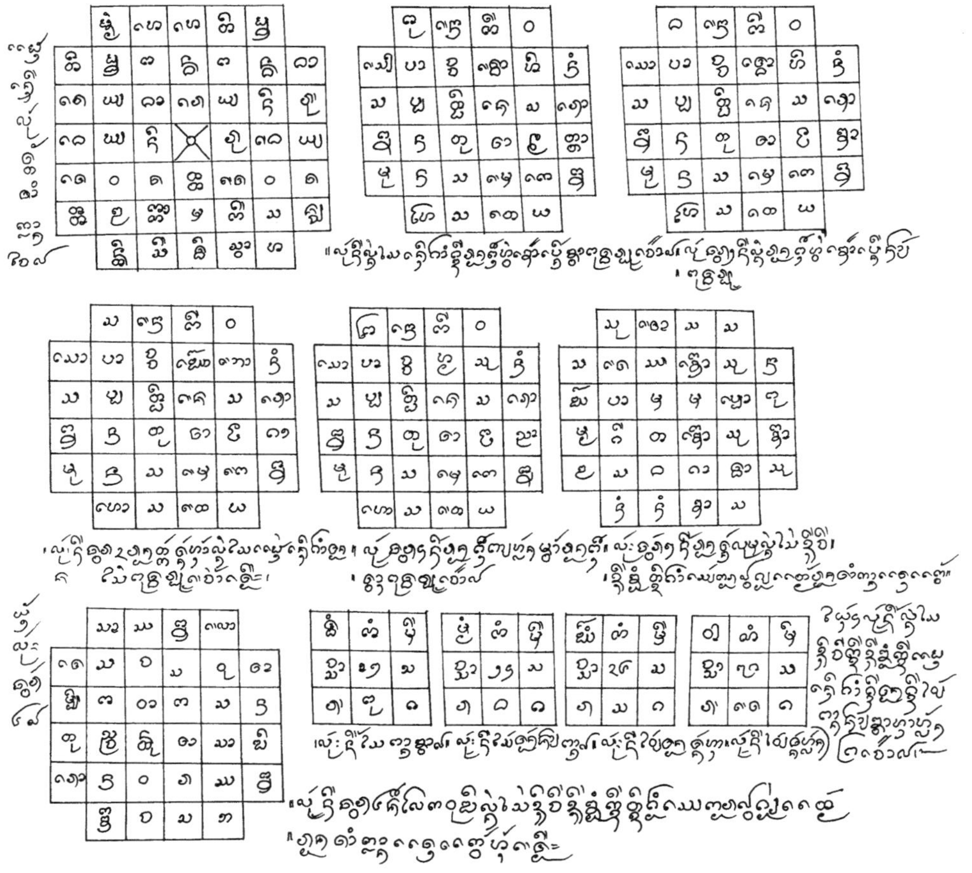

7.a. *Yan Phraphuttharūp*. Buddha image *yantras*, northern Thai script.

ment each other in Indian thought whether as the destructive/creative power of Lord Śiva or as the Buddha's conquest of Māra (in this case, Devadatta) and subsequent enlightenment victory.

2. *Buddho loke samuppanno*
   *hitāya sabbapāṇīnaṃ*
   *etena saccavajjena* [*saccavācena*]
   *sotthi me hotu sabbadā*

      The Buddha appeared in the world
      For the welfare of all living beings.

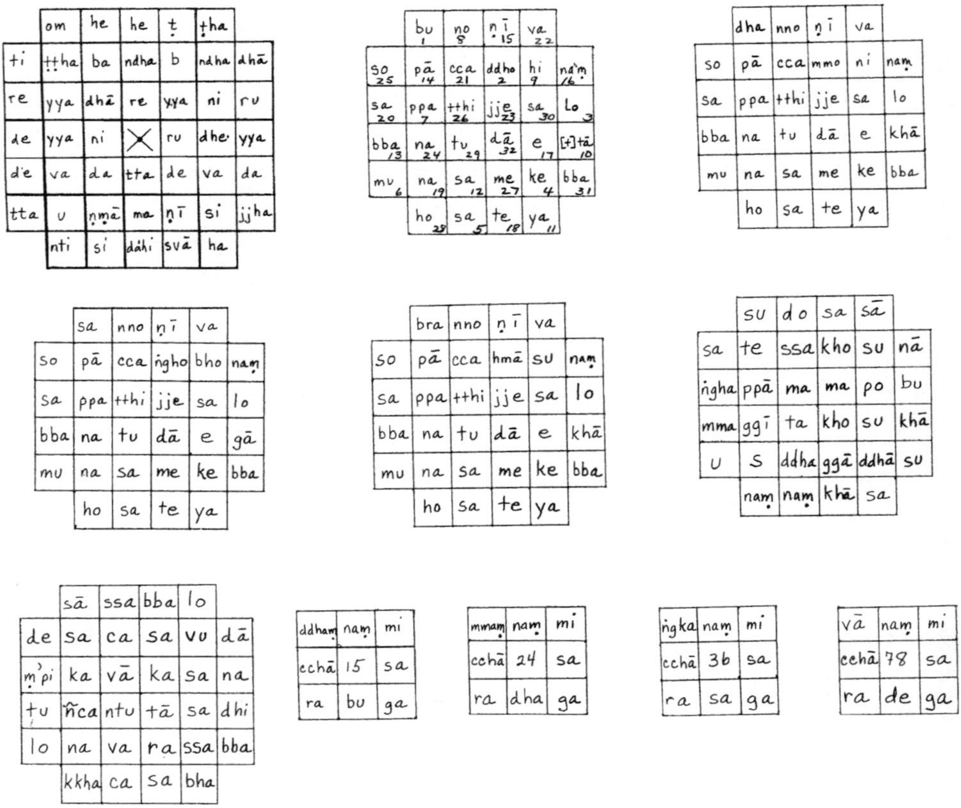


7.b. *Yan Phraphuttharūp*. Buddha image *yantra*s, roman script.

By this word of truth  
May I have good fortune forever.

3. *dhammo loke samuppanno*  
*sukhāya sabbapāṇīnaṃ*  
*etena saccavajjena* [*saccavācena*]  
*sotthi me hotu sabbadā*  
The Dhamma appeared in the world  
For the welfare of all living beings.  
By this word of truth  
May I have good fortune forever.

4. *saṅgho loke samuppanno*  
*bhogāya sabbapāṇīnaṃ*

*etena saccavajjena* [*saccavācena*]
*sotthi me hotu sabbadā*
The *saṅgha* appeared in the world
For the nourishment of all living beings.
By this word of truth
May I have good fortune forever.

5. *Brahmā loke samuppanno*
*sukhāya sabbapāṇīnaṃ*
*etena saccavajjena* [*saccavācena*]
*sotthi me hotu sabbadā*
Brahmā appeared in the world
For the happiness of all living beings.
By this word of truth
May I have good fortune forever.

6. *sukho buddhānaṃ uppādo*
*sukhā saddhamma desanā*
*sukhā saṅghassa sāmaggī*
*samaggānaṃ tapō sukho*
The Buddhas appeared for the welfare [of all living beings];
The preaching of the *dhamma* is for the welfare [of all living beings];
The fellowship of the *saṅgha* is for the welfare [of all living beings];
The dedicated practice of the religious path is for the welfare [of all living beings].

7. *sāsanassa lokassa ca*
*vuḍḍhi bhavatu sabbadā*
*sāsanaṃ'pi ca lokañca*
*devā rakkhaṇtu sabbadā*
May [the people of] the world
And the Buddhist religion prosper forever.
May the gods protect [the people of] the world
And the Buddhist religion forever.

8. *Buddhaṃ saranaṃ gacchāmi* (15)

9. *Dhammaṃ saranaṃ gacchāmi* (24)

10. *Saṅghaṃ saranaṃ gacchāmi* (36)

11. *Devā saranaṃ gacchāmi* (78)
I take refuge in the Buddha.
I take refuge in the *dhamma*.

I take refuge in the *saṅgha*.
I take refuge in the gods.

The numbers in parentheses following each refuge—(15), (24), (36), (78)—indicate birth days auspicious for enduring relationships, such as special friends or spouses. The correlations are as follows:

15 = (1) Sunday + (5) Thursday
24 = (2) Monday + (4) Wednesday
36 = (3) Tuesday + (6) Friday
78 = (7) Saturday + (8) Rāhu [Rāhu is an interlinear day marking the transition between the two halves of the seven-day week. It becomes the second twelve hours (noon to midnight) of Wednesday. Cosmologically, the number 8 marks the major and minor directions of the horizontal plane of the cosmos. The alternation between an odd- and even-numbered week (seven days/eight days) may also be construed as embracing the eternal alternation between life and death, light and darkness.]

The three refuges form the focus of the above Buddha image *yantra*. The yantric infusion of the three refuges into the image constitutes part of its auspicious power to grant succor, protection, and well-being. The *yantra* denotes that within the context of northern Thai devotional ritual the threefold formula of taking refuge in the Buddha, the *dhamma,* and the *saṅgha* becomes an act of truth, not simply a devotional affirmation. Yantrically recalling (*anussati*) the three refuges brings into the present moment an eternal truth, and in so doing a particular Buddha image instantiates the reality of the eternal lineage of the Buddhas in a specific place and time.

## Analysis

These texts emphasize four closely related elements: the ritual nature of fabricating Buddha artifacts; a pervasive esoteric apotropaism; the homologic relationship between *dhamma*(*kāya*) and *rūpa*(*kāya*); and the centrality of merit.

The actual fabrication of a Buddha image can be considered a self-contained ritual even though the image will undergo subsequent rites of consecration and emplacement. The construction follows a well-established, repeated spatial and temporal pattern. For example, temporally there are auspicious days for constructing a Buddha image. Spatially, a brick and plaster image is built according to a particular directional sequence; furthermore, the proportions of the image follow a specific pattern that corresponds to the bodily parts of the Buddha.[50] The parallel construction between image and reliquary is particularly noteworthy. Iconically both represent the Buddha and dhammic reality.

Physical and oral ritual gestures, such as the placement of *yantra* and chanting of *mantra,* accompany selected facets of the construction procedure. An image maker may invoke the presence of divine powers to assist him to perform his task, much as a priest when conducting a ritual: "May the Buddha enter the top of my head, Brahmā and the *devatā* my forehead, and Viṣṇu my heart."[51] *The Manual for Making a Buddha Image* clearly distinguishes between the ritualization of the construction of the image and the ritual for installing an image, even though overlaps between the two establish a continuity between image construction, consecration, and installation. In contemporary northern Thailand, the ritualization of image construction has been largely appropriated by the eye-opening ceremony of image consecration held within the precincts of a *wat.*

An esoteric apotropaism permeates the construction and consecration of Buddha images and includes auspicious days for building an image, the correspondence between chanted *gāthā* and the Triple Gem, and installing Phra Upagutta to protect the ceremonial proceedings from Māra's disruptive power. The heart of this apotropaism, however, lies in the use of *yantra* and *mantra.* Although the considerable literature on *yantra* and *mantra* quite naturally concerns Hinduism and Vajrayāna Buddhism in Central and East Asia, anthropologists and Buddhologists have studied apotropaic features of Buddhism in Southeast Asia as well.[52]

Nicola Tannenbaum, a cultural anthropologist whose work focuses on the Shans of northwest Thailand, argues that the basic Shan worldview in both its Buddhist and animistic guises is structured around the concept of power: "This basic axiom entails a number of corollaries concerning the distribution of power, how one gains power, consequences of having or failing to have power, how powerful beings behave, and so on."[53] One practical expression of this worldview is tattoos. Tannenbaum finds three general uses for tattoos in Southeast Asia—as a decorative sign of male maturity, a means to identify and control people, and magical protection and invulnerability to weapons. In the third use, tattoos are like medicine, "analogous to vaccinations against various diseases."[54] Apotropaic tattoos take the form of *gāthā* (Thai, *kāthā*), Pāli words either written out or encoded on the skin in yantric diagrams. The tattooer, either a Buddhist monk or a traditional teacher, recites *kāthā* while applying the tattoo.

The Shan, Tannenbaum discovered, classify tattoos with regard to their use: those directed toward others, causing them to like or fear the bearer; those that act on the bearer, increasing skill in speaking; and those that create a protective barrier around a person against injury from animals or weapons.[55] Of the first class, the Five Buddhas tattoo requires the bearer to keep the five precepts and to observe certain food taboos. It is administered on an elevated platform and requires the recipient to dress in white. Its power inspires fear and awe in others and protects the bearer from intentional harm by human beings and malevolent spirits. The tattoo itself is a series of *kāthā* inscribed in red over the heart, near the hairline, behind the ears, on the lips, cheeks, upper and lower arms, and back. Because the ink includes the exfoliated skin of a monk, it is thereby believed to engender in the recipient the qualities of the noble monkhood.[56]

In his study of Tantric aspects of Buddhist thought and practice in Cambodia, Laos, and Thailand, François Bizot challenges the conventional wisdom that Southeast Asian Buddhism should be viewed primarily through the lens of the Pāli textual traditions of Sinhalese Mahāvihāra Theravāda Buddhism. One facet of his research focuses on the use of *yantras*.[57]

Bizot and Tannenbaum agree that the apotropaic use of *yantra*s is widespread; however, while in Shan culture *yantra*s as power-protection are largely a male domain, Bizot's research reveals that *yantra*s are commonly used by men and women, monks and nuns. Y*antra*s became a cult, subject to a strict set of rules, governing taboos regarding the parts of the body, especially below the waist, and acts considered impure. The liquid used to inscribe *yantra*s varies, as does the objects on which they are written and method of application. Some may be inscribed on a betel leaf and ingested, written on a small metal scroll and worn around the waist or placed over a doorway, sewn as a *yantra* shirt, or written on a piece of cloth attached to a monk's robe.[58] Depending upon the circumstances, they are often used to procure a specific objective such as beauty, holiness, longevity, or invulnerability. *Yantra*s are written in Pāli inscribed in a variety of scripts, for example, *mūl* in Cambodia, *kham* and *yuan* in Thailand, *tham* in Laos, and the Burmese and Shan scripts in Myanmar.[59]

Bizot is especially interested in Buddha image *yantra*s composed of Pāli *mantra*s taken from the *tipiṭaka,* commentaries, and paracanonical works. As evidenced in *The Buddha Yantra* text, *The Manual for Making a Buddha Image,* and in Bizot's research, these *yantra*s may be inscribed on the body of the image (or the *chedī*) or on strips of metal or other materials and then applied to the image to empower and protect it. Bizot explores the historical development of this esoteric, apotropaic tradition from its probable Vedic and Hindu roots to its general use throughout Buddhist Southeast Asia. Of particular importance to the *buddhābhiseka* are the 108 *kāthā* eulogizing the qualities (*guṇa*) of the Buddha, the *dhamma,* and the *saṅgha,* the source for which appears to be a text entitled the *Ratanamālā* (The Garland of Jewels), versions of which are found in Myanmar, Thailand, and Cambodia. This unique Southeast Asian Pāli text has no apparent connection to the five texts entitled *Ratanamālā* in the Tanjur.[60] The earliest reference appears to be a Pagan inscription dated 1442 C.E.[61] The 108 *kāthā* are divided respectively into fifty-six letters (*iti pi so . . .* ), thirty-eight letters (*svākkāto. . . .* ), and fourteen letters (*supaṭipanno . . .* ) representing the powers (*guṇa*) of the Buddha, the *dhamma,* and the *saṅgha.* In its yantric acrostic form, "Praise to the Triple Gem," like the *yantra* that appears in this chapter, it is impossible to decipher without decoding the words to which the letters refer and knowing the correct word order.[62] This *kāthā* is chanted during the *buddhābhiseka* and in other ritual contexts with its power and meaning embedded in its dual esoteric-exoteric nature.

"When one constructs a Buddha image and chants as written in this text it will be *as though the Buddha himself is present,*" so concludes the *dhammakāya* section of *The Manual for Making a Buddha Image.* The Buddha image is a homologic structure: the eternal body of the Dhamma (*dhammakāya*) made visible in the bodily form of the Buddha (*rūpakāya*). Bizot and George Coedès, following the work of T. W. Rhys Davids, link the *dhammakāya* to the Yogāvacara tradition of Sri Lanka, a system that teaches the method by which a yogic adept can realize the state of the Buddha's omniscience.[63] The Sinhalese manuscript edited by T. W. Rhys Davids is a meditation manual indebted to the *Visuddhimagga* and the *Abhidhammatthasaṅgaha.* Caroline Rhys Davids speculates that it may have been brought to Sri Lanka in the seventeenth century by Thai monks invited by the Sinhalese *saṅgha* to reinstitute the higher ordination ceremony, and subsequently promoted by the great eighteenth-century reformer, Saraṇaṃkara.[64] Whatever the text's historical origin, its preamble suggests two aspects of meditation practice directly applicable to the *dhammakāya,* namely, that individual parts of the body have a true, hidden nature, and that individual sounds, syllables, or words such as A-RA-HAN likewise have a hidden meaning or reality, in the instance cited, Dhamma (A), Buddha (RA), Saṅgha (HAN).

Both Bizot and Coedès consider a Thai Pāli text entitled the *Dhammakāyassa Atthavaṇṇanā* to be an example of the Yogāvacara tradition. The text is a doctrinal abridgment in thirty paragraphs of Buddhist teachings homologically identified with twenty-six bodily parts and four elements of the Buddha's vestments. The order of the paragraphs is determined not by a logical or philosophical classification but by the arrangement of bodily parts beginning with the head and ending with the feet. This suggests a natural or a priori correspondence between the Buddha's teaching, namely, the *dhamma,* and the parts of the Buddha's body. Bizot, furthermore, notes that in the Khmer tradition the *dhammakāya* associates the thirty-two bodily parts with *mūlakammaṭṭhāna,* or meditation foci.[65]

Even though such a homologic tradition may have roots in early Vedism, the mythic, cosmological model represented by the *Puruṣa Sukta* underwent a significant transformation in subsequent yogic traditions, including Buddhism. The long-standing Indian tradition of auspicious bodily marks, canonized in the Theravāda tradition as the thirty-two major and eighty minor marks of the *mahāpurisa* (*Lakkhaṇa Sutta*), came to be linked to the *dhammakāya,* with possible origins in the cultic veneration of material signs of the Buddha. Although the identification of the *dhamma* with the body of the Buddha was the subject of wide-ranging philosophical speculation, it may also reflect the practice of putting fragments of scripture in *stūpa*s and Buddha images, a tradition popularized in the legend that King Asoka's 84,000 *stūpa*s enshrined both bodily relics and *dharma*s.[66]

While I have never witnessed the recitation of the *dhammakāya* at the eye-opening ritual of Buddha image consecration in Thailand and it is not found in contemporary anthologies of northern Thai *buddhābhiseka* texts, Bizot confirms its recitation in the eye-opening ritual in Cambodia.[67] He divides the ceremony into three parts: implanting the marks, opening the eyes, and the consecration.[68] In comparing it with the Yogāvacara tradition, Bizot likens the practice of the eye opening ritual to the Yogāvacara transformation of the body through meditation. The parallel between the transformation of the body through *samādhi* and the transformation of a material representation into the Buddha provides a striking insight into the operative significance of the meaning of the Buddha image consecration ritual.

In addition to the complex practical and symbolic procedures for fabricating and empowering Buddha images, *chedī,* and *wihān,* several passages in the Buddha image construction texts specifically outline the positive, meritorious benefits that result from the construction and consecration of Buddha images: consecrating a Buddha image guarantees power, prestige, and prosperity; performing the ceremony according to the stipulated instructions invests the image with immense power for the benefit and well-being of devotees and the monastery; following the right procedures for dedicating a *wihān* assures prosperity for both the monastery and village; installing a consecrated wooden Buddha image in a home shrine will assure success in this life, rebirth in heaven, and the eventual attainment of *nibbāna.*

Merit making (*puñña*; Thai, *bun*) makes an appearance in *The Manual for Making a Buddha Image,* but it becomes the focus of the blessings (Thai, *ānisong*) text. In contrast to the KBV the occasion that prompts the making of Buddha images in the northern Thai text is not the Buddha's absence but his presence. The *tathāgata* preaches a sermon on the meritorious blessings for making Buddha images that stresses two primary consequences of this act of *dāna*: future personal benefits ranging from avoidance of rebirth in a low class to the attainment of wealth, high social status, and various heavenly rewards; the prosperity of the town featuring a *saṅgha* of learned, well-disciplined monks supported by a pious laity. The text describes in some detail the meritorious significance of building or sponsoring the construction of a Buddha image calculated according to the cost and rarity of the materials from which the image is made. In an obvious reference to tension within the tradition regarding the efficacy of the cult of images, the text concludes with a cautious reminder that a pure heart and mind is of greater value than the merit garnered from making a Buddha image. The *dāna* of donating Buddha images and other gifts to the *saṅgha* takes its place along with keeping the precepts (*sīla*), listening to sermons, and developing the mental powers of loving kindness (*mettābhavanā*). In the final analysis, this anthology of texts about the construction and veneration of Buddha images encompasses a broad spectrum of beliefs and practices, including protective magic, the omnipresent reality of the Buddha, the efficacy of merit-making acts, keeping the precepts, and meditation.

# PART II

# 4

# THE RITUAL: OPENING THE EYES OF THE BUDDHA

> Whether it is understood as a certain kind of symbolic action, a form of stylized behavior, a self-contained dramatic frame, or a distinctive story of cultural practice, ritual . . . [plays] a salient role in the meaningful construction of personal and social worlds.[1]

> Do you know the tradition of the Netra Mangala? It is a ritual of the eyes. . . . It is always the last thing done. It is what gives the image life. Like a fuse. The eyes are a fuse. . . . Without the eyes there is not just blindness, there is nothing. There is no existence. The artificer brings to life sight and truth and presence.[2]

IN NORTHERN THAILAND, Buddha image consecration ceremonies (*buddhābhiseka*) can be held at any time; however, they usually occur after the end of the monastic rains retreat in October and before Visākha Pūjā, a festival that celebrates the Buddha's birth, enlightenment, and death. The *Buddhābhisekagāthā,* a sixteenth-century northern Thai text, specifically states that to instill into an image the powers achieved by the Buddha at his enlightenment it must be consecrated on the full moon night of the month of Visākha, the very time of the Blessed One's awakening.[3] Today, images are most often consecrated between late October and May to avoid competing with the end of the rains retreat celebrations and rice planting. The date is set in consultation with the major lay sponsor(s) who has purchased and donated the life-size image(s) to be consecrated, the abbot of the monastery where the ceremony is to be held, and the chief ritual officiant. The calendars of invited dignitaries such as government officials, business leaders, and distinguished monks must also be consulted. Because a large ceremony demands extensive planning and coordination, the date may depend as much on such practical considerations as available time and mutual convenience as on a religiously and astrologically auspicious time.

Buddha image consecrations may also be held in conjunction with the opening of a new image hall (*wihān*) or the building used for monastic business (*bōt*). If a damaged image is repaired or if an image is moved to a new location, it will be reconsecrated. Consecrations may also occur

8. Covering the eyes of a Buddha image prior to the *buddhābhiseka*. Wat Phra Kāew, Chiang Rai, Thailand.

specifically in conjunction with major Buddhist celebrations or *wat*-sponsored events: *ngan poy luang* (major event), *ngan chlong* (dedication ceremony), *ngan oprom sompōt* (dedication festival), *ngan buat phra* (ordination ceremony). In March 1990, at Wat Phra Kāew, Chiang Rai, an image consecration was included in a three-day *poy luang* celebration elevating a senior monk to a high ecclesiastical position. The occasion amalgamated a Buddha image consecration ceremony; a life extension rite marking the elevation of Somdet Phra Phuttachinawong, abbot of Wat Benchamabophit, Bangkok, to the rank of *saṅgha* governor of the northern region; and the dedication of the cornerstone of a new *wihān* to house a replica of the famed Emerald Buddha image. I have also attended monastic ordinations where small home shrine images and amulets were reconsecrated by placing them in the ordinand's alms bowl. By so doing they are resacralized through the auspicious power of the ordination ritual. In both examples the symbiotic relationship between the Buddha image and the monk parallels the ritual interaction between monks and the Buddha image during the *buddhābhiseka* and provides insight into how a material image (*paṭimā*) is transformed into the form of the Buddha (*buddharūpa*). In the story of the first Buddha image the interaction between the image and the Buddha authenticates the image's likeness to the Buddha. In a similar manner, during the *buddhābhiseka* the interaction between monks believed to have actualized the perfections (*pāramī*) associated with the Buddha's path and the image validates the images being consecrated as the Buddha's double.

From my observations the *buddhābhiseka* always occurs within the precincts of a *wat,* customarily in the main image hall (*wihān*), the largest building within the *wat* compound. At the far end of the rectangular hall one sees a large, previously consecrated Buddha image resting on a massive dais inlaid with colored glass. In front of this elevated platform a set of wooden altar tables holds various receptacles for incense, candles, and flower offerings brought by devotees. Large pillars in two parallel rows that run the length of the *wihān* support the vaulted three-tier roof, a distinctive feature of Thai temple architecture. The ceremony consecrating the *wihān* signals the building's completion, sanctification, and worthiness as a sacred space appropriate for religious ceremonies.

The *buddhābhiseka* ritual usually takes place between sunset and sunrise. Specific details may vary considerably: the exact duration of the ritual, texts recited and preached during the ceremony, the number of images and amulets to be consecrated, the number of monks involved, and the status of lay sponsors. Despite these variations, fundamentally *the ritual represents a mimetic reenactment of the night of the Buddha's enlightenment.* The timing of the event, the content of the ritual's most distinctive texts, and its dramaturgical aspects homologize the occasion with the story of the Buddha's enlightenment that progressed through the three watches of the night, culminating at sunrise. Furthermore, although the rituals may vary in specific details, they include four basic components: chanting, preaching, meditation, and the presentation of gifts to the *saṅgha* (*thawāi saṅgkhathān*). The following account depicts the setting and the ritual process of the *buddhābhiseka* compiled from several ceremonies.[4] In order to enhance and nuance the rite's richly textured meaning, I have woven analysis and interpretation into the narrative, concluding the chapter by focusing on the ritual's dominant motif, namely, making the Buddha present.[5]

## The Setting[6]

### *The* Bodhimaṇḍa

Consecration rituals most often occur within a specially constructed sacred enclosure inside the main image hall that recreates the *bodhimaṇḍa,* the place of the Buddha's enlightenment. The space is enclosed by a wooden fence (Pāli, *rājavati;* Thai, *rājawat*) extending several feet in each direction.[7] At each corner are placed stalks of bamboo and sugarcane, a

9. Image consecration setting. *Bodhimaṇḍa* in foreground. Temple image in background. Wat Mū'ang Man, Chiang Mai, Thailand.

nine-tier umbrella, a long banner (*tung*), a cluster of coconuts, and a large clay water jar covered with a piece of white cloth. Each jar is filled with water and small pieces of lotus root, sandalwood powder, turmeric, and kaffir lime peel. This water is called the "Buddha image consecration water" (*nām buddhābhiseka,* or *nām khamin som poy*), signifying water that is sacralized with the *khamin* root and *som poy* leaf. A web of cotton cord extends from the hall's previously consecrated, main Buddha image, stretching over the *bodhimaṇḍa* and forming a yantric canopy of 108 small squares.[8] This is the same sacred thread (*sāi siñcana*/water-lustration thread) held by monks during the *paritta* ritual that makes water holy (*nām mon*/water sanctified by *mantra*s).[9] The *sāi siñcana* plays a crucial role in transferring sacred power from a particular source such as a Buddha image to animate or inanimate objects. One lay devotee compared the *sāi siñcana* to an electric cord that conducts the power from a previously consecrated Buddha image in a lineage extending back to the original image commissioned by the Buddha himself, much like a cable conducts electricity from a generator. The power stored in the image is then released by the monks' chanting. Another interpretation is that the chant itself generates power that is carried along the *sāi siñcana* and "recharges" the image's power if it has inadvertently been drained.

The images to be consecrated are placed at the center of the *bodhimaṇḍa*. The largest rest on a bed of grass in front of a potted *bodhi* tree. Their heads are shrouded in white cloths and their eyes covered by beeswax. In front of the *rājawat* pedestal tables (*khan wai khrū*) are piled high with small cone-shaped banana leaf containers of fragrant flowers and incense, betel nuts and betel leaves, husked and unhusked rice. Also present are a set of monk's requisites (robes, alms bowl, fan, wooden bed, sleeping mat, water strainer, sewing box, and a small knife), a rack containing five royal emblems (Thai, *rājakakuthaphan;* Pāli, *rājakakudhabhaṇḍaṃ*), a cruciform stand with three mirrors attached, and a long-handled peacock fan.[10]

The royal emblems and the monastic requisites recall Prince Siddhattha's renunciation of his princely status in search of Buddhahood and denote the close, symbiotic relationship between powerful king and renunciant monk. The sword, staff, and other signs of monarchial power protect the *bodhimaṇḍa* from Māra and his army who seek to prevent the future Buddha from attaining his goal. The bed of grass on which the images rest recalls the offering given to the Buddha by the grass-cutter, Sotthiya, while the *tathāgata* was seated under the tree of enlightenment. In the legend of the Buddha's awakening the bed of grass miraculously becomes a diamond throne.[11]

The image's white head covering, the beeswax closures, the three mirrors, and the peacock fan are cues to the story of Prince Siddhattha's enlightenment and attainment of Buddhahood. The beeswax covering the eyes of the image and the white cloth shroud suggest the Buddha in his preenlightenment state or a saint in a state of *samādhi.* Just as Prince Siddhattha isolated himself from the distractions of the world in his quest for the answer to the question of suffering (*dukkha*), so also the statue must be sequestered in the process by which it becomes the Buddha's double. While a monk applies the beeswax to the eyes of image, he recites three times the following *gāthā:* "*nibbāna* eye, all-seeing eye, wisdom eye, Buddha eye, *dhamma* eye, *saṅgha* eye, precious eye, *svāha.*"[12] At the conclusion of the ritual the beeswax and head coverings are removed, symbolizing the fulfillment of the monk's act of truth as he covered the eyes, or the saint's awakening from *samādhi* as he renews contact with the world. The three mirrors represent the three knowledges that define the culmination of the *tathāgata*'s spiritual journey—*pubbenivāsānussatiñāṇa* (knowledge of his past lives), *cutūpapātañāṇa* (knowledge of the coming into being and passing away of all beings), *āsavakkhayañāṇa* (knowledge of the destruction of the mental intoxicants).[13] During the ritual performance the mirrors face the image but at its conclusion they are turned outward to face the congregants. The peacock fan recalls the legend that following the Buddha's *nibbāna* he was fanned by the gods in honor of his victorious achievement.

Beyond their narrative reference, these material objects allude to even more archaic levels of meaning. The miraculous emergence of the diamond throne infuses the Buddha's awakening with royal, cosmic import.[14] Similarly, the *bodhimaṇḍa* protected by the *rājawat* demarcates a sacred cosmos (*cakkavāḷa*), a significance reinforced by the intricate web of 108 squares stretching over the area. This ceiling or sky dome resembles a maṇḍalaic template joined to the earth through the conduits of sacred cord extending around its perimeter. The use of mirrors—a ubiquitous feature of Buddha image eye-opening rituals throughout Buddhist Asia—suggests that the process by which the image becomes the Buddha's double resembles an act of shamanic divination. The fanning of the image cools the alchemical heat generated by the ritual that metamorphizes mere metal, wood, or stone into the Buddha.

The Buddha image consecration ritual connotes an even more elemental transformation associated with birth and death. The mimetic reenactment of Sujātā's offering of milk rice resembles the act of first-feeding, signifying the image's "birth" as the Buddha. The term *maṇḍa,* meaning the essence of milk, points to Sujātā as the instrumental cause of the Buddha's enlightenment. The *buddhābhiseka* likewise contains analogs to

10. *Maṇḍala* design over the *bodhimaṇḍa*. Wat Chet Yot, Chiang Mai, Thailand.

death rituals. While a statue and a dead body are insentient, paradoxically both embody—at least potentially—a living spirit. Recent scholarship in Ch'an (Zen) studies explores the relationship between beliefs about death and the afterlife, the body, and iconographic representations of Buddhist saints. Traditional Chinese beliefs regarding the lingering presence of the soul and mortuary practices whose aim was to prevent the decomposition of the corpse may have influenced the Ch'an practice of mummifying revered masters,[15] a practice extended to icons and statues.[16] These practices included inserting jade or bone into the body's orifices in the belief that doing so prevented decay.[17] In Thailand after bathing the corpse and inserting betel nut and a coin in the mouth, the head or only the eyes and mouth may be covered with beeswax overlaid with gold leaf.[18] In the *buddhābhiseka* the statue of the Buddha is not unlike a dead body that is brought to life. Like funeral rites, the image consecration ritual can be seen as a rejuvenating act prior to which death or nonsentience is but a necessary prelude.[19] Other aspects of the *buddhābhiseka* imply that not only the body of the Buddha but also his image actually incarnates the *tathāgata*'s supernal qualities in a manner quite similar to beliefs regarding the postdeath remains of Buddhist saints in India, China, and Japan.[20] This interpretation underscores the strong parallel between bodily relics and images, notwithstanding references that either omit images from a list of kammically potent objects of veneration (*Milindapañho*, 341), or make a clear distinction between images and bodily relics on the grounds that an image is without foundation (*avatthuka*) because it lacks the physical connection with the Buddha of bodily and contact relics (*Kāliṅgabodhi Jātaka*).

## *Offerings to the* Guru

In front of the *bodhimaṇḍa* low, round tables called *khan tang* are piled high with small banana leaf cones filled with incense sticks and flowers, strings of dried betel nut, cowrie shells, bowls of husked and unhusked rice, and pieces of red and white cloth that represent traditional offerings given to honor one's teacher (*khan wai khrū*).[21] Theravāda Buddhist texts portray the Buddha as teacher, so it is appropriate that the Buddha image consecration ritual would include gifts honoring the Buddha in that role. The term *guru*, furthermore, contains an archaic meaning that includes the *tathāgata* as a *mana*-filled being who radiates fiery power (*teja*).[22] Tradition stipulates that the objects included in this presentation should be two large candles of one baht weight (15 grams), four small candles of one-half baht weight, fifty-six small cone-shaped banana leaf containers of fragrant flowers, one meter of white cloth, one meter of red cloth, 1,003 cowrie shells, 1,003 large betel nuts, four packets of betel

11. Offerings to the *guru* (*khan wai khrū*).
Wat Mū'ang Man, Chiang Mai, Thailand.

leaves, one bushel of unhusked rice, one large coconut shell measure of husked rice, 2 kilograms of bananas, one bunch of coconuts, a 108 baht weight silver container, one large water jar in which a figure of a serpent (Pāli, *nāga;* Thai, *nāk*) lies submerged, and several small figurines (ox, turtle, chicken, snake, elephant, horse, woman) placed appropriately on or around the offering table.[23]

The objects associated with the *khan wai khrū* are not arbitrary but convey specific meanings. The numbers 108 and 56 symbolize the power valencies radiated by the guardians of the eight directions, the four cosmic elements (earth, water, fire, air), and, in particular, the three gems—the Buddha, his teaching (*dhamma*), and the monastic order (*saṅgha*). Each is assigned a quality (*guṇa*) or a level of power. The *guṇa* of the Buddha is 56 and that number together with the *dhamma* (38) and the *saṅgha* (14) comprise 108, represented in the number of syllables when the combined qualities of the Buddha, *dhamma,* and *saṅgha* ("*iti pi so . . .*") are recited; hence, within the context of the ritual, these sacred numbers are not merely symbolized by objects and yantric-like designs but are actually generated by particular chant-recitations.

The water jar and the small figure of the *nāk* recall the episode in the Buddha story where, prior to the *bodhisatta*'s enlightenment, Mahākāḷa, a *nāga* king asleep on the bottom of the Nerañjarā River, awakens to witness Prince Siddhattha's *nibbāna.*[24] Because the *nāga* king was present at

Sakyamuni's enlightenment, King Asoka asks Mahākāḷa to make a likeness of the Buddha:

> The king spoke to him: "Let us behold the (bodily) form of the omniscient Great Sage whose boundless knowledge has set rolling the wheel of the true *dhamma*." The *nāga* king created a beauteous figure of the Buddha, endowed with the thirty-two greater signs and brilliant with the eighty lesser signs of a Buddha, surrounded by the fathom-long rays of glory and adorned with a crown of flames.
>
> At this sight the king was filled with joy and amazement and thought: "If such is the image created by Mahākāḷa then what must the real form of the *tathāgata* have been!" And more and more uplifted with joy for seven days without ceasing the king of wondrous power kept the great festival called the eye-opening ceremony (*akkhipūjā*).[25]

Because the serpent king's life span extends over the entire eon, Mahākāḷa links the Buddha Gotama to the preceding Buddhas of this age (*bhaddakappa*). The *buddhābhiseka* celebrates both the Buddha Gotama of our era and the eternal lineage of Buddhas from the beginning of time.

The small, crudely made clay figures in the water jar provide a mundane (*lokiya*) counterpart to the supermundane (*lokuttara*) Buddha images being consecrated. Such figurines are also associated with the *phithī sado khro,* a northern Thai good-fortune ritual traditionally a part of the *songkrān* (New Year) celebration. In the *phithī sado khro,* small doll-like figures of people and animals as well as articles of clothing are ritually consecrated, symbolizing the protection and renewal of life at the beginning of the new year.[26] Other *khan wai khrū* offerings represent objects necessary to maintain life. In premodern times, cowrie shells and betel nuts were used as currency. Rice, coconuts, and bananas sustain life and together with sugarcane and bamboo are central to the traditional northern Thai "life-extension" (*sū'pchātā*) rituals performed at times of illness, life transition, and village or town crises.[27] By incorporating these elements into the Buddha image consecration ceremony, the performative power of the ritual is further enhanced as a rite of passage by which the image becomes the Buddha.

The pervasive use of polarities—large and small, gold and silver, husked and unhusked rice, white and red—can be understood as the ritual's power to integrate opposites or may underscore the theme of transformation central to the meaning of the *buddhābhiseka.*[28] Recent anthropological studies of South Indian rituals associate the use of red and white cloth with heating and cooling, respectively, as in divining rituals related to illness and health.[29] Heat is associated with life and fertility, and because it can both create and destroy life, it must be balanced with cool. "In ritual, as in mythology, heat must be encompassed or surrounded by cooling things. Red substances symbolize 'heated' states and white substances 'cooled' ones."[30] White expresses well-being and indicates recovery and stability; red, as a color of vitality, is appropriate when something life-giving is about to occur.[31] Within the context of the *buddhābhiseka*, the offering of red and white cloth suggests that the ritual brings the image to life (i.e., heat) and then cools it by fanning in order to stabilize the transformation that has taken place.

## The Ritual Process[32]

Buddha image consecration rituals generally commence at dusk and conclude at sunrise. With the increasing popularity of the *buddhābhiseka,* crowds may gather well before an announced 7:30 P.M. starting time. Old and young, men and women, boys and girls, all ages and social classes crowd in, overflow the image hall, and spill out onto the front veranda and the surrounding temple compound. Early that morning monks and a lay committee prepared the premises, cleaned the hall, gathered the images and amulets to be consecrated, made arrangements for the monks invited especially for the occasion, and readied the requisite ritual paraphernalia.

### *Preliminaries*

The ceremony begins in the traditional way of most Buddhist rituals. Respects are paid to the Buddha (Thai, *wai phra*) by chanting the appropriate Pāli phrases honoring the Triple Gem ("*arahaṃ sammāsambuddho bhagavā . . .*");[33] the assembled congregation takes refuge (*saranaṃ gacchāmi*) in the Buddha, his teaching (*dhamma*), and the monastic order (*saṅgha*); then the monks "give" the precepts of sabbath observance to the assembled laity. The idiom for this verbal transaction is Pāli chanted by both monks and laity. The devotees are led by an experienced former monk known as the monastery teacher (*āchān* [Pāli, *ācariya*] *wat*).[34] Following the giving of the precepts the congregants join in a unison chant of homage and forgiveness (Pāli, *vandanā;* Thai, *kham kho khamā*):

I pay homage to the Buddha. May the Buddha forgive my wrongdoings.

I pay homage to the Dhamma. May the Dhamma forgive my wrongdoings.

I pay homage to the Saṅgha. May the Saṅgha forgive my wrongdoings.

I pay homage to preceptors and teachers. May they forgive my wrongdoings.

I pay homage to meditation subjects (*kammaṭṭhāna*).[35] May they forgive my wrongdoings.

I pay homage to the monastery boundary stones (*buddhasīmā*). May they forgive my wrongdoings.

I pay homage at all times to the *cetiya,* the relics enshrined in all places, the *bodhi* tree, and all Buddha images.

I pay homage to the Buddha's bodily relics, hair relics, the relics of the saints (*arahanta*), the *cetiya,* the *gandhakuṭi,* the 84,000 *dhammakkhandha,* and the footprints (*pāda cetiya*) of all the Buddhas in the Nāgaloka, the Devaloka, the Brahmaloka, Jambudīpa, and Laṅkādīpa.

The previously prepared offering trays are then presented to the Buddha image.

The formal beginning of the image consecration ceremony proper commences with the lighting of a tall, glass-encased candle before the *bodhimaṇḍa* performed by the chief officiating monk while the other assisting monks sit on the chanting platform in the order of their monastic rank and tenure. The candle, called the *thīan chai* (victory candle), corresponds to the height of the chief sponsor. Its wick is formed by the number of strands equal to the age of the sponsor. *Mantra*s written on pieces of paper are wound around the wick.[36] The head monk stands in front of the candle and chants:

By the power of the Omniscient Buddha, the supermundane *dhamma,* and the highest virtue-attaining *saṅgha,* may all suffering, calamities, and dangers vanish. May all beings live without injury.

Following this invocation, the chief sponsor of the event is invited to light the three large candles between the Buddha image altar and the *bodhimaṇḍa*. The middle candle is named the *thīan wipassī* (Buddha Vipassī candle) and the two on either side are called the *thīan mongkhon* (Pāli, *maṅgala*) *sāi* and *thīan mongkhon khwā* (the auspicious candles on the left and right). In the Theravāda tradition Vipassī is the first of the six Buddhas preceding Gotama.[37] The lighting of this candle honors the eternal lineage of eonic Buddhas, Gotama being the historical expression in this age.[38] The two *thīan mongkhon* represent the polarity between the mundane (*lokiya*) and transmundane (*lokuttara*), a distinction fundamental to Theravāda thought. The candles also symbolize the mutual interdependence of the Triple Gem and the lay patron. The height of the *thīan wipassī* equals the length of the leg of the sponsor, and the wick consists of fifty-six threads, the constituent qualities (*guṇa*) of the Buddha. The two *mongkhon* candles are to be as tall as the circumference of the head of the sponsor, and their wicks are formed of thirty-eight threads, the constituent qualities of the *dhamma*.

Once all of these preliminaries are complete—paying respects to the Buddha with offering trays, taking the refuges and the precepts, the explanation of the ceremony, honoring the sponsors, and the lighting of the various candles charged with symbolic meaning—the ritual of opening the eyes of the Buddha begins in earnest. By this time it is completely dark outside. The visual atmosphere created by the flickering candlelight illuminating the shrouded Buddha images is enhanced by the reverberating sound of the monks' chanting that continues through much of the night. Soon after the chanting begins, additional sponsors and distinguished guests are invited to light candelabras with sixteen and nine candles in front of the altar tables located in front of the *wihān*'s main Buddha image.

In addition to the victory candle and right and left *mongkhon* candles, three other candle arrangements embody specific Theravāda teachings. When the offering trays are presented before the Buddha image, five candles are lighted representing the five ascetics (*thīan hā pok*) to whom the Buddha presented his first teaching. Alternatively they can be interpreted as signifying the five Buddhas of the current age. A series of sixteen candles is said to indicate the sixteen levels of the Brahma heavens or, more generally, the sublime rewards to be gained by sponsoring the consecration of a Buddha image. A candelabra of nine candles is interpreted as the four stages on the path to Buddhahood and their corresponding fruits (*maggaphala*), culminating in *nibbāna* (*navalokuttaradhamma*). Taken together these *buddhābhiseka* candle arrangements symbolize the different meanings incorporated into the Buddha image consecration ceremony, from the hoped-for blessings of personal happiness resulting from such meritorious activity, to honoring one's religion, teachers, and parents, to the more sublime goal of enlightenment and equanimity.

## Paritta *and Image Consecration*

Following the lighting of the *thīan chai* and the two *thīan mongkhon* candles and the presentation of the offering trays to the Buddha image, the lay congregational leader (*āchān wat*)[39] invites the monks to begin reciting the *paritta* (*ārāthanā paritta*), known in Thai as chanting the *mantra* or *suat mon*. The monks respond by first inviting all the gods and supernatural beings (*chumnum devatā*) with a "chant that resounds to the highest heavens" (*suat sagge luang*):

> May the *devatā* that live in the heavens, the realm of desire (*kāmabhūmi*), the realm of form (*rūpabhūmi*), mountains, rivers, the palace in the sky, islands, towns, countryside, forests, houses, and paddy fields, the *yakkha, gandhabba,* and *nāga* that live in the water and on the land, may they all lis-

ten to the *dhamma* now preached by the righteous. Now is the time to listen to the *dhamma* preached by the righteous; now is the time to listen to the preaching of the *dhamma*.

Due to the importance of the Buddha image consecration ritual, the period of *paritta* chanting continues for several hours. The event's auspiciousness is underscored by the extended period of *suat mon* and the fact that highly revered, senior monks lead the ceremony. Since many texts will be recited, the *suat mon* is referred to as an "inclusive" (literally, "piled up") chanting of the *paritta* (Thai, *suat mon tang* or *suat tang lum*).[40] Texts will be selected from the standard northern Thai collections of the Pāli *paritta* called the Collection of Seven (*Chet Tamnān*) and the Collection of Twelve (*Sipsong Tamnān*).[41] In addition to selections from the traditional Pāli *paritta,* such as the *Maṅgala Sutta, Ratana Sutta,* and *Karaṇīyamettā Sutta,* which constitute the content of *paritta* chanting throughout Theravāda Buddhist cultures, major northern Thai rituals will include recitations unique to the region.[42]

Most monks invited to chant at Buddha image consecration rituals and other major ceremonies that I have observed have memorized all of the appropriate chants. Those who have not rely on a folio of chants collated by Phra Khrū Siriratanasunthorn, Wat Nantharām, Chiang Mai (*Pap Suat Mon Tan*), which does not delineate the texts by name. A particular *sutta* or *paritta* is recognized by its opening word or lines. For example, monks know that "*yanidhabhuta*" refers to the *Ratana Sutta* and that "*virupakkhe*" is the *Khandha Paritta.* Divisions among the *sutta* and *paritta* used in the *suat mon* are of secondary importance to the sense of the chant as a whole, even though a particular sequence will be followed, with each section initiated by the officiating monk. This observation, while seemingly of minor significance, raises an important question about the nature of *suat mon,* especially for the Western student accustomed to think in terms of specific written texts with titles. To approach *paritta* chanting in this way bifurcates what is perceived as an integrated, sacred whole. Comprehending the *dhamma* in a ritual context rather than as written text integrates the apocryphal 84,000 facets of the Buddha's teaching into a seamless unity at the level of oral/aural experience. In rituals with powerful positive kammic potency (*phithī kam*), the historical and literary aspects of the texts chanted are unimportant. In this context the power of the ritual experience depends less upon correspondences to a written text than upon sound uttered and heard. The *suat mon* is so quintessentially an oral/aural and visual experience that to observe monks chanting from a book is qualitatively different from watching them with closed eyes reciting continuously for an hour or more solely from memory.

In the *buddhābhiseka* the chanting of *paritta* and other recitations is primarily an affective rather than cognitive experience. As I sit with a congregation during an image consecration ceremony in a candlelit *wihān,* the sound of the chant washes over me like waves echoing into the dark silence of the night. As they recite, the monks hold the *paritta* cord (*sāi siñcana*) that extends from the Buddha image above and around the sacred *bodhimaṇḍa* enclosure. The chant continues unabated until the unison chorus pauses, only to be resumed again under the direction of the lead monk while the assembled congregation sits in silent, concentrated meditation.

## *Texts*

Although the specific *paritta* recited at the beginning of the image consecration ritual vary, they may include the following:[43] the *Aṭṭhavīsati Buddha Paritta, Mahāsamaya Sutta, Maṅgala Sutta, Ratana Sutta, Kalaṇīyamettā Sutta, Khandha Paritta, Mora Paritta, Dhajagga Paritta, Āṭānāṭiya Paritta, Mahāmoggallāna Sutta, Buddhajayamaṅgala Aṭṭhagāthā, Aṅgulimāla Paritta, Hiriottappa, Jayapañjara Gāthā,*[44] *Uṇhassavijaya, Maṅgala Cakkavāḷa, Dasa Pāramī, Sukho Buddho*. Together they represent a wide range of Buddhist teachings.[45] I have included translations from lesser known *paritta* with particular relevance to this study: *Jayamaṅgala Aṭṭhagāthā, Dasa Pāramī, Sukho Buddho,* and *Jinapañjara.* They highlight Buddhological concepts central to the Thai Buddhist worldview and to the *buddhābhiseka:* the Buddha as victor over evil personified by Māra; the Buddha as the embodiment of all perfections; and the Buddha, *dhamma,* and *saṅgha* as guarantors of mundane and transmundane happiness. The most unique is the *Jinapañjara* (The Victor's Cage), which depicts the transmutation of Buddhas, *arahants*, the *dhamma,* and various *paritta* into the body as protection from all forms of evil, as the symbols of royal power in a similar way protect the *bodhimaṇḍa* from Māra during the Buddha image consecration ritual. The assimilation of these powers into the body, furthermore, resembles the fusion of the person of the Buddha and the *dhamma* with the image, thereby transforming it from a mere material representation into a cult icon—the living presence of the *tathāgata.* These parallels reinforce the connection between the *paritta* and the Buddha image consecration ritual.

### *Buddhajayamaṅgala Aṭṭhagāthā* (The Auspicious Victory)[46]

The Buddha, full of great compassion, the refuge of the world, performed all perfections for the benefit of all beings, and attained supreme enlightenment. By uttering this truth may victory and auspiciousness be with you.

The Buddha conquered Māra at the foot of the *bodhi* tree. He brought delight to the Sakyan people. By this virtue may you be a conqueror; may you gain victory as did the Buddha on the auspicious, undefiled throne where all the Buddhas were consecrated. Such a victor is filled with joy.

May good fortune, good days, good times, good moments, a good watch of the night, and good devotion be with those who live a holy life. May good bodily acts, good verbal acts, good mental acts, and a good state of being lead to good consequences.

May all goodness come to you; may all the deities protect you; by the virtues of all the Buddhas may good fortune be yours forever.

May . . . by the virtue of all the *dhamma* . . . be yours forever

May . . . by the virtue of all the *saṅgha* . . . be yours forever.

### *Dasa Pāramī* (The Ten Perfections)[47]

Because of past causes, the Blessed One performed ordinary, superior, and supreme perfections of giving (*dāna*). He was endowed with the perfections of lovingkindness (*mettā*), compassion (*karuṇā*), sympathetic joy (*muditā*), and equanimity (*upekkhā*).

Because of past causes, the Blessed One performed ordinary, superior, and supreme perfections of renunciation (*nekkhamma*). He was also endowed with the perfections of lovingkindness. . . .

Because of past causes, the Blessed One performed ordinary, superior, and supreme perfections of wisdom (*paññā*). He was also endowed with the perfections of lovingkindness. . . .

Because of past causes, the Blessed One performed ordinary, superior, and supreme perfections of exertion (*viriya*). He was also endowed with the perfections of lovingkindness. . . .

Because of past causes, the Blessed One performed ordinary, superior, and supreme perfections of patience (*khanti*). He was . . .

Because of past causes, the Blessed One performed ordinary, superior, and supreme perfections of truth (*sacca*). He was . . .

Because of past causes, the Blessed One performed ordinary, superior, and supreme perfections of resolution (*adhiṭṭhāna*). He was . . .

Because of past causes, the Blessed One performed ordinary, superior, and supreme perfections of lovingkindness (*mettā*). He was . . .

Because of past causes, the Blessed One performed ordinary, superior, and supreme perfections of equanimity (*upekkhā*). He was . . .

Because of past causes, the Blessed One performed the ten perfections of all manners and kinds (literally, "ordinary, superior, and supreme") . . .

### *Sukho Buddho* (Happiness Is the Buddha)[48]

The birth of the Buddhas is happiness; listening to their *dhamma* is happiness; the harmony of the *saṅgha* is happiness; the religious duty of the assembly is happiness.

The ruler is supreme among human beings. Among all divine and human beings the one endowed with true knowledge and who practices it is superior.

The sun shines by day; the moon by night; a ruler with superior strength shines; the Brahman who attains the state of absorption shines; but the Buddha shines both day and night by his power.

To be free from illness is the supreme physical gift; contentedness is the supreme wealth; friendship is the supreme relationship; but, *nibbāna* is the supreme happiness.

### *Jinapañjara Gāthā* (The Victor's Cage)[49]

The Buddhas, the noble ones who drank the nectar of the four noble truths, having come to the victory seat, having defeated Māra on his mount;

These Buddhas, the twenty-eight leaders, the sovereign sages beginning with Taṇhaṅkara, are all established on the crown of my head.

The Buddha is established in my head, the *dhamma* in my eyes, the *saṅgha,* the mine of all virtues, is established in my chest.

Anuruddha is in my heart, Sāriputta on my right, Koṇḍañña behind me, and Moggallāna on my left.

Ānanda and Rāhula are in my right ear, Kassapa and Mahānāma are in my left ear.

Sobhita, the noble sage, sits in full glory, shining like the sun over the hair at the back of my head.

The great sage, a wellspring of virtue, Elder Kumāra-kassapa, noted for his gift of speech, is constantly in my mouth.

Five elders, Puṇṇa, Aṅgulimāla, Upāli, Nanda, and Sīvalī, have appeared as auspicious marks at the middle of my forehead.

The remaining eighty great leaders—victors, disciples of the victorious Buddha, sons of the victorious Buddha, shining with the majesty of moral virtue—are established in the parts of my body.

The *Ratana Sutta* is in front of me, the *Mettā Sutta* on my right, the *Dhajagga Paritta* behind me, the *Aṅgulimāla* [*Paritta*s] on my left. The *Khandha, Mora,* and the *Āṭānāṭiya Paritta*s are a roof over me. The remaining *sutta*s are a fortress wall [around me].

Protected by the seven fortresses of the Victors' realm, may all misfortunes within and without caused by such things as wind or bile be destroyed without remainder through the majesty of the eternal Victor.

In all that I do, I always dwell in the cage of the Self-awakened Ones; living grounded in the midst of the cage of the Victors, I am always guarded by all of the great noble ones.

Thus am I utterly well-sheltered and well-protected;
Through the power of the Victor misfortunes are vanquished;
Through the power of the *dhamma* hordes of enemies are vanquished;
Through the power of the *saṅgha* dangers are vanquished;
Guarded by the power of the true *dhamma* I live in the Victors' Cage.

## Paritta *and* Abhiseka

Monks chant the evening *paritta* (*suat charoen phraphutta mon*) seated in a lotus posture on a raised platform situated along the wall to the right of the main Buddha image in the *wihān*. A monk's alms bowl with a yellow beeswax candle attached to its rim faces the chief officiating monk. A *sāi siñcana* cord extends from the main temple image to the begging bowl. At the beginning of the *suat mon* the officiating monk passes the ball of sacred cord to the next monk and so on to each monk down the line. The monks hold the *sāi siñcana* throughout the entire *suat mon* period. At the beginning of the *Maṅgala Sutta* the head monk or the chief lay sponsor lights the candle and later extinguishes it in the begging bowl at the point in the *Ratana Sutta* where the text likens the destruction of becoming and the realization of the cessation of passions to the extinguishing of a flame.[50] Through the combined potency of the *suat mon*, the begging bowl, the *sāi siñcana* cord, and the ritual acts of lighting and extinguishing the candle at the appropriate times during the chant, the monks create *mantra* or holy water (*nām mon*). In ritual strategies more often associated with Tantra rather than Theravāda, ordinary water is charged with power through the interaction of sacred persons (monks), sacred words (*paritta/mantra*), symbolic actions, alms bowl, and consecrated cord. In a similar vein, Roger Jackson observes that the *pirit* ceremony as performed in Sri Lanka "reveals a number of features that call to mind elements found in Indo-Tibetan Buddhist tantric traditions, especially in *abhiseka* (consecration, empowerment, initiation) ceremonies."[51]

A monk's alms bowl and robe symbolize the essence of the monastic life. The homeless, celibate monk, the polar opposite of the householder who marries, has children, grows crops, and so on, produces no visible material goods. The begging bowl represents both the monastic state of nonattachment as well as the powerful qualities generated by the ascetic life. Holy or *mantra* water becomes one of the sacred (Thai, *saksit*) fruits of the *suat mon*, an especially important benefit of the *buddhābhiseka*. Because of the unusually long period of chanting during the consecration ritual, the presence of senior, highly venerated monks, and the large number of Buddha images and other holy objects in the *wihān,* the *mantra* water sacralized at Buddha image consecration ceremonies is believed to be especially efficacious. The sprinkling of the holy water signals the conclusion of the *abhiseka* as an auspicious seal of the ritual's completion.

The chant that concludes the evening recitation mirrors the ritual's beginning. The evening started by inviting the presence of various sacred powers and concludes with a chant *(Dukkhappatta)* that requests the extension of their blessing to all living beings:

> May all living beings who suffer be free from suffering, those who meet with danger be free from danger, those who are sorrowful be free from sorrow.
>
> May all divine beings (*devā*) approve of the merit we have accumulated so that by their accomplishments (*siddhi*) we may gain wealth. Give gifts (*dāna*) faithfully, observe the precepts continually, delight in meditation. May I be protected by the power of the Buddhas, the *paccekabuddhas,* and the *arahants.*

## Opening the Eyes of the Buddha

Midway into the evening, sometime before midnight, one or two additional periods of extended chant recitation occur that are unique to the ritual. One text recited is the Pāli "Buddha [Image] Consecration" (*Buddha Abhiseka*) (BA), a featured event in Thai image consecrations. The northern Thai vernacular version of the BA is also preached during the evening. A second text, the "Eye-Opening Sutta" (*Suat Bōek Phranet*) (SBN), is unique to northern Thailand. The SBN is a Pāli text with no northern Thai sermon version (*desanā*). Some informants speculate that the core of the traditional northern Thai consecration ritual may have been structured around an alternation between vernacular sermons and chanting the three sections of the SBN. Such a scheme would represent a symbiosis between esoteric and exoteric performative modes, an interactive movement between a highly distinctive form of Pāli chanting in a unique singsong cadence alternating with the preaching of stories about the life of the Buddha in northern Thai, comprehensible to a lay audience.

The SBN is usually chanted in one sitting lasting less than an hour unless performed by groups of monks from different *wats* in a manner similar to the *thet mahāchāt,* whereby monks display their skill at preaching the *Vessantara Jātaka.*[52] Because the *suat bōek* demands special training, teams of monks from different monasteries are often invited to demonstrate their proficiency in this chanting style, thereby lengthening its recital time.

12. Monks chanting the *suat bōek* during the image consecration ritual. Wat Phra Kāew, Chiang Rai, Thailand.

The SBN represents the most distinctive aural/oral aspect of the Buddha image consecration ritual. Its recitation and the participation of monk-meditators noted for their spiritual prowess greatly enhance the extraordinary nature of the event. If the SBN is omitted the ritual assumes a less auspicious, mystical ambience. Five or seven monks and novices perform the recitation seated around a low, round, wooden table upon which the lead monk has placed the text written on a traditional northern Thai mulberry paper album (*samut khoi* or *bap sā*). He directs the recitation with a baton, keeping the cadence by striking the *samut khoi,* a rhythmic device absent from all other ritual chants in Thai Buddhism.[53] The complexity of the recitation demands long hours of practice and requires voices capable of reaching both high and low ranges. Toward the end of the SBN the chant becomes especially unusual and dramatic, and when asked what makes the *suat bōek* chant so special, informants invariably mention its unique cadence that mimics the sounds of birds and animals.

The similarities between the BA and the SBN and the possibility that the BA may have been preached in the northern Thai vernacular as early as the fifteenth century lends credence to the view that chanting the Pāli BA during the *buddhābhiseka* could be a later development. The juxtaposition between the BA and the SBN points to the close relationship between preaching (*thet;* Pāli, *desanā*) and chanting (*suat*).[54] In the same vein, the *suat bōek* chant style and cadence recalls the preaching eloquence of the *āchān wat,* the northern Thai lay ritual leader, when he performs "spirit calling" (*riak khwan*) rites.[55] On these occasions, the voice of the *āchān wat* ranges from high falsetto to a low, gravelly basso.

The eerie cadence of the *suat bōek* sustains interest, keeps people awake during a long ceremony, and creates a mystical atmosphere consistent with the esoteric intent of the SBN, namely, to hyposticize the Buddha. The text can be cognitively understood as connecting the story of the Buddha's enlightenment and the consecration of a Buddha image, but *hearing* the *suat bōek* recited in the early hours of the morning after an all-night vigil evokes the palpable reality of that relationship. The chant becomes the medium through which the unseen reality of the Buddha (*dhammakāya*) is joined to the material reality of the image (*rūpakāya*). From this perspective, the monk practitioner's role could be considered shamanic. As the *mo khwan* (spirit doctor) and *āchān wat* call the spirits into a person's body during a spirit calling ceremony (*phithī riak khwan*), so the monks through their chant invoke the "spirit" of the Buddha into the image. In 1985, the late Kraisī Nimmhemindā, a Chiang Mai businessman and avid student of northern Thai culture, sponsored the construction of a Buddha image. For the consecration ceremony he invited an *āchān wat* to perform a *riak khwan,* "calling the spirit of the Prince Siddhattha," to be present at the ceremony. Monks who witnessed the event reported the invocation as idiosyncratic, but justified it on the grounds that the purpose of the *buddhābhiseka* is to en-liven, or in this case to "en-spirit," the Buddha image.

### *Sermons: "Ordaining" the Buddha*

During the all-night ceremony several sermons are likely to be preached depending on the head liturgist, the interests of the lay patrons, and the number of monks invited to deliver sermons. At least three texts are usually preached: the *Pathom Somphōt* (PS) (Pāli, *Paṭhama Sambodhi*) (The Buddha's Supreme Enlightenment); the *Buddha Abhiseka* (BA) (Consecrating the Buddha); and the *Dhammacakkappavattana Sutta* (Setting in Motion the Wheel of Truth). When image consecrations form part of a major celebration that lasts several days, additional sermons are included. In times past in large monasteries sermons were preached simultaneously in several image halls, a rare occurrence today.

Within the context of the Buddha image consecration ritual, sermons serve two major purposes: to instruct (*oprom*) the image and the congregants in the life story of the Buddha, and together with chant recitation and meditation, to empower the image. The BA and the SBN complement one another with their focus on the Buddha's attainments prior to,

13. Preaching a sermon during the image consecration ritual. Wat Mū'ang Man, Chiang Mai, Thailand.

during, and after his enlightenment. In the sermon form of the BA these attainments are called *ñāṇa*. *Ñāṇa,* as imperceptible aggregates of the mental powers of the Buddha, are implanted into the image, thereby imbuing it with a supernal range of spiritual perfections or *pāramī* (Thai, *tham hai saksit*).

The PS and the now rarely preached *Sitthāt Ōk Buat* (SB) (Siddhattha's Renunciation) elaborate details of the Buddha's life for the mutual edification of image and laity. SB is more frequently recited at the beginning of the monsoon rains retreat to highlight the paradigmatic role of Siddhattha's renunciation and enlightenment quest for the young ordinand entering the *saṅgha*. Its occasional use as a preached text during a Buddha image consecration ceremony denotes the connection between the rite of ordination and the consecration of a Buddha image. Both rituals are referred to as *buat phra,* "ordaining the venerable one," and are mimetic reenactments of the Blessed One's quest for *nibbāna*.

In northern Thailand and other Southeast Asian Buddhist cultures, the custom of novitiate ordination centers on a reenactment of Prince Siddhattha's renunciation. Although the details of the ceremony and its duration vary depending on the location, the cost, and the cultural awareness of the family, it is typically divided into three preliminary segments before the ordination proper:[56] first, the youth, referred to as a *nāk*

(Pāli, *nāga*), has his head and eyebrows shaved, is dressed in white robes, and then receives his saffron monastic robes from his appointed teacher (Thai, *āchān;* Pāli, *ācariya*); second, the *nāk* will be dressed in a royal costume emulating Prince Siddhattha and led in procession through the streets of the town or village; third, a spirit calling (Thai, *tham khwan, phuk khwan, riak khwan, sū khwan bāi sī*) will be held either in the ordinand's home or at the *wat*. The Thai word, *khwan,* may be derived from a similar word in archaic Chinese meaning soul or spirit. Presumably under the influence of the Buddhist concept of thirty-two bodily constitutents, Thai Buddhists enumerate thirty-two *khwan*. The core of many life-passage rites is the calling (*riak*), tying (*phuk*), or making (*tham*) the thirty-two spirits. Spirit calling rituals always involve an offering tray (*bāi sī*). When spirit calling rituals are connected with ordinations, large *bāi sī* will be pyramidal in shape and divided into five, seven, or nine tiers reminiscent of a *chedī*.[57]

After the spirit calling ritual, the *nāk* is carried or will ride, sometimes on a horse, in procession to the *wat,* where he dresses in monk's robes in preparation for taking monastic vows. The parallels between novitiate ordination and the legend of Prince Siddhattha's going forth are striking. Both represent the transformational structure of a rite of passage. In schematic terms a future king renounces his throne, embarks on a quest for a higher truth, accomplishes his goal, and is transformed into the fully enlightened Buddha. This transformational journey from prince to Buddha serves as one of the basic reference points for both ordination and the Buddha image consecration ritual. The *buddhābhiseka* incorporates the symbols of this journey from kingship to Buddhahood. At an even more elemental level, opening the eyes of the Buddha image transforms an insentient object from a material representation of the Buddha into the Blessed One's real presence.

Like the *buddhābhiseka,* ordination reflects the theme of transformation, especially with regard to the symbolism of the *nāga*. In the story of the Buddha's enlightenment the *nāga,* Mahākāḷa, witnesses Siddhattha's achievement of Buddhahood, and during the third week after the Buddha's enlightenment the *nāga* king, Mucalinda, shelters the Buddha during a rainstorm. Cosmogonies often homologize serpent and water as a symbol of fertile, (re)creative power, but in the case of novitiate ordination, the serpent, a reptile that renews itself by shedding its skin, is associated primarily with transformation. The reason the candidate for *sāmaṇera* ordination is called a *nāk* is given in the following etiological folk legend:

> During the Lord Buddha's time, a certain *nāga* or mythological snake, by its magical power turned itself into a man and became by ordination a monk. One day the *nāga* monk during a deep sleep turned into a *nāga* and was seen

> by brother monks. The matter was reported to the Lord Buddha, and the *nāga* monk had to relinquish his monkhood for no creature except a human being may be ordained as a monk. The *nāga* asked a favor of the Lord Buddha that his name as a *nāga* might be given as namesake to a candidate for monkhood in memory of the fact that it was once a monk.[58]

Stanley J. Tambiah interprets this legend adapted from the *Mahāvagga* as symbolizing a novice's renunciation of male virility, which he identifies with the serpent. While male sexual virility may characterize the serpent as a mythic archetype,[59] the *Mahāvagga* tale on which it is based suggests a different construction. In this version, the serpent's rationale for assuming human form is ultimately not to become a *bhikkhu* but to be reborn as a human being. In other words, the basic point of the canonical version of the story is transformation from a reptilian to a human form of life. This construction is further reinforced when the Buddha instructs the *nāga* how to be transformed into a human being—not by becoming a *bhikkhu,* but by the conscientious observance of the sabbath days, a duty incumbent on Buddhist laity.[60] In short, the story illustrates two kinds of transformation: from creature instincts to human behavior regulated by the Buddhist *sāsana,* and from a lay ethic governed by the norms of *sīla* to the monastic pursuit of nibbānic liberation.

### *The Performative Power of Meditation and Holy Monks*

The Buddha's extraordinary attainments during his enlightenment experience are at the heart of the BA. While it is being chanted, which takes about forty-five minutes, highly esteemed, senior monks sit in silent meditation around the *rājawat.*[61] An alms bowl filled with holy water rests in front of each monk, and a *sāi siñcana* cord connects the bowls to the *bodhimaṇḍa.* Some devotees believe that as the monks meditate their spiritual perfections (*pāramī*) and jhānic attainments—wisdom, compassion, divine eye—literally travel or "spread" (*phāe*) via the cord into the image.[62] In this way the image is charged simultaneously with the qualities of the Buddha enumerated in the BA and the spiritual qualities of venerable, esteemed monks who empower images and amulets through their own mental determination (*adhiṭṭhāna citta, bhāvanā citta*).

Historically meditation has always been linked with the life of the Buddha, monastic practice, and the attainment of jhānic powers and the spiritual virtues of calmness, equanimity, and insight. The Buddha's higher states of consciousness gained through meditation directly precede his awakening, and consequently, meditation, the quintessential activity of the Buddha's supreme achievement, is central to the story recited during the ritual. Furthermore, throughout the ceremony, laypeople and monks meditate. Some laypersons attend Buddha image consecrations precisely because the ritual provides an auspicious and powerful context for meditation. The monks who chant the *suat mon* also meditate, although not in the official capacity of those invited specifically for that purpose. At an image consecration ceremony held in Chiang Mai at Wat Chet Yot (Monastery of the Seven Spires) in December 1989, 108 monks, the *guṇa*-value of the three gems, meditated in shifts throughout the night because the small *wihān* could not accommodate them all at the same time. Revered monks, such as Khrūbā Phrohm and Luang Pū Lā, who attend by special invitation, implant (*plūk*) their *pāramī* into the images and also radiate their powers to the assembled congregants through the potency of their *bhāvanā* (meditation). This power is understood as an impersonal kind of *mana,* a quality derived from the accumulated virtue and mental states achieved by the Buddha. To this the monks also impart personal *mana,* specific qualities associated with their life stories, especially wisdom (*paññā*), lovingkindness (*mettā*), and compassion (*karuṇā*), as well as the mental powers for which they have gained an extraordinary reputation. As Luang Pū Lā was known for divine foreknowledge, it was believed that when he meditated during the *buddhābhiseka* ritual the quality of divine foreknowledge (literally, divine eye) was implanted into the Buddha image.

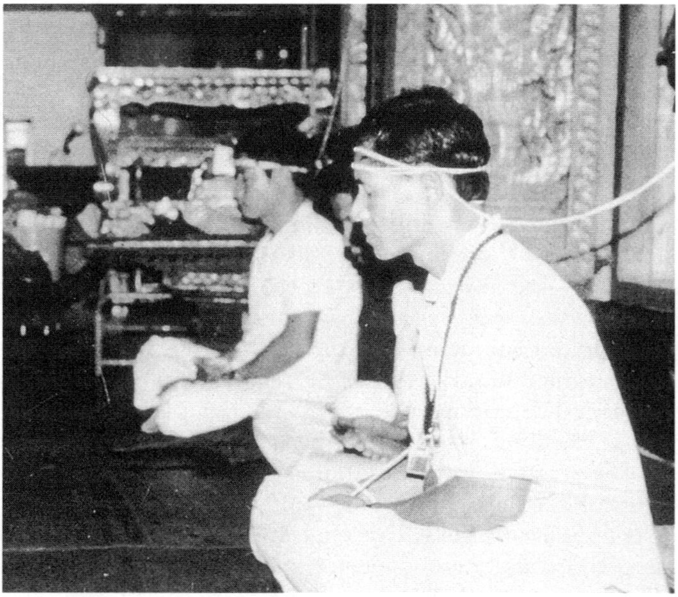

14. Laymen meditating while the *Buddha Abhiseka* is being chanted. Wat Pā Pāeng, Chiang Mai, Thailand.

Luang Pū Lā and other holy monks are highly revered by the assembled laity, who cry out, "*sādhu, sādhu,*" as they enter the *wat*. Congregants place articles of clothing on the floor for them to walk on, and prostrate as the monks bless them with holy water.[63] The power of the holy monks' sacred charisma is mediated through such physical objects, just as the living presence of the Buddha is mediated through images and relics. Their presence at the *buddhābhiseka* sanctifies and empowers images, amulets, holy water, and the sacred thread used in the ritual. Devotees retrieve and cherish these objects for the potency they believe derives from the monks' charisma. In particular, relics acquired from elderly monks are believed to ensure good health and long life as well as symbolize the longevity and truth of the tradition (*sāsana*).

Should the power of the *buddhābhiseka* to hypostasize the Buddha be interpreted merely as an exercise in apotropaic magic? Such a functionalist interpretation overly simplifies the complex socio-religious dynamics of the image consecration ceremony and ignores the Buddhist worldview underlying the ritual, namely, that reality is a continuum of the natural and supernatural, the sentient and nonsentient, the commonplace and the profoundly mysterious. The *buddhābhiseka* synthesizes these poles broadly construed as the mundane (*lokiya*) and transmundane (*lokuttara*) in such a way that actualizes realities unavailable to ordinary sense

15. Luang Pū Lā receiving a *dāna* offering. Image consecration. Wat Pā Pāeng, Chiang Mai, Thailand.

experience. The holy monks who implant their *pāramī* into the image are regarded as actualized beings who themselves serve as agents of actualization. They are believed to be living surrogates for the Buddha much as the image becomes the Buddha's double via the ritual.[64]

### *The Third Watch of the Night*

Because the Buddha's awakening occurred during the third and final watch of the night, the Buddha image consecration ritual concludes at sunrise with the last and final round of chanting. Throughout most of the night the congregants have been awake meditating and listening to chant recitations and sermons. As a consequence, by sunrise they experience feelings of exhaustion, euphoria, and great anticipation. In the *wihān* these feelings add to the already liminal atmosphere. The ceremony concludes with a reenactment of the Blessed One's final achievement and the events surrounding it: Sujātā's offering of milk and honey-sweetened rice, the attainment of Buddhahood, and preaching the first sermon to his five former disciples. Although the morning recitation is referred to as the second *suat charoen phrabuddha mon,* it is also called "opening of the eyes of the Buddha [image]" (*suat bōek phranet*) or chanting the "celebration of instructing the Buddha [image]" (*suat oprom somphōt phra*). At sunrise—the very juncture of night and day—the ceremony celebrates the Buddha's realization of the universal truth of the nature and cause of suffering. The divine beings are again invoked; respects are paid to the Buddha and his religion; forgiveness is asked for wrongs done; and, once again, the blessing of this auspicious ceremony is extended to all beings.

In the early morning hours, sweetened milk rice is prepared outside the *wihān* within a sacred enclosure set apart by a bamboo fence constructed for the occasion. This rice represents Sujātā's offering presented in a golden bowl to the Buddha when he was seated at the *nigrodha* tree.[65] The *bodhisatta,* having passed through a six-year "gestation" period of rigorous preparation, consumes the *madhupāyāsa* rice, an act that parallels the first solid food fed an Indian child six months after his birth.[66] This offering of milk rice mimetically reenacts the Sujātā episode from the legendary life of the Buddha but it can also be understood as a portent of Prince Siddhattha's birth as the Buddha. Just as a first-feeding marks a rite of passage, the offering of milk rice marks the *bodhisatta*'s cosmic passage to *tathāgata*-hood.

After mixing together rice, sesame oil, honey or palm sugar, and milk in a large cauldron, a group of prepubescent girls or nuns (*māe chī*) dressed in white stir the mixture over a wood fire. Once cooked, the sweetened sticky rice is divided and put into forty-nine bowls to simulate the Buddha's own act upon receiving Sujātā's gift and as a symbol of the

16. *Māe Chī* preparing sweetened milk rice as a part of the ritual reenactment of Sujātā's offering. Wat Mū'ang Mai, Chiang Mai, Thailand.

17. Forty-nine bowls of milk rice being offered to the Buddha images. Wat Mū'ang Man, Chiang Mai, Thailand.

forty-nine days the Buddha spent at seven different locations following his awakening.[67] When the rice is brought into the *wihān* the monks commence the morning chant. In addition to recitations from the northern collection of *tamnān*—"*iti pi so bhagavā arahaṃ* . . . ," "*bahum sahassaṃ abhinimmitasavudhantaṃ* . . . ," ending with "*yo kho Ānanda* . . ." and "*sukho Buddho,*"—the main texts are *Paṭiccasamuppāda* ("*avijja paccaya* . . ."), the *Maṅgala Udāna Gāthā* ("*anekajāti saṃsaraṃ* . . ."), the *Buddhānussati* (Recollections of the Buddha), and the *Dhammacakkappavattana Sutta* (Buddha's First Discourse).

As the *Maṅgala Udāna Gāthā* (Stanzas of Auspicious Joy) is being recited, a monk officiant uncovers the eyes and heads of the newly consecrated Buddha images, while chanting a *gāthā* in praise of the thousand-eyed Indra, the divine eye, and the eye of the Buddha, the *dhamma,* and the *saṅgha*. He then reverses the three mirrors that previously had faced the Buddha images. Now they shine outward, reflecting the Buddha's knowledge of his own past lives, the past lives of all beings, and the destruction of mental intoxicants. Finally, in emulation of the gods' legendary act honoring the Buddha, a monk "cools" the images with a long-handled peacock fan.

On behalf of the congregants, the *āchān wat* offers the milk rice first to the Buddha images, then to the monks as a *dāna* offering, and lastly to the assembled laity to share as a kind of communal meal. Throughout the evening the monks are also presented money donations arranged on wishing trees and gifts in kind, often a pail or basket filled with hand soap, a washcloth, razor, tea, canned fruit, a hand calculator, and other useful items. Regardless of their status, monks who are invited to preach and meditate will receive *dāna* in some form, but the honoraria for noted monks who travel some distance may be the equivalent of several hundred dollars. Among its many functions, the Buddha image consecration ceremony provides an especially auspicious venue for merit-making exchange—giving material gifts to the *saṅgha* in return for the gift of the *dhamma*.[68]

The lay devotees' offerings to the monks mirror Sujātā's offering to the Buddha, the most impressive dramaturgical reenactment that occurs during the *buddhābhiseka* ritual. Two of the titles given to the ceremony are *oprom phra,* to instruct the venerable one, and *buat phra,* to ordain the venerable one. The honorific, *phra* (Pāli, *vara*), is a generic term for monk, but also serves as a prefix for the Buddha, *phraphutta,* and Buddha relics, *phrathāt*. The ritual as *oprom phra* or *buat phra* reinforces the close association between image and monk within the performative dynamic of the *buddhābhiseka*.

The Buddha image consecration ceremony ends with a different kind of giving, the monks' final blessing to the assembled congregants (*hai*

18. The head shrouds being removed from newly consecrated Buddha images. Wat Mū'ang Man, Chiang Mai, Thailand.

19. The *abhiseka* of the Buddha images at the conclusion of the ritual. Wat Mū'ang Man, Chiang Mai, Thailand.

20. Luang Pū Lā preparing to *abhiseka* the congregants and the consecrated images and amulets. Wat Pā Pāeng, Chiang Mai, Thailand.

21. The water pouring ritual (*truat nām*) that concludes the Buddha image consecration ritual. Wat Mū'ang Man, Chiang Mai, Thailand.

*phon*) as they perform the water pouring ritual (*truat nām*) as a physical expression of the words recited:

> Just as overflowing rivers make the ocean full, so *dāna* given from this world reaches the dead. May all of your wishes be fulfilled immediately. May all your wishes be as complete as the full moon and the bright, shining gem.

After the final blessing, the congregants share the sacred objects used in or consecrated during the ritual—the sweetened milk rice, consecrated holy water, pieces of the *sāi siñcana* cord—and retrieve the images and amulets they brought to be reconsecrated.

### *Texts*

I close this section with three recitations chanted during the final eye-opening rite. The first represents the quintessential expression of the Buddha's enlightenment; the second incorporates the claim attributed to the Buddha in the *Mahāparinibbāna Sutta* that the Buddha's successor will be the *dhamma* and the *vinaya;* and the third highlights the Buddha as the locus for recollection (*anussati*).

#### *Maṅgala Udāna Gāthā* (Stanzas of Auspicious Joy)[69]

*Anekajāti saṃsāra* . . . Through many a birth I wandered in *saṃsāra,* seeking, but not finding, the builder of the house. Sorrowful is birth again and again.

O House-builder! You are seen. You shall no longer build this house. All your rafters are broken, your ridge pole is shattered.

My mind has attained the unconditioned; the end of craving is achieved.

#### *Yo Kho Ānanda* (O Ānanda)[70]

O Ānanda, monks, nuns, laymen and laywomen should lead lives according to the religious teachings. They should truly honor, respect, esteem, and worship the *tathāgata,* especially in moral practice.

O Ānanda, everyone should keep in mind my doctrine (*dhamma*) and the discipline (*vinaya*) which I taught and enacted. After my passing away they will be your teacher. Monks, I admonish you, all compounded things naturally are born and pass away. Practice diligently.

#### *Buddhānussati* (Remembering the Buddha)[71]

The virtuous monk should develop the four protective measures, namely, recollection of the Buddha, of lovingkindness, of loathsomeness, and of death. Wise, learned monks recollecting the boundless virtues of the one filled with virtue should develop meditation subjects such as the recollection of the Buddha.

He who has surpassed all defilements is called "purified in mind"; he is worthy to be worshiped continuously. The *muni* [the Buddha], well versed in and dwelling in the *dhamma,* attains knowledge, virtue, and insight (*vipassanā*). He perfects the precepts, is superior to others, speaks skillfully, and attains to the knowledge of the three worlds.

Superior to others, he tames all living beings, teaches benefits to the world, consists of all virtues, is capable of knowing the minds of others, understands the *dhamma,* has compassion for all living beings, exemplifies the perfection of generosity by giving away his most precious possessions for the benefit of himself and others. He is superior in wisdom, in the *dhamma,* and in contemplative understanding. The body of such a person has an appearance beyond all thought and description. It is the *dhammakāya.*

This is the *ñāṇa* of the recollection of the Buddha.

## Making the Buddha Present

> The ceremony recreates the story of Gautama in order to assure that the statue is confronted with the same experiences, so that the stone or the stucco can be—just as Siddhartha's body was—*transformed* by immortality.[72]

> For those who . . . make ritualized offering directed toward relics, the Buddha is experientially present and accessible in precisely the same ways that he was present and available during his lifetime.[73]

Recent studies of ritual, cult, and devotional belief and practice throughout Buddhist Asia have challenged the now clichéd and problematic distinctions between elite and popular religion, between monastic and lay piety, and the tendency of an earlier generation of Buddhologists to reify a rationalized form of early Buddhism that degenerated in response to the onslaught of popular cult.[74] Gregory Schopen disputes a two-tier model for interpreting Indian Buddhism that bifurcates monastic *nibbāna*-seekers and the pious devotion of Buddhist laity who worshiped images and relics. He marshals archaeological, epigraphic, and textual evidence to support the view that monks and nuns were early donors of images and *stūpa*s, and that these physical reminders of the Buddha were not merely *symbols* of the *tathāgata* but were considered to be his real, living presence.[75] Reginald Ray, while acknowledging the ground-breaking work of André Bareau on the *Mahāparinirvāṇa Sutra* and early Buddha biography, effectively reverses Bareau's rationalized, evolutionary historicism. Echoing Stanislaw Schayer's 1935 essay on the nature of a precanonical Buddhism, Ray argues that a cult of the presence of the Buddha and Buddhist saints preceded an anti-*stūpa* reaction found in the Pāli *sutta*s. Claims attributed to the Buddha that the *dhamma* and *vinaya* would be his successor and that his body should not be venerated illustrate this reaction. Ray finds the tendency to stress the absence of the Buddha to be a construction of later settled monastic communities, whereas the emphasis on the Buddha's presence is an expression of an earlier Indian Buddhist cult of saints.[76] In the field of East Asian Buddhism, Bernard Faure and Robert Sharf are among those challenging old paradigms and creating new ones along similar lines. Faure's work, in particular, details the complex range of issues relative to the cult of bodily relics and the bodies of saints in China and Japan.[77] While these recent trends in Buddhological scholarship enrich and enlarge the scope of Buddhist studies, the question can be raised as to whether the bugaboo of binary oppositions has been resolved or only reversed—a privileging of the epigraphic, the cultic, and the magical at the expense of the canonical text, the scholar-monk, and the philosophical.[78]

Among historians of religion and Buddhologists whose research focuses on culturally encoded Buddhism from India and Sri Lanka to Tibet, China, and Japan, the concept of *presence* has become a major hermeneutical perspective. Since presence also figures as a major theme in the ritual of Buddha image consecration in northern Thailand, I conclude this chapter by examining recent studies of relics and images in South and Southeast Asia in order to enlarge on the notion of presence as it applies to reminders of the Buddha and Buddhist saints. In the two subsequent chapters I will develop further the ways in which the *buddhābhiseka* makes the Buddha present by programming the image with the Buddha story and charging it with the power of the Buddha's enlightenment. Although analogies with the computer and storage battery may seem trite, they are quite apt. To instruct the Buddha image with the Buddha story is akin to programming a computer with a language, and infusing the image with the qualities, perfections, and powers of the Buddha is not unlike charging a battery. Both actions actualize what is potentially present and are part of the process by which the image becomes the person and the story of Sakyamuni Buddha.

The dilemma posed by presence as it relates to material signs of the Buddha, such as bodily relics or images (relic of commemoration or association), is whether or in what manner the deceased, parinibbāned Buddha is able to be present in a remainder or sign.[79] Solutions to this dilemma vary. An earlier generation of scholars regarded the cult of relics and images as a degeneration of the ethical and philosophical integrity of the Buddha and his early followers. Most contemporary scholars reject such historical dualism and a related opinion that associates relic veneration with lay piety in contrast to the monastic quest for wisdom and compassion. Richard Gombrich modifies this view by suggesting that while Buddhists in Sri Lanka know cognitively that the Buddha is not actually present in images and relics, affectively they act as though the Blessed One is truly present.[80] From his study of the cult of amulets in the Thai Buddhist context, Stanley Tambiah adopts a rather different position. He holds that the Buddha is both semantically and existentially present in relics and images. They possess the same fiery radiance as the Buddha himself and at the same time represent or point to the Buddha's truth or *dhamma* beyond form: "Buddhahood has to assume . . . mundane forms . . . so that beings . . . can apprehend the truth."[81] In his analysis of Pāla era Buddha images, in particular, Prajñapāramitā, Jacob Kinnard also integrates what he characterizes as symbolic and existential levels of meaning, claiming that the image simultaneously *symbolizes* and *is* the Buddha.[82] Referring to Jean Luc Marion's distinction between idol and icon, Kinnard proposes that unlike an idol, which limits the gazer's vision, the Buddha image is an icon that liberates the gazer's gaze to an invisible reality,[83] and in so doing is in "ontological communion" with the original Buddha.[84] Unlike Tambiah's emphasis on the fiery power of the Buddha's presence in relic and image, Kinnard regards the image as a sign of the Buddha that produces the realization of both the absence and presence of the *tathāgata* that "at once heightens the reality of his absence (and therefore graphically embodies *śunyatā*), while at the same time makes available his presence."[85]

Whereas for Kinnard a Buddha image evokes both absence *and* presence, for Malcolm David Eckel signs of the Buddha, such as an image, point primarily to the absent Buddha. Eckel constructs a study of the Indian Buddhist saint-philosopher, Bhāvaviveka, around Xuanzang's (Hsüan-tsang) pilgrimage to India in the eighth century.[86] The underlying theme of his monograph and an earlier article on Mahāyāna Buddhist ritual is the tension between the notion of absence as in the parinibbāned Buddha, the concept of emptiness, and presence.[87] When Xuanzang visits Buddhist sites in India, Eckel describes the Chinese pilgrim's primary experience of traces or reminders of the Buddha as one of the *tathāgata*'s absence rather than presence: "The key elements in Hsüan-tsang's experience, and the one that seems to have triggered his emotional response, was the sense of absence. . . . [He] had an acute sense that the Buddha he longed to see was not there. . . . The activities of worship and the physical image of the Buddha took second place in Hsüan-tsang's mind to a feeling that the crucial object of his devotion was absent."[88] Eckel observes that when Xuanzang sees an image of the Buddha, he regards the image as a sign of absence. Hence, the diary of the Chinese pilgrim's travels in northwest India reads like a map of ritual sites marking the Buddha's absence. Even when the Buddha *seemed* to be there in the form of a relic, image, or another trace, what Xuanzang felt was the Buddha's absence,[89] leading Eckel to conclude that absence trumps the Buddha's presence, whether that presence is constructed symbolically, indexically, or in other terms.[90]

In his study of the *Aśokāvadāna* John Strong interprets King Asoka's need to experience the *tathāgata* by constructing 84,000 *stūpa*s, his pilgrimage with the elder Upagupta, and his worship of the *bodhi* tree as attempts to create "a situation in which the Buddha, despite his *parinirvāṇa,* may in some sense be said to be present."[91] Utilizing Paul Mus's interpretation of Borobudur as a magical mesocosm for making the Buddha present, Strong argues that Asoka's 84,000 *stūpa*s, his establishment of pilgrimage sites connected with the life of the Buddha, together with his special worship at the *bodhi* tree all represented the king's efforts to this end. Strong's claim, that Asoka created a cultic milieu in which the absent Buddha was made present, rests on two assumptions, one pragmatic and the other ontological. Pragmatically, while Buddhists viewed the Buddha's *parinirvāṇa* as a kind of absence, in practice they utilized traditional techniques of contagious magic (a la Marcel Mauss) to overcome this absence. Ontologically, the notion that the Buddha has two bodies, a form body (*rūpakāya*) and a body beyond form (*dharmakāya*), meant that a true or complete experience of the Buddha must incorporate both bodies or levels. Asoka's 84,000 *stūpa*s can be seen as both *rūpa* and *dharma* forms of the Buddha. On one level, the relics assume the personal image of the Buddha, but on the other level they represent the dharmic reality of the world.[92] Likewise, when Māra transforms himself into the Buddha at the request of Upagupta, this act enables the saint to experience the Buddha both dharmalogically and rūpalogically. Here Strong's interpretation rests heavily on Mauss: "Māra has become a magical mesocosm in which Upagupta can grasp something of the absent Buddha. What he grasps, however, is not the total Buddha, but only one aspect of him, his *rūpakāya*. And this he now has put together with his vision of the *dharmakāya* which, as an enlightened *arhat* he has already achieved."[93]

Strong's views about the rūpalogical and dharmalogical aspects of early Indian devotional Buddhism—in particular, the Buddha image—grow out of his extensive study of the Sarvāstivāda *avadāna* tradition.[94] He argues that the Sarvāstivāda notion of time, in which *dharma*s exist in the past, present, and future, had profound implications for the worship of Buddha images: "When applied to the worship of the Buddha image . . . from a Sarvāstivāda perspective, though the Buddha cannot be said to be 'present' in an image, he can be said to be 'past.' In this light, images (*stūpas,* relics, bodhi trees) do not make 'present' something 'absent'; rather they . . . enable the worshipper to overcome the barriers of time."[95] Strong resolves the absence/presence dichotomy by claiming that the Buddha is experienced in his pastness rather than absence.[96] A Buddha image makes possible a religious experience "not of the Buddha's presence but of his pastness, i.e., his absence, his impermanence, his nonmanifestness in the here and now."[97] This philosophical resolution differs from either a Theravāda or a Mahāyāna view, "in which the Buddha's *rūpakāya* is seen either as gone entirely to destruction or as never having truly existed in the first place."[98] Thus, from a Sarvāstivāda perspective, Upagupta's experience of the Buddha's *rūpakāya* is interpreted as an experience in the present of the Buddha's past. Similarly, Xuanzang's account of witnessing the image of the Buddha in Gopāla's cave that for Eckel points to a Mādhyamikized absence-emptiness is regarded by Strong in Sarvāstivāda terms. When the Chinese pilgrim sees the shadowy image on the wall of the cave it has a mirage-like quality so that upon drawing nearer it gradually disappears.[99] Strong regards this story of Xuanzang and the shadowy image of the Buddha in the cave as an illustration of a Sarvāstivāda temporal perspective whereby the Buddha is visible only from a distance (his pastness), but that close up (in the present), he is absent.

Eckel and Strong both affirm the absence/presence polarity but interpret it differently. Eckel foregrounds absence, possibly because he is attempting to make sense of the "practice" of emptiness from a Mādhyamika perspective. In his study of the *Aśokāvadāna* Strong foregrounds presence even when, utilizing the Sarvāstivāda notion of time, it is the presence of pastness. Magical techniques offer one solution—the right rituals make absent persons present in their material remains and signs. One example is the perfumed offerings associated with *gandhakuṭī* that make the Buddha present rupalogically through the medium of a sense (i.e., olfactory) experience.[100] Ontologically, absence and presence devolve into experiencing the Buddha on both rūpalogical and dharmalogical levels. Dharmalogically the Buddha is always present; rūpalogically the Buddha may be either absent or present; but the Buddha is truly or most completely experienced as both *rūpa* and *dharma.*

On the basis of his study of the cult of relics in Sri Lanka taken primarily from Pāli *vaṃsa* literature, Kevin Trainor offers another solution to the dilemma using the doctrine of *kamma* and the conception of intention (*adhiṭṭhāna*).[101] The principle of *kamma,* whereby "one's present is understood to be shaped by the effects of one's past intentional actions, and one's future is likewise shaped by those past actions," provides, in Trainor's view, an explanation for the way in which the absent Buddha is made present.[102] *Vaṃsa* texts are replete with stories of the Buddha in which he predicts that his relics will appear or be discovered at such and such a time and place by such and such a person. Thus, "it is the operation of the principle of karmic effects that insures that the Buddha's intentions, expressed in the past in the form of predictions will necessarily be fulfilled long after his ultimate passing away."[103]

All three of these solutions to the dilemma of absence and presence tend to regard material signs of the Buddha as a text, that is, they propose doctrinal solutions to a seeming paradox—Mādhyamika emptiness, Sarvāstivāda two-body doctrine and theory of time, and Theravāda teachings regarding *kamma* and intention. Jacob Kinnard characterizes such doctrinal resolutions to the absence/presence contradiction as "binary analyses" and judges them problematical because they tend to become fixed doctrinal positions rather than emerge from the complexity of "metapractical discourse," where the issues are more ambiguous, and more existential and practical than ontological and metaphysical.[104] Kinnard finds in the Pāla-period *habitus* of Buddha images that the essential feature is the cognitive or imaginative act of making the Buddha present. In this imaginative act, doctrine is not static but in a dynamic relationship with practice—"two overlapping discourses that mutually inform one another."[105]

Although Eckel, Strong, Trainor, and Kinnard do not definitively clarify the meaning of the claim that the Buddha is present in relics, images, and other material signs, none interprets presence in a literal, physical sense. Gregory Schopen comes closest to holding this view. In a substantially documented study of fourth- and fifth-century Buddhist monasteries in India, Schopen argues that the Buddha was believed to be in actual residence in a monastery, a claim he supports with archaeological, epigraphic, architectural, and *Vinaya* evidence.[106] He holds that inscriptions as early as the first century C.E. may imply belief in the Buddha's post-*parinibbāna* presence in a monastery and that donatory and land grant inscriptions from the fourth and fifth centuries unambiguously support this view. He cites one such land grant inscription from Bāgh in Madhya Pradesh wherein parcels of land are given to the Buddha and monks of the monastery as though they were *personally* present to receive them,[107] and land grants from Valabhī in Gujarat indicate that Buddhas and monks "both were conceptually *considered residents* of a single kind of establishment."[108] For Schopen the perfumed chamber (*gandhakuṭī*), in particular, provides inscriptional and architectural support for his thesis. He claims that by the fourth and fifth centuries the perfumed chamber, a central cell in a Buddhist monastery reserved for the Buddha, was "an established part of Buddhist establishments everywhere,"[109] and that the evidence supports the view that "the Buddha was considered to be an *actual individual* within the monastic community."[110]

Schopen's study challenges what he regards as a "*śāstric*" overemphasis on abstract Buddhologizing. He proposes that the synchronism in the fourth and fifth centuries between the rise of abstract Buddhological theorizing and the language of personal presence and permanent abiding that typify his sources should be seen as mutually interdependent, possibly competitive, or even antagonistic.[111] His general argument, that the study of Buddhism—in this case, the nature of the Buddha—should include as wide a variety of relevant sources as feasible seems to me to be irrefutable. The debate centers on how one reads these sources. At issue is whether the presence of the Buddha in the monastery necessarily means that the Buddha is there physically as an actual, living individual; that he abides in the *gandhakuṭī* just as a monk abides in a neighboring cell. In his study of the *gandhakuṭī,* John Strong poses a different answer, one, in fact, that is supported by several of Schopen's own examples. Strong contends that the perfumed chamber should be seen as the "cultic abode of the Buddha,"[112] that is, at the *gandhakuṭī* devotees honor the Buddha with scented water, flowers, and so on. The perfumed chamber became a repository for floral tributes and other offerings to the Buddha as a stand-in for the Buddha himself, much as the Buddha image serves as a stand-in for the Buddha in the KBV. To be meritoriously efficacious, ritual offerings to the Buddha require his presence as the head of the *saṅgha,* either his actual living presence or in the form of image, bodily relic, footprint, *bodhi* tree, or *gandhakuṭī.* The Buddha's "real presence" does not require an actual individual in the perfumed chamber but a sense of the immediate, mysterious presence of the Buddha's wisdom, power, and compassion—those very qualities that constitute Buddhahood throughout time and space.

A summary of recent scholarship on the Buddha's presence supports the following general conclusions: reminders, relics, and traces of the Buddha (and Buddhist saints) are more than merely symbolic; they were variously believed to represent the living presence of the Buddha; veneration of these reminders is found in the early Indian tradition as well as late pan-Buddhist traditions; both monks and laity supported such veneration; and the veneration of relics prompted considerable sectarian debate. Controversy regarding the meaning of the Buddha's presence (or absence) in his signs has been part of the history of Buddhist thought and scholarship from the *Mahāparinibbāna Sutta* to the present. Diverse views reflect normative and scholarly agendas as well as the particular contexts on which these views are based, whether textual, epigraphic, or specific material signs such as Pāla images, pilgrimage sites, or consecration rituals. It is indisputable that philosophical notions influenced the way in which presence was interpreted; yet it is equally true that the Buddha's presence was experienced in meditation, devotional rituals, and pilgrimage in ways not exhausted by doctrinal configurations. Within these living situations ordinary devotees expect to meet the Buddha—much as King Pasenadi and his retinue did in the KBV—and that if the historical Buddha was absent there would be an equivalent stand-in. But what does "real presence" mean? This is a matter of interpretation contingent on the historical situation, sectarian philosophical agendas, and particular contexts. There is no definitive answer to the question of what presence means with regard to material reminders of the Buddha; however, in the *buddhābhiseka* the Buddha's presence ritually infused into the image is constituted by the jhānic powers he achieved on the night of his enlightenment and his full awakening to the truth of the *dhamma.* The means by which this happens could be characterized as a technique of contagious magic, and the explanation of how the Buddha is cognized as present in a material sign might be characterized as a metapractical discourse or interpreted in Theravāda or Sarvāstivāda doctrinal terms, but for the pious devotees who experience the sunset to sunrise *buddhābhiseka* ritual there is no doubt that the Buddha has been made fully present, hypostasized in an image.

# APPENDIX 4.1

## *PARITTA* AND *SUAT MON*

The chant (Thai, *suat*) is the single most pervasive element in Thai Buddhist ritual, including the northern Thai Buddha image consecration.[113] Monks begin the evening service with Pāli chants common to the ritual practices of all Theravāda Buddhist cultures. The majority of the texts recited were formulated in Sri Lanka as an "anthology of selected discourses of the Buddha compiled by the teachers of old . . . as a handbook for the newly ordained novice," known as the Book of Protection or *Pirit-pota* (Pāli, *paritta*).[114] The older Pāli name of the *Pirit-pota* is *Catubhāṇavārapāli,* literally, the text in four sermon sections. This anthology contains twenty-nine *sutta*s—the twenty-two *sutta*s of the *Catubhāṇavārapāli* plus an additional seven from various parts of the Pāli canon.[115] Lily de Silva suggests that because seven of the first nine *sutta*s are found in the *Khuddakapāṭha,* which is generally regarded as a type of elementary doctrinal manual, that both the *Catubhāṇavārapāli* and the *Khuddakapāṭha* may have evolved simultaneously to meet the demands of a growing Buddhist community. From the twelfth century, when the rulers of the emerging, powerful Burmese and Tai states favored the Sinhalese Mahāvihāra form of Theravāda, variants of the Book of Protection became the predominant handbook of ritual chants.[116]

The term *paritta* first occurs in the *Cullavagga* of the *Vinaya Piṭaka* wherein the Buddha exhorts monks to use the *Khandha Paritta* as an expression of lovingkindness (*mettā*) toward snakes, an entreaty against injury to animals, and for the protection and welfare of all beings.[117] The first recorded recitation of the *paritta* for the public good appears in the *Mahāvaṃsa*. During the reign of Upatissa (370–412), monks dispelled drought and disease from the island by chanting the *Ratana Sutta,* whereupon the king issued this decree: "Should there at any time be another affliction of drought and sickness in the land you should observe the ceremonies."[118] In the *Sāsanavaṃsa* the victory of Asoka's emissaries, Sona and Uttara, over the *yakkhinī* terrorizing Lower Burma was attributed to the chanting of *paritta.*[119]

*Paritta* handbooks exist in both Pāli and vernacular translations in all Theravāda Buddhist cultures.[120] In Thailand canonical texts consistently included in *paritta* rituals are the *Maṅgala, Ratana,* and *Karaṇīyamettā Sutta*s found in the *Khuddakapāṭha,* the first book of the *Khuddaka Nikāya.* Other *paritta* are taken from the four *nikāya* and the *jātaka* (e.g., the *Mora Paritta*) and commentaries.[121] Even though the content of each *paritta* varies, within their narrative frameworks each promotes the realization of a particular end or goal: the preaching of the *Maṅgala Sutta* enables countless *deva*s to realize the truth; the *Ratana Sutta* banishes evil spirits that cause sickness and pestilence from Vesali; the *Karaṇīyamettā Sutta* pacifies an evil spirit who torments five meditating monks; the *Dhammacakkappavattana Sutta* enables Koṇḍañña to reach the stage of stream-enterer (*sotāpanna*); the *Dhajagga Paritta* protects from worries and fears; and the *Aṅgulimāla Paritta* is recited to safeguard pregnant women.[122]

Regarding Sinhalese Buddhist practice, Hammalawa Saddhatissa observes, "Any social function, religious festival, or ceremony is incomplete without the recital of *paritta.*"[123] In Sri Lanka *pirit* chanting is classified into seven-, three-, and one-day *pirit*s, or designated specifically for protection against illness or misfortune. In Thailand meritoriously auspicious events will include the chanting of *paritta,* especially one or more of the three *sutta*s from the *Khuddakapāṭha.* Taking into account the texts, their narrative frameworks, and the ritual occasions in which they are chanted, Lynn de Silva outlines five distinct but interrelated meanings of *paritta* chanting: the power of presence of the Triple Gem (Buddha, *dhamma, saṅgha*); the power of an act of truth (*saccakiriya*) to ward off evil and disease; the power of lovingkindness (*mettā*) to promote beneficial physical and spiritual effects; the power of sound to engender tranquillity of mind, peace, and harmony; the power of virtue that grounds an upright and moral life.[124] Saddhatissa emphasizes the benedictory and apotropaic functions of *paritta* chanting, likening it to the chanting of *dhāraṇī* in Mahāyāna Buddhism and Vedic *mantra*s, especially those of the Atharavaveda.[125]

In Thai Theravāda Buddhism the term *suat* (chant) may derive from the Pāli verb *saheti,* which can mean "to perform or recite." In northern Thailand *suat* is colloquially equated with *sutta.*[126] Chanting during kammically efficacious rituals (Thai, *phithī kam*) is called *suat mon* ("reciting the *mantra*") or "reciting the Buddha's teaching (i.e., *sutta*) as *mantra*." This latter interpretation may be supported by the distinction made in Thai Buddhist chant between *suat mantra* and *veda mantra* (Thai, *ved mon kāthā*), which Thai interpreters freely acknowledge to reflect the influence of Brahmanism.[127] Assuming a Brahmanical influence, *suat mon* could be interpreted as the Buddhist form of *veda mantra.* While the content of *suat mon* is Buddhist, it has the purpose of *ved mon,* namely, to engender religious rituals (*phithī kam*) with protective, efficacious power (Thai, *tham pen saksit*; Pāli, *sakti-siddhi*).

In Thai Buddhism chant recitation forms a part of most ritual occasions with variations of style and cadence. Its purpose is to praise the virtue (*guṇa*) of the religion (*sāsana*), secure a blessing from objects of supernatural power such an image or relic, alleviate danger and hardship, propitiate the spirits (Thai, *khwan*), ensure the success of any ritual performance, or facilitate memorization of Buddhist scripture.[128] According to Manī Phayomyong, chanting can be classified according to different settings and purposes: (1) major ceremonies like a Buddha image consecration ceremony inclusive of many texts in the northern Thai *paritta* repertoire (*suat dang*); (2) an abbreviated version of the *suat mon* divided according to the days of the week as a type of monastic lectionary (*suat yo*); (3) to facilitate meditation, especially during the three-month rains retreat (*suat kammaṭṭhāna*); (4) to consecrate or open the eyes of Buddha images (*suat bōek phranet*); (5) for removing or transporting spirits from one place to another (*suat thon*); (6) for the enhancement and extension of life at crisis or transition periods (*suat sū'pchātā*); (7) during a funeral ceremony (*suat matti*); (8) after receiving *dāna* at funerals (*suat sisaya*); (9) in the *uposatha* hall (*suat niyatti*).[129]

The cadence of the chant significantly enhances the ritual experience. When chanting the *Abhidhamma* at funerals, a generally slow, almost mournful cadence is used. But in the *suat mon* that begins the Buddha image consecration ceremony the cadence is rapid and arresting. Cadence is as essential to chant as rhythm is to song, having an affective rather than a cognitive result. Cadence is used to create mood rather than rational understanding.

In Thailand five major cadence styles developed in response to different ritual occasions, sectarian distinctions, and historical influences.[130] These styles are *roy kāew, sangyōk, sarapanya,*[131] *makata*, and *suat bōek*. *Makata* style is used by the Thammayut sect founded by King Rama IV (Mongkut), who was a monk for over twenty-five years before he ascended the throne in 1851. The order that he established follows a stricter disciplinary code than the older, larger Mahānikāi order. *Makata* features a staccato, recitative cadence copied from the Mon monks with whom Mongkut studied. *Sarapanya,* with its slow, high-pitched, mournful, minor key cadence, is called *suat sop,* or funeral chanting.

*Roy kāew* and *sangyōk* are distinguished by the speed of the chant and the relationship between words. *Sangyōk* is slower with a slight pause between words, a style favored by Mahānikāi monks. *Roy kāew* is a faster cadence with the words flowing together and the rhythm determined by long and short syllables, with two short syllables equal to one long. The traditional style of northern chant, sometimes referred to as *suat phū'an mū'ang,* or "local chanting," closely resembles *roy kāew.* The *suat bōek* cadence, or chanting to open the eyes of the Buddha, differs from any other style. Informants speculate that its "singing cadence" (*tham nong rong plāeng*) may suggest a Chinese influence.

# APPENDIX 4.2

## MONASTIC BIOGRAPHIES: LUANG PŪ LĀ, LUANG PŪ WĀEN, KHRŪBĀ PHROHM[132]

Luang Pū Lā was born in 1898 and until his death in 1993 led the list of highly esteemed charismatic (*saksit*) monks in Chiang Mai Province. His fame rested partially on his long life since longevity is considered to be a sign of wisdom, extraordinary virtue, and spiritual power. His early life followed a common pattern. At age nine he became a temple boy at Wat Pā Tu'ng, his village monastery, and at eleven was ordained a novice. At eighteen he continued his studies at Wat Chetuphon in Chiang Mai, eventually returning to Wat Pā Tu'ng as abbot at age twenty-seven. A brief published biography describes how he practiced meditation while at the same time faithfully attending his predecessor, Khrūbā Pinta, in his old age.[133]

Extraordinary events leading to the attribution of supernatural powers are one of the defining characteristics of saintly monks. Luang Pū Lā's reputation follows this pattern. One day during the rainy season Lā told a group of novices at his *wat* that because of imminent danger they must immediately vacate their dormitory (*kuṭi*). Subsequently, a heavy rainstorm felled a large tree and crushed the wooden building. From that time on Luang Pū Lā was believed to have divine foreknowledge and was called "Divine Eye Venerable Lā."[134] In another apocryphal tale, on one sabbath day throngs of people came to see him, requesting sacred relics. Even though he had only a few on hand, those few miraculously multiplied in sufficient numbers for all of those present. Like other charismatic monks in Thailand, Lā's reputation inspired patronage by the country's elites, including the king and queen, who sponsored the building of a new ordination hall at Wat Pā Tu'ng and attended its dedication in 1989.

Lā's powers are believed to have resulted from his diligent practice of meditation: "He has a special insight into problems derived from his moral earnestness, wisdom, and practice of meditation. For this reason, we give him the title, Luang Pū Lā with divine foreknowledge."[135] "Devotees come to him to ask for sacred objects (*sing saksit*) such as holy water (*nām mon*) or to bless amulets (*sāek baw*) [to consecrate by blowing on the object]," observes his biographer. "Because of his lovingkindness (*mettā*), Luang Pū Lā never refuses. He has insight into the suffering of all beings because of his *tā thip* (divine foreknowledge)."[136] Lā's biographer, a university professor, writes that the saint accepted invitations to meditate (*pluk sek*) at ritual occasions because Lā viewed holy water, amulets, images, and relics in psychological, moral, and even pragmatic terms. He dispensed blessings "for the peace of mind of the people" who came to him in order to focus their attention on the truth of the Buddha's teaching.[137] Lā's devotees have a less rationalized view of his powers. They believe that when he participated in *buddhābhiseka* rituals he implanted his gift of divine foreknowledge into sacred objects and thereby made them efficacious.

Luang Pū Wāen is associated with the northeast Thailand meditation lineage of Āchān Mun (Man). Born in Lōei in 1888, at thirteen Wāen was ordained a novice at Wat Phothai, Banpong, Lōei Province. At age twenty he took his higher ordination (*upasampāda*) at the Mahānikāi monastery, Wat Sangtho, in Ubon, where his uncle was the abbot. In 1927 he was reordained in a Thammayut ceremony in Chiang Mai at Wat Chedī Luang in a ceremony presided over by Phra Upāliguṇūpamācariya, the noted abbot of Wat Bowomiwet in Bangkok.

Luang Pū Wāen's relationship with Āchān Mun, the founder of the modern forest monk tradition, is uncertain. Some claim that the Venerable Wāen accompanied Mun on his eremetic wanderings as a *dhutaṅga* (ascetic) monk while others see the *dhutaṅga* phase of Wāen's monastic career independent of Mun, who became his teacher only after 1927. For ten years the Venerable Wāen spent his rains retreats in forest retreats with Āchān Mun near Mae Rim, Chiang Mai Province. Later, his monastic career alternated between eremetic tours and monastic residency in northern Thailand; he settled eventually in 1962 at Wat Doi Māepang in Phrao. His prominence as a charismatic, holy monk was legitimated and enhanced by a visit from the Thai royal family in 1974, and they were in attendance at his death on July 2, 1985, at the age of ninety-seven.

Wāen's life has become the subject of hagiographic reconstruction. Tales of his miraculous powers are standard in the oral tradition and popular religious magazines. By general consensus he has gained *arahant* status. Wāen's biographies emphasize his extraordinary virtue and his supernatural attainments. As a novice monk he distinguished himself by following a strict ascetical regime, eating only one vegetarian meal a day and spending long hours in meditation. One biographer reports that the novice often spent the night meditating in a graveyard and that he practiced both walking and sitting meditation for several hours before setting out on his alms rounds at dawn.[138] Many claims about his rigorous lifestyle are coupled with stories of his extraordinary powers. Solely by the power of his preaching the spirit of a woman imprisoned in a demon (*asura*) was released to a better rebirth,[139] and the power of his lovingkindness (*mettā*) similarly affected a hungry ghost (*preta*).[140] When he was attacked by tribal peoples while living as a forest monk in the mountains of northern Thailand, he entered into a deep *samādhi* meditation and deflected their arrows.[141] The sick were cured of illnesses simply by drinking holy water (*nām mon*) he had consecrated.[142] During the year and a half between Wāen's death and his cremation it is claimed that his body did not deteriorate, and after the cremation his bones became relics (*dhātu*), assuming the green, emerald-like color of the relics of Buddhas and *arahants*.[143]

Khrūbā Phrohm, who died in 1988, was one of the Chiang Mai region's most acclaimed monks. In 1947 he became the abbot of Wat Phraphutthabāttākphā, a historic but abandoned forest monastery that was to thrive under his leadership. The monastery, located in Pasang District, became one of the largest in Lamphūn Province and one of the three most important monastic colleges in the north. Despite the monastery's fame, the Venerable Phrohm continued to live in a simple bamboo hut on the *wat*'s perimeter until age and infirmities required more care and comfort.

An imposing *chedī* enshrining Khrūbā Phrohm's relics dominates the *wat*'s landscape.

Khrūbā Phrohm has no direct link with the Āchān Mun tradition, but his sacred biography reveals conventions similar to those found in the biographies of monks associated with Mun. In 1898, Phrohm was born into a devout family of rice farmers. Ordained as a novice at age fifteen, he excelled as a student of the scriptures and as a meditator. After his higher ordination in 1918 he became one of the first northern monks to pass the newly inaugurated system of monastic exams administered from Bangkok. When faced with a decision whether to continue his studies in Bangkok or stay in the north as a forest monk, Phrohm chose the latter. At age twenty-four he began the life of a *dhutaṅga* monk, wandering the hills of northern Thailand, Laos, and Burma for over two decades. After making this decision he remarked, "I'm like a person escaping from prison, having been detained there many years."[144]

Typical of the sacred biographies of other Buddhist saints (*arahant*s), accounts of miracles and supernatural events compete with the rigor and purity of the kind of life Phrohm lived. Once when he was staying in a tiger-infested area of northeastern Thailand, a large beast approached the base of the tree where he was sleeping. The biographer recounts that the tiger sat gazing at the Venerable Phrohm for an hour before it went away. The amazed local villagers asked the Khrūbā how he had protected himself and he replied that he had not employed any special protective *mantra* but had simply extended the power of his *mettā:* "We believe in the virtue (*guṇa*) of the Buddha, are firm in our moral virtue, and extend our love to all sentient beings; may all beings be happy; may they not bring harm to one another; may all supernatural beings (*devatā*) who dwell in this forest live happily in heavenly gardens."[145] Khrūbā was spared because he had meditated on the virtues of the Buddha, the teachings of impermanence, suffering, and not-self with a single purpose—to follow the teaching of the Buddha. Phrohm taught, "Monks, we meditate not to deceive people or to have them worship or praise us. We practice control in order to abandon attachment, to strive for the cessation of suffering."[146]

# 5

# INSTRUCTING THE IMAGE

## Introduction and Analysis

As a gifted actor becomes the person he or she plays by identifying with the character portrayed in the drama, so the Buddha image becomes the Buddha's double after being instructed in the *tathāgata*'s life history. Biographical sermons preached during the *buddhābhiseka* perform a didactic function for image and devotees. Both image and participants relive the Buddha's history (Thai, *phutthaphrawat*) as it is rehearsed orally, reenacted, and symbolized during the evening's ritual. Recalling (*anussati*) the Buddha story in these different dimensions transports the narrative past into the present. The story of the Buddha becomes more than a legendary tale of the tradition's founder who lived and died 2,500 years ago. Like the sequential flow of the *jātaka*s, the story of the past merges into the present, instantiating in the *buddhābhiseka* a paradigmatic truth.

The northern Thai Buddha image consecration ritual includes one or more sermons (*desanā*) that relate the Buddha's life story as found in Pāli canonical scriptures (e.g., *Mahāvagga, Mahāsaccaka Sutta*) and commentarial accounts (e.g., *Nidānakathā, Madhuratthavilāsinī*). The sermons are intended to educate and inspire rather than precisely replicate Pāli prototypes. A sermon may stray so far from Pāli sources that it becomes an imaginative incorporation of local traditions and rhetorical conventions.

Two biographical sermons constitute the core of this chapter. The first, the *Paṭhama Sambodhi* (Thai, *Pathom Somphōt*) (PS) (The Buddha's Supreme Enlightenment), begins with the Buddha's *bodhisatta* existence as Prince Vessantara and rebirth in Tusita Heaven and continues to his rebirth as Prince Siddhattha, his renunciation of worldly life, and final attainment of enlightenment.[1] The second, *Sitthāt Ōk Buat* (SB) (Siddhattha's Renunciation), also begins with the Gotama Buddha's preexistence but extends the story beyond the great awakening to include the Buddha's death and the distribution of his bodily relics.[2] The PS is preached in most northern Thai Buddha image consecration ceremonies, while the SB traditionally was featured at the beginning of the rains retreat (Thai, *khaw pansā;* Pāli, *vassa*), the season of temporary ordinations. Monastic ordination and image consecration are linked in several aspects of the *buddhābhiseka* ritual, and both ceremonies can be seen as reenactments of the Buddha's story—the former highlighting the future Buddha's going forth and the latter his *nibbāna*. As a composite narrative, the PS and SB encompass more of the Buddha's life than the Pāli *Nidānakathā* (Ja-nidāna), which concludes its account with Anāthapiṇḍika's donation of the Jetavana Monastery, although the Ja-nidāna, or memory of it, informed the unknown author of the PS in particular. Together with *Bimbā Philāp* (Bimbā's Lament), an expanded account of the story of Yasodharā's response to the Buddha's return to Kapilavatthu, an episode that occurs in the Ja-nidāna (89–91), these texts paint a detailed picture of how northern Thai Buddhists remember the Blessed One.[3] The *buddhābhiseka* evokes the story of the Buddha, but it is by the ritual's performative reenactment that the Buddha is called forth into the present time.

It is still a widely held view that Indian Buddhism, including its depiction of the Buddha, developed from a prior "philosophico-mystical" doctrine to a "true religion, with a pantheon, mythology, hagiography and worship . . . due to the penetration of the Good Law among the mass of the people, who were more devout than well-informed."[4] A different view regarding the formation of the Buddha biography proposes that the traditional Theravāda version reflects a process of gradual historical development of biographical cycles divided into four periods: the Buddha's own lifetime (ca. 567–483 B.C.E.); the reign of King Asoka (ca. 275–236 B.C.E.); the formation of the written Pāli canon around the first century C.E.; and the compilation of the major Pāli commentarial life of the Buddha (ca. fifth century C.E.).[5] The Buddha legend evolved over time to incorporate four elements: stories of the lives of previous Buddhas and *bodhisatta*s precedent to Siddhattha Gotama; accounts of the Buddha's genealogy, birth, and youth; stories of the Buddha's enlightenment and the early years of his teaching; accounts of the final months of his life, his *parinibbāna;* and the distribution of his relics. The enlightenment receives the most attention in the Pāli scriptures. Episodes of the Buddha's awakening and his teaching arose in conjunction with particular pilgrimage sites as it did in the case of the cult of Buddha relics. The *Mahāparinibbāna Sutta* influenced biographers' construction of events surrounding the Buddha's death and legitimated the cult of relics included in later Buddha biographies. The cult of relics and images was subsequently elaborated in Theravāda chronicles (*vaṃsa*), especially in northern Thailand, where the vernacular chronicle genre (*tamnān*) rivaled the popularity of indigenous *jātaka*s.

Some narratives of the life of the Buddha end with the enlightenment or the sermon at Benares or with stories of conversions that served a paradigmatic function regarding the formation of the *bhikkhu saṅgha* and its relationship to the laity. The Ja-nidāna, for example, concludes with ordinations into the *saṅgha* and Anāthapiṇḍika's donation of the Jetavana grove where the Buddha recounts his past lives to his disciples. Similarly, the *Lalitavistara* ends with the sermon at Benares, and the life of the Buddha in the *Mahāvastu* concludes with several conversion narratives following the sermon at Benares. For these early narrators the career of the *bodhisatta* that culminated in the itinerant life of the ascetic, Gotama, the defeat of Māra, and the attainment of Buddhahood held the most interest.[6] Over time this spare construction of the Buddha biography expanded to include episodes beyond the Buddha's enlightenment to his death and events following the *parinibbāna.* Bumphen Rawin holds that however one constructs the historical development of the various facets of Buddha narrative—*sutta, apadāna, nidāna, aṭṭhakathā,* traditional lives, or modern biographies—each negotiates a balance between the transcendent (*dhammabhāva*) and the human (*manussabhāva*) aspects of the story, and that differing biographical genre may emphasize one facet over another depending on the historical and doctrinal contexts.[7] Although Bumphen does not address all of the complex historical and literary problems relative to the formation of sacred Buddha biographies, he offers a useful perspective on the function of Buddha biography as it is utilized in the context of the *buddhābhiseka*—a ritual whose purpose is to instantiate *bodhiñāṇa* (transcendental knowledge) and *dhammakāya* (the body of *dhamma*) in a Buddha surrogate.[8]

The PS and SB share similarities in narrative content but differ in distinctive ways. The PS appears in several Pāli versions as well as Thai, Tai Yüan, Tai Isān, Lao, and Khmer. Although ascribed to a Sri Lankan origin, the PS is known only in Thailand, Laos, and Cambodia.[9] The earliest extant manuscripts dating from the sixteenth century are found at Wat Lai Hin, Lampāng Province, Thailand. Of the several Thai versions that bear the title *Pathom Somphōt,* the best known was compiled by Somdet Krom Phra Paramānuchit-chinōrot in 1845 C.E.[10] In contrast to the Ja-nidāna— the oldest Pāli life of the Buddha that concludes with the Buddha's visit to Kapilavatthu, Sakyan ordinations into the order, and Anāthapiṇḍika's donation of the Jetavana grove—Paramānuchit's twenty-nine-chapter PS includes episodes from the expanded Buddha legend: his *parinibbāna;* the distribution of Buddha relics among the eight Indian rulers; the burial of the remaining relics by Mahākassapa and their subsequent multiplication and redistribution by King Asoka; the Buddha's prediction of the coming of the Buddha Metteyya; the binding of Māra by Upagutta; and reasons for the decline of Buddhism in India. Paramānuchit's narrative invites comparison with the *Mālālaṅkāravatthu* (MLV), a Burmese sacred biography written in 1773.[11]

A condensed, demythologized version of Paramānuchit's PS was later prepared by Somdet Phra Ariyawongsākhatayān (Supreme Patriarch Sā).

Sā's redaction, one serialized in a Buddhist periodical in the 1890s, was designed specifically for preaching. It presents the major events in the life of the Buddha, the basic teachings of Buddhism, the founding of the order, and the first Buddhist councils. Unlike Paramānuchit's PS, Sā's omits such mythic episodes as the binding of Māra by Upagutta and Buddhaghosa's prediction that Buddhism would disappear 5,000 years after the Buddha's enlightenment. In accord with the decree by King Chulalongkorn (r. 1873–1910) that monks should not begin sermons with this gloomy prediction, the Sā version emphasizes the Buddha's teaching as motivation for ethical behavior in this world rather than "fear that the religion's disappearance would obviate their salvation."[12] The most recent Thai PS is that of Supreme Patriarch Vajirañāṇavarorasa (1860–1921 C.E.), who revised and edited Sā's redaction. It is currently used in the national Buddhist studies curriculum for novice monks.

In northern Thailand the PS exists in a short *desanā* (Thai, *thet*) or sermon form in Tai Yüan designed for ritual use, which is translated in this chapter and designated as *Pathom Somphōt Thet* (PST). A longer, literary version apparently was first composed in Pāli and later translated into Tai Yüan. George Coedès reckons that the northern Thai or Lānnā edition may be the oldest—possibly the original *Paṭhama Sambodhi*—composed in Chiang Mai in the sixteenth century.[13] Like other traditional lives of the Buddha in Pāli and Sanskrit, the *Pathom Somphōt Lānnā* (PSL) is structured around the path to and attainment of Buddhahood, in particular, the defeat of Māra, the Buddha's awakening, and concludes with the sermon at Benares, omitting the *parinibbāna* and the distribution of relics.

Predictably, the longer, seven-fascicle version of the PSL includes greater biographical detail and hagiographic elaboration than its shorter, one-fascicle counterpart (PST) designed for preaching. PSL contains references to canonical texts such as the *Buddhavaṃsa* (Bv) to which the PSL acknowledges its indebtedness and references that are omitted in the PST. In addition to a more abbreviated narrative, PST also omits several events and episodes that appear in PSL and in the other standard lives of the Buddha.

Both the standard and abbreviated Lānnā versions of *The Buddha's Supreme Enlightenment* (PSL/PST) commence with the *bodhisatta*'s prior existences that are requisite for the development of the moral and spiritual perfections (*pāramī*) that lead to Buddhahood. The PSL excludes most of the Vessantara story while emphasizing the *bodhisatta*'s investigation of the five requisite conditions of rebirth in the human realm—time, continent, region, family, mother's age—from the vantage point of Tusita Heaven. PST departs from the standard list of five conditions, but like PSL, highlights the importance of human beings' willingness to receive the Buddha's teaching, a factor reiterated after the *tathāgata*'s enlightenment. At the very outset the two Lānnā versions of *The Buddha's Supreme Enlightenment* establish the main parameters of the story—the human, the divine, and the dhammic. Although both texts omit the story of Sumedha in the Bv which begins the *jātaka* commentary life of the Buddha, PSL makes specific reference to the Bv and both versions assume the epochal Buddhology requisite for the development of the moral and spiritual excellence (*pāramī*) of Buddhahood.

The two sentences allotted to the Buddha's conception and birth in PST are greatly expanded in the PSL, reinforcing the miraculous nature of these events: "The sick were cured; the blind could see; the deaf could hear; the lame became strong; the dumb spoke. Diamonds appeared in the sky, and the earth emitted beautiful rays. Creatures who were formerly foes became friendly and compassionate." Events of infancy and youth recounted at length in the PSL—the visit of the sage, Kāladevala; Siddhattha's naming ceremony; the vision of the *cakkavatti* gem wheel; the auspicious marks of the great being (*mahāsatta*); the miracle at the roseapple tree; Siddhattha's demonstration of archery skills—are absent from the shorter sermon text. Even Siddhattha's marriage, the birth of Rāhula, the episode of the four sights, and Kisā Gotamī's praise of Prince Siddhattha are truncated.

The great renunciation is similarly abbreviated to an outline form in PST. Excluded is the poignant dialogue between Siddhattha and his charioteer, Channa, as recounted in the PSL: "O Channa, if you really love me you will return to Kapilavatthu. If you do not love me then stay. My father and mother who love me deeply will die of a broken heart if they have no news of me. You must return home." And no mention is made of the death of Siddhattha's noble horse from sorrow as described in the PSL: "Once he lost sight of the great being (*mahāsatta*), Kanthaka could no longer bear the grief and sorrow he felt and his heart was shattered into seven pieces. After he died, Kanthaka was reborn as a deity (*devaputta*) in Tāvatiṃsa Heaven."

Instead, PST quickly moves to events surrounding the Buddha's enlightenment: Sujātā's *dāna;* Sotthiya's offering; a long section on Māra's attack of the Buddha at the throne of enlightenment; the witness of mother earth (Dharaṇī) and the *nāga* king, Kalana; and the *bodhisatta*'s perfection and Buddhahood. Excluded are the great being's encounter with King Bimbisāra and the discipleship of the five ascetics; the text also departs from the standard version of the *bodhisatta*'s five visions of his approaching enlightenment and Buddhahood. PSL expands Māra's attack on the Buddha at the tree of enlightenment by adding details about Māra's daughters—lust (*rāga*), aversion (*arati*), and attachment (*taṇhā*)—his mighty army, and a long exaltation of cosmic and miraculous events legitimating the Buddha's enlightenment.

Both Lānnā versions include the same sequence of postenlightenment events: forty-nine days spent at seven different locations in the vicinity of the *bodhi* tree and the conversion of two merchants, Tapussa and Bhallika, followed by the preaching of the *Dhammacakkappavattana Sutta* to the five ascetics. As well as more biographic detail and hagiographic elaboration, the PSL includes the Buddha's reconsideration of the law of interdependent co-arising and his indecision about whether or not to preach the *dhamma*.

In summary, both Lānnā versions of *The Buddha's Supreme Enlightenment* (PSL/PST) follow a similar sequence of events that begins with the *bodhisatta*'s precedent lives qualifying him for Buddhahood and concludes with the sermon at Benares. The victory over Māra and the achievement of enlightenment constitute the focus and climax of both texts. One can assume that PST was written as a distilled version for preaching within a specific ritual context, presumptively the *buddhābhiseka* ritual. In structure the PSL bears a closer resemblance to earlier lives of the Buddha (*Nidānakathā, Lalitavistara, Buddhacarita*) and the biography in the *Mahāvastu* than to either the eighteenth-century Burmese *Mālālaṅkāravatthu* or the nineteenth-century central Thai *Pathom Somphōt*. The PSL excludes the *parinibbāna,* the burial, Asoka's redistribution of the relics, and events associated with the development of the *saṅgha,* including admissions to the order, the donation of *ārāma,* and the councils.

Consistent with its ritual purpose, the condensed PST contains the essential components of the story that define the *bodhisatta*'s Buddhahood. The tale begins with an infinite, mythic time that reaches its historical apex in this eon with the appearance of Prince Siddhattha, the great being's (*mahāsatta*) awakening, and his early teaching. From the age of Dīpaṅkara to Vipassī and finally to the Buddha Gotama, this is the oft-told paradigmatic story that is taught to the Buddha image, the newly consecrated embodiment of this eternal truth. Any other text that might be preached during the *buddhābhiseka* ritual is secondary to the *Pathom Somphōt*. The *Dhammacakkappavattana Sutta* is occasionally preached in northern Thai, but is always chanted in Pāli at the conclusion of the eye-opening rite, where it stands as a doctrinal elaboration of the closing chapter of the PST.

*Sitthāt Ōk Buat* (SB) enriches and extends the Buddha story found in the PST. More important, the SB enhances the liminal, transformational nature of Buddhist rite of passage rituals, such as ordination, the period of intensive practice signified by the rains retreat, and opening the eyes of the Buddha image. Into this transformational scheme the SB incorporates the *parinibbāna* that signals the dissolution of Sakyamuni's physical body and at the same time anticipates the Buddha's continuing presence in relics and other material signs. With regard to the Buddha image consecration ritual, three elements in the SB are noteworthy: the episodes prior to Siddhattha's renunciation; Māra's challenge to the *bodhisatta*'s quest for Buddhahood; and the continuing presence of the parinibbāned Buddha in the form of relics following his cremation.

The hagiographic elaboration of the *bodhisatta*'s preexistence in Tusita Heaven, his conception, and his birth can be interpreted as fulfilling two aims implied by the terms *bhagavant* (Lord or Blessed One) and *tathāgata* (the Thus-Gone-One). The first portrays the Buddha as an extraordinary being worthy of worship (*pūjā*) by both gods (*devatā*) and human beings. His worthiness results from incalculable lifetimes of moral and spiritual perfection evidenced in numerous bodily signs and divine radiance. The *tathāgata* dimension complements these qualities. Siddhattha is foreordained to be a fully enlightened Buddha, not because sages and astrologers predict such a future, but because he follows an eonic, Buddhological pattern. His achievement is anticipated from the time of the Buddha Dīpaṅkara.

Māra, the lord of the realm of sense desire (*kāmadhātu*), attempts to thwart Siddhattha from his destiny as the conduit for the eternal *dhamma*. In SB Māra first challenges Siddhattha as he leaves Kapilavatthu, stalking him during his renunciant wanderings, and launching an aggressive attack at the moment of his enlightenment. The presence of Māra in the Buddha legend adds dramatic tension to the story at critical points.[14] Moreover, the Buddha's victory over Māra demonstrates his power over the forces of evil (*pāpimā*/evil one) and darkness (*kaṇha*/dark one). As a consequence, the Buddha embodies not only the wisdom achieved at his enlightenment but also power over the vast range of negative forces emanating from the realm of desire. In Thailand the Buddha image that symbolizes the Blessed One's victory over Māra (*māravijaya*) exceeds all others in popularity, indicating that the Buddha is worshiped as much for his power as for his wisdom. Within the context of the *buddhābhiseka*, Māra's role in both sermons and chants adds considerable drama to the Buddha's story. As the enlightened hero of SB glows with rays of omniscience, so the Buddha image radiates the power of the *tathāgata* over Māra, making that power available via appropriate ritual acts.

SB omits Māra's final encounter with the Buddha, which occurs three months before his death as recounted in the *Mahāparinibbāna Sutta*. Māra, having failed to obstruct Siddhattha's quest for and attainment of enlightenment, tries another strategy by declaring that the monks and nuns are sufficiently schooled in the *dhamma* and skilled in expounding so that the continuation and prosperity of the *sāsana* is guaranteed. Māra, in the guise of the Buddha, then appears before the monk, Sūra Ambaṭṭha, propagating the false teaching that the five aggregates (*khan-*

*dhas*) are permanent. Sūra is up to the challenge. Recognizing the falsity of this view, he unmasks Māra and drives him away.[15]

SB abbreviates the description of the cremation and the Buddha's relics. Although the text refers to cremating the Buddha's body in the manner of a world ruler, it omits the dispute among clan leaders over the possession of the relics and their eventual division into eight *stūpas* as recorded in the *Mahāparinibbāna Sutta*. Instead, the sermon only mentions the appearance of relics created by the element of fire, affirms the classification of three types of relics ranked by size, and makes additional reference to the enshrinement of the Buddha's hair relic in the Cūḷamāṇi *cetiya*. In this manner the SB uses the medium of the Buddha's bodily relics to connect the Blessed One's *nibbāna* and *parinibbāna*. The relic associated with his renunciation marks the Buddha's absence in preparation for the achievement of Buddhahood; his postcremation relics mark the *tathāgata*'s continuing presence after his physical death.

One episode in *Bimbā's Lament* (BP) that occurs in the Ja-nidāna and the Bv and its commentary deserves special mention for its relevance to the meaning of the Buddha image and the significance of the consecration ritual. It is the miracle of the jewel walk taken by the *tathāgata* when he returns to Kapilavatthu. This feat is performed in order to dispel any doubts harbored by the citizens of Kapilavatthu regarding his worthiness.[16] In this episode the Blessed One creates a double who walks on a crystal sky bridge surrounded by previous Buddhas. From this ascendent position he extends his arms to touch the sun and moon and then teaches the assembled citizens of Kapilavatthu. The Buddha's self-created double functions as his surrogate so convincingly that King Suddhodana asks the Lord Buddha's forgiveness for doubting him. All the Buddha's kinfolk then worship him as he descends from the sky. It is the Buddha's double, his image, that inspires awe and faith in the hearts of the assembled multitude in much the same way as the image functions in the KBV.

## Texts

### Pathom Somphōt (*The Buddha's Supreme Enlightenment*)[17]

*Namo tassa bhagavato sammāsambuddhassa . . . aham*. I pay respects to the Blessed One, the fully enlightened Buddha, to the virtuous qualities (*guṇa*) of the Buddha, the *dhamma*, and the *saṅgha* as handed down by the tradition since time immemorial.[18] The Buddha is the teacher (*satthā*) par excellence. He is supreme in the three worlds.[19] Through his resolve, he achieved enlightenment, brought happiness to the mundane world of rebirth, and attained the utter contentment of *nibbāna*.

Countless years ago he was born as Prince Vessantara. He gave away everything he possessed (*mahādāna*) and became a hermit, dwelling in the Himalayan forests. His generosity even extended to his willingness to relinquish his wife and children. At the sight of such generosity the earth quaked with a resounding noise, creating such a stir that in awe everyone's hair stood on end. At his death, the Lord was reborn in Tusita Heaven. There a host of celestial beings (*devaputta/devatā*), Indra, Brahmā, and others from the 10,000 universes gathered together under Mahābrahmā's leadership and built a palatial mansion (*vimānapāsāda*) for the great being (*mahāpurisa*) and paid their respects to him with the following invocation (*ārādhana*), *"Sabbasampatti saṇvidhāya pāramiyo asseto dhana dānena attano sambodhi pāpuṇissati"* [Having given away all wealth, being fulfilled in the perfection of *dāna,* he will attain full enlightenment on his own].

Through his perseverence the great being has achieved the thirty perfections (*pāramī*),[20] because it was his intent to become the refuge of the three worlds. The assembled beings invited the *bodhisatta* to be reborn into the human realm in order to awaken all beings to seek that state beyond old age and death, namely, *nibbāna.* By means of his supreme knowledge (*ñāṇa*), the great being contemplated the five conditions (*pañca vilokana*) required for him to be reborn in the human realm: that there be sufficient wealth, gold, silver, gems, servants, fields, and gardens; that the people be free from evil, backbiting, and the five fears of failure to fulfill the precepts (*sīla*); that the place (*Jambudīpa*) have sufficient rain; that the towns and villages be sufficiently populated and have enough food for their citizens; that the people have a life span between 100 and 1,000 years.[21] The *bodhisatta* would not be reborn among people who live less than 100 years because there would be insufficient time for the practice and realization of the fruit of the *dhamma;* nor would he be reborn among those with a life span of more than 1,000 years because they would be unable to comprehend the four noble truths and the truths of suffering (*dukkha*), impermanence (*anicca*), and not-self (*anattā*). Perceiving by his wisdom (*paññā*) that these conditions could be fulfilled, the *bodhisatta* descended from Tusita Heaven and was born in the womb of Mahāmāyā, the queen of King Suddhodana.

Thereupon, he entered his mother's womb by means of a vision (*nimitta*) of a white elephant. After ten lunar months in the womb, he was born on the full moon day of Visākha in the Lumbinī Forest. There he was attended by the *devatā,* Indra, Brahmā, and King Yama. After the *bodhisatta*'s birth, King Suddhodana asked his astrologers to name the baby. They called the great being Siddhattha. His mother died seven days after his birth. As the fully enlightened Buddha (*sammāsambuddha*) he had foreknowledge of his mother's death and of the condition of all beings. Siddhattha had reigned as prince for sixteen years when he married Yasodharā.

One day when Prince Siddhattha was riding in his pleasure gardens he encountered four sights: an old person, a sick person, a corpse, and a mendicant. That evening he returned to his palace and when he saw his concubines and dancers lying asleep on the floor, he was filled with sorrow (*saṃvega*) for the miseries of the material world (*rūpadhamma*). No one can escape suffering (*dukkha*), old age, and death. Resolving to become a mendicant (*pabbajjā*) to seek for a higher truth (*dhamma*), he called his servant, Channa, to prepare his horse, Kanthaka, and then he departed.

That same night, Yasodharā gave birth to Rāhula. Before departing, the great being contemplated whether to take a final look at his son. "If I return to see my son," he thought, "Yasodharā might try to keep me here and not let me go [literally, "will tie a rope around my neck and bind my arms and feet"]. Should I return, I fear that my resolve to become a mendicant might weaken. Therefore, I will not go back and allow Yasodharā-Bimbā to deter me. To see Rāhula might jeopardize my resolve [to renounce the world]; however, my dear son shall be known by the sign (*maṇḍala*) of Rāhu in the moon for all the world to see."[22] The Lord then stood in the doorway of the palace and took one last look at Bimbā lying on her left side with her right arm over Rāhula. Then, at daybreak in secret, he mounted his horse and accompanied by the *devatā* departed with his servant, Channa.

Then the forces of Māra appeared to impede the *bodhisatta*. Māra stood in the sky and said, "O Prince Siddhattha, seven days from now [I predict] you will be a world ruler and rule the four continents. You will have the seven jewels of this office including an elephant, a horse, the royal wheel.[23] You will become a great world ruler."

But the *bodhisatta* resisted Māra's temptations. On the night of his departure under a full moon he arrived at the banks of the Anomā River, where he shaved his head and began the life of a mendicant. At age twenty-nine during the month of Āsāḷhā he became a forest ascetic and he strove to realize the highest perfections (*pāramī-dhamma*).

The great being had five miraculous visions: (1) many blackheaded caterpillars covered his feet; (2) at the same time black birds from the four cardinal directions gathered around him and when both caterpillars and birds bowed down before the *bodhisatta* they turned white; (3) a tall plant grew up to the Mahābrahma Heaven; (4) the *bodhisatta* sat on top of a dung heap as tall as Mount Suniro (Sumeru); (5) tricolored moths flew around him.[24] The great being knew these visions portended that he would attain his resolve to become enlightened.

For six years, the great being practiced austerities. Then, on the full moon day of the lunar month of Visākha, a young woman named Sujātā presented the *bodhisatta* with sweetened milk rice (*madhupāyāsa*). After the *bodhisatta* had eaten, he put Sujātā's golden bowl in the Nerañjarā River and vowed, "If I am to attain enlightenment, may this bowl float upstream," and miraculously the bowl floated upstream. Then the great being knew that he would, indeed, become a Buddha. Kalana, a serpent king (*nāgarāja*), awoke from his watery slumbers, witnessed the bowl floating upstream, and knew that such a miracle could only be performed by someone destined to become a Buddha.

While seated under the *bodhi* tree the *bodhisatta* vowed to achieve supreme enlightenment (*sabbaññutāñāṇa*). *Nāga*s, *garuḍa*s, *kumbhaṇḍa*s [celestial beings classified with *yakkha*s and *asura*s] and *gandhabba*s [celestial musicians] offered him candles, incense, and trays filled with fragrant flowers. A host of celestial beings (*devaputta, devatā*), Indra, Brahmā, Yama, *garuḍa*s, *nāga*s, *kumbhaṇḍa*s, *gandhabba*s, and *yakkha*s sat down around the great enlightened being and worshiped him until the sound resounded to Brahma Heaven.

A Brahman named Sotthiya presented eight bundles of *kusha* grass as a gift (*dāna*). As soon as the Buddha sat on the grass, it was miraculously transformed into a diamond throne 14 cubits (Thai, *sok*)[25] high. While the great being sat facing the rising sun he attained the same reflective knowledge (*paccavekkhanañāṇa*) realized in the ancient traditions by those who had attained supreme Buddhahood.

At that time the forces of Māra who had gathered in the sky, angered by the great being's going forth, exclaimed, "O Prince Siddhattha, do not embark upon the mendicant life. In seven days you could become a world ruler (*cakkavattin*)." But the great being refused to be tempted. Lord Māra, whose heart was filled with evil (*pāpa*), had stalked the great being during the entire six years he pursued the renunciant's way. Thwarted in his attempts, Māra returned to his own kingdom of Paranimmitavasavattī and reflected, "Prince Siddhattha embarked on the mendicant life in order to become a Buddha. For the six years I hounded him he was unable to attain Buddhahood. The great being has achieved his goal at last and is seated on the diamond throne of enlightenment."

Māra then approached the diamond throne and said, "Siddhattha, this throne is not your domain. Descend from there at once. You cannot usurp my power. The throne is mine." To this remonstration the Buddha sat unmoved in silence. Māra grew exceedingly angry and marshaled his army with all their weapons. Māra's forces numbering several hundred thousand were fearsome. With Māra in the lead they came in a procession 12 *yojana*[26] long, 12 *yojana* wide, and 9 *yojana* high [i.e., about 85 miles in length, 85 miles in breadth, and 63 miles in height].[27] All the celestial beings (*devatā*), Indra, Brahmā, Yama, the *nāga*s, and the *garu-*

*ḍa*s were afraid and waited for the great being to save himself by launching a counterattack.

With their magical power Māra's army assumed awesome forms that aroused great fear. They carried spears and swords, bows and arrows, and raised a deafening cry.[28] They surrounded the great being in order to attack him, but due to his great merit (*puñña*) none of the weapons aimed at the great being harmed him. Next Lord Māra mounted a huge elephant named Tirantumeghala [var. Girimekhalā] who stood 250 *yojana* tall. Mounting the elephant's neck, Māra stood 3,000 *wā* [a *wā* equals 2 yards] high. With his magic power the evil one generated a thousand hands simultaneously, each holding a weapon, and charged toward the great being in order to strike the fatal blow.

*So bodhimaṇḍale mālāsane tassa samantato* . . . All the weapons Māra's army hurled at the Buddha were changed into flowers that fell as an offering at his feet. When Māra's forces looked up and saw the Buddha sitting in the middle of a lotus unafraid, encircled by a wheel like a lion king (*rājasiṅha*),[29] they fled, abandoning their attack on the diamond throne.

The Buddha reflected, "I embarked on the mendicant path and became a Buddha. Through diligent effort, I attained the thirty perfections. As Prince Vessantara in a previous life, my willingness to sacrifice my wife and children caused the celestial beings (*devatā, devaputta*), Indra, Brahmā to bless my great gift (*mahādāna*) with celestial water. From that time on such a blessing is a testimony to my enlightenment. I wrested this diamond throne from no one; it is a result of the store of my great merit."

While the Buddha was recalling (*anussati*) his past, a spirit (*viññāṇa*)[30] emerged from the earth in the form of a woman as beautiful as a celestial being, her hair heavy with water. She said to the Buddha, "O Lord full of merit. All the celestial waters that blessed your generosity (*dāna*) fell on my head and collected in my hair. None of it has evaporated because you knew that I would appear before you." Then Thoranī (Pāli, Dharaṇī)[31] wrung her hair dry. Miraculously the water that flowed from her hair was wider than the Ganges River and so powerful that it rolled over stones larger than mountains and scattered the forces of Māra.[32] Girimekhalā, Māra's elephant 250 *yojana* in height, was thrown to the ground.

Fearful, the evil-hearted (*citta-pāpa*) Māra cast down his weapons and prostrated before the Buddha, saying, "I pay homage to you, the leader of men, the noblest of men. In all the worlds, including the *deva*s, there is none comparable to you. Indeed, you are Buddha, teacher, defeater of Māra. You possess no evil dispositions and have crossed [to the farther shore]. May you convey others [to that shore]. O Lord filled with merit, I bow before you. You are supreme in the world, of unsurpassed wisdom and power, more sublime than all beings, the teacher of the world. You have transcended the five Māras: *khandha* (the five aggregates of human existence), *kilesa* (the depravities), [*abhi*]*saṅkhāra* (the basic components of embodied life), *devaputta, devatā,* (celestial beings), *maccurāja* (the king of death, i.e., Yama).[33] You have crossed the great floodwaters of desire (*kāma-ogha*), becoming (*bhava-ogha*), views (*diṭṭhi-ogha*), and ignorance (*avijjā-ogha*). I, Lord Māra, pay my respects to you, O great being." Then Māra and his army fled as bright rays (*rasmi*) emanated from the person of the Buddha.

Just as Māra and his army were fleeing, bright rays shining from the person of the Buddha in the form of a large red diamond wheel ascended into the heavens. The wheel measured 50 *yojana* in diameter and blazed with thousands of different colors as it descended to the horizon of the ocean, and then ascended again into the sky. At the center of the universe (*cakkavāḷa*), the *bodhisatta* shone with a splendid golden color. The Buddha sat on the diamond throne from which Māra's forces had fled, his radiance transforming the *bodhi* tree into silver.[34]

The celestial beings who had fled in fear of Māra witnessed the Buddha seated under the *bodhi* tree filled with the ten vital energies (*viriya*), and knew that he had defeated Māra's armies. They all joined in shouting the praises of victory (*jaya-gāthā*), "O most precious Lord Buddha, you have defeated Lord Māra." They then approached the Buddha on the throne of enlightenment under the *bodhi* tree. The *devatā*s, *nāga*s, *garuḍa*s, *kumbhaṇḍa*s, *gandhabba*s, *asura*s, Aiyavara [Śiva?], Indra, and Brahmā brought offerings of banners, flowers, whisks, fans, and containers of fragrant oil and consecrated water. They joined in the auspicious victory verses (*maṅgala-jaya-gāthā*), "*Jayo*. . . . Victory! Māra is defeated. The Lord Buddha is unscathed. Victory!" The divine celestial beings circumambulated the Lord Buddha three times to celebrate his release from suffering (*dukkha*), and Mahābrahmā placed a royal umbrella over the Buddha as protection.

Kalana, the *nāga* king, praised the virtue (*guṇa*) of the Buddha and Indra, the Lord of the celestial beings, worshiped (*pūjā*) him by blowing a conch shell. Five *devaputta*s played the harp, and the guardians of the four quarters (*lokapāla*) presented offering trays at the four directions to honor the Buddha's victory. Twenty-eight large *yakkha*s also offered victory trays to honor the Buddha's conquest of suffering, and tens of thousands of celestial beings throughout the universe joined together in a joyous chorus that resounded from the earth to the Brahma Heavens.

And thus it was that the Lord Buddha, having defeated Māra and his forces in the last watch of the night (*pacchimayāma*), attained the knowledge of the recollection of his previous existences (*pubbenivāsānussatiñāṇa*) from his first appearance innumerable ages ago to his enlightenment. As dawn approached, the Buddha understood the principle of cause and effect (*paccaya*), known by all the Buddhas, perceiving it both forward and backward, beginning with ignorance (*avijjā*) and ending with death; he comprehended the law of interdependent co-arising (*paṭicca samuppāda*) and the coming and going of the 10,000 universes and the 100 ages (*kappa*). When the Lord Buddha attained supreme omniscience (*sabbaññutāñāṇa*), the earth groaned and shook violently throughout 240,000 *yojana* and 100,000 ages, and the 100,000 universes trembled.

At the Lord Buddha's awakening, offerings of all kinds appeared. Following the tradition of previous Buddhas, he of unsurpassed merit uttered the following verse (*udāna gāthā*): "*anekajāti saṃsāraṃ sandhāvissaṃ* (traversing through *saṃsāra*'s many rebirths . . .)." According to the custom of enlightened ones, the Lord Buddha first sat on the diamond throne of enlightenment under the *bodhi* tree for seven days, where the bliss of his achievement (*samāpattisukha*) surpassed 100,000 years (*koṭī*). Second, he arose and walked to the north of the *bodhi* tree, where for seven days he gazed unblinking with his divine eye; therefore, the place is known as the shrine where the Buddha gazed without blinking (*animisa cetiya*). Third, he created a jewel walk (*ratana-caṅkamana*), where he spent seven days. Fourth, descending from this world the Lord Buddha entered a jewel abode (*ratana-ghara*) made by the *devatā,* where he contemplated the *tipiṭaka* [scriptures]. Fifth, the Lord Buddha spent seven days at the site where the serpent Mucalinda protected him from strong winds and rain. Sixth, the Lord Buddha went to the Ajapāla Tree, where he stayed another seven days. And, finally, the Lord Buddha spent seven days in the Rājāyatana Forest. During these forty-nine days the Buddha ate nothing and experienced only the joy of liberation (*vimuttisukha*). Later two merchants named Tapussa and Bhallika offered food to the Lord Buddha. That same morning Lord Indra offered water to the Buddha for washing his face, toothpicks for cleaning his teeth, and betel nut.

After the Lord Buddha accepted the food offered by the two merchants, the guardians of the four quarters (*lokapāla*) offered him four diamond alms bowls. The Buddha fused them into one bowl by the power of his mental resolve (*adhiṭṭhāna*), and from this bowl ate the food given by the two merchants. That day the two merchants took refuge in the two gems [Buddha, *dhamma*]. The Blessed One presented them with eight hairs from his head that they enshrined at their hometown and to which they made daily offerings.

In the tradition of all of the Buddhas who had attained enlightenment before him and by his own omniscience, the Blessed One had the foreknowledge that he would preach the *Dhammacakkappavattana Sutta.*

Knowing that the two sages, Uttaka and Attha, had already died, the Lord Buddha decided to preach the *dhamma* to his five former disciples, Koṇḍañña, Bhaddiya, Vappa, Mahānāma, and Assaji, and set forth to find them. Seeing the Blessed One approaching from a distance, they wondered whether or not the *samaṇa* Gotama had reached the higher stages of spiritual development (*magga/phala*). "Because we do not know if the *samaṇa* Gotama has realized omniscience (*sabbaññu-tāñāṇa*), we will not greet him until we know for certain." The Blessed One, perceiving that the five monks had reached this agreement among themselves, approached them. Unable to restrain themselves, each rose to greet the Lord Buddha, bowed down before him, and asked, "O respected elder, have your efforts been successful?" The Lord Buddha responded, "O sirs, why do you ask the *tathāgata* this question? This very day the *tathāgata* has attained omniscience and become a fully enlightened Buddha. Over the past ages (four *asankhaya* and 100,000 *mahākappa*) my previous lives (*paṭisandhi*) resulted in this lifetime to my attainment of *nibbāna,* the deathless state (*amata*), the overcoming of suffering, the truth of cessation (*nirodhasacca*), the four paths and their fruits (*magga/phala*), and the four noble truths. This will be my final existence."

Afterward, the Lord Buddha accompanied the monks to the Deer Park in the Isipatāna Forest near Vārāṇasī. The *devatā*s, Indra, Brahmā, *nāga*s, *garuḍa*s, *kumbhaṇḍa*s, *gandhabba*s, *asura*s, Lord Vessavana (Vaiśravaṇa), and the four *lokapāla*s gathered there to hear the Lord Buddha preach the *Dhammacakkappavattana Sutta.* A Mahābrahmā named Sahaṃpatimahābrahmā respectfully invited the Blessed One to preach the *sutta.* The Lord Buddha then preached to the five monks led by Koṇḍañña. He taught the middle path as the basis of the practice for all those who would follow the religious life, and noble eightfold path with right view as the basis for attaining the Emerald City, the deathless state, namely, *nibbāna.* The Blessed One taught the noble eightfold path for the benefit of all human beings to enable them to escape from endless rounds of rebirth and from all kinds of suffering. The truth taught by the Buddha—the four paths (*magga*), their fruits (*phala*), and *nibbāna*—sprang from his own knowledge and insight, not from anything he had heard or studied. The sequential teachings of the *Dhammacakkappavattana Sutta* are like 12,000 jeweled wheels of a carriage and for this reason it is called the *dhammacakka.* The Lord Buddha preached this *sutta* for the benefit of *devatā* and human beings.

After the Blessed One preached the *Dhammacakkappavattana Sutta,* many *devatā* from the earth, atmosphere, and the six heavens sang out in a mighty chorus that reached up to the Brahma Heavens. Everyone—*samaṇa* and *brāhmaṇa, devatā,* Māra and Brahmā, as well as ordinary human beings—bowed down in respect and cried together with one voice, "*Sādhu, Sādhu.*" To a depth of 240,000 *yojana* the earth groaned and trembled; Mount Sumeru and the oceans quaked; sounds of the rumbling earth penetrated everywhere; and a rainbow covered the world. When the *devatā*s heard the Lord Buddha's teaching, they attained the sublime states of stream-enterer, once-returner, and never-returner as a result of merit accumulated from over 100,000 *koṭi* together with Brahmā, who had accumulated merit for eighteen *koṭi*.

When Koṇḍañña heard the Blessed One preach the *Dhammacakka* during the month of Āsāḷhā he became an *arahant*.[35] Subsequently, Bhaddiya, Vappa, Mahānāma, and Assaji also attained arahantship. Thus, they are known as the five *arahant* disciples (*pañcavaggiya-bhikkhuarahantā*). After the Buddha preached the *Dhammacakkappavattana Sutta* he stayed in the Deer Park in the Isipatāna Forest, where he observed the rains retreat (*vassa*) for four months.

### Ānisong Pathom Somphōt (*The Meritorious Blessing for Copying or Listening to the* Pathom Somphōt)

All wise people who listen to the sermon (*dhamma-desanā*) called the *Pathom Somphōt* concerning the Buddha's way to and attainment of omniscience (*sabbaññutāñāṇa*) and follow its teachings will attain three kinds of happiness of which the deathless state (*amata*) of *nibbāna* is the highest. Whether you copy the text yourself, hire it done, give it as a *pūjā* offering, or simply listen to it, you will receive a great meritorious reward by being reborn either in heaven or as a human being greatly beloved by both *devatā*s and humans. You will be blessed with riches, power, prestige, beauty, a golden color, and great strength. Upon dying you will attain arahantship and become a *paccekabuddha* who has realized supreme enlightenment. Those who promote the *dhamma* in these ways will join the company of Metteyya, the future Buddha. They will realize the four stages of highest spiritual development (*magga/phala*); advance the *sāsana* (religion) for humans and *devatā;* achieve the Emerald City, namely, *nibbāna-dhamma;* and extinguish suffering (*dukkha*).

Remember the sermon of the *Pathom Somphōt* concerning the Lord Buddha's diligent practice for four *asankhaya* and 100,000 *mahākappa*s until he realized complete enlightenment and you will achieve the three kinds of happiness of which the state of deathless *nibbāna* is the highest.

[colophon] The *Pathom Somphōt,* the story of the enlightenment of the Lord Buddha, supreme in the world, is now complete. It was copied by the former monk, Gambhira of Wat Bān Nōi in the Suan Dok District together with his relatives in the Year of the Crow Culasakarāja 1225 (1863 C.E.).

## Sitthāt Ōk Buat (*Siddhattha's Renunciation*)

Homage to the teacher of both human and divine beings (*devatā*) who preached (*desanā*) out of his compassion (*mettā*) for the benefit of all the people in the world [literally, the realm of rebirth, *lokasaṃsāra*]. Having fulfilled the conditions for the attainment of enlightenment (*bodhisambhāra*) in mind, body, and speech for four incalculable ages (*asaṅkheyya*) and 100,000 eons (*mahākappa*), and having realized profound wisdom, he was reborn as Prince Vessantara. Having been reborn as a deity (*devaputta*) in Tusita Heaven for 4,000 divine (*dibba*) years, he was attended by 100,000 celestial nymphs (Thai, *nāng fā*). The gods of the 10,000 universes (*lokadhātu*) invited the Buddha to be reborn in Jambudīpa in order to attain omniscience and teach the *dhamma* to all beings. The Buddha, reflecting that the time had come to achieve the five extinctions (*pañcanirodha*),[36] set forth in the manner of the ancient traditions, acquiesced to their request and descended from Tusita Heaven to be reborn in the womb of Sri Mahāmāyā on the Thursday of the full moon day of the ninth lunar month.

Ten months later Mahāmāyā visited a pleasure grove [Lumbinī] with her attendants. Traveling by chariot, the queen entered the pleasure grove with her retinue and [her sister] Gotamī.[37] They came to a *nigrodha* tree with branches bending down to the ground, thereby creating a wide, shady area on all four sides. She stepped down from the chariot and grasped a branch of the tree with her left hand and Gotamī with her right hand. While the two beautiful sisters stood there, Mahāmāyā gave birth to the Lord Buddha, a child of unsurpassed beauty and as pure as dew on a lotus petal. The Lord Buddha then took seven steps to the north and spoke the following verse, "I am supreme in all the world." The entire universe up to the Brahma Heavens quaked. The guardians of the four quarters of the world came to care for Prince Siddhattha. Mahābrahmā descended carrying a white umbrella and a black antelope pelt to protect him as he emerged from his mother's womb.

Surrounded by all of his relatives, a clan numbering 103,000, Siddhattha shone forth as radiant as the sun. His father, Suddhodana, the ruler of the clan, was overjoyed to have a son. He brought Siddhattha into the palace and invited five Brahmans to predict his son's future.[38] The Brahmans who were skilled in *mantra*s and *śāstra*s examined the soles of the prince's feet and observed the 108 auspicious marks (*lakkhaṇa*). The first Brahman held up four fingers, the second held up three, the third held up two, and the fourth only one.[39] None, however, spoke. The fifth Brahman then paid his respects to Suddhodana and said, "O Lord of the People, your precious son born today, surpassing all in the three worlds, has realized the thirty perfections (*pāramī*). In his previous life he practiced unceasing generosity (*dāna*). Before he reaches old age he will renounce the world and seek enlightenment."

Suddhodana looked upon his child with pride and selected 30,000 exceptional children born on the same day to be his son's retinue.[40] The king then named his son Siddhattha. His mother, Sri Mahāmāyā, was able to care for him for only seven days before she died, whereupon she was reborn as a celestial being in Tusita Heaven and from thenceforth was known as the valiant Mahāmāyā.

After Mahāmāyā's death, her younger sister, Gotamī, felt great compassion (*karuṇā*) for Siddhattha's motherless state and attentively fed and cared for him. One day King Suddhodana went to plow the paddy field and took his son with him together with a large retinue. His aunt fed Siddhattha in the shade of a tree at the edge of the field, crooning a soft lullaby to comfort him. Just as the sun reached its zenith, the young prince fell asleep under the tree. Even though the sun moved across the sky, the shadow of the tree remained stationary, thereby protecting the child. The king observed this miracle from a distance. When he approached the child he paid homage to Siddhattha, exclaiming, "O great prince, I have witnessed a miracle. You are a person of great merit. The shadow of the tree did not move and so the branches continue to protect you from the sun." Suddhodana believed that a celestial being (*deva*) had prevented the shade of the tree from moving. He thought to himself, "This young prince is a person of unsurpassed merit. He will become a great lord." This was the first time the king paid homage to the Buddha.

On another occasion, King Suddhodana along with a large retinue of officials, attendants, minor wives, and Siddhattha's aunt, journeyed to see the sage, Devala, who possessed the power to look into the past for seven previous lifetimes.[41] The king, eagerly anticipating meeting the sage, held Siddhattha in his arms as he rode in the royal carriage from the city to Devala's Himālayan hermitage. Because of Siddhattha's extraordinary powers (*tejapāramī*) developed in past ages, the soles of his feet were covered with 108 auspicious signs, including blazing jeweled wheels. When Devala saw these signs on Siddhattha's feet, the sage looked into the past and predicted that the prince would become a Buddha who would teach human beings the way to escape from the power of Māra, uproot the darkness of delusion (*moha*), and destroy lust (*rāga*). Overcome with joy, the sage bowed down at the Lord's feet. Realizing that he, himself, would soon die, Devala began to weep. King Suddhodana noticed the sage's tears and asked, "Earlier you were joyful and paid homage to Prince Siddhattha; now you are weeping. Why are you crying?" The *ācariya* (teacher) replied, "O king, I predict that your son will be a great being (*mahāpurisa*), supreme in the three worlds. He has attained the thirty perfections (*pāramī*) including the five forms of charity (*dāna*), conquered rebirth (*saṃsāra*), and will reach the farther shore of *nibbāna*. For these reasons I am filled with happiness and pay homage to Prince Siddhattha. But when I considered my own future, I knew that I would soon die, leave this human realm, and be reborn into the formless realm (*arūpabrahmaloka*). When Prince Siddhattha becomes the Lord of all beings and preaches the *Dhammacakkappavattana Sutta,* it will be my misfortune to have died on the previous day. Because of the weight of my delusion (*moha*) I am unable to prevent this from happening and for this reason I wept." Upon hearing Devala's prediction that Siddhattha would attain enlightenment because of his great merit, King Suddhodana paid homage to his son for the second time. Then the king paid his respects to the sage and returned to the city.[42]

From that time on, King Suddhodana vigilantly shielded his son from all suffering or sorrow, but knowing that Siddhattha was a person of spiritual perfection and power, he feared that his son would renounce the world as predicted by Devala and the Brahmans. Thus warned of that possibility, the king ordered the city gate enlarged and reinforced. To prevent people from entering, he installed a large iron lock on the inside close to the top. When the gate was unlocked it made a telltale noise, and because it was so heavy it took a thousand people to open and close it. The king took all these precautions in order to prevent the prince from leaving during the night to embark on the life of a renunciant.

Time passed and Siddhattha continued to grow and mature. He enjoyed excellent health free from all illnesses. When he reached the age of sixteen his father was pleased to see that his son had become as handsome as a god. In order to encourage his son in worldly pursuits, he arranged for his marriage and consecration as one of the great world rulers of Jambudīpa. He summoned 30,000 rulers and said to them, "O kings! My son is now a grown man. The time has come for him to rule the kingdom as a mighty conqueror. Survey the world and find the most beautiful woman for my son to marry—one with green eyes, round supple fingers, fine complexion, a voluptuous figure, beautiful hair and eyebrows, and sensuous lips." All of the kings raised their hands (*añjali*) in respectful acceptance of the king's orders and departed. The officials (*senā* and *amātyā*), wise men, and Brahmans looked far and wide, in every country and every family for a suitable wife for Prince Siddhattha, a woman who was born on the same day as the prince. Finally, they discovered a woman of incomparable beauty, Bimbā by name, who resembled an angel (*devakaññā*) born in the human realm. She was the daughter of King Suppabuddha of the same lineage. The officials, wise men, and Brahmans sent word to Prince Siddhattha's father that they had found a suitable girl, Yasodharā [Bimbā] by name, the daughter of King Suppabuddha, Siddhattha's uncle.[43]

When the Sakyan nobles consulted among themselves, they voiced many objections to Siddhattha. "Earlier we heard," they said, "that Prince Siddhattha is extraordinary. However, he is but a person of ordinary ability. He is highly regarded only because of his royal status, not because he is learned in the arts and sciences (*silpa-śāstra*) or is a warrior capable of defending and defeating his enemies. We consider him to be unsuited to care for a wife and family. In our opinion he is unworthy of our daughter." And so it was that the Sakyans objected to the marriage proposal.

The officials and wise men who were sent by Suddhodana to find a wife for Siddhattha returned and reported to the king: "O King Suddhodana, we have a troubling report to make. The Sakyans consider Siddhattha to be an unworthy husband for Bimbā, accusing him of not being learned in the arts and sciences. Therefore, they refuse to give their daughter to him in marriage."[44] When King Suddhodana heard these criticisms of Siddhattha, the mighty ruler of Jambudīpa, he realized that the Sakyans were unaware of his son's true merit, and so he spoke to his wise officials: "Beat the large drum for seven days to announce throughout the city that Prince Siddhattha will demonstrate his archery skills at a special exhibition." The king's attendants did as they were ordered and beat the drum so loudly that it resounded throughout the four continents. Everyone, nobles and commoners, men and women, heard the announcement. King Suddhodana ordered the construction of a large pavilion for the use of royalty arriving to watch the event. The pavilion in which the bow was placed was constructed in the middle of a courtyard to prevent the crowds from getting too close to Prince Siddhattha and the special bow. The bow was called Sahassathāma because it took a thousand men to draw back the bowstring.

Thirty thousand members of the Sakyan clan and their leaders came. Officials dressed especially for the occasion installed white umbrellas and victory banners. They brought bananas and coconuts, various flowers including five kinds of lotus, and white, red, green, and gold cloth for the ceremony. There was abundant food and drink for all. Colorfully festooned elephants and horses processed; musicians beat drums and gongs, blew on conch shells, played xylophones, horns, and stringed instruments. The deafening sound carried to the highest heavens, and all enjoyed the festivities.

King Suddhodana invited his son, the future Buddha, resplendent in his royal finery, to descend from the pavilion. Prince Siddhattha thought to himself, "Now I must demonstrate my powers in the presence of all my relatives." Taking the mighty bow in his left hand, the prince easily drew back the bowstring with the little finger of his right hand and inserted an arrow into the bow. All 30,000 Sakyans were impressed at the size of the bow and arrow and looked on with rapt attention. Prince Siddhattha spoke politely to the assembled leaders and asked them, "O assembled lords, what target shall I aim for on top of the city wall? Quickly choose a spot." So King Suppabuddha, the father of Bimbā, placed a round disc on top of the wall a great distance away. "Shoot at that," he said. "We'd like to see if you are able to hit such a small target." The *bodhisatta* took the bow, aimed, and released the arrow. It made a sound louder than 100,000 claps of thunder. The arrow, true to its mark, hit the disc squarely in the center, then reversed its direction to return to Prince Siddhattha's hand. At that moment a tumultuous noise resounded from the heavens. When the 30,000 Sakyans heard the deafening roar they were struck dumb. Trembling, they bowed down before the *bodhisatta,* who then put aside the great bow and sat on the throne before all of the people present.

After Siddhattha demonstrated his archery prowess, King Suppabuddha directed Bimbā to dress in royal finery and enter the pavilion in procession with the 40,000 daughters of the Sakyan rulers. The king gave his daughter, Bimbā, in marriage to Prince Siddhattha, that together they might rule Jambudīpa. Prince Siddhattha was overjoyed with the youthful and beautiful Bimbā. King Suppabuddha bade Yasodharā [Bimbā] join Siddhattha on the throne surrounded by her 40,000 attendants. Following the ancient traditions, they reigned as king and queen with peace and justice.

For many years the *bodhisatta* governed the country wisely. Accompanied by his attendants, he enjoyed excursions into his royal gardens. At sunset he would return to the city in his chariot. One day when Bimbā was several months pregnant, Prince Siddhattha went on a tour of the royal pleasure gardens. Traveling in his chariot drawn by two horses and accompanied by a large retinue, Siddhattha observed an extraordinary sight, a supremely calm, peaceful mendicant who possessed the four noble truths and the knowledge gained from insight into the true nature of things (*vipassanāñāṇa*). The prince was so moved by this sight that he was determined to renounce the world, transcend suffering (*dukkha-cariya-kamma*), and teach others the path from the realm of rebirth to *nibbāna.* But he kept his vow a secret in his heart and continued as usual to spend time in his pleasure gardens accompanied by friends and attendants.[45]

After ten months the time came for Yasodharā [Bimbā] to give birth and she bore a son. Messengers entered the royal park to inform Prince Siddhattha. Upon hearing the news of his son's birth, the prince thought to himself, "This child is like a rope binding me to the realm of *saṃsāra* and suffering."[46] Outwardly he appeared to be happy at the birth of his child and returned to the city. Waking at midnight in the pleasant atmosphere of the moonlit chamber, Prince Siddhattha gazed on the 40,000 beautiful sleeping women. Their hair was disheveled; some resembled corpses with saliva dripping from their open mouths; others twitched their eyes and ground their teeth; some grunted like pigs with their hands draped over their foreheads. As some of the women slept their mouths sagged open and their feet jerked in a most hideous manner. They were lying packed on top of each another in utter disarray.

This disgusting sight reminded Prince Siddhattha of dead souls in a charnel house. At once he made up his mind to renounce the life of the householder and overcome defilement (*kilesa*). He must sever his attachment[47] to his wife and child, but because the *bodhisatta* loved his son he wanted to hold him and kiss the top of his head one last time before leaving on his quest for omniscience. The *bodhisatta* entered the sleeping chamber and drew aside the bed curtain to see Yasodharā with Rāhula suckling at her breast. He thought to himself, "If I pick up Rāhula, Yasodharā may awaken and beg me to stay and then I shall be detained even longer in this world of *saṃsāra*. Therefore, I must leave immediately to seek enlightenment." So, at midnight the prince woke his servant, Channa, and said, "Prepare my horse, Kanthaka; we must depart at once. I shall become a mendicant in order to build the raft of *dhamma* that will ferry all beings across the sea of *saṃsāra* to the farther shore of *nibbāna*." Channa arose quickly to prepare Kanthaka for the journey.

Prince Siddhattha was only twenty-nine when he renounced his kingship. He departed on a Monday under a full moon in the evening of the ninth lunar month. Kanthaka knew his master's heart and feared he would pursue the life of a homeless mendicant, so the horse sounded an alarm so loud that his neighing resounded over the city like the echo of a kettle drum. The celestial beings prevented the people of the city from hearing Kanthaka's loud neighing by plugging their ears with cotton. As Prince Siddhattha, Channa, and Kanthaka approached the eastern gate, they had the same thought: "If the gate is locked, Channa will hold onto Kanthaka's tail, the prince will sit astride, and together we'll fly over the city wall." It was during the third watch of the night that the *devatā* came and unlocked the gate, enabling the prince to leave the city.

As the prince departed, the evil-hearted (*citta-pāpa*) Lord Māra, vile and fearsome, came once again to tempt the prince with deceptive, sweet-sounding words. "O Prince Siddhattha, you are still youthful and handsome with many years to live before you reach old age. Why are you in such a hurry to renounce the world? Why leave your wife, Bimbā, called Yasodharā, beautiful as a jeweled flower, and your son, Rāhula, whose appearance surpasses the heavens? Yasodharā is still very young and Rāhula only a baby. When you left she was asleep, lying on her side cradling her child. When she awoke she reached out her hand only to find that her husband had already departed. She cried, was disconsolate and brokenhearted, grew pale and haggard, and wished to die. O Prince Siddhattha, please return to rule the city for just seven days. A jewel wheel[48] will appear and a hundred kings from the four continents will bow down before you. You will be the most powerful world ruler (*cakkavatti*) in the world."

After the *bodhisatta* listened to Māra's false flattery he replied, "O Lord Māra, I now see everything clearly. If I were to rule for seven days a jewel wheel would appear. A hundred kings would bow before me and I would be a great world ruler (*mahācakkavattin*). But I have grown disillusioned with the householder life. Therefore, I have decided to seek enlightenment and become a true ruler. Lord Māra, get out of my sight immediately!" Māra, annoyed that he had failed to change Prince Siddhattha's mind, turned and stalked off.

When the *bodhisatta* departed from the beautiful city with its golden palace, the *devatās* accompanying him illuminated his way with the beams from heavenly lamps and candles. The guardians of the four quarters protected the feet of Kanthaka as he raced through the sky, descending at the Anomā River. The *bodhisatta,* utterly delighted at the sight of a pure white island, walked out on the sand. With his left hand he grasped his hair and, holding his sword in his right hand, cut it off, casting his shorn locks into the air. Lord Indra, the ruler of the heavens, caught the *bodhisatta*'s hair and enshrined it in the Cūḷamāṇi *cetiya* in Tāvatiṃsa Heaven as a place of worship for Indra, Brahmā, and all other celestial beings. After Siddhattha cut off his hair, he took the eight monastic requisites presented by Mahābrahmā and put on the robes following the custom of all previous Buddhas.[49] Afterward he went for his alms in the city of Rājagaha. All the people, men and women, young and old, were amazed, saying, "Never before have we seen such a splendid, radiant (*rasmi*) person. What kind of being is he? He must be a god." They all eagerly rushed forward to put food into his alms bowl. When King Bimbisāra, who was in his palace, looked out and saw the future Buddha he was filled with an overwhelming sense of joy. Having received *piṇḍapāta* from the people of Rājagaha, the *bodhisatta* departed for Gandhāra Mountain, where he sat down on a rock to eat his meal.

King Bimbisāra, noticing that the monk had left the city, inquired as to his identity. Calling together his ministers and councillors, he told them to go to the foot of the mountain and ask him, "Who are your parents? What is your lineage? What is your caste? Where do you come from? Why have you renounced the world? Please answer these questions."[50] When the future Buddha heard that King Bimbisāra had inquired about him, his parents, ancestry, hometown and so on, he answered, "O Great King, listen to what I have to say. My father, the king of Kapilavatthu, is named Suddhodana. My mother's name is Mahāmāyā. I have relinquished the throne to pursue the practice of a world renouncer in order to attain enlightenment."

When he heard that Prince Siddhattha was the son of his friend, the king was overcome with joy and invited him to rule over his city, saying, "O prince, you are still young. You could be the ruler of Rājagaha. It is a large, magnificent city like Tāvatiṃsa Heaven, endowed with wealth, many elephants and horses, cows and buffalo, gold, silver, and much treasure, and beautiful women. There will be plenty of time when you are older, O prince, to renounce the world." The future Buddha responded by teaching the king the four sublime abodes [lovingkindness, compassion, sympathetic joy, equanimity], and then said, "I have no desire to rule for I have renounced the world in order to reach enlightenment." When King Bimbisāra heard Prince Siddhattha's refusal, he replied, "O prince, when you reach enlightenment and become the teacher of the world I would be honored to be the first to hear you preach." Then the prince bade farewell to King Bimbisāra and went to the Himālaya Forest to lead the life of an ascetic. Five mendicants observed Prince Siddhattha fasting in the forest and thinking that this sage (*muni*) would certainly reach enlightenment, decided to follow the ascetic until he attained *nibbāna*. Siddhattha continued to fast, growing weaker and weaker until he could no longer stand, whereupon the five hermits cared for him as he lay upon his bed.

Observing that Siddhattha was at the point of death and knowing it would be impossible for him to reach enlightenment, the five ascetics thought, "We have followed our leader's teaching but with little outward sign of success. Now is the time to leave him."[51] With the departure of the five ascetics, the future Buddha had no one to care for him, but still he continued to fast, growing ever weaker. When he lay down to meditate (*bhāvanā*), he looked like a withered tree that had been cut down for several days. Even in rain and under a scorching sun he still meditated, walking back and forth in an effort to reach enlightenment and help release others from the cycle of rebirth.

The *devatā* who dwelt in the Himālaya Forest watched over the *bodhisatta,* pleading with him, "O Prince Siddhattha, cease this fasting and resume eating so that you won't die." The *bodhisatta* refused to listen, so intent was he on attaining enlightenment, and the *devatā* out of compassion (*karuṇā*) continued to care for him. At that point the god Indra descended from Tāvatiṃsa Heaven to the place where the *bodhisatta* was meditating and there he began playing a three-stringed lute. As Indra played the first string the future Buddha observed, "The sound is too loud and shrill. The string is on the verge of breaking." As he plucked the second string he said, "I can barely hear the sound. The string is too loose." Finally, Indra plucked the third string and the prince exclaimed,

"The sound is beautiful. The string is neither too taut nor too loose." Indra then raised his clasped hands in respect and asked the future Buddha to break his fast and resume eating.

At that time the *bodhisatta* resided near the bank of the Nerañjarā River. One day, Sujātā, the daughter of a wealthy family, went for an outing with her retinue in the Himālaya Forest. There she saw a beautiful, green banyan tree where she believed a *devatā* was living. She swept the ground clean around the base of the tree and prayed, "O *devatā,* please give me a male child. If you grant my wish, I shall prepare for you a delicious rice mixture cooked with cow's milk." Then she returned home. Before long she gave birth to both a daughter and a son. In gratitude Sujātā wished to return the *devatā*'s kindness with an offering of milk rice (*madhupāyāsa* ). She had 500 cows drink the milk from 1,000 cows; 250 cows drink the milk of 500 cows; and so on until she took the milk from one cow and mixed it with new, carefully husked rice.[52] Taking only the finest grains she boiled them with the milk until perfectly cooked. At sunrise, Sujātā put the rice in a golden dish and carried it on her head to the banyan tree.

Just then, as the *bodhisatta* was wandering near the bank of the Nerañjarā River, he spied the beautiful banyan tree and sat down in the shade of its branches. At the same time Sujātā came to the Nerañjarā River and saw the future Buddha. Believing him to be the tree *devatā,* she presented her offering of milk rice. After accepting the golden bowl, the Buddha went to the bank of the Nerañjarā River, where he divided the rice into forty-nine portions and then placed the golden container in the river, where it miraculously floated upstream. Later the bowl sank to the bottom, where it struck the bowls of the three preceding Buddhas [Kakusandha, Konāgamana, Kassapa]. A *nāga* king who had been sleeping there since the time of Kassapa was awakened by the sound. Joyfully the *nāga* king reflected, "Oh, once again a Buddha has appeared to save the world."

Then the Buddha returned to the *bodhi* tree and, sitting down on the eight bundles of grass given as *dāna* by Sotthiya, he strove to achieve enlightenment that very day. The evil Lord Māra, residing in the sixth heaven, saw Siddhattha sitting on the throne of enlightenment. Angry and jealous he made haste to prevent Siddhattha from attaining his goal and to seize the throne of enlightenment for himself. Lord Māra assembled a large army of infantry and soldiers mounted on horses and elephants and carrying swords and spears, an army that extended for several *koṭi.* [The description of Māra's attack, Thoranī's witness on behalf of the Buddha, and the Buddha's ultimate victory has been omitted as it closely parallels the same events in PS.]

After defeating Māra, the Enlightened One radiated the seven divine rays (*rasmi*) throughout the universe. The victorious Lord Buddha, conqueror of Māra, teacher of the world, preached to all human and divine beings until he reached the age of eighty. He renounced the world when he was twenty-nine, spent six years in ascetic practice until he reached enlightenment, and then taught for forty-five years. Having transcended rebirth, he attained *nibbāna*.

The Lord Buddha went to a park near the town of Kusinārā, where he sat down in the shade between two trees. Foreseeing that he would reach his final *nibbāna* in the middle watch of the night before sunrise, the founder of the tradition (*sāsana*) called Ānanda to his side and out of his compassion (*karuṇā*) said, "O Ānanda, tell the king of the Mallas that before the morning sun reaches Jambudīpa, the Enlightened One will reach his final *nibbāna*." Following the Buddha's request, Mahānanda entered the town of Kusinārā to inform the king of the Mallas. At the time the king was in his palace consulting with his 6,000 advisers. Seeing Ānanda approach he rose to greet him and invited the monk to sit beside him on the beautifully adorned throne. He asked him, "*Bhante* . . . how have you been?" Mahānanda replied, "O great ruler, the Buddha is presently residing in a grove of trees in your kingdom. Far from his home and family, he is ill with dysentery and much weakened. The Lord, the Savior of all beings, has never been so sick. He asked me to inform you of his condition. The Lord Buddha, teacher of the three worlds, said that in the last watch of the night near sunrise, he will enter his final *nibbāna,* the Emerald City."

After hearing Ānanda's report, the king was filled with compassion for the Lord Buddha. Beating his chest he cried out to his officers and advisers, "O officials, the Lord Buddha, he who has conquered the realm of *saṃsāra,* is now residing in a forest grove near the city and will soon die. We had so little time to be with him, perhaps as a result of our limited merit." The king of the Mallas then ordered his officials to sound a gong throughout the entire city to summon everyone, both privileged and common folk, men and women. Upon hearing the news they all beat their breasts and cried out loudly in great sorrow, "Oh, the Buddha has come to our city but will soon die. How unfortunate for us that we were unable to present the Blessed One with offerings. Perhaps it is because we lack sufficient merit."

Having expressed their grief, they prepared offering trays of food and puffed rice decorated with sweet-smelling flowers and followed the king of the Mallas to where the Buddha lay ill. The king and his officials, attendants, wives, and concubines gathered together many different kinds of offerings—food, incense, flowers, and the requisites of the monastic life. With multicolored flags and banners the king mounted his auspicious royal elephant and, surrounded by soldiers, departed from Kusinārā. Arriving at the place where the Buddha was seated, the king circumambulated the Blessed One three times and presented him with offerings of flowers, puffed rice, scented oil, and other gifts. Sitting down near the Buddha, the king raised his hands in respect and then asked, "*Bhante bhagavatā* . . . O Blessed One, after you have passed into *nibbāna,* what should we do with your physical remains? Please, out of your great compassion, tell us what we should do."

Then the Blessed One, out of his great compassion, answered the king's question, "*Sādhu bho mahārājā* . . . Peace to you, O great king. After I die you must cremate my body in the manner of a world conqueror (*cakkavattin*)." Upon hearing the Enlightened One's request, the king of the Mallas, overcome with joy, sounded a gong to call together his soldiers mounted on horses and elephants to surround the area. A beautiful pavilion draped with banners and flags was prepared for the cremation.

The Buddha, seated between two *sal* trees in Kusinārā Park on a jeweled throne decorated with gold and silver, then preached his last sermon to about 700 human beings and *devatā,* saying, "O monks, remember well that all compounded things (*saṅkhāra*) are impermanent. Be diligent in the pursuit of the *dhamma*." In the last watch of the night on the full moon Tuesday of the month of Visākha the Buddha attained *nibbāna,* the Emerald City. The earth, in its great sorrow, quaked and resounded to a depth of 240,000 *yojana;* the oceans swelled, huge waves crashed against the shores; rain clouds darkened the earth, and the deafening crash of thunder and bursts of lightning inspired both awe and fright. Although no musicians could be seen playing instruments, the sounds of drum and gong, trumpet and conch shell, reverberated throughout the Himālayas, over Anotatta Lake, and to Mount Sinero [Sumeru], the king of mountains. This fanfare sounded throughout the cosmos (*cakkavāḷa*) from the Brahma Heavens to the Avīci Hell.

Both human beings and *devatā*s grieved over the Buddha's death (*parinibbāna*), crying, "There is no escape from evil (*pāpa-kamma*). Those who do evil will receive evil, but those who do good (*puñña*) will receive good. Those who do evil will be reborn in the four Apāya Hells and states of deprivation. Those who are devoid of good and blinded by delusion (*moha*) will be reborn in the Avīci Hell, while those who do good and are mindful will overcome ignorance (*avijjā*), transcend the cycle of rebirth, and attain heaven."

All kinds of human beings, Indra, Brahmā, Yama, *garuḍa*s, *nāga*s, Śiva [Thai, Phra Aisuan], *kumbhaṇḍa*s [supernatural beings ranked with *yakkha*s], *yakkha*s, *gandhabba*s [divine musicians], *deva*s, the *lokapāla* [guardians of the universe], the head of the *kinnarī,* and Rāhu all gathered together to express their sorrow at the death of the Enlightened One. Many kinds of forest animals were present when the Buddha reached his final *nibbāna*: elephants, horses, lions, tigers, large rhinoceroses, hog deer, barking deer, rabbits, monkeys, wild water buffalo; and creatures from the air and water, eagles, falcons, snakes, turtles, fish, crabs, shrimp, and clams.

Then the king of the Mallas ordered his soldiers and councilors to construct a funeral urn from costly wood and a pavilion for those who came to pay respects to the Buddha, a pavilion so richly adorned that it evoked the five pleasurable feelings. The area was made level, cleaned, and purified for the construction of a beautiful, multitier funeral tower (*pāsāda*).[53] When the gilded and bejeweled *pāsāda* was completed it shone with divine splendor.

To the accompaniment of heavenly music and dancing, Mahānuruddha Thera, the head of the *saṅgha,* Indra, Brahmā, and Yama paid their respects to the Buddha with offerings of flowers, puffed rice, candles, and incense. Afterward, Indra, Brahmā, and Yama anointed the head of the Buddha with holy water, wrapped his body in 500 layers of consecrated rose-colored silk cloth, placed it in the funeral urn, and carried it to the *pāsāda* accompanied by crowds of grieving human and divine beings. The supernal rays of the *pāsāda* reached to the Brahmaloka Heavens.

At that time a widow by the name of Marikā [Mālikā][54] fell to the ground before the funeral pyre, beat her breast, and cried, "O Prince Siddhattha, why did you die so soon? We Mallas had no opportunity to present offerings (*dāna*) to you. Perhaps this is a consequence (*vipāka*) of wrongdoing in past lives. Because I fear the king, I have not dared approach your body. Beating my breast in anguish, I wish to die. O Enlightened One, Teacher of the World, by the time I came to you, your life had ended. I am afraid of being reborn in hell (*apāya*). Time and again I have wanted to present offerings to you; now it is too late. You have already gone beyond this world of *saṃsāra.* I feel abandoned and filled with sorrow, distaught by your death. Now who will save us from the suffering and sorrow of hell and states of deprivation (*apāya*)? O Lord Buddha, whom none in the three worlds surpass, if you were still alive I would ask you to allay my fears and assure me of happiness."

At that time the officials and ministers of the Mallas together with all of the citizens and the divine beings—Indra, Brahmā, Yama, *garuḍa*s, *nāga*s, and Śiva—praised the widow, Mālikā. Their cries of "*Sādhu*" reached throughout the 10,000 universes, up to the six heavens, and finally to the Brahma Heavens. When the Lady Mālikā opened the cover of the golden coffin, she saw the precious remains of the Lord Buddha. Upon viewing the Buddha's remains, she performed *añjali* and cried out, "*Bhante* . . . O Lord Buddha, you are the supreme liberator of the world."

Mālikā removed her beautiful, priceless red stole [*mahālātāpasādhana*] and presented it to the deceased Lord Buddha as an offering, saying, "May I attain *nibbāna*."[55] After Mālikā had expressed her wish (*patthanā*), the Malla kings covered the Buddha's body with the royal stole. Crying "*Sādhu, Sādhu* . . . ," they carried the Buddha's body to the funeral pyre. As they did so, crowds of people gathered around the pyre to worship the body of the Lord Buddha.

The Malla kings, Indra, Brahmā, and Yama, lifted the golden casket onto the pyre. Circumambulating the funeral pyre clockwise, they worshiped the Buddha, beseeching his compassionate forgiveness. First the gods—Indra, Brahmā, and Yama—and then the people attempted to light the pyre, but it would not ignite as though it was wet. Both the gods and the people were amazed at this miracle. Unable to understand why this had happened, they approached the Venerable Mahānuruddha and asked, "*Bhante* . . . we are puzzled. Why didn't the body of the Buddha burn when we lit the funeral pyre?"

The Venerable Anuruddha entered into a state of meditative absorption (*jhāna*) and perceived with the divine eye that the Buddha intended to delay the proceedings until Mahākassapa, one of his first disciples, arrived to pay respects to his body. After the people and the *devatā*s heard what the Thera said, they waited for the arrival of Mahākassapa. While they were waiting, they assembled the requisite offerings to worship the Buddha—flowers, puffed rice, and sweet-smelling perfumes—and observed the five and the eight precepts. Meanwhile, Mahākassapa with a company of monks was traveling to see the Buddha. Along the way they met a sage carrying a *kannika* staff[56] and asked him, "O sir, is the Lord Buddha, the teacher of the three worlds, in good health?" The sage replied, "Gotama, your teacher, reached *parinibbāna* twenty days ago. A large number of men, women, and *devatā* are waiting for you around the funeral pyre." When he saw the *kannika* staff carried by the sage, Mahākassapa realized that he spoke the truth.[57] All *bhikkhu*s who had not yet attained arahantship lamented and wept. Subhadda, an elderly monk, admonished the weeping monks, saying, "Don't be sad because the Buddha has died. He has reached *parinibbāna*. He can no longer order us around. We can now do as we like." Mahākassapa heard the heretical words of the monk but kept them in his heart. Then he led the monks to the Buddha's funeral pyre, where they circumambulated the body of the Buddha three times. As he bowed to pay respects to the Lord Buddha, the Blessed One's feet, radiating divine light, miraculously emerged from the golden coffin to receive Mahākassapa's homage and then returned into the coffin.[58]

After Mahākassapa paid respects to the Buddha, the kings, Indra, Brahmā, Yama, *garuḍa*s, *nāga*s, and Śiva arranged the fire for the Buddha's cremation. The fire prepared by the human beings and the *devatās* consumed only the funeral pyre, leaving intact the bones of the Buddha. Miraculously the flames shot up into the sky and then fell back to the earth with the relics (*dhātu*) of the Buddha emitting supernatural rays of six colors that reached to the Brahma Heavens.

There are three sizes of Buddha relics: one as large as a bean seed; another, half the size of a grain of rice; and the third equal to a lettuce seed. The Buddha's hair, thirty-two teeth, and collarbone were not consumed by the fire. Indra and Brahmā enshrined the Buddha's hair relic [in the Cūḷamāṇi *cetiya* in Tāvatiṃsa Heaven]. Lady Mālikā was amazed to find that her stole also was not consumed by the fire. All of the *devatās* bowed down in respect at this miraculous event. This completes the *nibbāna* of the Buddha.

# 6

# EMPOWERING THE IMAGE

## Introduction and Analysis

The image consecration ritual not only rehearses the life story of the Buddha Gotama—the narrative of becoming a *tathāgata:* the experience of enlightenment, the antecedent factors leading to that experience, and its consequences that led the Buddha to teach the *dhamma*—but simultaneously infuses the image with the necessary qualities of arahantship and Buddhahood. This is accomplished by chanting the *Buddha Abhiseka* (Buddha [image] Consecration Sutta) (BA)[1] while nine or more monks sit in meditation facing the *bodhimaṇḍa* along three sides of the *rājawat;* and by chanting the *Suat Bōek Phranet* (Eye-Opening Sutta) (SBN), a text recited exclusively during the *buddhābhiseka* in a cadence unique to this *sutta* and this ritual. Both *sutta*s are recited in Pāli by two groups of monks invited specifically for this recitation. In the palpably mystical atmosphere created by the ceremony, this experience lends a dramatic, performative power to the ritual, further enhancing the sense of witnessing the very night of the Buddha's enlightenment. Translations of the two *sutta*s follow an introduction to the texts set within the context of the ritual.[2]

The BA begins with a terse, abbreviated sketch of the life of the Buddha, concluding with the victory over Māra, the realization of the nature of impermanence (*anicca*), and emancipation from suffering (*dukkha*). Central to the BA is the cognition of the truth of impermanence and the transcendence of the four kinds of feeling (mental and physical suffering and happiness) by means of mindfulness of breathing (*ānāpānasati*). From meditation emerge the various mental attainments and spiritual powers associated with Buddhahood, in particular, mindful awareness (*sati*) that constitutes the ground of insight meditation (*vipassanā*).[3]

While legendary and mythological embellishments enhance the dramatic nature of the Buddha's enlightenment, meditation is the sine qua non of the *tathāgata*'s achievement of *nibbāna*. In essence, both the BA and the SBN are meditation treatises. The performative power of the *buddhābhiseka* is reinforced when monks seated in meditation reenact the night of the Buddha's awakening while the BA is being recited. The monk-meditators function as surrogates for the Buddha, mimetically empowering the images within the *rājawat* with the mental and spiritual achievements that constitute Buddhahood.

Following a brief biographical sketch of Gotama Buddha, the BA describes the following: the four levels of meditative absorptions (*jhāna*); the higher knowledges (*abhiññā*); the four stages of sanctification of the lineage of the Ariya (*gotrabhū*); and the attainments acquired by the Buddha during the three watches of the night. The text concludes by implanting (*plūk*) all of these qualities into the images being consecrated.

**Jhāna.** *Jhāna*s are described in the Pāli *sutta*s, the *abhidhamma,* and commentary.[4] An early version is found in the *Bhayabherava Sutta,* the Discourse on Fear and Dread, an autobiographical *sutta* in the *Majjhima Nikāya* ( M I.4).[5] Calming the body (*passaddho kāyo*) and focusing the mind (*samhitaṃ cittaṃ ekaggaṃ*) are preconditions for acquiring the *jhāna*s. Sequentially the characteristics of each of the four *jhāna*s are: conceptualization (*vitakka*), discursive thought (*vicāra*), rapture and pleasure (*pītisukha*); moving beyond conceptualization and discursive thought but accompanied by concentration (*samādhi*), rapture, and pleasure; transcendence of rapture but accompanied by pleasure (*sukha*), equanimity (*upekkhā*), awareness (*sati*), and alertness (*sampajāna*); and abiding in pure equanimity and mindful awareness and the transcendence of feelings of pleasure and pain.[6] The *jhāna*s describe a process of mental purification and transformation culminating in the affective state of equanimity and the cognitive state of full awareness. In the *Bhayabherava Sutta* and the BA the four *jhāna*s do not constitute a goal but only a stage on the way to enlightenment, serving specifically as a prerequisite to the attainment of the higher knowledges (*abhiññā*).

**Abhiññā.** In the Pāli canon the *abhiññā* appear as conditions conducive to serenity, special wisdom, and *nibbāna,* and as refined mental powers including clairaudience, clairvoyance, and the certainty of emancipation.[7] According to the *Bhayabherava Sutta* during the three watches on the night of his enlightenment the Buddha achieves each of three *abhiññā,* namely, the knowledge of his previous lives, the knowledge of the arising and passing away of all beings, and the knowledge of the destruction of the cankers or mental intoxicants (*āsava*). In the BA, knowledge of the Buddha's past lives and of the kammic conditions of all living beings is followed by transcendence of the eight worldly factors—gain, status, praise, happiness, and their opposites.

In the standard account of the stages of the Buddha's enlightenment,[8] the higher knowledges are followed by knowledge of the nature of all compounded things (*saṅkhatadhamma*), namely, the knowledge of the interdependent and co-arising nature of things (*paṭicca samuppāda*) and their three fundamental, underlying traits—impermanence, suffering, and not-self. The BA affirms that the *jhāna*s and *abhiññā*s so defined are attained through the knowledge derived from insight meditation (*vipas-*

*sanāñāṇa*), thereby establishing a direct association between insight and absorption modes of meditation.

The *abhiññā*s also include *iddhi,* supernatural powers considered by some scholars to represent a pre-Buddhist thaumaturgical tradition that was incorporated into early Buddhism.[9] In the *Sāmaññaphala Sutta* (D I.78), a classic description of *iddhi* appears in a list of the fruits of the life of a *samaṇa*:

> He enjoys different powers: being one, he becomes many—being many, he becomes one; he appears and disappears; he passes through fences, walls, and mountains unhindered as if through air; he sinks into the ground and emerges from it as if it were water; he walks on the water without breaking the surface as if on land; he flies cross-legged through the sky like a bird with wings; he even touches and strokes with his hand the sun and moon, mighty and powerful as they are; and he travels in the body as far as the Brahmā world.[10]

Scholastic scholars arranged the *iddhi* into two categories, both represented above—the power of extraordinary movement such as flying through the air and the power of creation such as reduplicating oneself.[11] The Buddha as thaumaturge appears in the *Dhammapada* commentary (DhA 14:2), wherein the Blessed One creates miraculous signs of fire, water, and multicolored rays as well as counterparts of himself, and in the *Buddhavaṃsa* commentary, where the Buddha creates his double. This thaumaturgical tradition finds its way into the story of the creation of the first Buddha image and the *buddhābhiseka* ritual, which implants into the image the Buddha's miraculous *abhiññā* and *iddhi.*

**Paṭicca samuppāda.** The first appearance of the formula of interdependent co-arising in the BA departs from the classic twelve-stage formula: ignorance, mental formations, consciousness, name and form, six sense organs, contact, feeling, thirst, attachment, becoming, birth, old age and death.[12] Variations on the standard formula also appear in the Pāli canon. They represent the historical development of the *paṭicca samuppāda* formula but they do not alter its basic form and meaning. The interdependent co-arising paradigm teaches that all compounded things originate within an interaction among causes and conditions rather than through a strictly linear theory of cause and effect.[13] The BA considers ignorance to be the underlying cause of the cycle of causality but begins the linked formula with consciousness and so reverses the standard order between consciousness and mental formations. This minor variation serves to heighten the Theravāda view that "processes of the mind . . . [are] prior to the objects they process."[14] Variations in the formula have been interpreted as offering a meditator different ways to approach the complexities of the causal stream in order to master them.[15]

**Ariyamagga** (noble paths). At this juncture in the enlightenment accounts of the BA and the SBN, the four stages of spiritual perfection that lead to arahantship are inserted: stream-enterer, once-returner, never-returner, *arahant.* At each stage the Buddha contemplates the four noble truths and the three characteristics of existence. These attainments are associated with the knowledge achieved through insight (*vipassanā*), contemplation (*paccavekkhana*), and the path (*magga*), emphasizing once again the centrality of meditation for the path to spiritual perfection and insight into the true nature of reality.[16]

After achieving omniscience (*sabbaññutāñāṇa*), the Buddha utters the famous verses (*gāthā*) acclaiming his conquest over grasping (*taṇhā*) and the destruction of all mental intoxicants (*āsava*). Siddhattha becomes the Buddha, the Thus-Gone-One (*tathāgata*). The BA then repeats his attainments during the three watches of the night, the twelvefold formula of interdependent co-arising that the Buddha contemplates both forward and backward, and then repeats the victory *gāthā.*

Finally, the text instills into the image the qualities and accomplishments that constitute Buddhahood: the *pāramī* of the Buddha's previous existences; forty-seven states of knowledge (*ñāṇa*); concentration (*samādhi*); liberation (*vimutti*); the supermundane *dhamma;* the Buddha's numerous miracles; the power of the reliquary mounds (*cetiya*). Postenlightenment events included are: preaching the *Abhidhamma;* teaching the 84,000 sections of the *dhamma;* the first sermon (*Dhammacakkappavattana Sutta*); ordaining Yasa; converting Uruvela Kassapa; performing miracles at Kapilavatthu; teaching the *Cariyāpiṭaka* and the *Vessantara Jātaka;* and donating the Jetavana Monastery. In these events the qualities, actions, and teachings of the Buddha are assembled and appropriated into northern Thai devotional Buddhism and instantiated in the Buddha image.

**Ñāṇa.** The BA focuses especially on the Buddha's awakening, the stages leading up to this achievement, and the power of the extraordinary knowledge (*ñāṇa*) associated with it. In Pāli canonical literature the concept of *ñāṇa* is central to Theravāda thought and practice. *Ñāṇa* is used to describe the knowledge of past, future, and present, and the knowledge of the four noble truths and their function. Insight-knowledge (*vipassanāñāṇa*), a central concept in the BA, includes nine types of knowing: rising and falling of *dhamma*s, dissolution, fear, disadvantage, dispassion, the desire for deliverance, reflective contemplation, equanimity regarding all conditioned formations, and the natural order of things.[17] A precise, definitive translation of the term *ñāṇa* poses special difficulties. It denotes knowledge and is often so translated, but in the BA, its meaning expands to include a state of extraordinary, transcendent awareness, a transformative knowing that includes a state of being. Thus, when the Buddha attains various *ñāṇa*s they define or characterize the nature and power of his Buddhahood.

In the *buddhābhiseka* ritual context, the BA highlights the Buddha's enlightenment, especially the achievement of states of consciousness integral to the omniscience of complete awakening (*sabbaññutāñāṇa*). Buddhahood represents the culmination of eons of moral and spiritual perfections (*pāramī*) and numerous higher states of superior mental awareness and knowledge that come from meditation. The qualities comprising Buddhahood and *tathāgata*-hood enumerated in the BA are then instilled into the image through the agency of the monks who meditate while the BA is chanted. By both verbal and nonverbal performative action, the image is imbued with the efficacious power (*ānubhāva*) of the Lord Buddha.

The SBN also describes the night of the Buddha's enlightenment in terms of insight meditation, especially breathing awareness, mental absorptions (*jhāna*), the higher knowledges (*abhiññā*), and the stages of the noble path to spiritual perfection that occurred during the three watches of the night. The sermon version of the BA either eliminates or abbreviates much of the repetition found in the SBN, whereas the SBN expands the limited reference to breathing mindfulness in the BA to a full-scale description of the four foundations of mindfulness: body, feelings, mind, concepts. Further, the SBN elaborates the structure of the three watches of the night that provides a framework for the repetition of the higher knowledges, the three characteristics of existence, the four noble truths, the stages of spiritual perfection, and, most prominently, the forward and backward contemplation of the arising and cessation of the twelve factors of interdependent co-arising.

The SBN concludes with a unique *dhāraṇī* in praise of the Buddha, and a recitation in northern Thai of the Buddha's victory over Māra. The *dhāraṇī* emphasizes the esoteric nature of the northern image consecration ceremony found in the *dhammakāya,* the Buddha *yantra,* and other aspects of the construction and consecration of images described in chapters 3 and 4. The concluding recitation dramatizes the power of the Buddha and the consecrated Buddha image over the evil powers of the sensate world personified by Māra. While the *dhāraṇī* and the closing northern Thai chant have the appearance of addenda, they actually highlight the fundamental import of the *buddhābhiseka* ritual.

## Texts

### Buddha Abhiseka (*Consecrating the Buddha*)[18]

The Buddha, our great teacher, the Enlightened One, out of his great compassion (*mahākaruṇā*) for all beings, practiced the thirty perfections (*pāramī*). His resolve to realize the perfections began with his first birth and continued throughout his countless lifetimes. As Vessantara he practiced the perfection of generosity (*dāna*), relinquishing even his wife and children. After his death as Vessantara, the Enlightened One was reborn in Tusita Heaven.[19] There the deities (*devatā*) of the countless universes met and addressed him saying, "O thou of great resolve (*paṇidhāna*), the appropriate time has come for you to be reborn in the realm of human beings in order to be enlightened as the Buddha." Then, the *bodhisatta* departed from Tusita Heaven and was born into the family of the king of the Sakyas, having been carried in his mother's womb for ten months. Upon his birth he faced the north, took seven steps, and gazed in all directions and declared, "I am supreme in the three worlds."

The Enlightened One lived as a layman [Prince Siddhattha] for twenty-nine years. One day while traveling in his pleasure gardens he chanced upon four sights: an old person, a sick person, a corpse, and an ascetic. He was so moved by this experience that he gave away all his belongings and departed to become a hermit, residing in the forest on the banks of the Anomā River, where he practiced austerities for six years.

### The Enlightenment

On the full moon day of Visākha he received [a food] offering from a young woman named Sujātā which he consumed while sitting on the banks of the Nerañjarā River. That day the [future] Buddha cast his golden begging bowl into the river, where it [miraculously] floated upstream. In the evening the *bodhisatta* took eight clusters of *kusha* grass given to him by the Brahman, Sotthiya, and approached the auspicious *bodhi* tree that grew beside a road built by the gods (*devatā*). Spreading the grass under the tree he sat down and vowed, "Here shall I sit and not move until I am freed from all defilements (*āsava*) and from all forms of evil." Then, facing eastward as the sun set, he conquered the forces of Māra. Afterward, the *bodhisatta* sat in meditation practicing mindfulness of breathing (*ānāpānasati kammaṭṭhāna*), alternating exhaling and inhaling short and long breaths. While engaged in the mindfulness of breathing, the *bodhisatta* comprehended both physical and mental suffering (*dukkha*), overcame bodily and mental formations (*kāya* and *citta saṅkhāra*), and experienced both physical and mental rapture. His mind was so concentrated that it was freed from the four kinds of feeling: mental and physical suffering and mental and physical happiness. He perceived the impermanence of all things, the nature of *nibbāna,* and the freedom from all passion (*rāga*) and suffering.

### The Mental Absorptions (*Jhānas*)

While Prince Siddhattha was investigating (*vicāra*) breathing meditation he experienced supreme bliss. Persevering in this discipline, he concentrated his mind so intently that he was freed from all sensual defilements (*kilesa-kāma*) and sensual objects (*vatthu-kāma*). Freed from all taint of evil (*akusala-dhamma*), he attained the first stage of meditative absorption (*jhāna*), a state composed of thought conception (*vitakka*) and discursive thinking, physical and mental nonattachment (*kāyacitta-viveka*), and the rapture of bliss (*pītisukha*). He reached the second level of absorption, eliminating both *vitakka* and *vicāra* and attaining the rapture of supreme bliss. He experienced physical and mental joy (*kāyikacetasika-sukha*) as a result of unwavering concentration, realizing a wisdom characterized by equanimity (*upekkhā*), by five kinds of rapture, and devoid of passion. The third stage of mental absorption combines equanimity, unwavering mindfulness (*sati*), and contentment. Having attained this third *jhāna,* Prince Siddhattha contemplated the fourth in which both mundane happiness and suffering (*lokiya sukha-dukkha*) and all feelings of joy (*somanassa-vedanā*) and grief (*domanassa-vedanā*) are eliminated. He was suffused with equanimity (*upekkhā vedanā*), freed from suffering, and filled with pure mindfulness. The *bodhisatta* Siddhattha attained serenity and purity, totally eliminating the 1,500 major defilements (*kilesa*) and all the minor defilements (*upakilesa*). He took delight only in skillful action (*kusala-kamma*) and thwarted temptation by the eight worldly phenomena (*lokiya-dhamma*) [gain and loss, status and loss of status, praise and blame, pleasure and pain (A IV.157)].

### The Higher Knowledges (*Abhiññās*)

Regarding the higher knowledges (*abhiññā*), the Lord achieved the mental state in which he was able to recall his previous lives (*pubbenivāsānussattiñāṇa*). During the first watch of the night he recalled the family of his birth, the color of his complexion, his diet, his experiences of happiness and suffering, the span of his life, his death and rebirth, and each of his previous lives until his present existence. Then Siddhattha firmly resolved to become pure by eliminating all traces of defilement. With his mind pacified and pure he resisted temptation by the eight worldly phenomena. In the second watch he entered the absorption in which he realized the knowledge of death and rebirth of all living beings.

Prince Siddhattha, seeing all beings with the divine eye, transcended all human and divine capabilities, saying, "Some people harbor evil thoughts, do evil deeds, and speak evil words. Because of their evil thoughts they condemn the noble ones (*ariya*), and they reject the four noble truths.

When such human and divine beings die, they will be reborn in hell (*niraya*), where they will suffer in the four realms of deprivation (*apāya-bhūmi*). But when death comes to those with pure actions and a pure heart who lead virtuous lives and do not criticize the noble ones, they will be reborn in heaven."

The *bodhisatta,* perceiving that those who die and are reborn according to the consequences of their actions, with the good being rewarded with good and the evil with evil, sat in meditation, unaffected by the eight worldly phenomena. At that time the *bodhisatta* came to understand the nature of all compounded things which, because of ignorance, continually die and are reborn. Attachment to consciousness (*viññāṇa*) arises from attachment to mental formations (*saṅkhāra*) which, in turn, arises from attachment to name and form (*nāma-rūpa*). Because of the six sense spheres (*āyatana*), there arise the six kinds of contact (*phassa*), which lead to the six different kinds of feeling (*vedanā*). Grasping for existence (*bhava-taṇhā*) arises from clinging (*upādāna*), which leads to birth (*jāti*), old age and death (*jarāmaraṇa*), lamentation and suffering.[20]

The cessation of this process is the complete cessation of dhammic formations, which leads to the cessation of mental formations; . . . the cessation of name and form; . . . the cessation of the six sense spheres; . . . the cessation of the six modes of contact; . . . the cessation of the six kinds of feeling; . . . the cessation of craving, old age, and rebirth.[21]

## Stages of the Spiritual Perfection (*Ariyamagga*)

The *bodhisatta,* Siddhattha, having attained insight knowledge (*vipassanāñāṇa*) with a radiant wisdom like a great diamond (*vajira*), perceived the three common characteristics of existence—impermanence, suffering, and not-self—and the nature of the cause and effect of all things. Then the Lord attained the knowledge of the lineage of the Ariya (*gotrabhū*) and the knowledge that conforms to the highest truth preparatory to reaching the path of stream-enterer (*sotāpatti-magga*). There he overcame the limitations of views (*diṭṭhi*), doubt and perplexity (*vicikicchā*), and the ten fetters (*saṃyojana*) [the illusion of a self, doubt and perplexity, attachment to rules and rituals, sensual lust, irritation, passion for the realm of form, passion for formless realms, conceit, restlessness, ignorance] that constitute the body of ignorance.

By the knowledge of the stream-enterer (*sotāpannañāṇa*), its contemplations (*paccavekkhaṇa*) and its fruits (*phala*), the Lord perceived the four noble truths: there is suffering, the cause of suffering, the cessation of suffering, and the way to the cessation of suffering. By the knowledge of insight (*vipassanāñāṇa*), he contemplated the three characteristics of existence. He realized the awareness of the final stage of insight knowledge and the purification associated with wisdom, thereby achieving the condition of the once-returner (*sakadāgāmī*). Again he contemplated the four noble truths and the nature of suffering that characterizes the cycle of birth and death. He realized that craving is the cause of suffering, the end of rebirth is the end of suffering, and the path to the end of suffering. By the knowledge of insight, the Lord contemplated the three characteristics of existence of all compounded things.

The Lord reached the state of the never-returner (*anāgāmī*) in which he overcame all sensual desire (*kāma*), passion (*rāga*), and ill will (*byāpāda*). This was the knowledge of the fruit of the never-returner. By the knowledge of the contemplations, the Lord perceived the four noble truths: that rebirth is suffering; that craving is the cause of suffering; that *nibbāna* is the cessation of suffering; and that there is a path to the cessation of suffering. The Lord understood these truths perfectly. By the knowledge of insight he understood the three characteristics of existence and thus attained to the knowledge of the path of the *arahant*. Hence, the Lord attained to the knowledge of the fully enlightened one. His course was now complete, having achieved the knowledge of the fruit of the *arahant,* of the contemplations, and so on.

The *bodhisatta,* Siddhattha, perceived the four noble truths through the knowledge of the path and the contemplations, being purified from the effects of *saṃsāra*. Together with all the previous Buddhas he came to know the truth of suffering.

## The Enlightenment and the Watches of the Night

In his enlightenment the *bodhisatta,* Siddhattha, achieved the condition of omniscience, becoming the foremost in the world of human beings and gods, of Māra and Brahmā, and in the realm of religious practitioners (*samaṇa* and *brāhmaṇa*). He fully understood that this was the end of rebirth. He attained to the state of sublime bliss while seated under the *bodhi* tree, proclaiming, "Having realized the end of *saṃsāra,* I have destroyed all craving (*taṇhā*)."

"O house-builder (*gahakāra*) [i.e., *taṇhā,* the maker of this body of ignorance]! Before I was enlightened I traveled through many cycles of birth and death, and for an infinite number of lifetimes I experienced suffering. O house-builder! Now I have seen you. Hereafter you will no longer build this house [i.e., the five aggregates]. Having broken the crossbeams and destroyed the ridge pole of that house, I have attained to *nibbāna,* and am freed from all conditions. I have attained the knowledge of the destruction of the intoxicants (*āsavakkhayañāṇa*) in which all grasping (*taṇhā*) is destroyed."

The *tathāgata* reached this supermundane state (*lokuttara-dhamma*) through perseverance and effort. As one in whom the passions are extinct, the *tathāgata* extinguished all demerit (*pāpa*), and through his wisdom realized the *dhamma* of cause and not-cause. During the first watch of the night all of the *tathāgata*'s doubts disappeared.

At that time the Lord Buddha was able to recall his previous lives. With a pure heart devoid of defilements, he resisted the eight worldly phenomena. In the middle watch he was able to see the birth and death of all beings through his divine eye, superior to all human and divine beings.

"O *brāhmaṇa*s, all beings who are subject to evil *kamma*, those who speak and think in evil ways will be reborn in hell (*niraya*), and after death will suffer in the four states of deprivation (*apāya*).[22] Those who act and speak in beneficial ways, upon death will be reborn in the realm of a good destination (*sugati*)."

The Lord Buddha knew the condition of the life and death of all beings: those who are stubborn, superior or inferior, beautiful or ugly, punished in hell or rewarded in heaven according to their *kamma*. Then, the Buddha, having attained enlightenment (*anuttarasammāsambodhi-ñāṇa*), was suffused with calm and established in the skillful actions (*kusala-kamma*) so that he was unaffected by the eight worldly phenomena. In the middle watch of the night he attained to this state of omniscience.

At that time he understood the nature of conditioned reality, and that rebirth is caused by ignorance, which in turn depends on mental formations, which in turn depend upon consciousness, mind-body, the six senses, contact, sensation, craving, clinging, coming into being, birth, old age and death.

By insight knowledge the Blessed One contemplated the three characteristics of existence. The following day he eliminated all of the intoxicants (*āsava*), ignorance, the bonds (*saṃyojana*), and the five hindrances (*nīvaraṇa*). Then, attaining to the state of the fruit of the *arahant,* he perceived the four noble truths by means of the knowledge of the path and the contemplations, namely, that the cycle of birth and death is suffering. This noble truth has been realized by all the noble ones. By eliminating craving they eliminated suffering, and the cause of suffering, and realized the unconditioned (*nibbāna*). That is the cessation of suffering. The practice leading to the cessation of suffering is called [in Pāli] the *dukkha-nirodha-gāmini-paṭipadā.*

In the last watch of the night the Lord Buddha reflected both forward and backward on the law of interdependent co-arising (*paṭicca-samuppāda*) . . . and that all physical and mental suffering arises accordingly. The Lord Buddha, thereby coming to know the cause and cessation of all forms of suffering and being suffused with supreme bliss, exclaimed,

"O house-builder! Having identified you as the builder of this house, no longer will you be able to construct the five aggregates (*khandha*). All construction materials composing the 1,500 defilements (*kilesa*) have been utterly destroyed. I have reached *nibbāna* beyond cause and effect, the cessation of all defilements and the supreme transmundane state. All demerit has been consumed. I have entered the higher meditative absorptions and am freed from the intoxicants. The *tathāgata,* greater than all beings, has a radiance more brilliant than the sun shining in a cloudless sky."

The *tathāgata,* without physical blemish and free from all doubt, reached the farther shore of enlightenment. He overcame all evil, attained the bliss of the six kinds of seclusion, and realized *nibbāna*. He is free from anger and desire, cares for all living beings, and dwells in supreme bliss.

### Empowering the Image with the Qualities of the Buddha[23]

The Lord Buddha, filled with boundless compassion, practiced the thirty perfections for many eons (four *asaṅkheyya* and 100,000 *kappa*), finally attaining enlightenment. To that Buddha I pay homage.

May all the Buddha's qualities (*guṇa*) be invested in this image. May the Buddha's boundless omniscience be invested in this image until the Buddhist religion ceases to exist.

May all of the states of knowledge achieved by the Blessed One—analytical insight (*paṭisambhidā-ñāṇa*), perseverence (*dharana-ñāṇa*), the four perfect confidences (*vesārajja-ñāṇa*), the forty paths (*magga-ñāṇa*)—a total of seventy-seven different properties—be invested in this image.

May the boundless concentration and the body-of-liberation of the Buddha be invested in this image for 5,000 years during the lifetime of the religion.

May the supermundane truth discovered by the Buddha during his enlightenment under the *bodhi* tree be invested in this image for the 5,000 years of the religion.

May all the miracles performed by the Buddha after his enlightenment in order to dispel the doubts of all humans and gods be invested in this image for all time.

May the power of the reliquary mounds (*cetiya*) miraculously created by the Buddha at the places following his enlightenment in order that both humans and *devatā* might worship him be invested in this image for 5,000 rains retreats.

May the Buddha's powers acquired during his activities immediately after his enlightenment be stored in this image forever.

May the knowledge contained in the seven books of the *Abhidhamma* perceived by the Buddha in the seven weeks after his enlightenment be consecrated in this image for the remainder of the lifetime of the religion.

May the power acquired by the Buddha during the seven days under the Ajapāla Tree, the seven days at the Mucalinda Pond, and so on, be invested in this Buddha image for 5,000 rains retreats.

The Buddha returned to Ajapālanigrodha, where he preached the 84,000 stanzas of the *dhamma*. May they also be stored in this Buddha image. May the Mahābrahmā who requested that the Buddha preach come into this image.

The Buddha went to Vārāṇasī, where he preached his first sermon (*Dhammacakkappavattana Sutta*). May the knowledge embodied in this sermon be instilled in this Buddha image. The Buddha observed the rains retreat in the Deer Park, where he ordained Yasa. May the supernatural power of that event be stored in this image.

The Buddha preached to the ascetics led by Uruvela Kassapa and his brothers together with their retinues. May the supernatural power of their conversion be invested in this Buddha image for 5,000 rains retreats.

When the Buddha entered Kapilavatthu in order to teach his relatives, he performed many miracles. He flew through the air and walked on a pure crystal road. May the supernatural power of that occasion be instilled in this Buddha image for the lifetime of the religion.

Mahākassapa Thera approached the Buddha and inquired about the tradition of the Buddhas (*Buddhacarita*). The Buddha then preached the *Cariyāpiṭaka* to him. May the truth of this teaching become a part of this Buddha image for the remainder of the life of the religion.

The Buddha, the conqueror of Māra, descended from the air and sat under a mango tree, where he preached to the people of the Sakya clan so that they might pay respects to him. May the supernatural power of that event be invested in this Buddha image. The Buddha, referring to the miracle of the Pokkhara rainfall during the time of Prince Vessantara, preached the *Mahāvessantara Jātaka*. May the supernatural power of the *jātaka* also be instilled in this Buddha image for 5,000 rains retreats.

The Buddha entered Sāvatthi and stayed at the Jetavanārāma. He received this gift [the Jetavana Monastery] out of his great compassion for the lay disciple, Anāthapiṇḍika. There he preached to both human beings and gods. May the supernatural power of that occasion be invested in this Buddha image. The Buddha preached out of compassion for all living beings. May all his teachings be instilled in this Buddha image for 5,000 rains retreats.

The Buddha performed many marvelous acts, taught continually, and ordained monks into the noble path. May all the gods, together with Indra, Brahmā, Māra, and all people protect this Buddha image, as well as the relics (*dhātu*) and the religion (*sāsana*) for 5,000 years for the welfare of all human beings and gods. The sermon consecrating this Buddha image has been preached in thirty-eight stanzas (*gāthā*).

## Suat Bōek Phranet (*Opening the Eyes of the Buddha*)[24]

While seated at the base of the exalted *bodhi* tree the Blessed One defeated Māra and his powerful forces and attained enlightenment. I honor the Buddha, that supramundane being of infinite knowledge (*anantañāṇa*). The *tathāgata,* our teacher, out of sympathy for the world (*lokānukampa*), performed the thirty perfections (*pāramī*) from the time he vowed [to be the Buddha] until he was reborn as Prince Vessantara. The *tathāgata,* having fulfilled the *pāramī* of generosity during his life as Vessantara, was reborn in Tusita Heaven. After being invited by a multitude of *deva*s in the 10,000 universes . . . [to be reborn again in the human realm], he descended from Tusita Heaven and was reborn in the Sakya clan. After ten months he emerged from his mother's womb, [a prince] endowed with unsurpassing wealth. Turning toward the north, he walked seven steps; seeing no one comparable to himself in the 10,000 universes, he announced: "I am beyond comparison, the most exalted, priceless one in the world." [The prince] lived as a householder for twenty-nine years. Upon seeing four sights [an old person, a sick person, a corpse, and an ascetic], he abandoned his life of wealth and ease and embarked upon the homeless life. On the banks of the Anomā River he became a wanderer and for six years he undertook strenuous training in the Udumbara Forest. On the full moon day of the month of Visākha, after receiving milk rice offered by Sujātā, he ate it near the banks of the Nerañjarā River, spending the day in the great forest. That evening he was offered eight handfuls of *kusha* grass by the Brahman, Sotthiya. He spread it out under the *bodhi* tree, sat down, and vowed: "I will not depart from this seat until my mind has been liberated from the intoxicants (*āsava*)." Facing the east, before sunset he conquered the forces of Māra.

### Breathing Meditation and the *Jhānas*

Ascending the throne of enlightenment, he steadied his mind and trained it as follows,

"I inhale a long breath; I exhale a long breath;
I inhale a short breath; I exhale . . . ;

I shall inhale experiencing my entire body (*sabbakāyapaṭisamvedi*); I shall exhale . . . ;
I shall inhale calming my bodily constituents (*kāyasaṅkhāra*); I shall exhale . . . ;
I shall inhale experiencing joy (*pīti*); I shall exhale . . . ;
I shall inhale experiencing happiness (*sukha*); I shall exhale . . . ;
I shall inhale experiencing the mental constituents (*cittasaṅkhāra*); I shall exhale . . . ;
I shall inhale calming the mental constituents; I shall exhale . . . ;
I shall inhale experiencing the mind itself (*citta*); I shall exhale . . . ;
I shall inhale gladdening the mind (*abhippamodayaṃ cittaṃ*); I shall exhale . . . ;
I shall inhale calming the mind (*samathaṃ-*); I shall exhale . . . ;
I shall inhale releasing the mind (*vimocayaṃ-*); I shall exhale . . . ;
I shall inhale investigating impermanence (*aniccā-anupassi*); I shall exhale . . . ;
I shall inhale investigating detachment (*virāga-*); I shall exhale . . . ;
I shall inhale investigating cessation (*nirodha-*); I shall exhale . . . ;
I shall inhale investigating renunciation (*paṭinissagga-*); I shall exhale . . ."

These are the steps of tranquillity meditation (*samatha kammaṭṭhāna*) and mindfulness of breathing (*ānāpānasati*).

He undertook this strenuous training with a steady and firm awareness, a calm and unwavering body, and a concentrated and focused mind. Liberated from sensual passions and unwholesome elements he attained the first absorption characterized by reflection and investigation, detachment, joy, and happiness.

Stilling reflection and investigation he attained the second *jhāna,* a state devoid of reflection and investigation, imbued with mental tranquillity, peace, and happiness.

Attaining the third *jhāna* he became devoid of passion and suffused with equanimity. Full of mindfulness and awareness he experienced bodily joy, and dwelt in happiness contemplating the teachings of the noble ones.

Abandoning both joy and suffering, attaining the cessation of delight and lamentation, contemplating the absence of joy and suffering, he attained the fourth *jhāna* of absolute purity (*parisuddhiṃ*).

### The First Watch of the Night (*Patama Yāma*)

Thus, with his mind fully concentrated, completely pure, serene, uncorrupted; having transcended moral taint (*upakilesa*); being modest, vigilant, steadfast, and unswerving; in the first watch of the night having harnessed his mind he attained the knowledge of his previous lives as follows, "I had such and such a name, came from such and such a family, from such and such a caste, ate such and such food, experienced such and such joy and suffering, having reached such and such an age. Finally, I was reborn into this present existence."

In the same watch of the night with his mind fully concentrated, completely pure, serene, and harnessed he came to know the death and rebirth of all living beings. With his purified divine eye, he saw the condition of all living beings, saying, "Those beings who are characterized by evil bodily actions, evil speech, and evil thought, who hold the wrong view, who find fault with the noble ones (*ariya*), and who perform wrong actions, when they die will be punished in the *apāya* states of woe and be reborn in *niraya* hell. However, those beings characterized by good deeds, good speech, and good thought, who hold right view, who find no fault with the noble ones (*ariya*) and who perform right actions after they die will be reborn in a good destination."

With his purified divine eye (*dibbena cakkhunā*) he observed living beings dying and being reborn in low and high families, in good and bad castes, in good and evil planes of existence in accordance with their accumulated deeds.

In the first watch of the night with a mind fully concentrated . . . [as above], he developed insight knowledge (*vipassanāñāṇa*), that is, the great diamond knowledge capable of perceiving the three characteristics of existence and the successive factors of interdependent co-arising. From dependence on ignorance arise the mental formations [and so on following the standard sequence: consciousness, mind and body, the six sense bases, contact, feeling, craving, clinging, becoming, birth, old age and death, sorrow, lamentation, pain, grief and despair]. Thus arise the aggregates of suffering (*dukkhakkhandhassa*).

Upon the cessation of ignorance, mental formations cease; upon the cessation of mental formations, consciousness ceases; [and so on following the standard sequence: mind and body, six sense bases, contact, feeling, craving, clinging, becoming, birth, old age and death, sorrow, lamentation, pain, grief and despair].

Subsequently, the Blessed One attained the knowledge of the lineage of spiritual perfection (*gotrabhū-ñāṇa*): the knowledge of the path of stream-enterer which eliminates self-identity views, doubt, and indulgence in misguided rites and ceremonies; then the knowledge of the fruition of the path; then the knowledge of contemplative reflection.

With the aforesaid supreme knowledge of the path (*magga-ñāṇa*) and of contemplative reflection, the Blessed One perceived and understood the four noble truths as follows, "This is suffering; arising . . . ; cessation . . . ; path . . ." Once again, the Blessed One, having realized insight knowledge, contemplated the three characteristics of compounded things. Hence, he attained knowledge [of the factors of interdependent co-arising] in succession (*anuloma-ñāṇa*); the knowledge of purity (*vodāna-ñāṇa*); the knowledge of the once-returner which weakens sensual passion and ill will; then the knowledge of the fruit of the once-returner, and the knowledge of contemplative reflection.

With the aforesaid realization of the knowledge of the path and of contemplative reflection he saw and understood the four noble truths: "This is suffering [and so on] . . ." Once again, he realized the knowledge of insight, contemplating the three characteristics of compounded things, [and so on]. . . . He then reached the knowledge of the never-returner, which weakens all sensual passion and ill will, followed by the knowledge of the fruit of the never-returner and of contemplative reflection.

By the realization of the knowledge of the path and of contemplative reflection the Buddha saw and comprehended the four noble truths. Once again, the Blessed One realized the knowledge of insight awareness contemplating the three characteristics of compounded things [and so on]. He came to the knowledge of the path and fruit of arahantship which is the base of omniscience, eliminating all craving for form (*rūparāga*), passion for life in the formless realm, conceit, restlessness, and ignorance [and so on].

By the knowledge of the path and of contemplative reflection, by the pure vision into the compounded nature of things comprising twelve factors [of interdependent co-arising], the Blessed One saw and perceived the four noble truths. Becoming the Buddha, he attained supreme enlightenment (*anuttaraṃ sammāsambodhiṃ*) higher than all the *deva*s, Māra, Brahmā, *samaṇa*s and *brāhmaṇa*s, and all manner of divine and human beings. Then, the knowledge and vision arose (*ñāṇadassanaṃ udapādi*), "My emancipation [from defilements] is absolute; this is my last birth; now there will be no further becoming." Then, sitting on the throne of enlightenment, he breathed forth this joyful utterance (*udānaṃ udānesi*), "I traveled through *saṃsāra* with its many births, seeking but not finding the builder of this house. Painful is continuous rebirth. O house-builder, you are seen! . . . My mind has now attained the unconditioned and arrived at the end of all craving."

### The Second Watch of the Night (*Majjhima Yāma*)

He who sat at the base of the exalted *bodhi* tree defeated Māra and his powerful forces and attained enlightenment. I honor the Buddha, that supramundane being of boundless knowledge. In the second watch of the night with his mind fully concentrated, completely pure, serene, uncorrupted, having transcended moral taint, being modest, vigilant, steadfast, and unswerving, harnessing his mind he recalled his previous lives . . . In the second watch of the night with the mind fully concentrated [as above] he recalled the previous rebirths of all living beings: "O living beings, those whose actions, words, and thoughts are evil, who find fault with the noble ones and hold wrong views, when they die will be punished in states of woe and be reborn in hell. But, O living beings, those whose actions, speech, and thoughts are good, who find no fault with the noble ones and hold right views, when they die will be rewarded by good destinations." With his purified divine eye the Blessed One perceived that all living beings were in the process of dying and being reborn in low and high families, in good and evil castes, in good and evil states of being in accordance with their accumulated deeds.

In the second watch of the night with his mind fully concentrated [as above] the Blessed One reached the knowledge of the cessation of intoxicants and of insight. Having attained the knowledge of insight, he contemplated the three characteristics of all compounded things and saw in direct succession the factors of interdependent co-arising: [Here are repeated the twelve factors of interdependent co-arising and their cessation.] O living beings, all compounded things are impermanent, all compounded things suffer, all compounded things are without self." Then the Blessed One attained the knowledge of the stages of spiritual perfection: of the path of the stream-enterer which eliminates the view of self-identity [and so on as above]; of the fruit of the stream-enterer; and of the knowledge of reflective contemplation.

By the attainment of the knowledge of the path and of contemplative reflection the Blessed One perceived and understood the four noble truths as follows, "This is suffering . . . , the three characteristics of compounded things . . . , the successive factors [of interdependent co-arising] . . . , of purity . . ." Once again the Blessed One having realized the knowledge of insight awareness attained . . . the knowledge of the once-returner . . . and its fruit; . . . the knowledge of the never-returner . . . and its fruit . . . ; the knowledge of the *arahatta* which is the basis of omniscience eliminating all the defilements . . . and its fruit; . . . and the state of contemplative reflection which is omniscience.

With the realization of the knowledge of the path and of contemplative reflection, the Blessed One perceived and comprehended the four noble truths in forward succession as follows . . . [By the realization of the knowledge of the path, of contemplative reflection, and insight-knowledge of the twelve factors of interdependent co-arising and the four noble truths], he became the Buddha, attained supreme enlightenment, higher than all the *deva*s, Māra, Brahmā, *samaṇa*s and *brāhmaṇa*s, and all manner of divine and human beings. Then the vision arose, "My emancipation [from defilements] is absolute. . . . My mind has now attained the unconditioned and reached the end of all craving."

### The Third Watch of the Night (*Pacchima Yāma*)[25]

Seated at the base of the exalted *bodhi* tree the Blessed One defeated Māra and his powerful forces, and attained enlightenment. I honor the Buddha, the supermundane being of boundless knowledge.

The Blessed One spent the third watch of the night investigating the successive factors of interdependent co-arising in forward and backward order. Then the Blessed One, having attained this knowledge, breathed forth this solemn utterance, "When the truth appears to him who is forceful and vigilant, he will conquer the forces of Māra as surely as the sun shines in the sky."

The *brāhmaṇa* who refrains from bad deeds, who is uncomplaining, uncorrupted, and self-controlled, who has reached the end of knowledge, who has completed the religious path, is deserving of the word, Brahmā. Happy are those in the world who are content and at peace, who take joy in hearing the *dhamma,* and who are fully concentrated. Happy in the world are those who are nonviolent and who refrain from taking the life of any living being, for being devoid of greed brings happiness in this world. The elimination of sensual pleasure and the destruction of pride and egoism results in absolute happiness. I have known and overcome all beings; I am well versed in all the *dhamma;* I have discarded all things, extinguished all desires, attained liberation, and by my own effort I have achieved the higher knowledge (*abhiññā*). I have no teacher; no one is superior to me. In all the worlds, including the realm of the gods (*deva-loka*), I am beyond comparison. I have attained arahantship. I am the incomparable teacher of the world, the omniscient one who is calm and peaceful. I will proceed to the city of Kasi, where I will set in motion the wheel of the law (*dhammacakka*). In the world those who are blind need help. I who have conquered all evil will help them overcome the defilements. Therefore, I am called the conqueror of evil.

Then the Blessed One traveled to the Deer Park in Vāraṇasī, where the five ascetics (*pañcavaggiya bhikkhu*) resided. Upon his arrival the Blessed One sat on the seat prepared for him by those monks. After the Blessed One assured the *pañcavaggiya bhikkhu*s that he had attained enlightenment without relying upon a teacher, he preached to them the teaching of the wheel of the law.

[After the end of the section on the third watch of the night the manuscript from the Lai Hin Monastery praises the Buddha, first in what appears to be a *dhāraṇī* followed by a verse (*gāthā*). Because the Pāli is corrupt at this point, reconstruction of the *dhāraṇī* and *gāthā* sections of the text is difficult. The *dhāraṇī* appears to be a combination of the following words and syllables.]

The Buddha—of great achievement, of mystic power, of noble mind, and of noble action, illumines [the worlds]: *ja la ga ga la ka la ka li sīla sangho da da da dam da da da daṇḍo bhiyyo bhiyyo kim ka kum ka ke ka ka la litta līlā ralitta lammava lamma bhamara bhamara . . . suvaṇṇa va vaṇṇa vara vara vara dhara dhara dhara dhara dhara dhīra dhīra dhīra . . . dharaṇi dharaṇi dharaṇi dharaṇo dharaṇo . . . madhura madhura madhura madhuri madhuro madhura . . . amita satta ratanabhūta varasamudda medāvin maṇḍala bāhāracakkavala mahāsamudda . . .*

[The penultimate section of the text is the following Pāli *gāthā:*][26]

Having listened to these praises of that Muni, the great sage,
Being sanctified by his presence,
We reflect on the accomplishments of the lineage of the Buddhas,
The many rebirths of the Great Sage.
Reborn in the world as Vessantara,
He offered an incomparable *dāna.*
Rejoicing seven times,
The earth, the ocean, and Mount Meru quaked.
Departing for Tusita Heaven, that abode of joy and pleasure,
He dwelt in three palaces,
Surpassing the *deva*s in splendor.
Worshiped by Brahmā, Indra, and other deities,
The great elephant-like being, undefiled by old age,
Was praised by the thirty-two [gods]:
"This one is like a Buddha," they declared.
Happy and pure, after abiding in Tusita Heaven for one *kappa,*
He realized that the time had come to preach the Dhamma
And be reborn into the Sakya clan.

Pure, venerated by men and gods;
The Blessed One lived in three palaces,
Enjoying boundless wealth and endless pleasure.
Then the sage came to be known as the Buddha.
May the attainment of his final goal be established in this Buddha image.

Joyous is the birth of the Buddha;
Joyous is the proclamation of the Dhamma;
Joyous is the amity of the Saṅgha;
Joyous is their practice.
Trees begin to flower and fruits continuously appear on them;
Even barren trees bear fruit.
Innumerable drums beat endlessly as
The thirty-two gods of Tāvatiṃsa Heaven exclaim, "Sadhu,
The Buddhas are not inferior to Hari and the other gods."
May the noble Buddhas protect us from rebirth for a *kappa*.
I worship him, beloved by men and gods.
Beloved is he, the Buddha-Sun of great power.
The *saṅgha,* like a vast cluster of stars, are our great ones.
May their power protect us.
Gods and kings together take delight in this community.

[The final section of the SBN proclaiming the Buddha's victory over Māra is written and recited in the northern Thai dialect (Tai Yüan). In the following scene, the *devatā* or heavenly forces flee and the forces of nature—mother earth and wild animals—come to the Buddha's aid.]

The superior teacher who ascended and sat on the precious throne is thus called "*Satthā.*" Oh . . . Oh . . . this throne looks very beautiful and is of surpassing excellence; it arose to receive the Lord who is well known throughout the human world even up to the realm of Māra over yonder. Māra's army descended from the celestial plane called Paranimmitavasavattī, coming in continuous waves and creating fearsome sounds like a thunderstorm as though the Khong [Ganges] River was falling as rain from the sky. It seemed as if the whole world might be destroyed. The noise continued to reverberate. Human beings recalled that the rain poured down as Lord Māra's army descended from Paranimmita Heaven. Hundreds of thousands of Māra's soldiers marched in a single, long, continuous line. Just as they advanced to destroy the precious throne of the Enlightened One, in the middle of the deep jungle near a monastery a congregation of *deva*s waited with spears in hand and other weapons ready to engage Lord Māra's troops. But Māra's soldiers were so numerous that the *deva*s were afraid and fled to Lord Sakka's [Indra] palace.

At that moment only the Lord Buddha sat alone in deep meditation as though he had nothing to fear. The Blessed One, recollecting his perfections (*pāramī*), called to the *deva*s, "O *devatā,* O *devatā,* where have you all gone? Shall I descend from my precious throne?" Just then a bird flew by and cried out, "Be patient a little longer; you will attain happiness." After that a second flock of birds flew by and cried, "Continue to be patient; surely you will soon defeat Māra's army." Eventually, as the Buddha recalled his perfections, a celestial *devī* called Nang Thoranī (Dharaṇī), a powerful supernatural being, arose from underneath the precious throne near the Buddha's feet. With water wrung from her hair, she created a great river that flooded the monastery compound. In the middle of the river several kinds of creatures could be seen—crabs, fish, snakes, otters, turtles, sting rays, and giant crabs, all jumping and running about. Crabs, shellfish, whirligigs, and dragonflies attacked Māra's army so they could not escape the floodwaters. Māra's hordes threw away their helmets and abandoned all their weapons including bows and arrows, spears, and their elephants and horses right in the middle of the great river. All of them, commoners and nobility, the queen and the king, and the ministers cried out, fearing for their lives. With horrified faces Māra's army fled in disarray to the forests and mountains, dispirited for losing their precious throne to the only one capable of defeating Māra's forces.

When they had recovered, they all paid respects to the Blessed One. The Buddha, the greatest in the three worlds, shone resplendent in the Jetavana Forest. Gotama, supreme and beyond comparison, having defeated Māra's hordes, sat serene and victorious on the diamond throne.

# PART III

# 7

# THE BODY OF THE BUDDHA: POPULAR BUDDHISM AND BUDDHOLOGICAL THEORY

> Probably all would agree that understanding the way in which the person of the Buddha was understood is central to any attempt to characterize the Indian groups that came to coalesce around that person. In fact, understanding how that person was understood or perceived has . . . often times determined how a great many other matters [e.g., the Buddha image] were understood.[1]

BUDDHA IMAGE CONSECRATION RITUALS in northern Thailand begin with the lighting of two tall candles. The chief officiating monk lights the victory candle and the ceremony's principal patron the Vipassī candle. The victory candle represents the power of the Buddha's supreme enlightenment to overcome and dispel suffering, calamity, and danger. The Vipassī candle connects the particular image(s) being consecrated with the eonic Buddhas or *tathāgata*s, including the Buddha Gotama.[2] The first symbolizes the Buddha's victory over Māra; the second stands for the Buddha Vipassī, the nineteenth of twenty-four Buddhas in the *Buddhavaṃsa* (Bv) and the first of the six Buddhas preceding Sakyamuni Gotama in the *Mahāpadāna Sutta.* Vipassī may have been chosen as the representative eonic Buddha celebrated in the *buddhābhiseka* because his name is linked specifically with seeing. Furthermore, of the previous Buddhas, his is the only life story told in detail in the *Mahāpadāna Sutta.* The commentaries explain that he was given the name for three reasons: his sight was as keen by night as by day; his eyes were large; and he could perceive clearly after investigation.[3] Furthermore, because he embodied all the conditions of Buddhahood (*dhammatā*), Vipassī becomes its universal prototype. His life pattern mirrors that of Siddhattha Gotama.[4] Consequently, Vipassī's story mediates between Buddhahood as timeless-universal and historical-particular, a major Buddhological theme underlying the image consecration ritual.

This chapter examines three interrelated aspects of the *buddhābhiseka* ritual denoted by the lighting of the victory and Vipassī candles: the Buddha as omnipresent through time and particularized in history; the relationship between the Buddha and the *dhamma,* the form body (*rūpakāya*) and the *dhamma* body; and the Buddha image as an embodiment and mediator of power. Included is a translation and analysis of two northern Thai texts related to these themes: *Tamnān Kā Phū'ak* (The Chronicle of the White Crow) and *Tamnān Phra Silā* (The Chronicle of the Stone Buddha Image). The former incorporates folk traditions into a cult of the five Buddhas of the present age. The Stone Buddha, the cult image of Wat Chiang Man in Chiang Mai, is featured at the temple's annual Thai New Year festival (*songkrān*).

## Buddhas: Past, Present, and Future

> We find in this tract [the *Mahāpadāna Sutta* that recounts the story of seven Buddhas] the root of that Bīraña-weed which, growing up along with the rest of Buddhism, went on spreading so luxuriantly that it gradually covered up much that was of value in the earlier teaching, and finally led to the downfall, in its home in India, of the ancient faith. The doctrine of the Bodhisatta . . . drove out the doctrine of the Aryan Path. A gorgeous hierarchy of mythological wonder-workers filled men's minds, and the older system of self-training and self-control became forgotten.
> (T. W. Rhys Davids, Introduction to the *Mahāpadāna Sutta*).[5]

Even though Theravāda Buddhology gives preeminence to the historical Buddha in both text and practice, Theravāda reveals a surprising diversity comparable to Mahāyāna and Vajrayāna—much to the consternation of T. W. Rhys Davids and scholars of an earlier generation.[6] Whereas Vajrayāna developed a *maṇḍala* of five *dhyāni* Buddhas associated with the cosmological focal points of the center and cardinal directions, Theravāda delineated eonic Buddhological schemes that adumbrated five Buddhas of the present age with the twenty-five or twenty-eight Buddhas, including Gotama, who appear in the past, the present, and in the future as Metteyya. Similarly, although devotional rituals in Theravāda traditions are regarded as attending exclusively to the Buddha Gotama in contrast to the Mahāyāna and Vajrayāna worship of Amitābha, Vairocana, and others, the veneration of Buddhas and *arahant*s, especially Metteyya, the Buddha of the age to come, is present in all Southeast Asian Theravāda traditions.[7] The prominence of eonic Buddhas in Pagan[8] represents an extension of a tradition supported by archaeological evidence from Bhārhut, Sāñcī, Amarāvatī, and Nāgārjunakoṇḍa, as well as later diary reports by the Chinese pilgrims, Faxian (Fa-hsien) and Xuanzang

(Hsüan-tsang). Moreover, recent studies have called attention to a Khmer cult of the five Buddhas of this eon.[9]

Even though the twenty-four Buddhas prior to the Buddha Gotama portrayed in the Bv emerged relatively late in the Theravāda tradition, and may have been influenced by the earlier Jain doctrine of twenty-four *tirthaṃkaras* (ford-makers), the concept of previous Buddhas is present in the early strata of the Pāli canon.[10] Eight Buddhas, including Gotama and Metteyya, are mentioned in the *Dīgha Nikāya*. The Great Discourse on the Lineage of the Buddhas (*Mahāpadāna*) begins with Vipassī, followed by Sikhī, Vessabhū, Kakusandha, Koṇāgamana, Kassapa, and finally, Gotama. The *Nidānakathā* (Ja-nidāna), a fifth-century C.E. non-canonical text written as an introduction to the Pāli *jātaka* commentary, recounts the Bv's lineage of twenty-four Buddhas prior to the appearance of Siddhattha Gotama. The first or distant epoch that extends from the Buddha Dīpaṅkara to Vessantara is followed by an intermediate epoch which follows the future Gotama Buddha's departure from Tusita Heaven to his enlightenment. The final section of the narrative, the proximate epoch, starts with events of the Buddha's enlightenment and concludes with Anāthapiṇḍika's donation of the Jetavana Vihāra to the *saṅgha,* which are duplicated in form during the lifetimes of the six Buddhas preceding Gotama beginning with Vipassī.

The most complete account of Vipassī, the Buddha who is honored at the beginning of the northern Thai *buddhābhiseka,* appears in the *Mahāpadāna Sutta* as a story told by the Buddha Gotama to his disciples. The *sutta* begins with a brief, stereotypical description of each of the seven eonic Buddhas that includes their clan, life span, enlightenment tree, two major disciples, assemblies of monks, names of their parents, and capital city. In the second section of the text the narrator describes the life of Vipassī that mirrors in considerable detail the life of Gotama: the *bodhisatta*'s descent from Tusita Heaven; the miraculous birth; the thirty-two marks of the great person; the four sights that prompt the future Buddha's renunciation; the quest for enlightenment that incorporates an explanation of interdependent co-arising; teaching the *dhamma;* founding the *saṅgha* and commissioning them to go forth out of compassion for the world. Unlike Gotama, Vipassī delivers his first teaching not to five ascetics but to King Bandhumā's son and chaplain in a graduated discourse that begins with generosity, morality, the rewards of heaven, the corruption of sense desires, the profit of renuniciation, and the four noble truths.[11] Subsequently, Vipassī preaches the same message to a crowd of 84,000, who then receive ordination. After six years the monks who were commissioned to itinerate for the welfare of both *devas* and humans return to the royal capital of Bandhumatī to recite the *vinaya.* On that occasion, Vipassī teaches the synopsis of Theravāda *dhamma:* "Do no evil; cultivate the good; purify the mind; this the Buddhas teach."

The *Mahāpadāna Sutta*'s depiction of the life of the Buddha Vipassī authenticates Gotama Buddha "as having a distinguished lineage of Great Beings whose life story and saving message were virtually identical to his own."[12] Gotama and his predecessors follow a universal, paradigmatic pattern. The truth of Gotama Buddha's enlightenment is validated, not by a divine figure or an institutional authority, but by its repetition of the universal pattern.[13] By paralleling the story of the Buddha Vipassī, Gotama's life story represents an ontological, universal truth or, in the terms of the text, the basic principles of reality (*dhammadhātu*).[14] The Vipassī story serves as a paradigm because it adheres to "rules" of nature, namely, the way things really are (*dhammatā*).[15]

The Ja-nidāna and the Bv bring together what Frank Reynolds refers to as the *jātaka* and Buddha lineages and rebirth traditions in Theravāda Buddhology.[16] The former relates stories from the past in which the future Buddha Gotama is the usual protagonist. Because the Buddha narrates his own rebirth lineage, the stories presuppose the Theravāda epistemological claim that at his enlightenment the *tathāgata* attained the knowledge of his previous lives. The extensive Pāli *jātaka* tradition includes stories from the *Suttapiṭaka;* the *jātaka* commentary; the *Cariyāpiṭaka* (Cp) (Basket of Conduct), thirty-five verse stories illustrating seven moral and spiritual perfections (*pāramī*);[17] and extracanonical collections.[18] The tradition focuses on the development through countless previous lives of the perfections necessary for Buddhahood. Among the more than 200 canonical *jātaka*s the last ten of the *jātaka* commentary illustrate the normative list of *bodhisatta* virtues.

Prince Vessantara is the final and most celebrated of the future Buddha's *jātaka* rebirths prior to his appearance as the Buddha Gotama. In the Ja-nidāna, Vessantara represents the perfection of selfless generosity (*dāna*) and, as the penultimate appearance of the *bodhisatta,* is the summation of the moral and spiritual qualities required for Buddhahood. As Vessantara personifies *dāna,* so Sumedha in the Bv lauds generosity as the first great perfection on the path to Buddhahood.[19] Taken together, the story of Sumedha at the beginning of the Bv narrative of the twenty-four eonic Buddhas and the story of Vessantara that concludes the Ja-nidāna connect the Buddha and *bodhisatta* lineages that frame Theravāda Buddhology. Through their distinctive lineages, both Sumedha and Vessantara prefigure the Buddha Gotama.

The *bodhisatta* perfections illustrated by the final ten narratives in the *jātaka* commentary differ in sequence from the Bv, the Cp, and the Ja-nidāna. The list begins with the story of Temiya, who represents renunciation, and concludes with Vessantara, who exemplifies selfless generosity.

The order of the *jātaka* stories denotes that such supreme generosity is attained only at the end of a long process of moral and spiritual achievement culminating in Buddhahood.

The most fully elaborated Buddha lineage in the Pāli canon appears in the Bv, a late addition dating from the third or second century B.C.E.[20] Although the bulk of the Bv consists of verse stories of the previous Buddhas, each narrated by Gotama in a prior rebirth after the manner of the *jātaka,* the chronicle begins with Sumedha, a Brahman ascetic, who is destined to become Gotama Buddha. Dīpaṅkara's prediction that Sumedha's vow to become a Buddha will be realized creates the story's most dramatic moment.

At the beginning of the narrative we find Sumedha engaged in meditation at Dhammaka Mountain after leaving the city of Amarāvatī to "seek the peace that is unaging, undying, secure."[21] Meanwhile, the people of a neighboring area invite Dīpaṅkara and 400,000 steadfast followers to visit them. Sumedha, knowing that the citizenry are repairing the road that Dīpaṅkara and his retinue will travel, offers his assistance. Before he can finish the section of the road he has been assigned, Dīpaṅkara arrives. Sumedha quickly lies down in the mire, creating a human bridge so that the *tathāgata* can pass by without being soiled, even at the sacrifice of his own life. Prostrate at Dīpaṅkara's feet, Sumedha makes his vow of Buddhahood. Dīpaṅkara recognizes Sumedha's spiritual potential and predicts: "Do you see this very severe ascetic, a matted hair ascetic? Innumerable eons from now he will be a Buddha in the world."[22] Dīpaṅkara foretells many of the major turning points in the future Buddha's life: his renunciation and departure from Kapilavattu; the practice of austerities; Sujātā's offering of milk rice at the Ajapāla Tree and his journey to the Nerañjarā River; attaining enlightenment at the foot of an Assattha Tree; the names of his father and mother, chief attendants, and disciples. A similar pattern appears in each of the subsequent chapters.

Each account of the twenty-four Buddhas preceding Gotama includes common elements from the legend found in the story of the Buddha Gotama. However, details differ, such as the height of the *tathāgata*s, their life span, their years as householders, the time spent in ascetical practices, the kind of tree under which they achieved enlightenment, the names of their chief attendants and disciples. Even though Buddhahood is acknowledged as an individual achievement requiring eons of preparation, the stories replicate a pattern authenticated by a previous Buddha as, for example, Sumedha's determined intention and Dīpaṅkara's confirming prediction (*vyākaraṇa*).

Buddhologically, the Bv narrative of Sumedha's aspiration to Buddhahood and Dīpaṅkara's prediction of his success reflect the Theravāda understanding of the eonic Buddhas as the same and yet unique. In each of the stories the future Buddha aspires to Buddhahood in the form of a particular aspirant—such as the Brahman Sumedha, the noble Vijitāvin, the Brahman Suruci, or the *nāga* king Atula. The Buddha of that age under whom the vow is made then predicts in the same eleven verses that the aspirant will become a Buddha. By this repetitive device, the Bv reinforces the authority of the Buddha Gotama, but the repetition also reflects the seeming paradox underlying Theravāda Buddhology, namely, that even though the eonic Buddhas are individually distinctive, yet they are the same. While each aspirant is a different character in the narrative, all the eonic Buddhas use the same formula to predict the aspirant's future Buddhahood. Buddhahood requires identical qualities and characteristics, even though each eonic Buddha has a different name, a different life span, and so forth. In the formulation of the *Kathāvatthu* (XXI.5), Buddhas do not differ with regard to any quality that defines their Buddhahood but only in terms of accidental characteristics such as body, age, and radiance.

This same pattern of difference and identity, universal and particular, is found in the northern Thai *buddhābhiseka*. In the act of consecration the image becomes the Buddha Gotama and, as symbolized by the Vipassī candle, stands in the lineage of the *tathāgata*s. The mechanism of repetition that creates the lineage of the Buddhas in the Bv occurs in the *buddhābhiseka* with the reenactment of the Buddha story, which serves to extend the lineage, not in the mythic time of the Bv, but in the present existential time of those who venerate the Buddha in the form of his image. The image makes concretely real the confidence expressed in the Bv that if we "fail of the dispensation of this protector of the world" then another will appear who will teach the *dhamma* for the welfare of all sentient beings. As seen in the KBV story of the first Buddha image and in this ritual, the image functions in this capacity.

The twenty-four Buddhas also appear in the Theravāda cultic tradition, especially in *paritta* (protection) recitations. In Sri Lanka the twenty-four *vivaraṇa*s (permissions, unveilings) are a popular subject for temple murals; and the twenty-four Buddhas are honored in the Suvisi Vivaraṇa Pūjā Näṭum, a ritual dance performed on special Buddhist sabbath days in the Kandyan region of the island.[23] The dance usually lasts an entire night, although on major merit-making occasions it may extend from three to seven successive nights. The standard venue is the terrace around the *bodhi* tree in a temple compound surrounded by framed pictures of the twenty-four Buddhas arranged in chronological order. In each picture the future Buddha Gotama kneels before one of the twenty-four Buddhas in the posture of receiving the *vivaraṇa*. While the performers dance to Kandyan drums, they sing songs narrating the stories of each Buddha depicted. At the end of each dance segment, the chief dancer approaches the appropriate picture and makes offerings of flowers and incense to invoke the blessing of the Buddhas on the assembled congregation.

The scene of the future Buddha Gotama kneeling before the eonic Buddhas asking them to unveil (*vivaraṇa*) the promise of Buddhahood is akin to the aspirant who seeks ordination from the Buddha, an *arahant,* or a senior monk. The act of admission into the monastic order, so central to the path toward the realization of *nibbāna,* achieves its extraordinary importance within the life of the Theravāda community by reenacting this primordial scene. In the *buddhābhiseka* ritual, devotees approach the Buddha image with the same general wish; as the statue is transformed into the Buddha, they too, hope to receive a similar blessing, not of Buddhahood but of health, welfare, and eventually *nibbāna.* Here we find a parallel between the vow or earnest wish to become a Buddha (*paṇidhāna*) and a more generalized sense of wish (*patthāna*) that pervades Theravāda merit-making rituals which are directed toward achieving a material end, a better rebirth, and *nibbāna.*[24]

In mainland Southeast Asia the cult of the five Buddhas of the present age (*bhaddakappa*) beginning with Kakusandha and ending with Metteyya is more prominent than the veneration of the twenty-four Buddhas. The cult appears in Myanmar, Thailand, Cambodia, and Laos, and undoubtedly reflects a well-established early Indian tradition as confirmed by sculptural and inscriptional evidence from the Indian sites of Amarāvatī, Nāgārjunakoṇḍa, and Ajaṇṭā.[25] An Asokan inscription states that the king doubled the size of a *stūpa* associated with the Buddha Kassapa, Gotama's immediate predecessor.[26] In Pagan, the base of a small *stūpa* dating from the sixth to seventh centuries is embellished with four figures identified by Pyu and Pāli inscriptions as Koṇāgamana, Kakusandha, Kassapa, and Gotama.[27] Moreover, scholars assume that in the twelfth-century Ānanda temple the configuration of four colossal standing Buddhas at the center of the cruciform temple facing outward at the cardinal directions represents the Buddhas of the present age, and that in five-sided temples the fifth Buddha, Metteyya, is also included.[28]

In Thailand, Cambodia, and Laos, the cult of the five Buddhas has continued into the modern period. The five Buddhas appear in temple murals, as miniature figures, and in symbolic representations. For example, in Cambodia five candles and incense sticks are used to honor the five Buddhas as are five kinds of offerings. The four cardinal directions and center are also said to symbolize the five Buddhas.[29] Adhémard Leclère observed that in the Cambodian Buddha image consecration ritual the five Buddhas were represented by five wooden lotus buds arranged in a fan shape and placed between the previously consecrated temple image and the one being consecrated.[30] I was informed that the lighting of five candles during the northern Thai Buddha image consecration ritual honors the Triple Gem, teachers, and parents. At an earlier time, however, the five candles could have symbolized the five Buddhas of the present age, a meaning now lost to local memory.

Formerly the cult of the five Buddhas was widely known in Thailand and found expression in art, ritual, legend, and literature. Many texts began with the salutation, "Homage to the Buddha! To the Five Buddhas I pay homage!"[31] Even today booklets on the five Buddhas continue to be published in Thai.[32] A *jātaka* story of the five Buddhas of the present age is included in the appendix to the northern Thai collection of *jātaka*s known as the Fifty Jātakas (*Paññāsa Jātaka*), composed in Pāli sometime between the fifteenth and sixteenth centuries.[33] A northern Thai version of the story, *Tamnān Kā Phū'ak* (TKP) (The Chronicle of the White Crow), is found in monastery palm leaf manuscript collections and continues to be produced as a sermon printed on heavy paper folded accordian style.[34] In northern Thailand the story was preached at the end of the monastic rains retreat in October before the festival of the floating boats (Thai, *loi krathong*).[35] In the Tai region of China's Yunnan Province it is preached at the beginning of the rains retreat, a traditional time for young men to enter the *saṅgha* in honor of their mothers, a key element in the story and an important social value of ordination.[36]

The theory of previous Buddhas developed in the Theravāda tradition to authenticate the Buddha and his message, mirrors the Buddhist cosmology, universalizes the life pattern of a Buddha-to-be, and commends the power of an aspiration or vow (*paṇidhāna*).[37] However, the cosmological aspect of multiple Buddhas requires further consideration.

While there are eons without a Buddha, in the Bv's worldview the way of the Buddhas and the *dhamma* have always existed: "Since the Buddha (Gotama) and Dhamma are identifiable it follows that a Buddha must be timeless, transcending the eons both as to the past and the future."[38] In later Pāli texts this view led to a proliferation of Buddhas.[39] The *Jinakālamālīpakaraṇaṃ* (Jinak) (The Sheaf of Garlands of the Epochs of the Conqueror), an early-sixteenth-century Pāli chronicle composed by the Venerable Ratanapañña in Chiang Mai, begins with an account of several Buddhas prior to Dīpaṅkara. It opens with a story of aspiration parallel to that of Sumedha's in the Bv. The future Buddha Gotama, who is living in the kingdom of Gandhāra and supporting his poor mother by selling firewood, embarks on a sea journey intent upon improving their circumstances. On the seventh day of the journey the ship is wrecked but the young man heroically saves his mother at the risk of his own life. Mahābrahmā beholds the scene, "This, indeed, is a great being of firm endeavor and altruistic intentions," and arouses in the young man a noble aspiration: "I will become enlightened and enlighten others; I will become released and release others; I will cross over and take others."[40]

After recounting several additional lives, the Jinak then enumerates sixteen incalculable ages with hundreds of thousands of Buddhas prior to the appearance of Dīpaṅkara and his three immediate predecessors mentioned in the Bv. The Jinak's account is indebted to the *Saddharmālaṃkāraya,* an early-fifteenth-century Pāli prose text written in Sri Lanka. The author, Dharmakīrti, begins with stories of the future Buddha's mental aspiration to attain Buddhahood prior to his birth as Sumedha and mentions hundreds of thousands of Buddhas prior to Dīpaṅkara.[41] The Buddhas of the Bv, Jinak, *Mahāpadāna,* and *Saddharmālaṃkāraya* are eonic Buddhas who embody a timeless Buddha lineage.

On one level the mythological complexity that came to define the doctrine of former Buddhas in the Theravāda tradition seems to make the specific Buddhas cited in the Bv and *Mahāpadāna* redundant, a logical extension of the repetitive similitude of their stories. From another perspective, however, the "world now teeming with *bodhisatta*s"[42] may have encouraged the development of a cult of Buddha images that blended Buddha devotionalism with astrological and calendric time. In any case, the proliferation of Buddhas of past, present, and future can be interpreted from several perspectives. Philosophically it can be regarded as the Buddhological expression of the Theravāda modal view of time that considers past, present, and future not as completed realities but as modes on a continuum.[43] By universalizing the Buddha Gotama's story through the lives of previous Buddhas, in particular, Vipassī, Theravāda devotional veneration of Gotama is linked to the Buddhas of all ages. The mythic proliferation of Buddhas can be seen as conceptually consistent with the emergence of sets of Buddha images in many different postures (*mudra*s) found in northern Thai ritual practice.[44] Whereas the stories of previous Buddhas mirror that of Gotama Buddha, the variety of Buddha images offers a visual narrative of episodes from the Buddha's life. For example, one set represents the Buddha's seven stations during the seven weeks following his enlightenment. Other sets are associated with astrological and calendric time: Buddhas of the nine planets (the seven visible planets plus Rāhu and Keta) are correlated with the seven days of the week, the twelve months of the year, and the twelve years of the astrological cycle.[45]

The origin of these sets is obscure, although the iconography of the seven stations is well known in north India, Myanmar, and northern Thailand. In the mid-nineteenth century Rama III (r. 1824–51) commissioned the head of the Thai *saṅgha,* Paramānuchit-chinōrot, to codify forty postures from the life of Gotama Buddha, a number consistent with the sum total of the Buddhas of nine planets, seven days, twelve months, and the twelve-year cycle. In northern Thailand the two most prominent sets are the images of the Buddha's seven stations following his enlightenment, first enshrined at Chiang Mai's Wat Chet Yot (Temple of the

Seven Spires) modeled on Bodhgayā, and the Buddha images of the days of the week correlated with the nine planets.[46] The latter have become increasingly popular in contemporary northern Thai practice. Pilgrimage monasteries, in particular, have a set of the Buddhas of the days of the week or "birthday" Buddhas (*phraprajamwankoet*) that devotees patronize.[47] It is the custom to deposit a money offering in a replica of a monk's alms bowl in front of the image of one's birthday, light candles, and repeat a *gāthā*. From this act the devotee derives the following benefit:

> Do this *pūjā* for your well-being, for success in business, and for physical beauty. If illness befalls you, make a banana leaf container (*krathong*). Put forty-nine balls of sticky rice in it and place a small umbrella in the middle. Then offer the *krathong* to the main image in the temple, light the candle of your birthday Buddha, free an animal, and give offerings to the monks. This will lead to a good result. Repeat the following *gāthā: Da Ka Da Tha Ra Ka To Āraham̩ Da Ka Vā Nirodho Sabbadā To Vinassantu.*[48]

The sets of Buddha images that represent the life of the Buddha Gotama do more than expand the iconographic representation of the story. Like the narratives of the Buddhas of the past, present, and future, they replicate the Buddha paradigm throughout time. The immense production of Buddha amulets and votive tablets in Thailand can be viewed similarly, as literally filling space and time with the presence of the Buddha.[49] Buddha images synthesize paradigmatic, narrative, and iconographic levels of truth and in so doing mediate the universal and the particular to the lives of individuals for whom the Buddha is not just a distant ideal but a present refuge, protector, and grantor of boons.

## Buddha-body and Dhamma-body

> The very same path by which Vipassī went,
>
> By that very path Sikhī, Vessabhū,
>
> Kakusandha, Koṇāgamana, and Kassapa [went].
>
> By that straight path went Gotama.
>
> Free from craving, devoid of grasping,
>
> The seven Buddhas plunged into ending.
>
> By them, who had become *dhamma*,
>
> Such, this *dhamma* was taught.
>
> (*Theragāthā* 490–91)[50]

> The *dharmakāya* which had been understood as meaning one who experienced or was in possession of the *dharma* or truth came to mean one in whom the truth itself was embodied or one whose body was the *dharma* itself.[51]

The *buddhābhiseka* not only enhances our understanding of the Theravāda conception of multiple Buddhas, but also the two-body theory (*rūpakāya/dhammakāya*) that has been central to Buddhological speculation throughout the history of Buddhist thought. Lighting the Vipassī candle that initiates the *buddhābhiseka* ritual represents multiple Buddhas and sets in motion the timeless truth of the *dhamma,* the eternal law of interdependent co-arising taught by Vipassī ninety-one *kappa* ago.[52] Vipassī prefigures this truth realized by the Buddha Gotama at his enlightenment, the same truth that will be ritually implanted in the Buddha image. The *Dhammacakkappavattana Sutta* brings the ceremony to its dramatic conclusion as the first rays of sunlight illumine the image through the temple's eastern doorway. Having mimetically reenacted the Buddha's enlightenment, the image (*buddharūpa*) now embodies the *dhamma* distilled in the formula of cause and effect and the Buddha's first teaching (the four noble truths and the eightfold noble path) intoned by the monk-ritualists at the conclusion of the ceremony.

The *buddhābhiseka* ritual reaffirms the traditional Theravāda view of the historical Buddha revered as the teacher of the truth (*dhamma*) he perceived on the night of his enlightenment. Even though the ceremony celebrates the historical Buddha, it challenges the view that Theravādins perceive the *dhammakāya* and statements that identify the Buddha and the *dhamma* as only symbolic or metaphorical.[53] The Buddha image embodies the *dhamma* in a manner customarily associated with more esoteric forms of Buddhism that employ the ritual techniques of *yantra* and *mantra.*[54] The fabrication of a Buddha image traditionally ends with a mantric strategy for infusing the form of the image (*rūpa*) with the *dhammakāya.* The *Tamrā Kān Kosāng Phraphuttharūp* (The Manual for Making a Buddha Image) concludes the *dhammakāya* section by stating: "Altogether these [twenty-six] characteristics of the Buddha are called the *dhammakāya.* If one constructs a Buddha image and recites this text, it will be the same as *though the Buddha himself was present.*"[55] Regarding the image as the *dhamma* does not mean that the material form which impacts on the sense of sight to create a visual image is itself the Buddha, but rather that to be the Buddha the image must be the *dhammakāya:* "It serves no purpose to see the Buddha in his material body (*rūpakāya*), in his corruptible body (*pūtikāya*); he should be seen in his *dharmakāya.*"[56] As the consecration ritual makes so abundantly clear, the Buddha image in its concrete particularity mediates simultaneously the timeless lineage of the *tathāgatas* to any given moment in time and the *dhamma* as absolute truth (*dhammatā/lokuttara*) to the lived reality of mundane (*lokiya*) existence.

Over twenty years ago, Frank E. Reynolds observed that scholarly interest in the subject of conceptions of the bodies of the Buddha focused primarily on interpreting the emergence and meaning of the doctrine of the three bodies of the Buddha in Mahāyāna, while virtually ignoring the Theravāda traditions of Sri Lanka and Southeast Asia.[57] As a counterbalance, Reynolds analyzes the concept of multiple Buddha bodies in terms of the polarity between *rūpakāya* and *dhammakāya* that he regards as the two basic Buddhological realities on which Theravāda has historically been grounded.[58] Furthermore, following the work of Maryla Falk, George Coedès, Louis Finot, and F. L. Woodward, Reynolds points to another Buddhological perspective on the fringes of mainstream Theravāda—possibly reflecting Sarvāstivāda influence—that merges the multiple bodies of the Buddha into a single *dhammakāya*.[59] With probable pre-Buddhist, yogic roots, this subtradition emerged as a community of interpretation and practice in northern Thailand, Laos, and Cambodia after the middle of the second millennium. Referred to as Yogāvacara, it apparently was taken to Sri Lanka by Thai monks in the eighteenth century coincident to the time of Saraṇaṃkara's reforms of the Siṅhalese *saṅgha*.[60] Although this subtradition has much in common with Brahmanic, Upaniṣadic, and Indian yogic teachings and anticipates later Mahāyāna conceptions of the body of the Buddha, it retains a normative Theravāda flavor that emphasizes Buddhahood as a product of a series of attainments rather than conceiving of the Buddha body in ontological terms.[61]

If we examine the Theravāda concept of Buddha bodies vis-à-vis the *buddhābhiseka* ritual, we find that the Buddha's *rūpakāya* and *dhammakāya* are ineluctably merged into one reality. It is not my purpose to contend that the ritually created body of the Buddha is a proto-Mahāyāna notion or to debate the possibility that the ritual's Buddhology reflects Yogāvacara or Sarvāstivāda tendencies. My claim, rather, is that through the ritual process of giving the *dhamma* a body we gain a clearer picture of the meaning Southeast Asian Theravādins ascribe to the Buddha image and, by extension, to the Buddha himself.

Generally it is thought that the earliest theory of the bodies of the Buddha was twofold—the Buddha's physical form (*rūpakāya*) and his body of teachings (*dhammakāya*).[62] Furthermore, this distinction has been correlated with the controversy between those for whom the Buddha's legacy was his teaching (*dhamma*) and those who venerated the Buddha's physical presence—his person during his lifetime and after his *parinibbāna* his relics and other material representations. Some scholars identify the first with the tradition's early monastic orientation and the second with lay devotional piety that emerged with the growth of Buddhism during the Maurya period.[63] Others regard the polarity between the two bodies not as a two-tier historical model divided between monastic and lay sensibilities but as a long-standing debate that pertains throughout the history of the tradition.[64] Controversy over the nature of the Buddha certainly existed before his death[65] but his absence that resulted from his *parinibbāna* became a matter of debate and intense Buddhological speculation. In the KBV, which can be read as a foreshadowing of the Buddha's *parinibbāna,* the Buddha's temporary absence prompts King Ajātasattu to build the first Buddha image. In the *Mahāparinibbāna Sutta* the Buddha's death elicits two responses that formed the crux of the disagreement over how the Buddha was to be remembered and venerated after his death, that is, his permanent physical absence. In the *Mahāparinibbāna Sutta* the Buddha authorizes both the *rūpakāya* legacy that identifies the Buddha with his bodily person and the *dhammakāya* legacy that identifies him with his dhammic realization and teaching. On the one hand, the Buddha instructs his disciples to venerate his bodily remains in the manner of a *cakkavattin* by enshrining his in *stūpa*s erected at crossroads (D II.142). And, on the other, he instructs Ānanda that true homage of the *tathāgata* comes from practicing the *dhamma* (D I.138), suggesting that after his death "the teacher" will be the *dhamma* and the *vinaya* (D II.154). According to legend, the first legacy led to the construction of eight *stūpa*s in eight Indian kingdoms of the day (D II.167), subsequently the relics contained therein were redistributed by King Asoka to 84,000 locations throughout Jambudīpa.[66] The second legacy refers to the Council of Rājagaha held after the Blessed One's *parinibbāna,* where the *saṅgha* recites the *dhamma* and the *vinaya.*[67]

The socio-historical logic that identifies these two legacies with the lay and monastic communities respectively has been challenged.[68] Although the historical sociology of the *rūpakāya* and *dhammakāya* polarity is contested, both Pāli and Sanskrit sources offer evidence of an ongoing debate between rūpalogical and dhammalogical contenders with wider implications for Buddhist practice beyond its Buddhological significance.[69] From the Pāli sources evidence appearing to identify the Buddha and the *dhamma* has been interpreted as advancing a position in opposition to those who venerate signs of the Buddha, especially his relics: *Saṃyutta* III.120, "Whoever sees me sees the *dhamma;* whoever sees the *dhamma* sees me"; *Milindapañho* III.5.3, "Whoever sees the *dhamma,* he sees the Blessed One, for the *dhamma* was preached by the Blessed One; by the *dhammakāya* the Blessed One can be pointed out for the *dhamma* was preached by him." Early Mahāyāna sources reveal a simliar point of view: "The *tathāgata* cannot be seen from his form-body."[70] *Avadāna* texts offer a different perspective, in which the two *kāyas* are complementary, "a total experience of the Buddha appears to involve a double vision focusing in some way on the Blessed One's *rūpakāya,* on the one hand, and his *dharmakāya* on the other."[71]

As the Theravāda tradition evolved, the concepts of *rūpakāya* and *dhammakāya* came to incorporate different meanings. The most immediate references are to the physical body of the Buddha that manifests the thirty-two major and eighty minor marks of the great being, and to the Buddha's teachings. The Buddha's body was not seen as a corruptible, material object but as a body formed as a consequence of many lifetimes of moral and spiritual perfection that was manifested in physical traits such as a golden radiance.[72] The Buddha also attained a meditation or jhānic body, described metaphorically as a reed drawn from its sheath, a snake from its skin, or a sword from its scabbard.[73] This mind-made body resonates with the exact likenesses of himself (*nimmita-buddha*s) that the *tathāgata* created during his three-month absence while he was preaching the *Abhidhamma* to his mother in Tusita Heaven,[74] an event echoed in the story of the construction of the Udayana sandalwood image. Beyond interpreting the Buddha's *dhamma* body as his teaching, it came to be identified with the eight stages of path attainment—stream-enterer, once-returner, never-returner, *arahant,* and their fruits. In the Vism, Buddhaghosa understands the *dhammakāya* to be the five components of the Buddha's path and realization: moral virtue, concentration, wisdom, liberation, and the knowledge of liberation (*vimuttiñāṇadassana*). Other references link the Buddha to the *dhamma* not only in the sense of the Buddha's teaching, his perfections, the path to and realization of *nibbāna,* but also *dhammā,* meaning the way things are in their ultimate, true nature, namely, impermanent, interdependent, and co-arising: "The *dhammā* are rooted in the Buddha; have the Buddha as their guide; have the Buddha as their protector" (*Bhagavam mūlakā no bhante dhammā bhagavaṃ nettikā, bhagavaṃ paṭisaraṇā*).[75] This statement plus claims that identify *paṭicca samuppāda,* the *dhamma,* and the Buddha—"Whoever sees interdependent co-arising [*paṭicca samuppāda*] sees the *dhamma;* whoever sees the *dhamma* sees interdependent co-arising," and, "Whoever sees the *dhamma* sees me; whoever sees me sees the *dhamma*"[76]—point to a substantive, organic relationship among the different layers of meaning ascribed to *rūpakāya* and *dhammakāya* but without implying a metaphysical absolute. Nalinaksha Dutt suggests, however, that such claims provided the impetus for the Sarvāvastivādins and the Mahāyānists to develop their metaphysically oriented theories of *dharmakāya.*[77]

In a similar vein, Paul Harrison contends that the passages in the *Aggañña Sutta* (D III.84) where *dhammakāya* and *dhammabhūta* appear as designations for the Buddha are devoid of ontological significance. On the grammatical grounds that these terms are adjectival compounds, he states, "the followers of the Buddha . . . claim to be his sons, not because they have been engendered by his physical body, but through being the offspring of the *dhamma* because the Buddha is *dhamma*-bodied or has the *dhamma* as his body (*dhammakāya*); the Buddha is the *dhamma* itself (*dhammabhūta*)."[78] In short, the Buddha is embodied in the *dhamma;* and the *dhamma,* in turn, is embodied in the Buddha. In devotional Buddhism and the practice of relic veneration a similar equation is found in the mutual identity among the 84,000 bodily relics of the Buddha enshrined by King Asoka, the 84,000 *dhamma*s, and the 84,000 atoms of the body.[79]

From these theoretical considerations, we move to practice, for the image consecration ritual is effectively the mechanism by which the Buddha body (*buddharūpa*) and the *dhamma* body become one reality. In the Cambodian consecration ceremony the ritual infusion of the material form of the image with the *dhamma* plays a major role.[80] Transforming the image into a *dhamma* body becomes a ritual enactment of the scriptural claims that the Buddha has the *dhamma* as his body (D III.89) and that whoever sees the Buddha sees the *dhamma* (S III.120). In the Khmer context, *dhammakāya* denotes two interdependent meanings: the body as the receptacle for the *dhamma* and the *dhamma* as the collective body of the Buddha's teachings.[81] The *dhammakāya* also incorporates the equivalent of the thirty-two bodily parts of the great person (D II.16–17; M II.136–37) identified as the thirty-two *kammaṭṭhāna* (bodily meditation subjects). As the Buddha transformed his own body into the *dhammakāya* through the practice of *kammaṭṭhāna,* so also the image is transformed into the same *dhamma* body through a specific ritual process that involves the meditation of charismatic monks. In the *buddhābhiseka* the inclusion of monks seated in intense meditation before the Buddha images to be consecrated denotes that the power of their own *kammaṭṭhāna* attainment is used to the transform the image into a *dhammakāya.*

The mantric transformation of the material form of the image into a *dhammakāya* occurs at either the beginning or end of the Khmer consecration ceremony. A group of monks seated in front of a new Buddha image recite the doctrinal counterparts of the body and robe;[82] the chief officiant mimes shaving the head and facial hair of the image in a symbolic reenactment of the future Buddha's renunciation-cum-monastic ordination while the five basic meditation subjects (*mūlakammaṭṭhāna*) are recited; the chief officiant opens the eyes of the image by touching them with a needle as he recites the eye-opening formula; lastly, a previously consecrated Buddha image is placed behind the new image and the verses of consecration are chanted that charge the new image with the perfections (*pāramī*) of the previously consecrated image, thereby transforming it into the *dhammakāya*.[83]

The image's body parts and robe correspond to specific doctrinal concepts whereby the statue becomes the *dhammakāya*. From the concept of the "body of doctrine" derives the notion that the making of all corporal representations must correspond to the specifications of the teachings concerning the auspicious signs that characterize the one who has attained perfect, complete enlightenment.[84] It is this metamorphosis that enables a representation made of wood or bronze, already rendered "living" by the opening of the eyes, to become a figure worthy of veneration. To effect this transformation, the chief officiating monk recites the designated formulas of the *dhammakāya* while touching the specific bodily part with the tip of his finger in order to infuse into the image the marks of Buddhahood.[85]

Despite some variation, it is reasonable to assume that the Khmer and Thai *dhammakāya* formulas were modifications from a root text.[86] Neither version exactly matches the thirty-two bodily marks of the great person. Each rendering refers to twenty-six or more parts of the body, including three or four elements of monastic attire, yet, for both, the formulas establish a nonhierarchical relationship between the rūpic and dhammic elements of the Buddha/Buddha image.[87]

The noble head denotes omniscient wisdom (*sabbaññutāñāṇa*); the hair, *nibbāna;* the forehead, the four meditation states (*jhāna*); the forehead mark, diamond-like foreknowledge; the eyebrows, the blue disc of visual meditation (*kasina*); the eyes, the divine eye, eye of wisdom, all-seeing eye, Buddha eye, and *dhamma* eye;[88] the ears, divine auditory hearing; the nose, knowledge (*ñāṇa*)[89] of the lineage of sanctified beings (*gotrabhū*);[90] the cheeks, knowledge of the path and fruit of liberation; the teeth, knowledge of the thirty-seven constitutents of liberation; the lips, knowledge of the mundane and transmundane (*lokiya/lokuttara*); the eye-teeth, knowledge of the four paths; the tongue, knowledge of the four truths; the jaw, unlimited knowledge (*appaṭihatañāṇa*); the neck, realization of supreme liberation (*anuttaravimokkhādhigamañāṇa*); the throat, knowledge of the three characteristics of existence; the arms, knowledge of the four assurances (*catuvesārajjañāṇa);*[91] the fingers, knowledge of the ten recollections (*dasānussatiñāṇa*);[92] the chest, knowledge of the seven factors of enlightenment (*sattabojjhaṅgañāṇa*);[93] the breasts, knowledge of the inclinations (*āsayānusayañāṇa*); the abdomen, knowledge of the ten powers (*dasabalañāṇa*);[94] the navel, knowledge of interdependent co-arising; the buttocks, knowledge of the five powers of the five faculties (*pañcaindriyapañcabala*); the thighs, knowledge of the four perfect efforts (*catusammāppadhāna*); the legs, knowledge of the ten paths of meritorious action (*dasakusalakammapatha*); the feet, knowledge of the four bases of mystical power (*caturiddhipāda*); the *saṅghāṭī* robe, knowledge of moral virtue, concentration, and wisdom; the *cīvara* robe, knowledge of shame and fear (*hiriottappañāṇa*); the outer robe, knowledge of the eightfold path; the belt, knowledge of the four foundations of mindfulness.

Some correlations bear a specific doctrinal significance or a numerical correspondence, while in others a parallel is drawn between a human organ and a supernatural organ such as the divine ear. The purpose of the *dhammakāya* is not to establish a symmetrical hierarchy between the various elements of the path, attainments, and goal incorporated into the form of the Buddha's body (*buddharūpa*), nor to dissolve the separate parts of the body of the Buddha into a metaphysical, universal Buddha body. Rather, from the perspective of the *buddhābhiseka* for which it was undoubtedly created, the text becomes one of the key elements in the transformation of a mere physical likeness of the Buddha into the *tathāgata*'s real presence.

The *buddhābhiseka* can be interpreted as a ritual process that transforms an image (*buddharūpa*) into the *dhammakāya* by integrating paradigmatic, narrative, and iconic modes of understanding. I am adapting the first two terms from Jerome Bruner and the third from Charles Peirce as used by Mark R. Woodward and Robert L. Brown.[95] Bruner defines paradigmatic as a formal system of description, explanation, and general causes that transcends the particular.[96] Narrative, by contrast, strives to integrate the timeless and general with the particulars of experience, and locates that experience in time and space.[97] The Buddha image consecration ritual in northern Thailand and Cambodia dramatizes the story of Gotama Buddha, especially the night of his enlightenment, not only as a narrative in a given place and time but also as a timeless or paradigmatic truth. Furthermore, as a mimetic process the ritual does more than dramatize paradigmatic and narrative modes of meaning; it embodies them in an icon. The icon synthesizes the paradigmatic and narrative modes and in doing so becomes more than both. As Robert L. Brown points out in his study of representations of the Buddha's life at *stūpa* sites in India and Southeast Asia, they are much more than a "visual narrative."[98] They are iconic in the sense that they serve the principal purpose of the monuments of which they are a part, namely, to actualize or make the Buddha present. Similarly, through the *buddhābhiseka* the Buddha image becomes an icon; more than a mere representation or symbol, it is the functional equivalent of the reality itself, namely, the *dhammakāya*.

## Buddha Images, Kings, and Power

> *Bhakti,* the seed in Buddhism long before its efflorescence in the Mahāyāna, must have constantly demanded some token of the Lord that could be sensed, loved, and cherished. . . . For the emergence of the Buddha image, there was indeed a psychological background in preparation over several centuries.[99]

Sukumar Dutt's psychological explanation for the origin of the Buddha image rings true to modern ears but runs the risk of overlooking a different meaning of the image and the reality it represents. The ritual in which images are consecrated or brought to life embodies one of the fundamental polarities underlying the tradition's understanding of its founder: that the Buddha is simultaneously a morally perfect saint whose principal virtue is salvific wisdom, and a conqueror with supreme power.[100] The most pervasive forms of the Buddha image in Thailand—the meditation (*samādhi*) and victory over Māra (*māravijaya*) postures—reflect this paradox. The former represents the defining moment of the Buddha's supreme enlightenment; the latter, the future Buddha's conquest of Māra's armies at the *bodhi* tree.

The power of the Buddha image, as of the person himself, derives from the Buddha's extraordinary spiritual accomplishments, a sacred power seen as coterminous with but not in opposition to the secular power of the world ruler (*cakkavattin*). Genealogically, this connection is made in the *Aggañña Sutta,* Mhv, and Vism by linking Gotama Buddha with the Mahāsammata, the progenitor of all world rulers.[101] Both Buddha and *cakkavattin* have in common the same thirty-two marks of the great person. Furthermore, the power of the world ruler derives from the same *bodhisatta*-like qualities formed over many lifetimes—generosity, high moral character, self-sacrifice, self-control, kindness, nonanger, nonviolence, and patience—not solely the power of the sword. Both the iconography of Buddha images and royal patrons that supported their construction reflect the close relationship between Buddha and *cakkavattin.* In northern Thailand images of the Buddha are venerated both for the sacred power that flows from the Buddha's extraordinary achievement and the secular power of kingship that protects the image and the community of monks.

The close relationship between Buddha and king appears in early Indian Buddhist texts and is depicted iconographically in Buddha images: "All these early images [in stone] from Mathurā and the surrounding area are closely related with the local *yakṣa* figures and with Kuṣāṇa emperors. They belong to the same world, where the concepts of overlordship, of fame and fortune (*bhāga*) predominate."[102] In affirming the close and complex relationship between the concept and symbolism of the universal ruler and the Buddha, Robert L. Brown contends that in art, "it is the royal and supramundane nature [of the Buddha] that predominates."[103] Buddha images dressed in royal regalia appear as an important motif in Southeast Asia and earlier in India. During his wanderings in India, Xuanzang (seventh century C.E.) reports seeing royally adorned Buddha images, and the famed *māravijaya* image at Bodhgayā wears royal regalia over monastic robes.[104] Why Buddha images were clothed in royal attire has given rise to several interpretations that connect them with theories about the Buddha as *cakkavattin,* Mahāyāna Buddhology, and local beliefs in the divinity of kings.[105] The most commonly accepted etiology of such images in Theravāda Southeast Asia concerns the story of King Jambupati:

> According to legend, Jambupati was so important in his own estimation that he would not listen to the teachings of the Buddha. Furthermore, he became jealous of King Bimbisāra of Magadha, and caused the latter great anxiety through the exercise of magic powers. In order to protect King Bimbisāra, who was a great patron of his religion, the Buddha changed himself into another universal emperor, a *rājādhirāja,* even more glorious than King Jambupati. He enthroned himself in a dazzling imaginary palace, and invited the king to come to visit him. By the time Jambupati had passed through the splendid series of gateways and outer courtyards of this palace, he became so awed and humble that his heart was ready to receive the Buddha's teachings. The Buddha then instructed him and even allowed his pupil a glimpse of his relatives in hell and in heaven so that he could visualize the pain in *saṃsāra.* Jambupati abandoned his throne, became a disciple, and eventually attained *nibbāna.*[106]

In the well-known story of the Buddha Gotama, Prince Siddhattha renounces his kingship to follow the path to Buddhahood; however, as the legend of King Jambupati demonstrates, the Buddha's power exceeds that of the universal ruler.

In northern Thailand, Buddha legends document the *tathāgata*'s ongoing presence in the region through a legacy of material signs—bodily relics, footprints, and images. Kings and *arahant* monks accompany the Buddha on a journey through the region. Kings, as in the *Mahāparinibbāna Sutta,* mediate his material signs, while monks mediate the *tathāgata*'s teaching. According to the northern Thai legendary chronicles (*tamnān-nidāna*), King Asoka bears witness to the Buddha's visit to the region and protects the Buddha's gifts of bodily signs. Northern Thai monarchs followed King Asoka's example. The Jinak recounts the history of the founding of Buddhism in northern Thailand as one where kings support the *sāsana* through the enshrinement of relics and images that become the palladia of Tai and Lao kingdoms. Legends of the Emerald Buddha, the Lion Buddha, and the Stone Buddha images discussed in this chapter disclose how Buddha images become efficacious as loci of political and cosmic power.

The Emerald Buddha image now resides in the royal chapel of the Grand Palace in Bangkok, where crowds throng to venerate the image as the protector of the Chakri dynasty and the nation. The most auspicious times are the three occasions when the image's attire is changed: summer royal attire consisting of a diamond crown, upper arm bangles, wrist bracelets, and a long necklace set with precious stones; a rainy season monk's robe of gold inlaid with gems and a golden headdress decorated with jewels and cloisonné; and a gold filigree cloak for the cold season.[107] The seasonal dress illustrates the paradox of the dual power of monk and king.

According to legend, the Emerald Buddha image was made in India.[108] The Venerable Nāgasena, desiring to propagate the Buddha's *sāsana*, with the aid of Sakka (Indra) and Vissakamma, made an image of the conqueror from a precious gemstone of miraculous power.[109] After honoring the image for seven days, Nāgasena resolves that seven jewels will enter the image at the top of the head, forehead, heart, hands, and knees.[110] After traveling throughout Theravāda Buddhist Asia, the image is eventually enshrined at Wat Chedī Luang, Chiang Mai's most prominent royal monastery at the time, by its most illustrious monarch, Tilokarāja (r. 1441–87). There the image becomes the preeminent guardian of the city, especially venerated during the April New Year festival to ensure the onset of the monsoon rains and guarantee the prosperity and security of the region for the coming year.[111]

Two Lion Buddha image traditions exist in northern Thailand; one ascribes the image to a Sinhala origin and the other to a northern Thai provenance associated with the Seven Spires Monastery (Wat Chet Yot) in Chiang Mai built by Tilokarāja. The legendary account of the Lion Buddha (*sīhaḷapaṭimā*) as given in the *Phra Buddha Sihing* chronicle and the Jinak traces its origin to Sri Lanka.[112] Like the Emerald Buddha, the Lion Buddha is embued with an intrinsic power that is conferred through the supernatural agency of a *nāga*. Because the serpent had observed the Buddha when the *tathāgata* visited the island, the *nāga* was able to form a likeness that sculptors used to make the image.[113] The Lion Buddha image was brought to Thailand in the thirteenth century, where it and subsequent replicas become palladia for the major Tai principalities of Sukhōthai, Ayutthaya, Chiang Rai, and Chiang Mai. Typical of the praise given the image is that rendered by Mahābrahma, the ruler of Chiang Rai (1345–1401):

> The world is full of merit, the world is full of virtue! What a person requires, he obtains; so do I. The statue of Buddha known by the name of Phra Sihiṅga [Lion] has come to me! None of Jambūdvīpa's sovereigns has more merit than I. Today I have realized everlasting happiness. My wish to obtain Phra Sihiṅga has at last been gratified.[114]

The Phra Buddha Sihing image was taken to Bangkok in 1795 and enshrined in the Buddhaisawan chapel (now a part of the National Museum). Annually, during the April New Year celebrations, the Lion Buddha image is moved from the chapel to the adjacent royal parade grounds, where thousands of devotees honor it as one of the country's most illustrious and powerful Buddha images.

The Lion Lord image at Wat Phra Singh in Chiang Mai dates from the late fifteenth or early sixteenth century, the period in which most images of this particular style were produced. A. B. Griswold connects what he calls the Lion Lord image with Tilokarāja's sponsorship of the building of the Seven Spires Monastery (Wat Chet Yot) founded in 1455, also known as Wat Bodhārām, a reference to its prototype at Bodhgayā in India.[115] The king was a great supporter of Buddhism, restoring old monasteries and building new ones, projects that required a considerable production of Buddha images. The prototype of the Lion Lord image was the great cult image at Bodhgayā in the *māravijāya* posture, called the Lion of the Sakyas. Griswold regards replicas of this image in the Pāla-Sena style that were installed at the seven spires of Wat Chet Yot as symbolizing the seven sites where the Buddha spent the seven weeks following his enlightenment.[116] The Phra Singh Buddha image that served as a palladium image for the princes of Chiang Mai is of the Lion Lord type. In this image Griswold sees a full embodiment of the demeanor of the power of the universal monarch:

> Though they wear the monastic robe, they are charged with memories of the Universal Emperor. Their faces are majestic to the point of arrogance. They convey no sense of meditation or spirituality, self-denial or kindliness. They "call the Earth to witness" with an air of command that will not take "no" for an answer. They are alert, aggressive, self-indulgent and self-satisfied authoritarians.[117]

In contrast to my own view of the complementarity between the power of the renunciant and the king, Griswold finds the imperial demeanor of the Lion Lord Buddha image at odds with the monastic ideal of worldly renunciation: "Springing from dreams of power quite alien to the Hīnayāna, they [the Lion Lord Buddha images] are strangely incongruous as 'reminders' of the Sage of the Sakyas."[118]

Today in Chiang Mai, the Lion Lord Buddha and the Stone Buddha images are especially venerated during the New Year festival, where relics and images undergo rituals of renewal.[119] Thai New Year (Thai, *songkrān;* Sanskrit, *saṅgkrānta*) signals the transition from the dry season to the onset of the monsoon rains and the planting of paddy rice. Both home and temple ceremonies marking the passage from old to new include rites of purification and rituals symbolizing the annual renewal of both time and space, especially the fertility of the earth. In a festival of sympathetic magic, the images are processed through the streets of Chiang Mai to protect the region and ensure its prosperity.

In Chiang Mai, the Stone Buddha and the White Crystal Buddha images enshrined at Wat Chiang Man are honored at the New Year festival for their power of life renewal and regeneration.[120] The inscription on the base of the White Crystal Buddha image states that it was made in 1874 C.E. by Chao Inthanon, then ruler of Chiang Mai. According to the legendary chronicle of the White Crystal Buddha (Phra Setaṅgamaṇī), the image originated during the time the Buddha was residing in northern Thailand.[121] The legend recounts the day when the Lord Buddha was on his morning alms rounds and a householder named Khun Sāen Thong offered himself and five nieces as his servants. The Blessed One refused, advising Khun Sāen Thong to have his seven-year-old niece ordained as a nun. The Buddha then prophesied that at that place the city of Chīmai (Chiang Mai) would be founded 837 years after his *parinibbāna.* As a memorial of the event, Khun Sāen Thong had the likeness of the Buddha and his prophecy engraved on a stone and buried it at the source of the Māe Khā River to the west of Suthep Mountain.

In another legend the image was made by the god Vissakamma from a white crystal gemstone provided by the god Indra and given to the sage Vasudeva, the guardian of Suthep Mountain overlooking the Chiang Mai valley, as a reward for paying homage to the Buddha relics enshrined in the Cūḷamāṇi *stūpa* in Tāvatiṃsa Heaven.[122] The crystal image is also reputed to have been the palladium of Queen Cāma, the first ruler of Haripuñjaya (modern Lamphūn). This connection to the Mon at Haripuñjaya continued until the kingdom fell to Mangrai, who then made Chiang Mai his capital in 1298. According to the legend, Mangrai and his Tai forces sacked Haripuñjaya but, to the king's amazement, the chapel of the White Crystal Buddha remained intact. In the tradition of the Mon rulers of Haripuñjaya, Mangrai installed the White Crystal Buddha image in a shrine on his palace grounds. In 1380 C.E. King Kū'nā initiated the custom of anointing the image during the New Year ceremonies, a tradition that continues to this day.[123] In 1479, King Tilokarāja constructed a chapel for the image at Wat Chedī Luang, where previously he had enshrined the Emerald Buddha image.

The Stone Buddha image, whose legendary history concludes this chapter, embodies both the power of the state, namely, the palladial power associated with kingship, and the power of nature as life-giving rain. Its power comes from the attribution that at the request of King Ajātasattu seven bodily relics of the Buddha miraculously entered various parts of the statue, thereby transforming the image into the Buddha's *rūpakāya*. The *ye dharmā* inscription around the image also bears witness to the image as the Buddha's *dhammakāya*. Finally, the legend connects the Stone Buddha image not only with kings but with three holy monks who enable the Buddha's supernatural powers (*iddhi*) via the image to act for the benefit and happiness of human beings in a manner quite similar to the charismatic monks who ritually actualize the Buddha's presence during the *buddhābhiseka*.

## Texts

### Tamnān Kā Phū'ak (*The Chronicle of the White Crow*)[124]

#### Introduction

The *Tamnān Kā Phū'ak* follows a traditional *jātaka* structure with a story of the past framed by one of the present. Like many *jātaka* tales, the story incorporates an eclectic blend of elements from folk and Buddhist traditions, including etymological wordplay on the names of the five *bodhisattas*. In the story these names are linked to animals who care for them: Kakusandha—*kukkuṭī* (hen), Koṇāgamana—*nāga* (serpent), Kassapa—*kacchapa* (turtle), Gotama—*go* (cow), Metteyya known in Thai as Phra Sī An—*sīha* (lion).[125] Peter Skilling notes that the association of Metteyya with a lion points to a Thai venue for the text.[126]

Five distinctive elements are integrated into the legend: the story of the past, appropriated from folk tradition, tells of a white crow who is the mother of the five Buddhas of the present age; the cult of Buddha relics, taken from the Ja-nidāna, represented by the story of two merchants who are given a hair relic by the Buddha that frames the tale of the white crow; a folk Buddhology with roots in popular Buddhist piety that complements the more formal eonic Buddhology of the *Mahāpadāna* and Bv; an etiological hermeneutic that explains the origin of the small clay lamp with a crow's foot-shaped wick widely used in northern Thailand during religious festivals; and an ethic of mutual love and concern that marks the relationship between the crow mother and her *bodhisatta* sons. As a sermon the text integrates diverse and sometimes seemingly contradictory elements into the same story to delight and edify its lay audience: the practice of renunciation; a familial ethic of mutual love and concern; the veneration of Buddha relics; and a quintuple Buddhological worldview that contains a cult of the Buddhas of the present age (*bhaddakappa*).

In Thailand during the festival of the floating boats in November, small clay lamps, incense, and flower offerings are placed on small "boats" (*krathongs*) fashioned from banana stalks and floated down streams and rivers. The clay lamp with a white cotton wick in the shape of a crow's foot is interpreted as a reference to the mother of the five Buddhas of the present age. A different theory views the festival as an occasion to pay respects to the spirits of deceased ancestors, especially in memory of mothers.

The preaching of the *Tamnān Kā Phū'ak* may coincide with the celebration of the *Vessantara Jātaka* (*Thet Mahāchāt*), also held in November. If the event continues for three days it may begin with preaching the TKP followed by the *Phra Mālai,* the *Vessantara Jātaka* on the second day, and conclude on the third with the BA account of the Buddha's awakening. The order of these preaching texts can be schematized in this way: the TKP establishes a cosmic Buddhological framework coupled with two aspects of popular Buddha cult, the veneration of relics and the lighting of small votive oil clay lamps; the *Phra Mālai* relates a pious monk's visions of the heavens that reward the doers of good deeds and the hells that punish evildoers;[127] the story of Vessantara celebrates the moral principle of generosity that is fundamental to all merit-making rituals; appropriately the sequence concludes with Prince Siddhatttha's journey to enlightenment, the subject of the BA. This preaching sequence continues to be followed at Wat Phrathāt Haripuñjaya in Lamphūn with the last event, the preaching of the BA, accompanied by the reconsecration of the monastery's Buddha images and *chedī.*[128]

### Salutation

*Namo Tassatthu . . . Satthavo . . .* Attention! Listen all of you of surpassing intelligence to the words of the Fully Enlightened One, the Lord Buddha. I shall preach to you in its entirety the sermon entitled *Phradīp Din-Kā* (The Crow's Feet Lamp). It is a story about the five Lord Buddhas who were born of the same mother.

### Story of the Present

*Atha kho bhagavā rājāyatane viharati tapussa-bhalliko . . .* Once upon a time before the Fully Enlightened One, the Lord Buddha, had attained his *nibbāna* he was staying beneath a mango tree. At the time two merchant brothers resided in the city of Uttaradhammavatti on the bank of the Samudarasagara River. In the neighboring city of Suvaṇṇabhūmi a thousand measures of rice fetched a thousand measures of gold. Wishing to take advantage of a favorable price, the two merchants took 500 carts [loaded with rice] to sell in Suvaṇṇabhūmi. As they proceeded along the way, they came to the [mango grove] where the Buddha was practicing austerities. A group of divine beings (*devatā*) [who had been watching over the Buddha] spoke to the merchants, "The Lord Buddha has been fasting for forty-nine days. Please prepare food and drink and present it to him as *dāna*."[129]

The two merchants were delighted and prepared a thousand balls of rice mixed with honey and palm sugar (*madhupāyāsa*). After accepting the offering of sweetened sticky rice, the Buddha presented each of the merchants with four hair relics (*kesadhātu*). The merchants, overcome with delight, gratefully paid respects (*añjali*) to the Blessed One and said, "O Fully Enlightened Lord Buddha, where should we enshrine the hair relics you have given to us?" The Lord Buddha who was able to survey the entire universe (*cakkavāḷa*) with his divine eye replied, "O merchant brothers, enshrine the hair relics on top of Mount Siṅgkuttara where dwelt the three previous Buddhas, namely, Kakusandha, Koṇāgamana, and Kassapa. Long ago the five Buddhas predicted that they would be born the children of a white crow during the first world eon (*kappa*)." The Buddha fell silent and said no more.

The two wise merchants bowed down at the feet of the Buddha, saying, "O Lord Buddha, the conqueror of Māra, knower of the foundation of the three worlds and this tale (*tamnān*) which we have never heard, we invite you, O most precious Lord, tell us the story of the time when you and your brothers were born the children of the white crow."

## Story of the Past

The Buddha then preached as follows, "*Pubbepi kāle mahāmūlabhaddakappo atisetakāko pañca bodhisatto ahosi* . . . In a former time, at the beginning of the first *kappa* (eon), there was a white crow mother who nested in a tree on the bank of the Ganges River. Soon she gave birth to five children [eggs] and attended to them every day without once leaving the nest. As time passed she became more and more hungry until at last she was forced to leave the nest in search of food. After she left a severe rainstorm arose, uprooted the tree, and hurled her nest into the swirling, raging torrents of the Ganges. The eggs were swept out of the nest, each one carried away by the raging waters.

"In the meantime, the mother crow, having refreshed herself with food, flew back to the nest only to discover that both nest and eggs were gone. Brokenhearted she flew in search of her young [the eggs], crying out for them in white crow language. She looked under every stone and every blade of grass, fearing that her babies had perished in the raging waters. After flying everywhere looking for her children who had been blown into the river, the exhausted mother crow lamented, 'O my children whom I love so dearly [referring to the five *bodhisattas*], where can you be? When I bore you in my womb and nursed you in the nest I protected you from all possible harm. Now you are in extreme danger, and I have flown far and wide looking for you. Oh, my dears, you must have been carried away into some far country. If I cannot find you I shall surely die [of grief]. May the *devatā* bring you back to me. Perhaps you have been eaten by fish or turtles. Here am I, alone, without anyone to help me find the five of you. Oh, woe is me; the sorrow of it all if you are dead.'

"*Tadā* . . . The mother white crow continued to fly back and forth in search of her beloved children. She flew high up into the sky, down to the water, over sandy beaches and fields, and even into caves both far and near but failed to find them. She gave up hope, unaware of what evil she might have done [in past lives] to deserve such a fate. Flying back and forth time and again until utterly exhausted, she died of a broken heart. She was then reborn in the Suddhāvāsāmahābrahma Heaven as a result of the meritorious power (*teja-puñña*) of her five children, and her sorrow was transformed into happiness. She dwelt in a golden mansion (*vimāna*) for 106,008 *kappa* as a result of the merit (*puñña*) generated by her deep concern (*citta-cetanā*) for her children, whose *bodhisatta* merit over many lifetimes kept her from falling from Ghaṭīkāramahābrahma[130] Heaven. She presented a lotus offering [from the Ghaṭīkāramahābrahma Heaven] to her *bodhisatta* sons when each of them attained enlightenment.

"Now I shall explain to you what happened to the five children of the white crow when the eggs were swept into the Ganges River. Kakusandha was carried by the waters to the edge of a forest where the queen of the chickens was foraging for food. Upon seeing the egg she was moved by pity and cared for it with her own [eggs]. Shortly thereafter, the shell cracked and to the queen's utter joy a male child emerged.

"*Dutiyo* . . . Koṇāgamana was carried by the river's current to a sandy island. A mother serpent (*nāga*) saw the egg that was carried by the current washed ashore. She gathered it up and when a male child was born, she looked after it with her whole heart.

"*Tatiyo* . . . Kassapa was swept onto another sandy island where a mother turtle came upon the egg and cared for it. In a short time a male child was born and the mother turtle was unstinting in her love and care.

"*Catuttho* . . . Gotamo [was found by] the queen of the cows who was walking along the shore [at the time of the storm]. Spying the egg lying there she cared for it out of her great sympathy and compassion. Soon the shell broke open. The male child that was born was much loved by the mother cow.

"*Pañcamo* . . . [The fifth child was Sī Ariya Metteyya.] The raging current carried him onto a narrow, sandy island where [he was found by a lioness].[131] Seeing the egg she cared for it, and when a male child was born she loved and nurtured him. Because of the perfection of their meritorious power and virtue (*teja-puñña-sīla*) each had acquired in previous lives, they were all born at the same time on the same day although in a different place.

"For twelve years the five [*bodhisatta*s] were loved and cared for by their foster mothers. At the same moment, they resolved to become hermits (*ṛṣi*) in order to train their minds (*bhāvanā*). Each reassured his foster mother, 'Please do not be sad or upset [that I'm leaving]. Rejoice, instead, that I am embarking on the mendicant path (*samaṇadhamma*) for the purpose of training the mind. Please do not prevent my departure. I seek the liberation that will enable me to conquer the evil of this world (*pāpaloka*).'

"Each animal mother who had cared for her foster child so long and lovingly gave her permission, saying, 'Oh, my dear child, your decision to become a hermit in the forest concerns me very much. Dangerous animals live there—rhinoceroses, elephants, tigers, and bears—yet I realize that the seekers of wisdom also dwell in the forest. Go with my blessing and best wishes for your safety. Because of your surpassing merit (*puñña*) you will attain *nibbāna*. I ask only one thing of you. Please promise (*paṭiñña*) me that you will remember your family name and lineage (*nāmagotra*) after you have attained supreme enlightenment.'

"*Tadā* . . . Then, after promising to honor their mothers' request, each of the five princes separately took leave of his foster mother at the same time on the same day. Each of the five went into the forest where they ate the fruits of the forest, followed the discipline of an ascetic, engaged in rigorous mental training, and wore the white robes of a hermit-sage. Each succeeded in overcoming the intoxicating passions of the senses (*kilesa*) and, thus, transcended evil (*pāpadhamma*). Soon all five [of the *bodhisatta*s] attained to an extraordinary state of mundane knowledge (*lokiyañāṇa*) which led them to the transmundane state (*lokuttaradhamma*) of *nibbāna,* a condition of supreme happiness. One day as they wandered in the forest both far and near to gather food, it so happened that all five found themselves under the same beautiful *nigrodha* tree with broad-spreading branches located on the top of Siṅgkuttara Mountain. After exchanging greetings, they asked each other where they had come from, who were their fathers and mothers, and the month and time of their birth. When they discovered they had the same white crow as a mother, the five Blessed Ones were delighted to learn they were brothers. They resolved to find their mother, but they had no idea of her whereabouts or even if she was dead or alive.

"'Let us swear a solemn oath (*saccakiriyā*) on our mother's name that we shall dedicate ourselves to a hermit's life of discipline and meditation and resolve to practice diligently and steadfastly until we attain omniscience (*sabbaññutāñāṇa*). Let us shout so loudly that our vow will reach the Mahābrahma Heaven. Once we have reached enlightenment, our mother, the white crow, will appear before us.'

"*Tadā* . . . Thereupon, the vow of the five Blessed Ones, having been made with such steadfastness and determination, reached to the Mahābrahma Heaven. At that very instant Ghaṭīkāramahābrahma, realizing (literally, knowing in her heart) [that her five children were calling to her], transformed herself into a very large white crow with beautiful full wings and tail and appeared in front of the five morally pure (*sīlaparisuddha*) sages.

"They addressed their mother as follows: 'Is this [white crow] our mother, with the beautifully feathered wings and tail, who left us to look for food and returned to our nest after we had fallen into the water of the Ganges before we learned to fly?' The crow listened to her children's query and then replied, '*Piya puttā* . . . Dear children, the crow you see before you is, indeed, your mother. I heard your solemn oath and immediately flew down from my heavenly golden palace (*pāsādadibbavimāna*) and now appear before you as your white crow mother. By your merit (*puñña*) I was able to come here.

"'O my beloved children, [in my previous life] when I was a white crow I built my nest on the top of a tree by the river bank. One day hunger forced me to go out in search of food even though it greatly troubled me to leave you. After I departed, a severe rainstorm arose and by the time I could return to my nest, the five of you were nowhere to be seen. The water of the Ganges had overflowed its banks; I was heartbroken. Had I not gone this might not have happened. I did not know what had befallen you. Weeping, I searched everywhere. I looked high and low along the riverbank, but you were nowhere to be seen. I returned brokenhearted and died, to be reborn in the Suddhāvāsāmahābrahma Heaven. After I heard of your desire to see me, I was able to come down from heaven and appear before you as a crow because of your virtue (*guṇa*).'

"*Sī pañca bodhisatta* . . . The five *bodhisatta* hermits now knew how they had lost their mother and were overjoyed to be reunited with her. In response they respectfully prostrated themselves before her. Then the five hermit sages said to each other, 'Because of the circumstances of our birth and childhood, we did not have the opportunity to honor our mother and repay her for her boundless compassion (*karuṇā*). Let us, then, make a replica of our mother's footprint to which we can pay our respects, which others can praise, and which will be meritorious in the future. Please, [mother], do this for us out of your love and compassion.'

"Ghaṭīkāramahābrahma, the mother of the five [Blessed Ones], looked into the future and saw that [such a replica] would become a connecting link (*upanidāna*) [to the Brahma Heavens] and provide a means of salvation for both human and divine beings. Therefore, she replied, '*Sādhu* . . . I am happy to comply with the wishes of my five divine children. You may make a replica of my feet in remembrance from now and forevermore. It will bring merit to you and honor to your mother.' Ghaṭīkāramahābrahma then took strands of cotton and twisted them into three small lengths the shape of a crow's foot. She gave them to her five holy children to make into a votive lamp to use for *pūjā* to honor their mother from that time until they reached enlightenment. Whoever in Jambudīpa and the three worlds pays respects to the mother of the five [*bodhisatta*s] using the votive lamp in the shape of the foot of the white crow will reach *nibbāna*.

"'This place is the most precious in all the world,' they said. 'Let us make a replica of our mother's foot so we can pay respects to her now and in the future. We vow that as long as we pursue the ascetic discipline in the forest we shall come regularly to the foot of this *nigrodha* tree. If one of us cannot come he should send word. This site has an unparalleled significance for it is surrounded by ninety-nine mountains. The five of us, as saviors of the world, should construct a special place here for the enshrinement of relics (*dhātu*) as a witness to our vow.' After making these resolutions they returned to their separate places to continue their ascetic disciplines in order to transcend impurity and sin (*kilesapāpadhamma*). They lived solely on forest fruits, determined to reach enlightenment and transcend the world (*loka*). They performed *pūjā* with the offering lamps whose wicks were made in the shape of a crow's foot.

"At the end of each month the five brothers returned to the agreed upon meeting place. Each shared with the others what he had done [during their time apart]. Then they returned to their separate places and continued their practice. At their death all five were reborn in Tusita Heaven, there to be attended by heavenly young maidens. After 5,000 years they were reborn into the human realm. The eldest of the five, due to the great merit (*puñña*) he had accumulated, became the very first fully enlightened Buddha (*sammāsambuddha*) in the three worlds. He took the name, Kakusandha, according to the promise he had made to his foster mother that he would preserve her name for posterity. Perceiving that her son had attained enlightenment, by the power of her divine eye and knowledge of former lives, his mother, Ghaṭikāramahābrahma, the white crow, made an offering of a beautiful golden staff which she placed in the shade under the *nigrodha* tree for the good fortune of human and divine beings (*devatā*).[132]

"In due course, the second brother, having been reborn in the human realm, attained enlightenment so that he might help others transcend rebirth and gain *nibbāna*. As he had promised his foster mother he took the name, Koṇāgamana, so that her name would be remembered. According to the agreement the five brothers had made when they were forest ascetics, he fashioned a drinking vessel and placed it in the shade under the *nigrodha* tree for the benefit of both human and divine beings.

"The third brother, after being reborn in the human realm, conquered Māra and attained the knowledge of the divine eye. According to his promise he took the name, Kassapa, so that his foster mother's name would be preserved for posterity. He became a fully enlightened Buddha dedicated to helping all sentient beings transcend rebirth and gain *nibbāna*. As he and his brothers agreed when they were ascetics, he made a beautiful saffron robe (*cīvara*) and placed it under the *nigrodha* tree.

"*Cattutho* . . . Then the fourth ascetic due to the power of his meritorious actions (*puññakiriyā*) was reborn as Prince Siddhattha. At age twenty-nine he renounced the householder life to seek instruction in the religious life. Ghaṭīkāramahābrahma, his mother, took robes from her heavenly abode and gave them to her son, the Lord Gotama. As he had promised his foster mother, after his enlightenment [the fourth ascetic] took the name Gotama."

### Story of the Present

"O merchant brothers, eight relics (*dhātu*) are to be found near your town. The guardian tree deities (*rukkhadevatā*) will tell you where they are located. You can see three of them now. They protect the town and are the shining light of the *tathāgata*'s religion (*sāsana*). All who have faith in my religion should pay unceasing respect (*pūjā*) to these relics. By doing so they shall reach *nibbāna*.

"O merchant brothers, after my religion has endured for 5,000 years the fifth [of the Buddhas] will be reborn as a prince in the royal city of Ketumatī as a result of his great merit. There he will practice diligently to overcome all sin and evil (*kilesapāpadhamma*) through his meritorious power. Ghaṭīkāramahābrahma will give *dāna* gifts of bowl and robe to her son, the lord of the three worlds. Reflecting on the promise made to his foster mother during his previous existence, he will take the name of Sī Ariya Metteyya. As he and his four brothers had agreed and with the help of the *devatā* he will build a very large reliquary (*cetiya*) so that both human and divine beings can pay their respects (*sakkārapūjā*) [to the relics]. Whoever wishes to achieve the path and its fruit (*maggaphala*) should honor the relics of the five Buddhas either by worshiping at the *cetiya* or, if it is too far to travel, then by doing so in one's mind. In this way one sees the *tathāgata*."

*Desanāvasāne sotapattiphalādiṁi* . . . At that time the two merchants and the assembled human and divine beings attained to the stage of the stream-enterer (*sotāpattiphala*) upon hearing the Sermon of the White Crow. The teaching about the making of the crow's-foot lamp and the names of the five Buddhas is now concluded.

### Dedication

Those who sponsor the writing of this text, who copy it, or who give it in *pūjā* will receive a great and unceasing reward (*phalānisaṃsa*). All of their wishes will be fulfilled by honoring the five Buddhas in this way. Everyone should listen attentively to the story of the white crow and the enlightenment of the five Buddhas. Everyone, male or female, who listens to this sermon will reach the highest heaven, the immortal state of *nibbāna*.

## Tamnān Phra Silā (*The Chronicle of the Stone Buddha Image*)[133]

### Introduction

The earliest reference to the Stone Buddha occurs in a chronicle written in 1785.[134] According to this account the image was made at the order of King Ajātasattu of Magadha seven years after the Buddha's death. Seven of the Buddha's relics distributed after his cremation were placed in the image. From northern India the image was taken by three monks first to Sri Lanka, then Myanmar, and the Siamese city-states of Nakhorn Sīthammarāt, Lampāng, and finally Chiang Mai, where Tilokarāja enshrined it at several monasteries before eventually installing it in the Emerald Buddha shrine at his palace. During the sea journey from Sri Lanka to Thailand the miraculous power of the Stone Buddha image caused rain to fall when there was a shortage of fresh water. Much of its subsequent history is simply a panegyric to the rainmaking powers of the image.

The Stone Buddha is a stele on which the Buddha is depicted standing on a lotus, holding his robe with his left hand. His right hand is stretched out toward a small elephant kneeling in front of him, and on the right is his disciple, Ānanda, holding a monk's staff in his right hand and an alms bowl in his left. The scene represents the episode in which the Buddha subdues Nālāgiri, the wild elephant that Devadatta sets loose in an attempt to kill the Blessed One. A semicircular inscription around the figure of the Buddha has been translated and its provenance determined by J. E. Van Lohuizen-De Leeuw. It is the *ye dharmā* formula in a north Indian script similar to others found on Buddhist sculptures dating from the Pāla period: "Of all phenomena sprung from a cause the Tathāgata has told the cause and also their cessation. Thus spoke the great mendicant."

### Salutation

I pay homage to the sun, the Buddha, who realized the four noble truths, who made the lotus bloom, and who aroused faith in the hearts of human beings. I respectfully pay homage to the nine supramundane *dhamma* and the *pariyattidhamma,* ten altogether, which eliminate the darkness of delusion.[135] I respectfully pay homage to the eight noble *arahanta* monks who were ordained by the Buddha who conquered the five kinds of evil Māra. Now I shall relate the traditional story of the Buddha image that was built of *bimbakāra* stone by King Ajātasattu so as to inspire the faith of all people.

### The Origin of the Image

Seven years, seven months, and seven days after the Lord Buddha passed away, King Ajātasattu commemorated the occasion with a grand offering to the community of monks headed by the Venerable Mahākassapa and by worshiping the Buddha's relics. It was King Ajātasattu's custom to provide *dāna* regularly to the assembled monks. The wise king, who was the greatest among all people in the city of Rājagaha, wanted to construct a Buddha image. He ordered his workers to remove a *bimbakāra* stone from the bottom of the ocean and carve it into an image of the Buddha making his alms rounds in Rājagaha and taming the elephant named Nālāgiri by his compassion.[136] The elephant was carved in a kneeling position on the right side with the figure of the Venerable Ānanda holding an alms bowl on the left. All three figures were carved on the same stone slab.

The Buddha image measured one *khuep* [the length from the end of the thumb to the tip of the middle finger when the hand is spread flat] and 4 inches in height; the three figures together are one *khuep* in width.[137] King Ajātasattu and all the *arahanta* monks placed the image on a throne and put seven bodily relics of the Buddha (*sarīradhātu*) into a golden casket. Prostrating themselves three times before the image they made the following request, "May the relics enter this Buddha image." Miraculously, of the seven relics, one entered into the head, one into the forehead, one into the chest, two into the shoulders, and another two into the knees.

No sooner had the relics entered the Stone Image than it performed a miracle, ascending into the air to a height visible to a large crowd and then descending onto the throne. Delighted at such an astounding sight, Ajātasattu instructed his people to prepare a place for the image on a high cliff out of reach to those on foot. An altar was built below so that the pilgrims could make offerings and worship (*sakkārapūjā*) the image.

### Three *Theras* Venerate the Stone Buddha Image

Sometime later three elders embarked upon a preaching mission to pay homage to the relics as well as to the Stone Image. The names of the three monks were Sīlavaṃsa, Revata, and Ñāṇagambhīra. In their quest to find the relics and the Stone Image, the three elders wandered in all directions until they arrived at the city of Rājagaha. Spying the image enshrined on the high cliff, they worshiped it at the altar located below. After making a wish that the image would descend from the mountain, the three monks laid their outer robes (*saṅghāṭī*) one upon another on the ground. Prostrating themselves in veneration three times, they called upon the power of the Buddha with this *gāthā,* "O Lord Buddha, you who attained enlightenment and conquered the five evil Māras, filled with great compassion toward all beings, may you lead us to the extinction of all defilements, that is, to *nibbāna.* O Stone Image in the form of the Lord Buddha, the refuge of the world, endowed with supernatural powers (*iddhi*) we invite you to act for the benefit and happiness of all human beings ruled by kings in countries both great and small."

Immediately the Stone Image ascended into the air and descended upon the robes prepared by the three venerable monks. Overjoyed by this miracle, they proceeded to inform King Ajātasattu of this extraordinary event. The king said to the three elders, "Venerable sirs, if by its great compassion the Stone Image desires to help people in other countries, then it should be transported there. Please take the image with you." The venerable monks agreed.

### Travels of the Stone Image: Sri Lanka

King Ajātasattu presented a magnificent offering to the Stone Image and to the three elders before they boarded a ship for their journey. After many days and nights the elders finally arrived at the island of Sri Lanka. Being informed that three monks had brought the Stone Image to his country, the king of Anurādhapura invited them to bring the image to his palace. There he worshiped the image, consecrating it with fragrant water. Then, suddenly, because of the miraculous power of the Stone

Image, a heavy rainfall ensued. The king was so overjoyed by this miracle that he wanted to place the image in a shrine attended by the three monks. Responding to the king's request, the three elders said, "Mahārāja, this image is intended for the benefit of both kings and commoners in both large and small countries beyond the sea. We will now take the Stone Image to the city of Haripuñjaya so that they, too, may earn merit."[138]

Upon hearing this, the king of Anurādhapura presented an offering to the three elders, who then embarked on a ship with the Stone Image. After many days and nights the ship's water supply ran out while it was still in the middle of the ocean. No sooner had the monks made an offering to the image and lustrated it with consecrated water than a heavy rain poured down due to the powerful qualities (*guṇa*) of the Stone Image. With their water supply replenished, the people on board ship rejoiced exceedingly at such good fortune.

### SOUTHERN SIAM: NAKORN SĪTHAMMARĀT

The ship continued to sail on the high seas for many days and nights until it arrived at the port. The elderly Sīlavaṃsa placed the Stone Image in his alms bowl and carried it with him as the three monks journeyed overland.[139] Each took turns carrying the image until they arrived at the city of Lakhaeng. Hearing of the arrival of the three elders and the Stone Image, the king of Lakhaeng invited them into the city. After the king made an offering to the image and lustrated it with consecrated water, a heavy downpour immediately fell upon the city.

Thankful and filled with joy, the wise king of Lakhaeng desired to enshrine the Stone Image in his city. Reporting to the king all that had taken place, the three elders spread their *saṅghāṭī* robes on the ground, and invited the image to appear there as it had done previously. Once again the Stone Image miraculously ascended into the air and descended onto the robes prepared by the three venerable monks.[140] Dazzled by such a wonder, the king bade farewell to the three elders as they continued on their journey to their next destination.

### NORTHERN SIAM: SATCHANĀLAI, LAMPĀNG, CHIANG MAI

Once again the Venerable Sīlavaṃsa put the Stone Image in his alms bowl, and the monks continued their travels until they reached the city of Satchanālai [an important thirteenth-century Tai city-state near the famed capital of Sukhōthai]. The king of Satchanālai eagerly made an offering to the image and then sent the elders again on their way. Traveling north overland they eventually arrived at the city of Lampāng. The Stone Image remained there for many years until the reign of Mū'n Dong. When Mū'n Dong sent messengers to inform King Tilokarāja [r. 1441–87] of Chiang Mai of the miraculous image, the king immediately sent an emissary to bring it to his kingdom to be enshrined at Wat Pā Dāeng.[141]

At that time Venerable Mahāñāṇabodhi was residing at Wat Pā Dāeng. King Tilokarāja ordered Mū'n Khambha Wiangdin [a government minister] to carry the Stone Image to Wat Pā Dāeng and offer it to Phra Mahāñāṇabodhi. Afterward, the Venerable Mahāthera asked all the Buddhist devotees to worship the image with various offerings and lustrate it with consecrated water. Once again a heavy rainfall miraculously occurred. At the time a high-ranking officer named Mū'n Nangsū' Vimalakitti was in charge of religious affairs. He ordered a temple (*vihāra*) constructed at Wat Mū'nsān and moved the Stone Image from Wat Pā Dāeng to Wat Mū'nsān so that the Buddha's religion (*sāsana*) might flourish and prosper. Later the Venerable Mahāthera Buddhañāṇa, the abbot of Wat Mū'nsān, brought the image to Wat Suan Dok when he transferred to that temple, but for reasons unknown it was returned to Wat Mū'nsān.[142]

King Tilokarāja of Chiang Mai was a powerful, brave, and righteous monarch known for his strong support of the Buddha's religion. It was his wish to have the sacred image installed in his palace. In preparation for transporting the Stone Image to the palace, the king ordered his officers to plant banana trees and sugarcane, and to erect lamp posts along both sides of the road from the palace to Wat Mū'nsān. The posts were decorated with a variety of flowers and small, triangular-shaped flags. After these preparations the image was carried in grand procession by a large number of government officials and commoners. It was enshrined in the Emerald Buddha tower inside the palace compound in the Year of the Goat, 837 C.S./1475 C.E. That evening, after being enshrined in the tower, the Stone Image performed many miracles in the presence of all the people and the king. It is said that the image, about the size of a coconut, floated in the air above the beautifully decorated roadway.

At such an awesome sight, the crowd rejoiced. Raising their hands above their heads the people shouted, "*Sādhu, Sādhu.*" Overjoyed, King Tilokarāja made a costly offering to the image. Throughout his reign the king continuously cared for the Stone Image, maintained the Buddha's religion, supported monasteries, and provided monks and novices with the four requisites. Since then the tradition of worshiping and lustrating this most venerated image has been observed annually. In particular, if the monsoon rains do not fall at the seasonal time, a rainmaking ritual will be held highlighted by a ceremonial bathing of the image.

After Tilokarāja's reign, all his successors continued to observe these royal traditions. Wise men should care for the Stone Image and fervently worship it. This act of veneration will bring benefit and merit to oneself both in this life and in future lives until one reaches *nibbāna.* Here ends the story of the Stone Buddha Image.

### The *Gāthā* for Worshiping the Stone Image

"Those who pay homage to the beautiful Stone Buddha image endowed with great, miraculous power will attain *nibbāna.* Therefore, I shall always pay homage to the image. May all of my illnesses disappear; may I be free from all dangers; may all material gain be mine by the power of the Stone Buddha."

# 8

# CONSECRATION TRADITIONS IN OTHER BUDDHIST CULTURES: REASSESSING THE *BUDDHĀBHISEKA*

> The divine image, whatever it be, has no liturgical value if it has not been consecrated; it is not a holy thing, no spiritual force issues from it, it remains a lifeless object which will never be able to establish any living and direct relation with those who pray. (Giuseppe Tucci)[1]

BUDDHISM'S IMPRINT THROUGHOUT ASIA is as much one of Buddha images and other material signs as monks teaching the Buddha's *dhamma*. The *Jinakālamālīpakaraṇaṃ* describes Buddhism's historical journey from India and Sri Lanka to northern Thailand via the peregrinations of six different Buddha images. Because Buddhist devotional religion centers upon material representations of the Buddha's presence, in particular, Buddha images, consecration rituals have been an essential part of the tradition as it spread from India to Japan. As the renowned Tibetologist, Giuseppe Tucci, observed, they enable the devotee to establish a direct, living relationship with the Buddha.

Even though rituals to consecrate Buddha images developed attributes unique to particular cultures, their sine qua non remained "enlivening" and "dhammacizing" the image. The image is enlivened by opening its eyes; it is dhammacized by imbuing it with the ontological truth realized by the Buddha. Neither can occur without transforming the mere appearance or form of the Buddha image into the Blessed One's real presence. This chapter examines the common features that characterize the Buddha image consecration ritual drawn from its enactment in Sri Lanka, Cambodia, Myanmar, Tibet, Korea, China, and Japan, and the ritual's syncretic nature as demonstrated primarily in its Khmer expression. In this comparative analysis my purpose is not only to discern shared meanings among several Buddhist consecration traditions but also to highlight the two most distinctive features of the northern Thai *buddhābhiseka*: the prominence of the Buddha story in sermon and chant, and the crucial role of holy monks whose meditation serves to implant *buddha pāramī* into the image (*plūk sek*). The first constitutes the narrative template that makes the image the Buddha's *succedaneum*; the second empowers the image with vital, enlivening power.

## Auspicious Eyes: Enlivening the Image

> Before the *eyes* are made, it is not accounted a God, but a lump of ordinary metal, and thrown about the shop with no more regard than anything else. But . . . the *eyes* being formed, it is thenceforward a God.[2]

When Robert Knox witnessed a consecration ceremony in Ceylon in the seventeenth century, he observed that the eyes of the Buddha image were the key element to the ceremony's ritual significance. For this reason throughout Buddhist Asia the ritual is called the eye-opening ceremony. The northern Thai *phithī bōek phranet* (eye-opening ceremony) literally uncovers the eyes of the newly consecrated images that were closed throughout the ritual by beeswax and a white cloth head shroud. The uncovering of the eyes that occurs at the ritual's conclusion signifies the Buddha's omniscience (*sabbaññū*) symbolized by divine eyes mantrically infused into the image. This discussion of auspicious eyes focuses primarily on the Sinhalese *netra maṅgalya* or *netra pinkama* (the meritorious act of [opening] the eyes of the Buddha image) but also draws upon examples from other Buddhist traditions, and concludes with a consideration of the importance of eye and gaze as it applies to images and the consecration ritual.

The origins of the Sinhalese Buddha image consecration ritual are obscure. From references to the term, *akkhipūjā* (ritual of [opening] the eyes [of the Buddha image]), in the *Mahāvaṃsa* (sixth century C.E.) and Buddhaghosa's *Samantapāsādikā,* Richard Gombrich concludes that the *netra pinkama* originated prior to the fifth century C.E.[3] The *Cūlavaṃsa* records that in the twelfth century the king himself performed the rite of putting eyes into the Buddha image.[4] In the modern period, the eye-opening ritual (*netrapratiṣṭhapāna*) is performed as the centerpiece of a ceremony preceded by offerings to a variety of protective deities (*sadaṅga pūjāva*) and followed by a rite of purification *(śānti karaṇāva*). The ceremony includes the recitation of *paritta* and may begin with the KBV as an etiological justification for the making of Buddha images. The length of the event varies, depending on the extent of *pirit* chanting and additional elements that may be incorporated into the festival but, as in the case of the northern Thai ritual, opening the eyes of the image near sunrise is the climax.

Preceding the eye opening offerings are made at altars outside of the image hall (*vihāra*) to eight Brahmanical gods that include Indra, Agni, Yama, Varuṇa, and their attendants, or to the eight Bhairavas, but the core of the deity *pūjā* takes place in the image hall before the Buddha image that sits on a *yantra* fabricated of rice grains.[5] Young men dressed as Brahman priests perform the ritual following the prescriptions for *mantras* and *stotras* found in the *Sadaṅga Vidhiya*. The *yantra* is divided into a number of squares.[6] Upon each square (*kalaṣṭhāpāna*) rests a pot filled with rice and covered with a betel leaf and a coin. The first syllable of the name of the deity to whom the offering is proffered is traced on the ground beneath the pot. In the ceremony Richard Gombrich witnessed, the ritualist (*bās*) invoked the planetary deities, Śakra, Brahmā, Viṣṇu, and Maheśvara (Śiva), by placing the offering pots within the *yantra*.[7] Finally, the ritualist placed an Indra post (*indrakīla*) shaped roughly like an umbrella in a brass pot at the center of the *yantra* altar.[8] After offering incense and water and reciting Sanskrit verses at each of the altars, the ritualist walked clockwise around the image hall ten times accompanied by drumming and music as he proceeded to make an offering before the sword protector (*kadgapāla*) altar.[9]

Brahmanical elements are also found in the northern Thai eye-opening ceremony, but not to the extent given deity *pūjā* in the Sinhalese ritual, which bears a striking resemblance to the *kumbhaṣṭhāpana* of the Hindu image consecration and to the Sinhalese exorcism rites (*bali* and *śānti*) that invoke the protection of planetary and other deities.[10] Consequently, Gombrich considers the apotropaic significance of the Sinhalese Buddha image consecration ceremony to be uppermost. He contends that the event combines two fundamental ritual mechanisms for averting trouble or danger: "either Buddhist monks may chant certain sacred texts (*pirit*) that are believed to have apotropaic power; or Buddhist lay specialists may perform ceremonies to placate minor deities."[11] In his view, the distinctive parts of the *netra pinkama*—the deity *pūjā* and the transformation of the statue into a cult image by the act of opening its eyes—have a common apotropaic meaning.

For Gombrich the actual ritual of making or emplacing the eyes of the image indicates that the danger to be averted is the power associated with the final act of painting the eyes. After the ceremony invoking the presence of divine beings and the chanting of the *mahapirit,* the artist invited to paint in the eyes is sequestered in the image hall.[12] A white cloth is hung in front of the face of the Buddha image while a relic is placed in a hole in its back by the chief incumbent priest. Standing on scaffolding in front of the new image, the artist then paints in the eyes not by looking directly at the image but at its reflection in a mirror held by his assistant.

When the act of painting the eyes is completed, a white cloth is wrapped around the artist's head. So blindfolded, he is led from the image hall to perform a series of purificatory acts to dispel the power unleashed by the act of transforming the image from a material object into a representation of the Buddha. By these ritual acts the artist transfers this potentially dangerous power onto a scapegoat. In a ceremony observed by Hans Ruelius, the artist slashed a tree with a sword, thereby releasing a milky sap, an act that resembles the *bali* exorcism ritual.[13] Afterward, he washed his face with milk from a bowl that he subsequently broke on the horns of a bull tethered near the tree in the temple compound. The bull was then symbolically driven away, although in practical terms the animal constitutes the major portion of the artist's payment.

Richard Gombrich agrees with A. K. Coomaraswamy that the fundamental meaning of the *netra pinkama* derives from the extraordinary power of the eye and gaze of the image and by association, the artist as well. In Coomaraswamy's view both the mirror and the *indrakīla* are intended to absorb the dangerous power of the image's eyes: the mirror receives the gaze of the image and the *indrakīla* functions as a scapegoat for this gaze. Similarly, the dangerous power of the artist's eye is transferred to the bull.[14] For Gombrich, the purpose of the concluding purificatory rites associated with eye and gaze is to ensure that no harm results from unintentional mistakes in the ritual.[15]

Ruelius offers a different interpretation. In his view the apotropaic aspects are secondary to the ritual's basic intentionality of transforming a mere statue into a cult icon. From this perspective, the mirror is used not to absorb the dangerous power of the image's eyes but to symbolize this transformation.[16] The mirror represents the Buddha's absence and by the act of painting the eyes the artist divines or conjures the Buddha's presence into the image. Mirror and image, in Ruelius's analysis, have less to do with apotopaism than with the polarity of absence and presence, specifically the polarity of *dhammakāya* and *rūpakāya*. For those gathered to witness the ceremony outside the *vihāra,* the image behind the closed doors is literally absent from view. But once the eyes are painted and the doors opened, the Buddha is fully present in both a form-likeness (*rūpa*) as well as in essence (*dhamma*).[17]

Fear of the evil eye in the Sinhalese consecration ritual appears to be absent from the northern Thai ritual as it is currently performed. Its prominence in Sri Lanka may be explained as an appropriation from exorcism rituals. I have proposed that covering the eyes of the Buddha image during the *buddhābhiseka* may be interpreted through the lens of transformations: a mimetic reenactment of the Buddha's journey to enlightenment; a saint in *samādhi*; an alchemical type of transformation of the image into the Buddha's double; the symbolism of death and rebirth. The mirrors used in the northern Thai ritual refer specifically to the Buddha's awakening and, hence, the *dhamma,* not to exorcism. Ruelius's interpretation of the *netra pinkama* locates its core meaning closer to its northern Thai counterpart. He argues that eye and gaze should be viewed from the perspective of the ritual's master structure, namely, the transition from the liminal, potentially uncontrolled power of making a statue of the Buddha into a cult icon, namely, as both *rūpa-* and *dhamma-kāya.*

Buddha image consecration rituals in most traditions commonly include painting in or opening the eyes of the image. Gregory Schopen finds a clear reference to the empowerment of a Buddha image by painting its eyes in the *Ratnaguṇasaṃcayagāthā* dating from before the fifth century C.E.[18] Opening the eyes of the image is the focal point of Laotian consecration ceremonies,[19] and in Cambodia the Buddha image consecration ritual reaches its culmination when the chief priest mimes pricking the eyes of the image in an act called "opening the eyes of the venerable one."[20] The Chinese term for the consecration of a Buddha image is *kaiyan* (*kaigen* in Japanese), literally meaning "to open the eyes."[21] In China the eyes are opened after the statue has been symbolically inspirited (*ru shen*) by placing embroidered threads of five colors, coins representing dragon eyes, a round mirror, and other objects into the image.[22] Japanese annals dated 671 C.E. record that a statue or painting ceases to be a simple material object and becomes an icon charged with sacred power after the rite of consecration called the *kaigen-kuyō.*[23]

The tensions between iconism and aniconism in the Zen tradition, extensively explored by several scholars in recent years,[24] find expression in a story about an eye-opening ceremony held at Mampuku-ji, the main temple of the Obaku school of Zen during the summer of 1663:

> On one occasion at Obaku-san [Mampuku-ji], they held the ceremony for opening the eyes of the images of the sixteen arhats. That day, the images were divided into two sections, one set to the east and the other to the west. Zen Master Mu-an (J. Mokuan Shōtō, 1611–1684) and Zen Master Chi-fei were conducting the consecration ceremony of the images. Mu-an was a stern but gentle person and so one by one he opened their eyes, politely offering incense, bowing and reciting the appropriate Dharma words. However, Chi-fei, without offering incense, without bowing and certainly without reciting the Dharma words, abruptly raised an iron fist and *bang, bang* struck the images right between the eyes saying, "These monks' eyes are already open!"[25]

The earliest known reference to the Tibetan term for eye opening (*spyan-dbye*) appears in a Dunhuang (Tun-huang) cave inscription dated 834–835 C.E.[26] Opening the eye of the image plays an important but secondary role in Tibetan consecration rituals which Yael Bentor considers to be a historical artifact appended to the primary substance of the ritual as the transformation (*sādhana*) of both image and practitioner. Tibetan ritual authorities liken the opening the eyes of the image to opening the eyes of a blind person so that he or she may be able to enter the city, "so by opening the eye of an image it is able [to act] for the sake of sentient beings." And, in like manner, "the ritual of eye opening is appended because its aim is the commitment to look on the trainees (*gdul-bya*) with a compassionate eye until the end of *saṃsāra*."[27] The Tibetan emphasis on compassion resolves the paradox of invoking the presence of the Buddha in a particular image when the Buddha's eternal omnipresence is the doctrinal norm.

The Korean ritual, "Painting the Eyes of the Buddha Image," similarly rationalizes the paradox of the universal *dharma* beyond form with the embodied *dharma* by appealing to the concept of the Buddha's loving-kindness:

> This patron has specially arranged this Dharma feast of painting the eyes and has respectfully prepared incense, lamp, and offerings. Open five eyes, ten eyes, a thousand eyes, and endless eyes. The essence of true Dharma is formless, the body of Dharma body is signless. Due to formlessness, it contains the Dharma realm as its form. How can there be the [thirty-two] marks and [eighty] signs? Also, since it pervades space as its body, it originally does not have the designation of eyes and ears. But in order to help the deluded beings in worlds as numerous as the sands of the Ganges and to save the suffering creatures in countries as many as specks of dust, [the Buddha] manifests thirty-two marks and is adorned with eighty signs. [We] implore the Tathāgatas to employ great loving-kindness towards all sentient beings.[28]

The centrality of opening the eyes of the image in consecration rituals throughout Buddhist Asia derives from the importance of *vision,* which stands at the very heart of Prince Siddhattha's enlightenment story and of the achievements of Buddhist meditation. In the first sermon, "Turning the Wheel of the Dhamma," the four noble truths are gained from knowledge (*ñāṇa*) and eye/vision (*cakkhu*). Throughout the discourses the Buddha's awakening is referred to as the purification of knowledge and vision (*ñāṇa-dassana*): "Thus, *nirvāṇa* in its oldest sense is attained when it is seen; and it is seen . . . by the 'eye' of insight (*paññā, prajñā*)."[29] In the Pāli tradition the eye is associated with three types of knowledge: the flesh eye (*maṃsacakkhu*) with insight into form (*rūpakāya*), the divine eye (*dibbacakkhu*) with insight into the mind-made body (*manomayakāya*), and the wisdom eye (*paññācakkhu*) with insight into *nirvāṇa*.[30] The Mahāyāna tradition adds two additional eyes, the eye of *dharma* and the Buddha eye, although the Buddha eye is also referred to in the Pāli tradition.[31] In the Tantric tradition the *uṣṇiṣa* and the *ūrṇākośa* as well as the thirty-two bodily marks of the Buddha function as a diamond eye (*vajranetra*) emanating streams of light and illuminating the worlds.[32]

When linked to eye and vision, insight denotes both the cognition of the true condition of things, and mental and physical power. Three interconnected *sutta*s in the *Majjhima Nikāya* that relate the Buddha's quest for and attainment of enlightenment associate the Buddha's vision with knowledge and power. In the *Ariyapariyesanā Sutta* the Buddha realizes the truth of conditionality and interdependent co-arising by *seeing* and, after surveying the world "with the *eye* of a Buddha," *sees* that "there are beings with little dust in their *eyes*," meaning that they are capable of understanding this truth.[33] The Buddha's attainments on the night of his enlightenment—the four meditative absorptions (*jhāna*s) and the three visions (recollection of his past lives, the passing away and reappearance of all beings, and the destruction of the defilements) are manifested by such physical effects as a bright or golden skin color (*Mahāsaccaka Sutta*).[34] And the *Bodhirājakumāra Sutta* discloses what must have been a strongly held view that physical contact with the Buddha's body conveys or transfers power to the devotee. In the narrative, Prince Bodhi invites the Blessed One for a noon meal. When the Buddha stops at the foot of the palace stairs the prince says, "Venerable sir, let the Blessed One step on [this] cloth, let the Sublime One step on the cloth, *that it may lead to my welfare and happiness for a long time*."[35] In this tricollage of *sutta*s from the *Majjhima Nikākya,* the Buddha's attainment of the three visions ("eyes") is extended to include the eye of compassion (*karuṇā*) and two physical attributes. The first is a bodily radiance described as a golden hue and irradiating rays (*rasmi*). The second attribute is a power that upon contact can be transferred to devotees for their welfare and happiness.[36]

A belief in the power of eye and gaze with its consequences for images and rituals of consecration appears in many religious traditions. The common experience of everyday eye contact and the fascination of a prolonged look and fixed regard came to be embodied in ritual practice, not simply as a means of expressing the feeling of love or reverence, imposing silence, or signifying consent, but as "a means also of participating in the essence and nature of the person or object looked at."[37] In Hinduism the term for this participation is *darśan,* a mutual "seeing" between devotee and image or devotee and saint. As Diana Eck observes regarding Hindu images, "The prominence of the eyes of the Hindu images also reminds us that it is not only the worshiper who sees the deity, but the deity who sees the worshiper as well. The contact between devotee and deity is exchanged through the eyes."[38]

One of the differences among Buddhist and Hindu consecration rituals is the varied use and import of eye coverings. In the northern Thai rite the head including the eyes of the image are covered with a white cloth, while in Sri Lanka the artist who paints in the eyes is blindfolded as he is led out of the space where the image is sequestered. In northeastern Thailand the custom of blindfolding an ordinand prior to novitiate ordination is parallel to "blindfolding" the image in the *buddhābhiseka.* A similar tradition occurs in Tibet. Tucci likens the ninth stage of the Tibetan ritual that includes blindfolding the eyes of the image to monastic initiation: "the band is taken from his [the image] eyes so that he may, like a person being initiated, gaze on the *maṇḍala* whose essence he must partake."[39] In Korea the head of a Buddha image is covered with a white cone during the consecration rite.[40] And, in an act reminiscent of Sinhalese practice, a Hindu priest is blindfolded when he transfers the "life substance" (*brahmapadārtha*) from old Jagannātha images to newly carved ones in the Purī Navakalĕvara ceremony.[41]

In Hindu consecration rituals even after the breath of life (*prāṇa*) is established in the image, the eyes must be ritually opened with a needle or the stroke of a paintbrush.[42] In the Babylonian rite of image consecration it is only after the eyes are opened with a twig of tamarisk that the priest chants, "Image that art born from the holy; Image that art born in heaven."[43] Opening the eyes of an image transforms what was a mere statue into a cult icon and in so doing brings the image to life; but, above all, opening the eyes gives the image an ontological status so that *darśan* can take place. In the Buddhist case when the eyes are opened, the image fully represents not only the form (*rūpa*) of the Buddha but also the Buddha's essential reality (*dhamma*). To truly gaze on the image of the Buddha is to see the Buddha and to see the Buddha is to see the *dhamma,* the theme to which we now turn.

## Dhammicization: Image and Reality

The northern Thai *buddhābhiseka* reaches its climax with the ritual reenactment of the *tathāgata*'s realization of the *dhamma,* the truth of the cause and cessation of suffering expressed in the formula of interdependent co-arising (*paṭicca samuppāda*), whereupon the eyes of the image are opened. The attainment of the eye of wisdom (*cakkhupaññā*) in the third watch of the night is the ritual's sine qua non. The Buddha's enlightenment represents the negation of craving (*taṇhā*) and mental defilements (*kilesa*), but it also represents the attainment of the knowledge of "things as they really are." Consequently, to claim that the Buddha image represents the Buddha means that the image also represents the *dhamma,* the fundamental causal principle that underlies reality.

The connection between image and reality is readily apparent in the simplicity of the Burmese ceremony.[44] In Myanmar the Buddha image consecration ritual is called the *anekaza* (Pāli, *anekajāti*), the first word of the first stanza of the *Dhammapada,* 153–54, considered to be the first words uttered by the Buddha immediately following his enlightenment, "Through the round of many births . . ." Customarily the Burmese image consecration rite is held in the morning, either in the home for a home shrine image or in a monastery or temple if the image is to be installed there. The hour-long ceremony has four major components: offerings to the image of flowers, incense, banners, and flags; the chanting of several *paritta* texts, in particular, the *Maṅgala Sutta, Mettā Sutta, Ratana Sutta,* and *Pubbhana Sutta;* the *anekajāti saṃsāraṃ* (the *Buddhābhiseka Maṅgala Udāna Gāthā*); and the recitation of the twelvefold formula of interdependent co-arising. At its conclusion the monks are fed the noon meal as an act of merit making. There appears to be no requisite number of monks mandated to participate in the rite, and in a simple home ceremony only one or two monks may be present. The core texts used in the consecration ritual focus on two aspects of the Buddha's enlightenment: the transcendence of craving (*taṇhā*) and consequently of the ceaseless rounds of rebirth; and, the realization of the interdependent and co-arising nature of reality, especially as it defines the cause and cessation of suffering.

In a manner consistent with later philosophical developments in Indian Buddhism, Mahāyāna and Tantrayāna traditions preserve and expand the Buddhological, cosmological, and ontological referents represented by the Buddha image. In addition to the principle of causation that appears in all consecration rituals, the most important are the three-body doctrine (*trikāya*), the concept of universal Buddha nature/realm (*dharmadhātu*), the notion of emptiness (*śunyatā*), and the doctrine of two truths.

In her detailed study of the Tibetan ceremony for consecrating *stūpa*s and images, Yael Bentor distinguishes between later Tantric and historically precedent *sūtra* elements of the ritual. In her discussion of the latter she includes the infusion of the principle of *praṭītya samutpāda* into the material receptacle through the verse, *ye dharmā hetuprabhavā/hetuṃ teṣām tathāgato hy avadat/tesāṃ ca yo nirodha/evaṃ vādī mahāśramaṇaḥ* ("Those *dhammas* which arise from a cause/The Tathāgata has declared their cause/And that which is their cessation/Thus the great renunciant has taught"). Archaeological evidence indicates a widespread use of the *ye dharmā hetuprabhavā* formula as a reliquary inscription dating from at least from the second century C.E. and extending to 1200.[45]

In the Tibetan consecration ceremony, infusing the *ye dharmā* verse in a Buddha image or a *stūpa* occurs as grains and flowers over which the verse has been recited are scattered on the object to be consecrated.[46]

This practice is cited in the Tanjur in the writings of Atiśa (982–1055), who observes, "One recites the *mantra* of interdependent origination three or seven times onto grain or flowers, and offers them [to the receptacle]."[47] By the seventeenth century this feature of the Tibetan ceremony was ritualized by placing a mirror inscribed with the *ye dharmā* verse on top of a mound of grain. The grain, symbolically infused with the formula through the agency of the mirror, becomes the medium for transferring the sacred verse to the object being consecrated. In the main part of the annual ritual reconsecrating the Kathmandu Bodnath *stūpa* observed by Bentor in 1988, the head ritualist recited *ye dhar*[*mā*] over a hundred times while holding a *dhāraṇī* thread that extended to the mirror. Afterward an assistant poured consecrated water over the mirror, thereby transmitting the sacred formula into the grain that was then thrown over the material receptacle.

The use of a mirror as a ritual implement to infuse the *dharma* into an image or another material receptacle is found in East Asian and other Buddhist traditions, although its meaning varies according to different cultural and doctrinal contexts.[48] On December 29, 1993, the Tian Tan Buddha image was installed at the Po Lin Monastery in Hong Kong. The world's largest outdoor bronze seated image of the Buddha is situated on Muk Yu Hill overlooking the Pearl River delta and the South China Sea. The climax of the consecration occurred when the officiating monk symbolically washed the face of the image with a towel, painted the eyes with a brush moistened with cinnabar, and reflected a beam of light from a bronze mirror onto the statue's face. These ritual gestures and accompanying recitation opened the *dharma* eye of the Buddha. The Venerable Chih-ding, abbot of the Hsu-yun Temple in Honolulu, interprets the use of the mirror as instilling the universal Buddha nature into the image so that it can shine the light of the Buddha's compassion on all sentient beings and free them from suffering.[49]

This evidence makes clear that the employment of the mirror in Buddha image consecration rituals denotes multiple meanings. However, as a pan-Buddhist symbol, Alex Wayman summarizes that the mirror functions in three ways: as a metaphor for the mind, a simile for the *dharma*s, and a predictive instrument.[50] In the Pāli *sutta*s the defiled mind is compared to a mirror-like pond made turbid by defilements; Yogācāra thought likens the relationship between store-consciousness and evolving perceptions to a mirror and reflected images; in Tantra a two-sided mirror represents the phenomenal mind (*manas*) of multiplicity and the pure consciousness (*buddhi*) devoid of images. Of particular significance for this study is the identification made in the *Saṃdhinirmocana Sūtra* between the image in the mirror and the image's model.[51] The same identification occurs in legendary narratives of the first Buddha image found in the diaries of Faxian, Xuanzang, the KBV, the *Vaṭṭaṅgulirāja Jātaka,* and the legend of the origin of the Mahāmuni image in Mandalay. By most accounts, the Mahāmuni image so perfectly mirrors the Buddha that devotees consider the copy the same as the original: "There on the top of the hill [King] Thagyarmin and his retinue saw to the creation of the image, the likeness of the Buddha to the utmost perfection. The finished image was then enthroned on a bejeweled seat. When the people came to look at the image, they bowed down in deep reverence thinking that it was the Buddha in person."[52]

The mirror enables the reflected image to "take hold" of the *dharma* in the phenomenal world.[53] It serves to signify the way things are in their true nature, as well as a ritual agency by which that reality enters the material receptacle. This reality is conceptualized in a manner that reflects the philosophical principles of different Buddhist traditions—interdependent co-arising, emptiness, the universal Buddha nature—or the numerous Buddhas and *bodhisattva*s that populate the Mahāyāna and Tantrayāna cosmologies. In the Korean ritual, "Painting the Eyes of the Buddha Statue," the three bodies of the Buddha as well as the five cosmic Buddhas and *bodhisattva* families are invoked into the image:

> Namu pure Dharmakāya Buddha Vairocana
>
> Namu complete Sambhogakāya Buddha Rocana
>
> Namu hundreds of thousands Nirmanakāya Buddha Śakyamuni
>
> Namu Eastern Buddha Akṣobhya
>
> Namu Southern Buddha Ratnasambhava
>
> Namu Western Buddha Avalokiteśvara
>
> Namu Northern Buddha Amoghasiddhi
>
> Namu five *bodhisattva* families.[54]

In the Tibetan ritual the mirror provides a temporary abode for the Buddhas or *jñānasattva*s being ritually instantiated into a Buddha image or *stūpa.* In some instances, the ritual actions of the consecration may be performed on the mirror itself, located in the center of a *maṇḍala* constructed for the occasion, rather than on the image or at the *stūpa.*[55]

The widespread use of a mirror in shamanistic rituals for predictive and divining purposes has led Alex Wayman to propose that its appearance in Buddhist literature may reflect a shamanistic origin. The term "mirror-face" (*ādāsa mukha*), as found in the story of a king with predictive powers (*Gāmaṇicaṇḍa Jātaka*), and the use of the term *mirror of the law* in the *Mahāparinibbāna Sutta* that gives a noble disciple the ability to predict victory over negative states of retribution, might represent a Buddhistic transformation of an ancient Indian practice of mirror divination.[56] Another parallel is found in China, where bronze mirrors were used as occult devices to discern and reproduce divine reality. The back of the mirror imaged the world through a set of icons (*hsiang*) arranged in a *maṇḍala* form, enabling the ritualist to manipulate iconically the cosmic structure underlying manifest phenomena.[57]

In Buddha image consecration rituals the mirror symbolizes the Buddha's simultaneous absence and presence, the profound mystery of a reality that is both form (*rūpa*) and formlessness (*arūpa*); however, it also functions as an instrument of ritual divination by conjuring this reality into the image. At the conclusion of the northern Thai ceremony the three mirrors that faced the new Buddha statues during the course of the night's ceremony now are reversed to face outward, signifying that the three knowledges constitutive of the Buddha's awakening have been invoked into the image.[58]

## Transformation: *Sādhana*

I have argued that the concept of transformation is central to the northern Thai *buddhābhiseka* and all other Buddha image consecration rituals. The Tibetan ceremony (*rab gnas*), in particular, is an outstanding example for understanding the transformative significance of the ritual. As a form of *sādhana* (means of achievement) the *rab gnas* transforms both the material objects being consecrated and the ritual participants into surrogates for deities and enlightened beings. This transformative process finds an analog in the northern Thai *buddhābhiseka,* where charismatic monk-meditators are one of the instrumental means by which the Buddha is hypostatized in his image.

In the Dge-lugs-pa tradition of Tibetan Buddhism, the most widely used consecration manual was composed by Khri-byang Rin-po-che (1901–81) based on a text written by the first Panchen Lama in the early seventeenth century. The manual stipulates a three-day ceremony for the consecration of images, *stūpa*s, and other material receptacles.[59] On the first day, rituals to prepare both the performers and the receptacles for the Buddhas, *bodhisattva*s, and titular deity (*lha*) are held; the central and most elaborate part of the consecration ritual occurs on the second day; and the event concludes on the third day with propitiatory, final rites. The major sequences of the ritual include transforming the ritual performers into a chosen Buddha, for example, Vajrabhairava; dissolving the receptacle into emptiness; visualizing the chosen Buddha (*yi-dam, iṣṭadevatā*) out of emptiness; inviting the enlightened being (*ye shes sems* *dpa', jñānasattva*) into the receptacle; unifying the visualized image (*dam tshig sems dpa', samayasattva*) and the enlightened being into nonduality (*guyis-su-med-pa, advaya*); transforming nondual emptiness into the original appearance of the receptacle; requesting the *ye shes sem dpa'* to remain in the receptacle. The explicit parallel transformation of ritual practitioners and material forms such as a Buddha image into the actual presence of the Buddha constitutes one of the most remarkable features of the Tibetan consecration ritual. This dual transformation resolves the apparent dilemma of ascribing to the human ritualists the power to localize the universal Buddha body, for only by being transformed into a titulary deity or chosen Buddha (*yi-dam*) are they able to transform a Buddha image or a *stūpa* into the very reality of the Buddha. Regarding the Chinese consecration ritual Lawrence G. Thompson makes an analogous point: "The key to understanding the consecration ritual is to keep in mind that its magic is performed not by man, but by the deity . . . [indicated by] the fact that the deity is consulted by man before any and all procedures in image making and animating."[60]

For Bentor the key to all Tantric ritual, including consecrations, is *sādhana,* whereby ordinary reality and actual reality—emptiness, suchness—are merged. In essence, consecration instantiates the universal Buddha nature (*dharmakāya, dharmadhātu*) through the agency of ritual transformation. Both ritual performers and receptacles—images, *stūpa*s, *than-ka*s, books—are transformed by means of visualization, focused concentration, and the performative power of chant.

Three central Mahāyāna philosophical notions underlie the ritual: the three bodies (*trikāya*) of the Buddha, emptiness (*śunyatā*), and the doctrine of two truths. The doctrine of absolute and relative truth serves to explain the paradox created by the instrumental agency of the ritual itself, namely, making present in a particular material receptacle that which is already present. Ultimately, the universal Buddha body permeates the four quarters of the universe, but at the level of relative truth the ritual localizes the presence of the Buddha in reliquary and image for devotional purposes and the accumulation of merit for the donor-patron. The universal *dharmakāya* is transmuted into a particular form (*nirmanakāya*), which makes possible interaction between the Buddha and human beings.

Tibetan Buddha image consecration is a process parallel "to that of transforming oneself into one's chosen deity by means of a *sādhana* practice, or to that of generating a deity in front of oneself, or in a vase, the receptacle transformed into the nature of the *ye shes sems dpa* [enlightened being]."[61] Bentor compares the process whereby an image becomes an embodiment of a deity to a meditator's attainment of Buddhahood by means of deity *yoga* achieved by visualizing complex *maṇḍala*s that eventually lead to the meditator's dissolution into nondual emptiness.[62] In this journey of spiritual perfection, meditators visualize the dissolution of the cosmos into a *maṇḍala*. While meditating on the *maṇḍala*, they merge with a titulary deity (*yi-dam*), dissolve into clear light, and then return to conventional reality, resuming the form of their *yi-dam* in order to save sentient beings from the wheel of rebirth. Likewise, by means of the consecration ritual the Buddha's universal reality or *dharmakāya* is instantiated in a particular form for the benefit of all humankind. In Tucci's still poetic prose, "The centre of these liturgies always means the priest's spiritual experience: he is the miracle-worker, because he finds again and causes to shine in his own soul the universally luminous consciousness which is the womb of all things: the gods themselves."[63]

Richard Payne interprets the transformative visualization technique of *mikkyo* in the Japanese Vajrayāna tradition (Shingon) through the lens of analytical psychology.[64] From this perspective, visualizing a deity such as Mahāvairocana is regarded as an intrapsychic transformation in which the practitioner realizes his inherent enlightened or *dharmakāya* nature. In the context of the consecration ceremony, *sādhana* creates a realm wherein the Buddha becomes manifest. The ritual is a preenactment or preactualization of the seemingly paradoxical creation of a reality already present. Payne likens this preenactment to a mimetic process in which one acts as if one already possessed a given quality in order to allow that quality to emerge.[65] In northern Thailand the mimetic process serves two purposes: the narrative construction of reality whereby the image becomes the Buddha's double through a reenactment of the night of the Blessed One's enlightenment; and the transference of the power of the first Buddha image and its living representatives, the charismatic monk-meditators, into the consecrated image.

The Vajrayāna concept of *sādhana* provides insight into the role of the holy monks who during the northern Thai image consecration ritual are seated around the *bodhimaṇḍa*, absorbed in meditation, as the *Buddha Abhiseka* is chanted. Ideally, they embody the charisma of *arahanta* monks whose biographies testify to the extraordinary power of their wisdom, lovingkindness, and jhānic attainments such as the divine eye. As *sāvaka-buddha*s they embody the *pāramī* associated with Buddhahood. The ritual techniques of the *buddhābhiseka*—chant, meditation, sacred cord—provide the means by which these powers are then transferred into the newly consecrated images.

## Syncretization: Buddha, Gods, and Ancestral Spirits

By their very nature, culturally embedded religious rituals including the Buddha image consecration ceremonies are syncretic. They incorporate diverse religio-cultural elements in unique and distinctive ways. For example, the Sinhalese *netra pinkama* begins with a *sadaṅga* ceremony, a magical sacrifice appropriated from the *kumbhapratiṣṭha* of Hindu consecration ceremonies. Offerings are presented to many Brahmanical and Hindu deities on a *yantra* made of rice grains on which have been placed several pots.[66] Of the several northern Thai *buddhābhiseka* rituals that I have observed, only two were preceded by a similar rite. The *buang sangwoey thewadā* (Thai) (propitiatory offerings to the gods) is conducted at an altar located in front of the building where the evening image consecration will be held. A table holds a variety of vegetable and meat offerings to a host of Brahmanical deities and protective forces (Thai, *chao thī*) which may include the spirits of powerful figures in northern Thai history.[67] In the absence of such a rite, however, offerings will be presented to the guardians of the universe (*lokapāla*) and to Phra Upakut (Pāli, Upagutta) to protect the ritual space from evil forces.[68] Whether identified as Brahmanical or animistic, these rites are thoroughly integrated into the religious practices of northern Thai Buddhists.

The Buddha image consecration ritual in Cambodia offers a striking example of the syncretic or incorporative nature of Buddhism as a lived tradition.[69] For François Bizot the ritual reflects a Khmer religious culture prior to the dominance of Cambodia's modern Theravāda tradition under Thai influence "that pertains to a collection of beliefs that appeared in practically all of Buddhist Indochina: a congruence of Vedic Brahmanism and Tantrism. Today it typifies the teaching of the Mahānikāya [sect] but reflects a much earlier time and rests on a common ground that until today resists complete identification."[70] Regarding Tibetan Vajrayāna consecration rituals, Tucci holds a similar view: "Vajrayāna continues India's old magical intuitions; the liturgy of *pratiṣṭha* tends to establish the divine presence in the consecrated object in the same way as the ritual of the *agnicaya* transformed the altar into a magical replica of Prajāpati. As Paul Mus has justly recognized . . . many Buddhist ideas . . . are not abberant plants but push their roots deep into the soil of pan-indian religious experience."[71] In support of the view that Buddhist consecration traditions evidence archaic Indian sensibilities, Jan Gonda finds that in the case of Hinduism a fundamental continuity pertains in the meaning of *pratiṣṭha* from early Vedic texts to much later sectarian *sūtra*s, *purāṇa*s, and *tantra*s.[72]

Bizot considers the Buddha image consecration ritual to be an amalgam of the popular belief that the Buddha imbued his image with his ten perfections (*pāramī*) to protect his teaching for 5,000 years coupled with the belief in a cult of guardian figures—heroes killed in battle and deceased kings—who have become protectors of the religion (*sāsana*). It is these guardian deities who "take possession of the image during the consecration rites . . . [and] receive the food offering made each morning to the central image of the Buddha in the *vihāra*."[73] Bizot suggests that the cult of the Buddha image incorporates a cult of the gods of the human realm (*devatā manussaloka*) and ancestral guardian deities and, correspondingly, that many Angkor monuments were intended for the worship of the spirits of parents and ancestors.[74]

In Cambodia, Buddha image consecrations occur between March and July or on the last day of the lunar month of *bhadrapad* (August/September) that coincides with the gathering of offerings (*pind*) for the dead, a ceremony related to the Brahmanical sacrifice for living beings or ancestors (*bhūtayajña* or *pitṛyajña*).[75] The earlier period occurs during the planting of paddy rice and the beginning of the lunar New Year, ensuring that the protective power (*pāramī*) of both the Buddha and ancestral guardians will result in agricultural fertility, communal harmony, and well-being. If the ceremony occurs during the month of *bhadrapad,* the Buddha image will appease the starving spirits of the dead and thereby calm their painful wanderings.[76]

The Cambodian Buddha image consecration ritual, as in Thailand, closely follows the story of the Buddha from the stages of Prince Siddhattha's renunciation and departure through the watches of the night of the Buddha's enlightenment. However, the Khmer ritual expands the dramatic elements. Emulating Prince Siddhattha's departure from the royal palace, the image is taken to the monastery in a colorful procession; Māra's attempt to prevent Siddhatta's departure from Kapilavattu is mimed; the hair of the Buddha image is symbolically cut off; milk rice is prepared and presented to the image;[77] and Māra's attack on the Buddha under the *bodhi* tree is reenacted.[78]

The ritual comes to a climax when the officiating monk symbolically opens the eyes of the image by lightly scratching them with a needle, and then touches specific body parts of the statue while he recites the appropriate Pāli stanzas that will infuse the physical body of the Buddha image (*rūpakāya*) with the *dhamma*.[79] Afterward, the monks call on the *pāramī* of the previously consecrated and empowered temple image to enter into the new image.[80] Whereas the canonical *pāramī*s or *pāramitā*s refer to virtue, equanimity, lovingkindness, and other moral and spiritual perfections, in the following passage the term represents the power of the very body of the Buddha and, by extension, his image. *Pāramī* in this sense closely resembles the Hindu concept of a god's *śakti*. Invoking Buddha relics to reside in the Buddha image is an especially dominant theme in the following recitation.

Then convene two renowned Theras, experts in consecration (*abhiseka*) marks (*lakkhaṇa*) of Buddha [statues], to come recite the invitation formulas of the "power" (*pāramī*) of the noble "relics." For a layperson to utter (these formulas) would be improper, for, lacking in morality (*sīla*), he would not know how to proceed. Monks should be convened to recite the invitation of the power (*pāramī*) of the "relics"(*dhātu*), [by saying] this:

> Hands joined, we pay homage to the excellent feet (*buddhapāda*) of the Greatest Jinasrī [conqueror],
> that the *devatā*, men, *yakkha*, and poets (*kavi*) together venerate with deep devotion (*bhakti*).
>
> I pay homage to the lips (*oṣṭha*) of the Buddha, the Satthā who revealed the teaching and tames all beings;
> By the strength of my respect, may misfortune (*upadrab*) be removed [and] may tragedy spare us.
>
> First, setting our mind to do meritorious acts and gifts, and to practice both abstaining from thoughts and creating them,
> We invite the priceless, noble relics of the Satthā from all of the places where they have been deposited
> To come rapidly—quick-quick!—without delay;
> Enter this magnificent statue of the Buddha, radiant, adorned (*rocanā*) with radiant colors.[81]
>
> The noble relics of the Jinasrī from all of the cities on the precious isle of Laṅkā,
> From Jambudvīpa, from [the world of] the Nāga (*bhujaṅganāgā*), from the abode of Paradise—
> I invite [them], these noble relics of the Jinasrī, to enter inside of the statue (*paṭima*) promptly and quickly.
>
> The magnificent upper right canine tooth, deposited in the Paradise of the Thirty-three (*traitriṅs*),
> The superb lower right canine tooth, deposited in the Isle of Laṅkā,
> The Satthā's upper left canine tooth in the city of Gandhāra,
> The Jinasrī's left canine tooth, especially beautiful, deposited in the world of the Nāgas,
> I invite them to come together quickly to enter into the statue (*paṭimā*) adorned (*racanā*) with radiant colors.
>
> The Jinasrī's right collar bone relic, deposited at Siṅhaladvīpa,
> The Satthā's left collar bone relic, deposited in the multicolored abode of Brahmā,
> The noble hairs and gleaming brows (*uṇṇāloma*), whose light radiates in the distance, deposited in the city of Pāṭaliputra,
> The Jinasrī's minor relics (*sākhā*) such as the eyes, hairs, and the forty noble teeth,

The noble nail relics, I invite them to enter into the statue of the Buddha immediately.

The Jinasrī's halo (*ketumālā*), radiant, incomparably beautiful,
The noble luminous halo (*bāmappabhā*) radiant with light—white, blue, yellow, red—magnificent,
The unique and splendid pale green light of six colors (*chabbaṇṇaraṅsī*), all around in a circle (*cravāt*),
Shining in the air (*veha*) with clarity, in the ten directions, exposing its various lights (*vivaraṇa vivdha rasṅī*),
Like the auspicious (*suostī*) mountain of gold, or still yet, like a perfect rainbow,
I invite the lights of the Satthā to gather together to enter into the statue of the Buddha immediately.

The ten forces of the knowledge that should be known (*ñāṇañeya*), the ten powers (*pāramī*), the ten supreme powers (*paramatth pāramī*),
The nine supranormal states, the eighty-four thousand *dhamma* of the Jinasrī,
The profound, magnificent knowledge, more profound than the ocean,
The meditative absorptions (*jhāna*), the knowledge that should be known,
The radiating wisdom that perceives all the ordinary *dhamma* (*samdāy*),
The noble heart, immensely pure and profound, perceives all places with clarity in all the worlds,
The preaching of the noble *dhamma* to save the countless beings in all regions and cities who have taken refuge [in the Buddha],
I invite the *dhamma* of the Jinasrī to come together to enter the statue immediately.

The lower robe arranged with care, the upper robe, the over robe, the vest, the belt,
The yellow light so beautiful that its reflection is like gold, or the frangipani flower, or even the magnificent pomegranate flower,
The alms bowl, the fan, the prayer rug, the three complete and perfect robes (*cīvara*) offered with devotion,
The pedestal of multicolored gold, of sparkling lights,
I invite the statue to be the substitute.

We consecrate (*abhiseka*) the jewel [that is the image] of the Buddha, in such a way that it is perfect and sits enthroned as the master of the three worlds.

The previous Buddhas, numbering more than a hundred thousand, countless ([*a*]*sankheyya*) like [the grains of] sand in the ocean,

The true Si-ārya, the noble Buddha who will attain enlightenment in the future,
The Arahant, numbering more than a hundred thousand, so numerous that they cannot be counted,
Whose glorious merits (*puñña*) and powers (*pāramī*) save beings in all abodes by offering them the three gems,
I beg the powers (*pāramī*) of these Buddhas and of all the Arahants, with their fiery-like energy (*ṭek tejaḥ*),
To enter the statue so that its power (*cesṭā*), its victory, its strength, and its [power to grant] good fortune may be increased.[82]

The monks' ritual action emulates the legendary attribution that prior to his *parinibbāna* the Buddha placed his *pāramī* in an image:

—Eh, *anak,* euy! The Noble One has entered Nibbāna, but it is as though he resides in this place—how is it possible that he resides here?—Eh, *anak,* euy! Because the religion of the Noble One will not last more than a total of 5,000 years, at the very moment he entered into the final Nibbāna, the Lord commanded the ten *pāramī* to protect the religion of the Master forever. Today, *anak,* euy! The exalted persons use gold, silver, earth, and wood in order to make the *braḥ jīv* [Lord of Life] that one calls statues of the Buddha. —When the Noble One entered into the noble Nibbāna, he deposited the appropriate *dasapāramī* into a statue of the Buddha for the protection and maintenance of the religion for 5,000 years.[83]

In addition to the *pāramī* of the Buddha, the image also incorporates the protective power of many gods and spirits, "masters of the territory and constant leaders of the social community" that are symbolically represented by an altar to Indra (*indrakīla*) and ritually transferred into the Buddha image.[84] The protective powers of the souls of the dead and of ancestral and tutelary deities who occupy the earth, trees, and waters, variously referred to as *bhūt, ārak, khmoc, brāy,* are also infused into the image. For Bizot, via the consecration ritual, Khmer Buddha images incorporate diverse, archaic traditions of sacred power. Here "one is in the presence not only of pre-Buddhist remnants but also of shared foundations, both pre-Aryan and proto-Indochinese, that go back to an era of civilization frequently identified as Austro-Asiatic. . . . Tree, stone or manufactured body, all of equal importance, can be manifestations of divinity. In the guise of vital function the substance of a deceased person is captured by incantation and buried within the image."[85]

The precise nature of the distinctive elements integrated into particular cultural forms of the Buddha image consecration ritual will vary; however, Bizot's analysis of the Khmer case demonstrates that the ceremony's meaning cannot be confined to a narrow Theravāda hermeneutic. But does this imply that the ritual should not be regarded as authentically "Buddhist"? For A. K. Coomaraswamy the Sinhalese eye-opening ritual was grossly antithetical to the Theravāda view of the Buddha:

> The ceremony would seem to be rather Hindu than Buddhist in origin; the underlying idea seems to be an endeavor to secure good "conditions" at the time of . . . consecrating the image as a medium which shall put the worshipper in touch with the unseen god whose symbol is thus set forth, and this is rather a Hindu than a Buddhist idea; for Southern Buddhism does not regard Buddha as a still existent personal God, and would not have been likely to originate such a ceremonial in connection with a mere memorial.[86]

Coomaraswamy's claim that an authentically Theravāda Buddha image consecration ritual could only be a "mere memorial" grows logically from his demythologized view of the Buddha: in Theravāda Buddhism the Buddha is not regarded as a "still extant personal God"; the *buddhābhiseka* ritual hypostasizes the Buddha in an image; therefore, Coomaraswamy reasons the ritual must have been derived from an outside influence like Hinduism. This study challenges such an ahistorical view and argues that it distorts not only the meaning of the Buddha image but of the Buddha himself.[87]

## Conclusion: Stories and Saints, Icons and Images

My comparison of Buddha image consecration rituals throughout Buddhist Asia finds a set of common themes or meanings that highlight enlivenment (opening the eyes of the image), dhammicization, and transformation. Furthermore, from a cultural perspective these rituals are inevitably syncretic or accretive. Although Buddha image consecration rituals have more in common than not, differences include both doctrinal and historical variables. In this concluding section two of the most distinctive—although not unique—features of the northern Thai Buddha image consecration ceremony deserve to be emphasized: the narrative construction of the Buddha image, and the charismatic intervention of monk-meditators. In becoming the Buddha's surrogate or double, the image is programmed with the story of the Buddha. In comparison with other Buddhist consecration traditions, the northern Thai *buddhābhiseka* highlights to an unusual degree the story of the Buddha's path to awakening.[88] The narrative structure of the northern Thai ceremony that recapitulates the events of the Buddha's enlightenment experience leads me to conclude that the *buddhābhiseka* transforms the image into the living reality of the Buddha by means of a narrative-based, performative mimesis. The ritual creates a cult icon by the mimetic repetition of the events that constitute Buddhahood. A second distinctive feature is the participation in the evening-long ritual by renowned, charismatic monks who embody in their person and story the mystical powers of mind and consciousness that the Buddha himself achieved during the night of his awakening. These monks function as living Buddha surrogates who, through the medium of the various performative mechanisms of the consecration ritual, transfer their extraordinary qualities into the Buddha image. Because of their spiritual attainments they represent a meditation or jhānic body in the likeness of the Buddha himself (*nimmita-buddha*). In the *buddhābhiseka,* the image becomes that same likeness.

The centrality of the story of Sakyamuni Buddha's enlightenment in the northern Thai *buddhābhiseka* ritual is consistent with the Theravāda focus on the historical Buddha rather than the cosmological or mythological Buddhas common to Mahāyāna and Tantrayāna traditions. This focus does not disregard the Buddhological complexity of the Theravāda tradition in Thailand; however, ample support for the prominence of the historical Buddha is found in the abundance of northern Thai legendary lives of the Buddha that include vernacular *jātaka* tales and chronicles (*tamnān*). This extensive literary tradition of Buddha narratives forms the core of northern Thai devotional sensibility, especially stories that connect the living Buddha with his material signs. The Buddha's visits to northern Thailand create a *buddha-desa* (Buddha-land), a presence guaranteed by relics, images, footprints, and other reminders foretold in these Buddha histories (Thai, *phuttha tamnān*).[89] The conspicuous role of the Buddha story in the northern Thai image consecration ritual is both logically consistent with the Theravāda celebration of the Buddha Gotama and in harmony with northern Thai devotional sentiment.

This narrative construction of the Buddha's presence in his image is supported in recent work by Juliane Schober on the Mahāmuni image in Mandalay and Robert L. Brown on *jātaka* iconography. Schober sees the Mahāmuni image as an iconic and ritual continuation of the Buddha biography.[90] When linked to the biography of the Buddha, the legend of the construction of the Mahāmuni image authenticates and perpetuates the sacred biography of the Blessed One. Thus, for Schober, "the rituals and myths of the Mahāmuni . . . accomplish two aims simultaneously: they place local contexts and actors within a universal Buddhist cosmology, and they locate a continuing biography of the Buddha in . . . Arakan and Upper Burma."[91]

In his analysis of bas-relief *jātaka* scenes at Bhārhut and Sāñcī and of the Ajaṇṭā paintings, Robert L. Brown argues that these visual narratives were not meant to be read linearly but iconically. Taking a clue from Ajaṇṭā Cave 16 with its large seated Buddha image referred to by an inscription as a "temple with a Buddha inside," Brown interprets the wall paintings of the *jātaka*s and scenes from the Buddha's life as hypostasizing the presence of the Blessed One: "They are there to indicate, to make 'actual,' the Buddha through his life and history . . . and perhaps are best seen as allowing the Buddha through his 'history' to participate with the monks and lay worshipers."[92] I make a similar claim about the nature of the Thai *wat,* the site of most devotional activities. With a larger than life size Buddha image on a high altar at the far end and representative murals from the Buddha's life and the ten *jātakas* on the two side walls, the preaching hall (*wihān*) is regarded as the abode or dwelling place of the Buddha. The large size of the *wihān* and its rectangular shape allow ample space for public ceremonies that commonly include listening to sermons, traditionally based on *jātaka* stories and Buddha histories (*tamnān*). The *wihān* as a physical structure and ritual space can be read as a narrative edifice that brings devotees into a personal relationship with the person of the Buddha and his story manifested quintessentially in his icon.

Saints' lives, apocryphal or historical, are an essential feature of popular Buddhist devotionalism as is the reverence for living, charismatic, holy monks. Like the Buddha, holy monks are represented by their story, their physical presence when alive, and their relics and consecrated images if deceased. These living monk-saints bring to the *buddhābhiseka* the charisma of their *pāramī* that through the performative power of the ritual is infused into the newly consecrated image. Their presence and the well-known stories of their spiritual achievement enliven the image in the same manner as the Buddha story that is chanted and preached through this recapitulation of the night of the Buddha's enlightenment. All who crowd the consecration hall become participants in *le grand narré* made contemporaneous through the mimetic reenactment of the Buddha story and the presence of living saints who, like the icon itself, demonstrate Buddha *pāramī* by their lives.

# APPENDIX 8.1

## HINDU OR BUDDHIST?

Even though Hindu theism differs substantially from Indian Buddhism, the Hindu consecration (*pratiṣṭha*) of deity images, temples, and other sacred objects shares commonalities with Buddhism. Within their respective worldviews, both Hindu and Buddhist consecration rituals utilize the polarities of absence and presence, formlessness and form, universal and particular, both philosophically and in practice. For both traditions, the ritual for infusing life into the image (*prāṇapratiṣṭha*) makes an image into a cult icon, an object of devotion worthy of worship.[93] In both Hinduism and Buddhism the mental-spiritual power of the ritualist/priest/*ācariya* complements various ritual strategies for invoking the "omnipresent divine" and infusing it into material representations.[94] Furthermore, in both traditions rituals for bringing an image to life illumine the fundamental meaning of the devotional cultus.[95] Hindu *pratiṣṭha* "charge[s] a physical object with spiritual presence, or change[s] its perceived nature in such a way so that is 'seen' thenceforth after its sanctification as essentially different from . . . before its consecration."[96] After *pratiṣṭha* the image is the deity, not merely a symbol of it.[97] In referring to the Śrīvaiṣṇava tradition, Vasudha Narayan observes, "the image [becomes] an actual and real manifestation of the deity, neither lesser than nor a symbol of other forms [of Viṣṇu]. It is wholly and completely God, though it does not exhaust his essence."[98] Jan Gonda, however, argues that while *some* Hindus believe that through the rite of consecration an image becomes a container of life and supernormal power, others—and in his view the right view—hold that "the ceremony merely serves to ennoble the worshiper, to realize . . . God's presence in the image, so that it becomes an effectual means of contact between the divinity and himself."[99]

Complex Hindu consecration rituals extend over several days. The *Vimānārcanakalpa* of the Vaikhānasa school of ritual practice requires twenty-five steps;[100] the *Kapiñjala-saṃhita* of the Pañcarātra tradition summarizes a program of sixteen discrete steps;[101] and the *Kāmikāgama* of the Śaiva Siddhānta includes twenty-two constituent rites.[102] Richard H. Davis divides the Śaiva Siddhānta rites into five stages: selecting materials and fabricating the image following precise iconographic and iconometric guidelines together with the recitation of *mantra*s that invoke the deity into the image; the initial awakening or eye opening in which the priest uses a golden needle to draw the outlines of Śiva's three eyes; the sculptor opens the eyes with a diamond needle and the priest anoints the image's eyes with unguents, presents it with offerings, bathes, and adorns it; circumambulating the image around the village and then bathing it again to further purify it; decorating a pavilion and installing the image there, then followed by a final water affusion or *abhiṣeka*.[103]

The sixteen steps of the Pañcarātra consecration tradition described in the *Kapiñjala-saṃhita* take place over a three-day period. The preliminary rites of the first day include preparing a pavilion and fire-pits for the *homa* rituals and other purification rites using water and grain. An elaborate ritual bath marks the second day. Using cleansing liquids (milk, curds, ghee, honey, and earth) the priest touches various parts of the image's body and opens its eyes. The image is placed on a bed of grain, honored with sandalwood paste and flowers, and covered with a cloth, after which fire sacrifices are performed inviting the forms of Viṣṇu and other deities to enter a series of pots. After invoking the cosmic person (*puruṣa*) and performing additional fire sacrifices, the priest touches parts of the image to infuse them with the qualities of *jīva, prakṛti, buddhi* while invoking breath (*prāṇa*) and bringing the image to life. The ceremony concludes on the third day with the purification of the temple precincts and the installation of the image in the *sanctum sanctorum.*[104]

Opening the eyes of the image occurs as the third step in the Vaikhānasa deity image consecration. It is commonly understood that with this ritual act the image ceases to be simply a material object and has begun the process of becoming fully divine. By the conclusion of the ceremony the image has become a god, fit to receive offerings and graciously bestow blessings.[105] Following ceremonies of cleansing and purification (*bimbaśuddhi*), the *ācariya* summons Viṣṇu and his entourage to enter a series of water pots prepared for this purpose. The *pratiṣṭha* is fully consummated when Viṣṇu, immanent in the water, is infused into the image through the *abhiśeka.*[106]

In her study of Hindu images and rituals of image consecration Joanne Punzo Waghorne concludes that the "embodiment of divinity" is the central feature not only of Hinduism but to the study of all religions.[107] Although the discrete details of image consecration ceremonies in Buddhism and Hinduism point to substantial differences in worldview and ritual performance, an examination of these rituals in several Buddhist traditions, as well as Hinduism, supports Wanghorne's position that rituals of consecration animate material representations with a reality that is ultimately beyond form, thereby making that reality accessible to human beings. When these signs cease to embody this reality, they revert to mere symbols, rather than—in the Buddhist case—being a mirror of the *dhamma.*

# EPILOGUE:

## "IF YOU MEET THE BUDDHA, KILL HIM!"

The religion of practical benefits permeates and upholds the religious tradition.[1]

The following announcement appeared in the January 27, 1999, issue of *Thai Rath,* Thailand's largest national newspaper:

**King Taksin Savior of the Nation Amulet**

The Maw Sukhā Association, Bān Bu'ng district, Chonburi Province has designated Sunday, January 31, 2542 B.E. [1999 C.E.] at 3:39 P.M. as the auspicious day for casting the "King Taksin Savior of the Nation Amulet (Phra Kring)."[2] Luang Pho Sawat[3] will lead the ceremony which will include offerings to the spirit of King Taksin to ask permission to make the amulet, and the consecration of gold leaf squares with 108 *yantra*s written on them along with others with 14 magic spells that will be used to make the "hearts" (Thai, *hua chai*) of the Phra Krings to enhance their miraculous power.

The King Taksin Savior of the Nation Amulet was commissioned by Luang Pho Sawat to celebrate and honor the wisdom of King Taksin who freed the Thais from the Burmese, to provide a powerful, auspicious talisman infused with the power of the Buddha especially for wealth and good fortune, and to increase the courage, strength, and industriousness necessary to overcome economic threats and dangers following the example of the victorious King Taksin who successfully defended the nation.

The Maw Sukhā Association is sponsoring the casting of the King Taksin Savior of the Nation Amulet in honor of Luang Pho Sawat's 92nd birthday. The amulets to be cast include 92 in gold at a price of 29,999 baht [$850], 1,492 in silver at 900 baht [$25], 1,292 in quality gold alloy at 1,299 baht [$37], 2,492 in gold finish at 300 baht [$8], 999 in a metal alloy at 300 baht [$8], 592 antiqued amulets three inches wide at 699 baht [$20], 592 gold plate amulets three inches wide at 999 baht [$28], 592 blackened Phra Saṅgkajjāi of wealth three inches wide at 699 baht [$20], 592 gold-finished Phra Saṅgkhajjāi of wealth three inches wide at 999 [$28], 999 good luck gold finished rabbits at 100 baht [$3] [1999 was the year of the rabbit.]

Everyone who comes will receive a free lucky rabbit charm that will help to ease economic distress.[4]

A few months earlier, an editorial by Sanitsuda Ekachai, noted social critic and assistant editor of the *Bangkok Post*, contained these observations:

> The latest trend in the world of charms is amulets made of mammoth ivory. In an open marketing blitz, the jewelry company importing the fossilized ivory to produce the charms recently placed a half-page advertisement in the newspapers. In one corner is a replica of an ivory coin bearing the image of King Chulalongkorn, who posthumously has become the god of wealth for today's Thai entrepreneurs. On the back of the coin is a yantra, an ancient symbol believed to ward off danger. In another corner is a photograph of Luang Por Uttama, a well-known elderly monk, who has sanctified the coins with magical powers. The background color is glowing saffron, the same as monks' sacred robes. Strengthens charisma and powers, proclaims the banner.
>
> The ad reveals how Thailand's capitalist spirit blends so well with old world beliefs in supernatural powers. And how Buddha's sons have become the tools of commercializing Buddhism. Elephants also are a national symbol of ancient glory. In a society where we are constantly seeking superlatives to reassure ourselves of grandeur, who can resist the idea of owning the ivory of the world's biggest and oldest elephants? In days past, charms usually boasted only one particular magical power, such as to ward off danger or attract the opposite sex. That's no longer the case. Today's talismans must offer a hodge-podge of magic, like the 7-Eleven one-stop-shop around the corner.
>
> Responding to clients' varied needs, the anti-harm symbol on the coin offers safety while the mammoth ivory gives a sense of sanctity and uniqueness. The image of King Chulalongkorn, apart from promising business success, helps the coin owners feel closer to the center of prestige and status. The monk's blessing, meanwhile, makes them feel it's all right for Buddhists to turn a deaf ear to Buddha's teaching on self-reliance. Monks used to monopolize amulet-making, but with big money available in the amulet business, they are being edged out. They are used only as ritual performers and thus receive only the crumbs of the profits.[5]

The newspaper announcement and editorial offer sharply contrasting attitudes toward the cult of images and other material representations of the Buddha, holy monks, gods, and kings that has come to dominate the contemporary religious ethos of the country.[6] The cult of King Rāmā V (Chulalongkorn), which originated at the equestrian statue of the king in front the national parliament building in Bangkok, has mutated into home and restaurant shrines and shopping center shops specializing in

Rāmā V memorabilia similar to stores selling traditional religious paraphernalia. The veneration of Rāmā V has spawned a more broadly based cult of other royal images in cities throughout the country: the statue of Queen Cāma in Lamphūn, of King Mangrai in Chiang Rai, and the more politically potent promotion of the veneration of the current king, Bhumiphol, Rāmā IX.

The cult of material signs of charismatic monks both living and deceased—relics, amulets, images—surpasses even those of royal images and icons. Popular religious magazines are filled with testimonials of the miraculous power of material representations of highly revered monks and tout the market value of particularly potent amulets and images. The most popular amulets—Phra Rod, Phra Somdet, Phra Nāng Phyā, Phra Sum Ko, Phra Phong Suphan—cost several hundred thousand baht, even though technically amulets are not "bought" (Thai, *s'u*), but only "rented" (*chaw*).[7] Trade in religious objects is reputed to have a nationwide commercial value second only to real estate. The economic importance of the cult of charismatic monks has prompted Peter Jackson to label it Thailand's new "prosperity religion" that flourished during the economic boom days of the 1980s and early 1990s.[8] Although the contemporary cult of amulets and images reflects the current economic and social atmosphere, the practice is not new to Thai Buddhism.

The modern amulet cult in Thailand may trace its origin to the reign of King Mongkut (1851–68) with influence from Tantric ritual practice. Although the cult today may appear modern, its roots are ancient, as evidenced by the discovery of small embossed, clay votive tablets and *dhāraṇī* seals at Nālandā, Bodhgayā, and other holy Buddhist sites in India.[9] From as early as the Mon-Dvāravatī period (ca. sixth–thirteenth centuries), large numbers of votive tablets have been found throughout Thailand. In the Sukhōthai kingdom (ca. 1240–1438) terra-cotta and metal votive tablets were often "placed in clay or ceramic containers together with other sacred objects such as relics and Buddha images, and laid in the relic chamber of a stūpa."[10]

The tension seen in contemporary Thai Buddhism between those who venerate images, amulets, and relics for their magical power and those who either reject outright or regard with skepticism such belief and practice is found in every age of Buddhism. Even though the *Mahāparinibbāna Sutta* legitimates the cult of the Buddha's bodily relics and pilgrimage to the places of the Blessed One's birth, awakening, first teaching, and death (D II.141), this motif is balanced by the admonition that the person of the Buddha is not to be worshiped. After the Buddha instructs Ānanda that his *parinibbāna* is without marks, he teaches the *bhikkhus* that following his death they should take refuge only in the *dhamma* (D II.100), and that the proper way to honor the *tathāgata* is by practicing the *dhamma*

(D II.138), not by paying homage with flags, flowers, and so on. I use as the title of this epilogue the Zen *kōan,* "If you meet the Buddha kill him!," as an example from Buddhist teaching and practice that illustrates opposition to the veneration of Buddha images and other material signs of the *tathāgata* and belief in their supernatural powers.

As a counterpoint to this study of the ritual empowerment and veneration of the Buddha image, this epilogue gives voice to a selected group of contemporary Thai critics of these practices. The Thai preoccupation with the supernatural, especially the cult of images and amulets that has burgeoned in recent years, has produced a strong negative reaction among urban, educated, reformist monks and laity. Some critics point out the cult's crass commercialism while others see it as a profanation of authentic Buddhism; however, all critics share a common suspicion of magical and supernatural practices ranging from astrology to the cult of relics and material icons.[11] Here I shall focus on three notable critical appraisals: P. A. Payutto's (Phra Dhammapiṭaka) critique of the cult of the magical and supernatural; Bhikkhu Buddhadāsa's interpretation of the Buddha and Buddha images; and the radical iconoclasm of Phra Bodhirak's controversial Santi Asok movement. Each occupies a distinctive niche in the increasingly pluralistic world of Thai Buddhism. As the foremost scholar in the *saṅgha,* Payutto represents a normative Thai Theravāda position; Buddhadāsa's innovative interpretation of the *dhamma* has been a major influence on contemporary reform Buddhists, both lay and clerical; and the Santi Asok movement, a middle-class, utopian, sectarian group on the periphery of Thai Buddhism, is noted for its critical, iconoclastic posture toward mainstream Thai Buddhism in general and magical cults in particular.

## P. A. Payutto (Phra Dhammapiṭaka)[12]

Bhikkhu P. A. Payutto, regarded as the dean of monastic scholars in the Thai *saṅgha,* was ordained a novice monk in 1950 at age eleven and by 1961 had passed the ninth and highest level of Pāli studies. The following year he graduated from Mahāchulālongkorn Buddhist University at the top of his class and in 1964 was appointed as deputy secretary-general of the university, a position he held until 1974. That same year he resigned from a two-year tenure as the abbot of Wat Phra Phirain in Bangkok in order to devote himself full-time to scholarly work. The magnitude and profundity of his scholarship is unrivaled among Thai Buddhist scholars of his generation. The first edition of his magnum opus, *Buddhadhamma,* was published in 1971 and the 1986 version of the book "is widely viewed as the most significant Thai contribution to Buddhist scholarship in the last two hundred years."[13] Payutto has produced two Pāli dictionaries of major significance and enduring value, and he served as an editor of the newest edition of the Thai Pāli *tipiṭaka* and the Mahidol University CD-ROM Pāli canon. In addition, his numerous books and essays embrace a wide variety of subjects, including Buddhist education and Buddhism and science.

Payutto's scholarship emphasizes thoughtful, engaged attention (*yoniso-manasikāra*) over against mental laziness, carelessness, and inattention (*pramāda*).[14] It is from the perspective of sustained investigation and attentive understanding that he criticizes blind faith in the miraculous power of spirits, deities, sacred objects such as images and amulets, and magical rituals believed to offer protection and guarantee good fortune. Payutto acknowledges that recent events, in particular the 1997 economic crisis, have increased Thai obsession with magical practices;[15] however, he bases his criticism of the veneration of sacred objects and personified external powers in the rationality of the Buddhist worldview and the Buddha's insistence on self-reliant empirical investigation to discover the true nature of things.

In response to the upsurge of magical cults in Thailand, Payutto has been invited to express his opinion on magic, occultism, astrology, and the veneration of amulets. Of particular interest are a 1993 interview and a 1997 rains retreat talk.[16] The former, printed under the title, *Sing Saksit, Devakru't, Pāthihān* (Sacred Objects, Efficacious Deities, and Miracles), was his response to the question: "there seem to be two positions today: one that believes Buddhism means teaching the truth (*sacca-dhamma*); the other that miraculous powers are a useful strategy and point to the time of the Buddha when *arahant*s used miracles to convince people. What is your opinion on this matter?"[17] An abbreviated, free translation of Payutto's published response follows.

## *Sacred Objects, Efficacious Deities, and Miracles*

P. A. PAYUTTO

This is a very uncertain time. If Buddhism isn't practiced correctly, its basic principles will be eroded and at the same time it will have a negative impact on Thai society. We must adhere to the basic principles of Buddhism.

During the time of the Buddha, people believed that *arahant*s had miraculous powers. The Buddha combated this belief. There's a paradox here, however. The Buddha used miraculous power (*iddhi*) to overturn *iddhi*. But it's important to keep in mind that after the Buddha did this he didn't continue using *iddhi*. After the Buddha defeated those who used *iddhi*, they abandoned its use and practiced the miracle of the Buddha's instruction. When they practiced it they encountered the truth, namely, the cessation of *dukkha,* which is the biggest miracle of all. This is the first principle that we must keep in mind.

Today, people see great value in miracles (*iddhi-riddhi-pāṭihāriya*). The miraculous and magical are becoming increasingly popular. We must adhere to the Buddha's principle of using *iddhi* to overturn *iddhi* rather than praising *iddhi* and reveling in it. When someone continues in this erroneous practice, we should correct this mistake and find the means to lead him in the correct way. In this case we appeal to the Buddhist principle that people develop and thrive through moral virtue (*sīla*), concentrated attention (*samādhi*), and wisdom (*paññā*). It's difficult to convince someone who's fixated on *iddhi* to move beyond it. We also have to realize that people are at different stages of moral and intellectual development and act accordingly. It's very difficult to influence the great majority of people who only have a faint understanding of the *dhamma.*

The second issue is the ability of the teacher. The Buddha's method for dealing with *iddhi* was to remove the dust from people's eyes so that they could see what the Buddha intended. This is difficult. We must be clear about our own purpose. If one uses the cult of deities, the miraculous and magical, in order to draw a person from attachment to such practices, and uses the principles of Buddhism to enter into the *dhamma,* then it's not objectionable. But, if such things are used in a way that deepens one's attachment so that one becomes completely enamored by them, then these practices are unacceptable.

One must carefully scrutinize to see whether or not magical practices contradict the principles of Buddhism. There are three principles to keep in mind. The first is *kamma,* the principle of cause and effect, namely, that results come from action. The principle of cause and effect—that good results come from good actions and vice versa—is a rational way to proceed. Belief in the miraculous is based in magic, a means to nurture and appease the spirits (Thai, *khwan*), and arises from a person lacking the strength of mind and reason. Clearly, magical practices based in a fatalistic belief that things are in the hands of the gods or the spirits, and that by appeasing them one can sit idly by doing nothing, contradicts the principle of *kamma.* This is destructive to the individual, society, and to Buddhism. But, if these practices actually promote confidence and effort to act for the good, rather than lack of awareness and neglect (*pramāda*), then they're useful.

The second principle is the emphasis on education, training, and the development of one's self. The reason for ordaining as a monk is to train oneself but, beyond that, Buddhism holds that everyone has the responsibility to develop and improve one's behavior, conduct, mind, and knowledge. If people are so absorbed in the miraculous and magical that they cease trying to improve themselves in body and mind, then the magical and miraculous must be rejected. But if they are used as a bridge to right action and do not inhibit self-development in the areas of *sīla, samādhi,* and *paññā,* then they are acceptable. We must distinguish between inner development and external agency, and also between attributing causes to external, magical forces versus understanding them in terms of the principle of cause and effect. Because the Buddha intended that we should develop mature minds and understanding, he did not promote belief in miraculous powers that would encourage people to place their hope in external objects for consolation.

People vary in their physical and mental abilities. In the midst of day-to-day dangers, struggles, and an uncertain future, it's understandable that some turn off their minds and turn to magic. This lack of mindful awareness may produce an even greater danger; however, if such beliefs do not contradict the laws of *kamma,* and magical practices are not inconsistent with the principles of education, they may be of some temporary value to relieve anxiety. Eventually they must be rejected, however. We need to scrutinize ourselves and to help others pursue the right path.

The third tenet is to understand the meaning of the supernatural or sacred power (*saksit*). Buddhism arose at a time when belief in the supernatural was widespread. This included the foolish belief in many gods with miraculous, protective powers. All that was necessary was to appease the gods through propitiatory offerings. In reality, their supernatural powers reflected the three *kilesa*s—greed, anger, and delusion. The gods were seen as angry, quarrelsome, and destructive deities who injured others. In images they were depicted as erotic, cruel, and fierce with multiple heads, eyes, and arms carrying all kinds of weapons. Their supernatural power derived from *kilesa.* However, Buddhism arose and offered a challenge: it associated sacred power with wisdom (*paññā*) and virtue (*guṇa-dhamma*). In Buddhism the supernatural (*saksit*) in the highest sense refers to purity (*parisuddha*), wisdom (*paññā*), and virtue. The Buddha is depicted in images as a human being, not displaying various supernatural powers but embodying the *dhamma,* equanimity, and lovingkindness—as one who inspires contentedness, happiness, and wisdom. To respect the supernatural in the Buddhist sense means to overcome the mental and moral defilements (*kilesa*) of greed, anger, and delusion; to understand the natural law of causality that we all can perceive; and to act virtuously and compassionately.

We must move beyond an understanding of the supernatural associated with externalized gods—Viṣnu, Śiva, Indra, Brahmā, and so forth—who personify the power of grasping, conceit, and mental defilements, appealing to them for help. We should turn instead to the Triple Gem and be firm in the supernal qualities of the Buddha, the *dhamma,* and the *saṅgha,* and develop moral virtue according to the principle of *kamma.* We should strive to improve ourselves following the sound principles of training and education, of *sīla, samādhi,* and *paññā.* If the supernatural is understood in this way, consistent with the principles of *kamma* and sound training aimed at overcoming mental and moral defilements and the achievement of purity, understanding, and compassion, then the supernatural is consistent with the teachings of Buddhism. Otherwise, teachings and practices regarding the supernatural, miraculous, and magical should be rejected.

• • • • •

As the above essay makes clear, despite his criticisms, Payutto holds the view that magical practices may have an *instrumental justification* if they lead to positive actions in terms of the Buddhist principle of cause and effect, or if they have a short-term therapeutic value. He approves only of "instructional miracles" that lead Thai Buddhists to wisdom and understanding and promote a self-reliant investigation of the truth.

## Buddhadāsa Bhikkhu[18]

Phra Dhammakosāchān, better known by his self-appointed monastic name Buddhadāsa Bhikkhu (Servant of the Buddha), was one of the most influential Thai monks of the twentieth century. Born on May 21, 1906, as Nguam Panich, he was ordained in 1926. By 1928 he had passed the third and final level of the monastic Dhamma curriculum and was invited to teach at the Wat Boromathāt monastery in Chaiya. After spending two years in Bangkok (1930–32) studying Pāli, Buddhadāsa became disenchanted with rote learning, distracted by the noise of the city, and dismayed by the lax behavior of Bangkok monks. In the spring of 1932, the year Thailand changed from an absolute to a constitutional monarchy, he returned to Chaiya, where shortly thereafter he established a forest monastery, Suan Mokkhabalārāma (The Garden of Empowering Liberation), known as Suan Mokkh. Buddhadāsa swiftly acquired a reputation for keen intellectual prowess, teaching ability, and innovative interpretation of Theravāda doctrine. His plain language unencumbered with technical monastic jargon and his rational, demythologized interpretation of Buddhist teachings appealed to the new urban elites. Suan Mokkh grew and expanded as Buddhadāsa's fame as a *dhamma* teacher spread, and even after his death in 1993 it continues as a center of Buddhist practice in the tradition of its founder.

Buddhadāsa's censure of the cult of amulets and images differs from Payutto's in both technique and substance. In contrast to Payutto, whose criticism of the cult of images and amulets is grounded in the principle of cause and effect and the mental attitude of thoughtful investigation and wise attention, Buddhadāsa takes a Buddhological approach to the problem. He demythologizes the Buddha and deconstructs veneration of the Buddha as a cult object in order to awaken his Thai audiences from their ignorant, "dogmatic slumbers." To venerate a Buddha image as though the historical Buddha were actually present totally misconstrues the true nature of the Buddha. Only when one attains the same understanding of reality the Buddha achieved does one then truly *see* the Buddha. In this sense, the Buddha is within us, not an external figure or force to be worshiped.[19] This distinctive Buddhological perspective underlies Buddhadāsa's critique of popular Thai devotional attitudes and practices.

### *Who Sees Me Sees the* Dhamma

Buddhist rituals in Thailand usually begin by taking refuge in the Buddha, the *dhamma,* and the *saṅgha.* In his 1971 Māgha Pūjā talk at Wat Suan Mokkha, Buddhadāsa provoked his audience to reconsider the meaning of going to the Buddha for refuge as follows: "Most Buddhists repeat the formula, *Buddhaṃ saranaṃ gacchāmi,* in parrot-like fashion without really meaning it or because they believe that it produces merit. The first is stupid; the second is false."[20] He then interprets "going to" the Buddha using the Thai terms *thu'ng* (attain) and *thū'* (abide in): "If we vow that we are going to attain and to abide in the Buddha, it means that we attain and abide in the Buddha in our heart and mind at every moment."[21] "Going for refuge to the Buddha expecting a boon or as an act of merit-making cannot relieve suffering (*dukkha*). Only when our minds are fully aware (*satipaññā*) of the Buddha's presence, are we then able to overcome suffering."[22]

Buddhadāsa's statement regarding attaining and abiding in the Buddha should not be read as a metaphysical claim. The Buddha, in his view, is not present as a universal Buddha body (*buddhakāya*), but as the *dhamma-vinaya.* "Whoever sees me [the Buddha] sees the *dhamma;* whoever sees the *dhamma* sees me [the Buddha]." This canonical statement attributed to the Buddha stands at the very core of Buddhadāsa's understanding of the meaning and significance of the person of *tathāgata.* To know the Buddha, indeed, to "be with" the Buddha, is to know and to be with the *dhamma.* The real Buddha, claims Buddhadāsa, speaks in terms of the *dhamma* (*dhammādhiṭṭhāna*).[23] The true character, quality, or essence (*guṇasampatti*) of the Buddha is the *dhamma.*[24] To attain and abide in the Buddha, therefore, means to attain and abide in the *dhamma.*

Buddhadāsa explains the relationship between the Buddha and the *dhamma* in terms of the Buddha's mind or consciousness (*citta*), and the Buddha's inherent quality or nature (*guṇa*). Because the Buddha perceived the *dhamma* by his mind or *citta,* the saying, "to see the Buddha is to see the *dhamma,*" means that when one sees the *dhamma,* one sees with the mind of the Buddha. *Citta,* in this usage, connotes what is essentially or truly the Buddha, for what defines the Buddha, namely, his awakening, is a matter of mind or consciousness. To venerate the Buddha means, for Buddhadāsa, to have achieved the Buddha's understanding of the *dhamma.*

At his *nibbāna* the Buddha embodied the essential quality of the *dhamma.* Buddhadāsa understands this quality to be constituted by purity (*parisuddhiguṇa*), tranquillity (*santiguṇa*), and wisdom (*paññāguṇa*).[25] To truly attain and abide in the Buddha, therefore, is to understand the *dhamma* with purity, tranquillity, and wisdom. We achieve this condition when we truly comprehend the four noble truths and, thereby, overcome depravity (*kilesa*). For most of us this experience is brief, often momentary. Only with the attainment of arahantship does it become a permanent state of being.[26]

## *Everyday Language/*Dhamma *Language*

The second major principle that informs Buddhadāsa's views about the nature of the Buddha is his distinction between two levels of language and, hence, two levels of understanding: conventional or ordinary language and truth or *dhamma* language (Thai, *phāsā khon/phāsā tham*).[27] For Buddhadāsa all particular representations of the Buddha, even the Buddha as a historical person, are limited to the conventional or ordinary level:

> As you know, the Buddha in everyday language refers to the historical Enlightened Being, Gotama Buddha. It refers to a physical man of flesh and bone who was born in India over two thousand years ago, died, and was cremated. This is the meaning of the Buddha in everyday language. Considered in terms of *dhamma* language, however, the word Buddha refers to the truth that the historical Buddha realized and taught, the *dhamma* itself. . . . Now the *dhamma* is something intangible. It is not something physical, certainly not flesh and bone. Yet the Buddha said it is one and the same as the Enlightened One. Anyone who fails to see the *dhamma* cannot be said to have seen the Enlightened One. Thus, in *dhamma* language the Buddha is one and the same as that Truth by which he became the Buddha, and anyone who sees the Truth can be said to have seen the true Buddha. . . .

> Again the Buddha said, "The *dhamma* and the *vinaya* which I have proclaimed . . . these shall be your teacher when I have passed away." So the real Buddha has not passed away, has not ceased to exist. What ceased to exist was just the physical body, the outer shell. The real teacher, that is, the *dhamma-vinaya,* is still with us. This is the meaning of the word Buddha in *dhamma* language.[28]

Buddhadāsa's distinction between *phāsā tham* and *phāsā khon* does not necessarily mean an outright rejection of representations of the Buddha either as a historical person or material signs such as Buddha images. Depending on the insight or mind of the viewer they may lead one to a deeper level of understanding. Suan Mokkh graphically illustrates this point of view. Mural depictions of the Buddha appear on the walls of the spiritual theater and Buddha images are found in the outdoor *dhamma* sanctuary for the purpose of promoting a deeper insight into the nature of the Buddha and the *dhamma.* Thus, while Buddhadāsa rejects a naïve, uninformed belief in representations of the Buddha, like Payutto he acknowledges that they may serve a positive function.

Despite his relative tolerance toward iconographic depictions of the Buddha, Buddhadāsa roundly criticizes the conventional Thai attitudes toward their popularity: "If we understand the Buddha only as a historical person who lived in India more than 2000 years ago, or as a statue in a temple, or as an amulet around our neck, there is no way that this Buddha can abide in our heart and mind or that we can become the Buddha."[29] Buddhadāsa's rhetorical method often resembles that of the Zen master he praised in a 1989 Visākha Pūjā talk at Suan Mokkh who likened the Buddha to horse manure: "In Thailand we're afraid to make such a statement for fear of offending someone. However, it points to a profound truth, namely, that everything is conditioned whether it's a beautiful lotus or horse shit."[30]

He directs his sharpest attack against the many magical beliefs and practices surrounding relics, amulets, images, and shamanistic invocations of the spirit of the Buddha. He ridicules those who pray to Buddha images for a new car or having a child as though the image were possessed by the Buddha's spirit or ghost (Thai, *phī*),[31] and he has little regard for the common practice among Thai Buddhists of wearing Buddha amulets in the belief that they offer protection from danger or bad luck. Further, he directs sarcastic barbs at the many popular religious magazines that print stories of the miraculous powers of various material representations of the Buddha and at those who invoke the Buddha's presence at seances: "It's laughable if they say that they invite the spirit of the Buddha from Tāvatiṃsa Heaven, and it's totally absurd to claim that the spirit of the Buddha can return from *nibbāna!*"[32]

## Phra Bodhirak and Santi Asok

Santi Asok, a utopian, communalistic movement on the margins of the Thai Buddhist mainstream, was founded in the early 1970s by Phra Bodhirak. Born on June 5, 1934, in Sisaket, northeastern Thailand as Monkol Rakpong, he later changed his name to Rak Rakpong. After enjoying a successful career as a movie producer, TV host, and songwriter, at age thirty-six he abruptly changed his lifestyle. He gave away his house and most of his belongings to family and friends, dressed simply, and walked barefoot. Eventually he resigned from his job, feeling with that act he was "free from any form."[33] Shortly thereafter, on January 27, 1970, Bodhirak had a profound mystical experience—"a brilliant flash occurred within me, a brightness, openness, and detachment which could not be explained in human terms. I knew only that my life opened up before me and that the whole world seemed to be revealed."[34] He interpreted the experience as a revelation of the truth of the Buddha's *dhamma*.

On November 7, 1970, he was ordained a Thammayut monk, but from the beginning his monastic career was controversial. On the basis of his revelation he claimed to be a once-returner (*ariya sakadāgāmin*) and established a center near Nakorn Pathom that he called Asoka's Land (Dan Asok). He resigned his Thammayut ordination and was reordained in the Mahānikai order, but on August 6, 1975, he severed all ties with both national orders of the Thai *saṅgha*. Bodhirak continued to establish "People of Asok" branches in Bangkok, Sisaket, and Nakorn Sawan. The movement grew rapidly. By 1974 it numbered more than 10,000 core members with thousands more attending Santi Asok meetings. The support of Major General Chamlong Srimuang, then the mayor of Bangkok and later an MP with the Phalang Dhamma (Power of Dhamma) Party associated with Santi Asok, gave the movement a high visibility.[35]

Bodhirak's outspoken criticism of mainstream Buddhism, corruption and immorality in the *saṅgha,* politics, and society together with the possibility that Santi Asok might gain political power through the Phalang Dhamma Party, produced sharp negative reactions from liberal reformers who considered Bodhirak too authoritarian and moralistic, and from the conservative *saṅgha* hierarchy who were distressed by his unorthodoxy, defiance of national *saṅgha* law, and unauthorized claims to spiritual attainment. Bodhirak's effrontery led the Supreme Sangha Council to defrock him in November 1988. All attempts to work out a compromise failed and on May 9, 1989, he was expelled from the *saṅgha* by government decree. For several years Bodhirak's case was deliberated in the courts but eventually the decision was upheld and the case closed in December 1995. Bodhirak still leads a monastic lifestyle, even though under *saṅgha* law he is not officially recognized as a monk.

From the beginning Santi Asok adopted an iconoclastic position vis-à-vis conventional Thai Buddhist practices, in particular, icon veneration. It rejects the ritualistic use of Buddha images, the widespread custom of wearing amulets, and the commerce in religious artifacts. Like Payutto and Buddhadāsa, Bodhirak finds Thai Buddhists' preoccupation with the cult of sacred objects to be contrary to the Buddha's teachings, but while Payutto's critique is grounded in the rationality of cause and effect, and Buddhadāsa's is formulated in terms of a sophisticated Buddhological epistemology, Santi Asok's rejection of the veneration of images grows out of its broad socio-cultural iconoclasm legitimated by its interpretation of early Buddhism.

Santi Asok rejects the use of Buddha images and amulets on the grounds that early Buddhism was essentially an ethical religion devoted to observance of the precepts (*sīla*) and the pursuit of the *dhamma.* A 1989 essay in the Santi Asok periodical, *Saeng Sūn* (Light of the Void), promotes the now contested view that images of the Buddha arose only under the influence of Greek theism in northwest India several hundred years after the Buddha's lifetime.[36] Citing the *Mahāparinibbāna Sutta,* the anonymous author contends that the Buddha authorized memorials to be erected at the locations where the Blessed One was born, reached enlightenment, preached the first sermon, attained *parinibbāna,* and for those worthy of *stūpa* commemoration including Buddhas, Paccekabuddhas, Arahants, and Dhammarājas, but that *cetiya*s enshrining the Buddha's bodily relics, relics of use, relics of association, and relics of the Buddha's *dhamma* occurred only after the Buddha's *parinibbāna.* Appealing to the authority of Pāli *sutta*s, the article states that the Buddha forbade images to be made of himself primarily because he was not to be venerated in the same manner that theistic religions worship gods and angels. Rather, the Buddha taught the way of *kammaniyama,* namely, that one's future for better or for ill depended solely on one's own deeds, and, that the miracle of overcoming suffering resulted from respecting the *dhamma,* not venerating objects to which miraculous powers are ascribed. The true representative or surrogate of the Buddha, then, is the *dhamma-vinaya,* not images, amulets, or relics.

A classical expression of Santi Asok's ethical iconoclasticism is the way the movement has transformed the traditional Thai amulet consecration ceremony (*phithī plūk sek phra*) from a ritual empowering objects to the moral empowerment of the Santi Asok community. Lay disciples, monks, and nuns gather together for an intensive training retreat that has none of the conventional magical, protective properties associated with amulet consecration. The thirteenth "consecration" held in 1989 involved nearly

2,500 participants.[37] During the week-long retreat everyone was required to attend *dhamma* lectures and follow a strict set of rules governing all aspects of personal behavior and group interaction. An article praising the powerful personal impact of the retreat on all the participants concluded with a gloss on the Thai words in the essay's title, "Genuine Buddha Image Consecration":

> *Plūk* (arouse). My life inscribed on a new path
> *Sek* (consecrate). My heart aflame with the truth of the *Dhamma*
> *Phra* (image). Polished with self-knowledge
> *Thāe* (genuine). Seeing the truth of the path (*magga*) and its fruit (*phala*)[38]

Payutto, Buddhadāsa, and Bodhirak offer counterpoints to the cult of Buddha images and the Buddha image consecration ritual at the center of devotional Buddhism in contemporary Thailand. Marshaling rational, Buddhological, ethical, and historical arguments, their critiques are contextual and distinctively modern; however, they are certainly not unique in the history of Buddhism. As the *Mahāparinibbāna Sutta* so aptly demonstrates, from its outset the Buddhist tradition has accommodated both those who venerate the person of the Buddha in material form and those who exclaim, "If you meet the Buddha, kill him!"

# NOTES

## CHAPTER 1. BUDDHA AND BUDDHA IMAGE

1. See Appendix 4.2 for the life story of the abbot of Wat Phraphutthabāt-tākphā.

2. The term *chedī* is derived from the Pāli, *cetiya*. Technically *cetiya* can refer to various types of structures related to veneration of reminders of the Buddha and Buddhist saints. In Thailand a *chedī* is a stepped, pyramidal structure or *stūpa* that most often functions as a reliquary. According to orthodox Theravāda classification there are four categories of *cetiya: dhātu-cetiya* containing bodily relics; *dhamma-cetiya* containing the *dhamma* in the form of palm leaf texts; *paribhoga-cetiya,* physical objects associated with the Buddha such as alms bowl, robe, footprint; and *uddesika-cetiya,* objects that function as substitutes for *paribhoga-cetiya,* such as replicas of footprints and bas-reliefs of great events in the life of the Buddha. Earlier classification was threefold, omitting *dhamma-cetiya*. See Alexander B. Griswold, *What Is a Buddha Image?* 2d ed. (Bangkok: Fine Arts Department, 2511 B.E./1968 C.E.), 14–15.

3. For a general discussion of images, see John S. Strong, "Images," in *The Encyclopedia of Religion* (New York: Macmillan, 1987), 5:97–104. See also David Freedberg, *The Power of Images: Studies in the History and Theory of Response* (Chicago: University of Chicago Press, 1989), whose extensive analysis incorporates various interpreters of modern Western art and culture, e.g., Benjamin, Bourdieu, Saussure, Goodman, Barthes.

4. Freedberg, *The Power of Images,* 234.

5. Ibid., 201.

6. Ibid., 28.

7. Ibid., 77, quoting Hans-Georg Gadamer, *Truth and Method,* trans. and ed. G. Barden and J. Cumming (New York: Seabury, 1975), 126.

8. Ibid., 25, quoting Nelson Goodman, *Languages of Art: An Approach to a Theory of Symbols,* 2d ed. (Indianapolis: Hackett, 1976), 259.

9. See Strong, "Images," 102.

10. Freedberg, *The Power of Images,* 5.

11. Ibid., 430, quoting Roland Barthes, *Camera Lucida: Reflections on Photography,* trans. R. Howard (New York: Hill and Wang, 1981), 119. "Immersion" here is Walter Benjamin's term but it appears analogous to Buddhist notions of contemplation and recollection.

12. Dorothy H. Fickle, *Images of the Buddha in Thailand* (Singapore: Oxford University Press, 1989), vii; Luang Boribal Buribhand and Alexander B. Griswold, *Thai Images of the Buddha,* 4th ed. (Bangkok: Fine Arts Department, 2514 B.E./ 1971 C.E.), 3.

13. In Thailand the *wat* functions as both a monastic dwelling place and a locus for lay religious observance. For a discussion of the structure of the *wat,* see Donald K. Swearer, *Wat Haripuñjaya: A Study of the Royal Temple of the Buddha's Relic, Lamphūn, Thailand* (Missoula, Mont.: Scholars, 1976).

14. A major contribution to this debate can be found in Gregory Schopen, "Archaeology and Protestant Presuppostions in the Study of Indian Buddhism," *History of Religions* 31, no. 1 (August 1991): 1–23. See also Charles Hallisey, "Roads Taken and Not Taken in the Study of Theravāda Buddhism," in *Curators of the Buddha: The Study of Buddhism Under Colonialism,* ed. Donald S. Lopez Jr. (Chicago: University of Chicago Press, 1995).

15. Richard Gombrich analyzes the dual constructions of the Buddha as human and god in terms of a cognitive, logically consistent, and canonically correct perspective versus an affective perspective which he sees as a consequence of the Buddha becoming the "victim of a personality cult." See Richard F. Gombrich, *Precept and Practice: Traditional Buddhism in the Rural Highlands of Ceylon* (Oxford: Clarendon, 1971), 82. Gombrich's extensive research on the construction of the Buddha in Sinhalese Buddhism, to which I am indebted, figures prominently in chapters 1, 5, and 8 of this work. In the above citation he does not escape from the tendency in modern scholarship to reify an "original Buddha(ism)" which, in this case, is associated with the terms *cognitive, logical,* and *canonical.*

16. See Susan L. Huntington, *The Art of Ancient India: Buddhist, Hindu, Jain* (New York: John Weatherhill, 1985), 70–73, and "Early Buddhist Art and the Theory of Aniconism," *Art Journal* 49, no. 4 (winter 1990): 401–8.

17. See Reginald Ray, *Buddhist Saints in India: A Study in Buddhist Values and Orientations* (New York: Oxford University Press, 1994).

18. *Papañcasūdanī* V. 73. Steven Collins, *Nirvana and Other Buddhist Felicities: Utopias of the Pali Imaginaire* (Cambridge: Cambridge University Press, 1998), 246.

19. Richard F. Gombrich, "Kosala-Bimba-Vaṇṇanā," in *Buddhism in Ceylon and Studies on Religious Syncretism in Buddhist Countries,* ed. Heinz Bechert (Göttingen: Abhandlungen der Akademie der Wissenschaften, 1978), 304–34. The date of the text is uncertain, although A. K. Coomaraswamy notes that a sixteenth- to seventeenth-century Sinhalese translation was recited prior to painting in the eyes of the Buddha image. My discussion of the text is based on Gombrich's article. For the Chiang Mai *jātaka* version, see Padmanabh S. Jaini, ed., *Paññāsa-Jātaka,* vol. 2 (London: Pali Text Society, 1983), and Padmanabh S. Jaini, trans., *Apocryphal Birth-Stories* (*Paññāsa-Jātaka*), vol. 2 (London: Pali Text Society, 1986). Jaini also discusses the text in "On the Buddha Image," in *Studies in Pāli Buddhism,* ed. A. K. Narain (Delhi: B. R. Publishing Corp., 1979), 183–87. He proposes that the writer(s) of the story may be perpetuating a tale whose literary life first appears in the early-fifth-century travel diary of the Chinese pilgrim, Faxian (Fa-hsien).

20. Gombrich, "Kosala-Bimba-Vaṇṇanā," 296.

21. Ibid., 298. Accounts of the Buddha image acting as the Buddha's animated double are not unusual. One early legend occurs in the *Dhammapada* commentary (DhA 14:2, "The Twin Miracle"), where the Buddha displays miraculous signs of fire, water, and rays of six colors and creates counterparts of himself. E. W. Burlingame, trans., *Buddhist Legends,* Harvard Oriental Series, 30, pt. 3 (Cambridge, Mass.: Harvard University Press, 1921), 35–56, especially 45–52.

22. See the *Mahāparinibbāna Sutta* (D II.142).

23. Others hold that Buddhists may have borrowed the idea of making a Buddha image from the Jains. See U. P. Shah, "A Unique Jaina Image of Jīvantasvāmi," *Journal of the Oriental Institute* 1, no. 1 (1951): 71–79; John E. Cort, "Bhakti in the Early Jain Tradition: Understanding Devotional Religion in South Asia," *History of Religions* 42, no. 1 (August 2002): 59–86.

24. See John S. Strong, *The Legend of King Aśoka: A Study and Translation of the Aśokāvadāna* (Princeton, N.J.: Princeton University Press, 1983), chaps. 3 and 4.

25. For an example from northern Thailand, see Donald K. Swearer and Sommai Premchit, *The Legend of Queen Cāma* (Albany: State University of New York Press, 1998).

26. The Emerald Buddha image served as the palladium for many Tai monarchs. See Frank E. Reynolds, "The Holy Emerald Jewel: Some Aspects of Buddhist Symbolism and Political Legitimation in Thailand and Laos," in *Religion and Legitimation of Power in Thailand, Laos, and Burma,* ed. Bardwell L. Smith (Chambersburg, Pa.: Anima Books, 1978), 175–93. The image is currently housed in a chapel in the royal palace of the Chakri kings in Bangkok. The growing popularity of the Emerald Buddha image, in particular, the enshrinement of copies in the restored *chedī* at Wat Chedī Luang, Chiang Mai, and Wat Phra Kāew, Chiang Rai, mirrors what I regard as the original function of the image of the Emerald Buddha, namely, as a sign of a ritually legitimated loose hegemony among Tai states in northern Thailand. The presence of temples of the Emerald Buddha (Wat Phra Kāew) in early northern Tai states of Chiang Khong, Chiang Rai, and Lampāng attests to this ritual linkage.

27. Robert L. Brown, "The Miraculous Buddha Image: Portrait, God, or Object?" in *Images, Miracles, and Authority in Asian Religious Traditions,* ed. Richard H. Davis (Boulder, Colo.: Westview, 1998), 43.

28. David Eckel emphasizes this point in his interpretation of Xuanzang's reaction to the Buddha's absence when the Chinese pilgrim visits the *bodhi* tree. Malcolm David Eckel, *To See the Buddha: A Philosopher's Quest for the Meaning of Emptiness* (San Francisco: HarperCollins, 1992), 57–58.

29. Gombrich, "Kosala-Bimba-Vaṇṇanā," 298. The same point is made in the story of The Twin Miracle, where the image is commanded by the Buddha to teach the *dhamma* in his absence (Burlingame, *Buddhist Legends,* 51).

30. Scholars who hold the view that early Buddhism was aniconic cite this saying from the *Saṃyutta Nikāya* to support the notion that after the Buddha's *parinibbāna* the *dhamma* stands in his place. For further support of this interpretation they cite the Buddha's teaching in the *Mahāparinibbāna Sutta* that after his death the *dhamma* will be his successor. On the relationship between *rūpakāya* and *dharmakāya,* see Gadjin M. Nagao, "On the Theory of Buddha-Body (*Buddhakāya*)," *Eastern Buddhist,* n.s., 6, no. 1 (May 1973), especially 25–30. See also John S. Strong, "The Transforming Gift: An Analysis of Devotional Acts of Offering in Buddhist Avadāna Literature," *History of Religions* 18, no. 3 (February 1979): 221–37.

31. For the argument of image as double, see Bernard Faure, *The Rhetoric of Immediacy: A Cultural Critique of Chan/Zen Buddhism* (Princeton, N.J.: Princeton University Press, 1991), chaps. 7 and 8.

32. The notion that the Buddha is present in the monastery is corroborated from several perspectives. See Gregory Schopen, "The Buddha as an Owner of Property and Permanent Resident in Medieval Indian Monasteries," *Journal of Indian Philosophy* 18 (1990): 181–217.

33. In classical Luang Prabang (Laos) *vihāra*s such as the royal monastery Wat Chiang Thong, the central Buddha image is flanked by two *dhammāsana* or preaching platforms. A Buddha image sits on the platform to the right of the central statue, while monks preach from the platform to its left. This parallel arrangement suggests that the Buddha image and the monk on the preaching platform are twin or equal teachers of the *dhamma,* a notion akin to the relationship between the Buddha and his image in the KBV.

34. Donald F. McCallum, *Zenkōji and Its Icon: A Study in Japanese Religious Art* (Princeton, N.J.: Princeton University Press, 1994).

35. Ibid., 180.

36. Ibid., 181–83.

37. Ibid., 182.

38. See William P. Alston, *Philosophy of Language* (New York: Prentice Hall, 1964), 50–61.

39. For Peirce on icon, index, and symbol, see Charles Peirce, *Collected Papers,* vol. 2, ed. Charles Hartshorne and Paul Weiss (Cambridge, Mass.: Harvard University Press, 1931), para. 247, 248, 307. The cult of Buddha images in northern Thailand incorporates all three meanings.

40. Charles Morris, *Signification and Significance: A Study of the Relations of Signs and Values* (Cambridge, Mass.: The MIT Press, 1964).

41. Kevin Trainor, personal communication, April 22, 1996.

42. Stanley Tambiah uses the term *indexical icon* in his study of figures and emblems of saints and the Buddha to mean the objectification of their power and virtue in these signs. Stanley J. Tambiah, *The Buddhist Saints of the Forest and the Cult of Amulets* (Cambridge: Cambridge University Press, 1984), 336.

43. Jaini, trans., *Apocryphal Birth-Stories* (*Paññāsa-Jātaka*), vol. 2, 110.

44. Although the *apadāna* is considered to be one of the last books added to the Pāli canon, its dates have not been determined. K. R. Norman opines that because many of its 547 verse legends are mythological in nature, the collection is late; however, he also notes that references to the worship of *thūpa*s, shrines, and relics found in the *apadāna* also occur in the *Theragāthā* and *Therīgāthā,* which he dates between the fifth and third centuries B.C.E. See K. R. Norman, *Pāli Literature* (Wiesbaden: Otto Harrassowitz, 1983), 90. For the *apadāna* contribution to Buddha biography and relationship to the *stūpa* cult, see Jonathan S. Walters, "Stūpa, Story, and Empire: Constructions of the Buddha Biography in Early Post-Aśokan India," in *Sacred Biography in the Buddhist Traditions of South and Southeast Asia,* ed. Juliane Schober (Honolulu: University of Hawai'i Press, 1997).

45. Thanissaro Bhikkhu (Geoff DeGraff), personal communication, December 27, 2000. Thanissaro lists the following services to the Buddha mentioned in the *apadāna:* donating food, a lamp, a candle, cloth, flowers, an elephant, flags, incense, a golden seat; praising the Buddha's wisdom; protecting the Buddha with a sunshade; receiving the triple refuge and the five precepts; making *añjali;* cover-

ing a *chedī* with gold, and so on. Many of these services continue to be offered to Buddha images.

46. Kevin Trainor, personal communication, April 22, 1996. See also Trainor, *Relics, Ritual, and Representation in Buddhism: Rematerializing the Sri Lankan Theravāda Tradition* (Cambridge: Cambridge University Press, 1997), 30.

47. H. A. Giles, trans., *The Travels of Fa-Hsien* (Cambridge: At the University Press, 1923), 30–31. This variation enhances both the mythological (Tāvatiṃsa Heaven) and the ethical (filial piety toward one's mother) dimensions of the tale. In the story of The Twin Miracles the Buddha's visit to Tāvatiṃsa Heaven to preach the Abhidhamma to his mother figures into the creation of the Buddha's double.

48. See Alexander Coburn Soper, *Literary Evidence for Early Buddhist Art in China* (Ascona: Artibus Asiae, 1959), 259–68; Martha L. Carter, *The Mystery of the Udayana Buddha* (Napoli: Instituto Universitario Orientale, 1990); Gregory Henderson and Leon Hurvitz, "The Buddha of Seiryōji: New Finds and New Theory," *Artibus Asiae* 19, no. 1 (1956): 5–55; Donald F. McCallum, "The Saidaiji Lineage of the Seriyōji Shaka Tradition," *Archives of Asian Art* 41 (1996): 51–67.

49. Soper, *Literary Evidence,* 259.

50. Ibid. Kosambī and Śrāsvastī competed with each other as popular Buddhist pilgrimage sites. Under Mathurā influence from the second century B.C.E. Kosambī came to supersede the earlier prominence of Śrāsvastī.

51. Ibid., 259.

52. John C. Huntington, "The Origin of the Buddha Image: Early Image Traditions and the Concept of Buddhadar Śanapunyā," in *Studies in Buddhist Art of South Asia,* ed. A. K. Narain (New Delhi: Kanak, 1985), 32.

53. Ibid., 33–34. J. Huntington suggests that the tradition recorded by Faxian of a Buddha image being taken to Sāṅkāśya, the reputed site of the Buddha's descent from Tāvatiṃsā Heaven, may reflect the historical importance of Sāṅkāśya as a pilgrimage site from the time of Asoka. Huntington believes that a small steatite plaque found at Sāṅkāśya with an image of the Buddha on it may memoralize this event.

54. Soper, *Literary Evidence,* 260.

55. For a translation of this text, see Robert H. Sharf, "The Scripture on the Production of Buddha Images," in *Religions of China in Practice,* ed. Donald S. Lopez Jr. (Princeton, N.J.: Princeton University Press, 1996), 261–67.

56. Ibid., 265.

57. Ibid., 262. Sharf links this text with other Chinese scriptures that detail the merit acquired through specific acts of piety, 262.

58. Soper, *Literary Evidence,* 261.

59. Ibid, 263. In East Asia the sandalwood image of Shaka at the Seiryōji temple in Kyōtō claims to be the original Udayana image. From the above textual evidence Soper concludes that by the second century C.E. a lively propaganda literature supporting the building of Buddha images had developed; the prominence given to King Udayana suggests that this enterprise was centered at Kosambī; Kosambī monks were propagating these texts under the influence from Mathurā; and by this time Śrāvastī, the old Kosala capital, had been eclipsed.

60. Samuel Beal, trans., *Si-Yu-Ki: Buddhist Records of the Western World,* 2 vols., by Hiuen Tsiang [Hsüan-tsang/Xuanzang] (London: Kegan Paul, Trench, Trübner and Company, Ltd., 1884; reprint, Delhi: Oriental Books Reprint Corporation, 1969), 235–36. Page citations refer to the reprint edition.

61. See, in particular, J. Huntington, "The Origin of the Buddha Image," and O. C. Gangoly, *The Antiquity of the Buddha-Image: The Cult of the Buddha* (1938; reprint, Calcutta: Bani, 1965), 1–21. Page citations refer to the reprint edition.

62. The following discussion is based on Lewis R. Lancaster, "An Early Mahāyāna Sermon about the Body of the Buddha and the Making of Images," *Artibus Asiae* 36 (1974): 287–91.

63. Ibid., 289.

64. Trainor, *Relics, Ritual, and Representation in Buddhism,* 94.

65. Ja. IV, 228. Italics mine. Quoted in Gangoly, *The Antiquity of the Buddha-Image,* 8. Gangoly queries the authenticity of this quote but observes that variants are found in the *Avadāna Śatakam* (#54) and in Xuanzang. In the northern Thai *Tamnān Doi Ang Salūng,* (The Chronicle of Water Basin Mountain), even the Buddha's excrement and mucus are enshrined as relics. I analyze this text in "Signs of the Buddha in the Northern Thai Chronicles," in *Wannakam Phutthasāsanā Nai Lānnā* [Buddhist Literature in Northern Thailand], ed. Phanphen Khrū'ngthai (Chiang Mai: Silkworm Books, 2540 B.E./1997 C.E.), 278–92.

66. See Gregory Schopen, "Monks and the Relic Cult in the *Mahāparinibbānasutta:* An Old Misunderstanding in Regard to Monastic Buddhism," in *From Benares to Beijing: Essays on Buddhism and Chinese Religions in Honour of Prof. Jan Yün-Hua,* ed. Koichi Shinohara and Gregory Schopen (Oakville, Ont.: Mosaic, 1991).

67. Gangoly, *The Antiquity of the Buddha-Image,* 10, citing *Bodhisattva Avadāna Kalpalatā* VII, vs. 69. Bibl. Indica Edition.

68. Ibid., 11. See also John S. Strong, *The Legend and Cult of Upagupta: Sanskrit Buddhism in North India and Southeast Asia* (Princeton, N.J.: Princeton University Press, 1992), chap. 5.

69. Gangoly, *The Antiquity of the Buddha-Image,* 10. My translation. Gangoly's is "We take refuge in you of divine sight."

70. For a thought-provoking study of signs (material representations) of the Buddha drawn from Xuanzang (Hsüan-tsang)'s pilgrimage, see Eckel, *To See the Buddha.*

71. Ananda K. Coomaraswamy, *The Origin of the Buddha Image* (1927; reprint, New Delhi: Munishiram Manoharlal, 1972), 1–42. See Klemens Karlsson, *Face to Face with the Absent Buddha* (Uppsala, Sweden: University of Uppsala, 1999), chap. 1.

72. Alfred Foucher, "L'Origine grecque de l'image du Bouddha," *Annales du Musée Guimet* 38 (1913): 231–72; Alfred Foucher, "The Beginnings of Buddhist Art," in *The Beginnings of Buddhist Art and Other Essays in Indian and Central-Asian Archaeology,* ed. Alfred Foucher, trans. L. A. Thomas (Varanasi: Indological Book House, 1972), 1–29.

73. For a brief outline of the two positions, see J. E. van Lohuizen-de Leeuw, "New Evidence with Regard to the Origin of the Buddha Image," *South Asian*

*Archaeology 1979,* ed. Herbert Härtel (Berlin: Dietrich Reimer Verlag, 1981), 377–400.

74. Coomaraswamy, *The Origin of the Buddha Image,* 12.

75. Ibid., 11–12.

76. Ibid., 27. Lohuizen-de Leeuw, "New Evidence with Regard to the Origin of the Buddha Image," refines the Coomaraswamy thesis.

77. Ibid., 37.

78. The date for the life of the Buddha is highly relevant to the historical origin of the first Buddha image. The Theravāda tradition accepts 544 or 543 B.C.E. as the date of the Buddha's death. The so-called corrected long chronology (486 to 477 B.C.E.) with minor variations is widely accepted by Western Buddhologists. Others, especially from Japan, propose a short chronology that places the death of the Buddha at 368 or 383 B.C.E., one hundred years before the accession of King Asoka. See Heinz Bechert, ed., *When Did the Buddha Live? The Controversy on the Dating of the Historical Buddha* (Delhi: Sri Satguru, 1995).

79. J. Huntington, "The Origin of the Buddha Image," 24–25.

80. Ibid., 37–41. Huntington has utilized the work of Jean Przyluski, *Legends of the Emperor Asoka.* My discussion follows Huntington's account.

81. Ibid., 40.

82. Ibid., 41. Huntington also detects a hint in the narrative for a monastic convention of Buddha image production. Gregory Schopen advances this position in "On Monks, Nuns, and 'Vulgar' Practices: The Introduction of the Image Cult into Indian Buddhism," *Artibus Asiae* 49, nos. 1/2 (1988–89).

83. Ibid., 46–48. Italics mine.

84. Ibid., 49.

85. See Vidya Dehejia, "Aniconism and the Multivalence of Emblems," *Ars Orientalis* 21 (1991): 45–66; S. Huntington, "Early Buddhist Art and the Theory of Aniconism"; S. Huntington, *The Art of Ancient India;* Susan L. Huntington, "Aniconism and the Multivalence of Emblems: Another Look," *Ars Orientalis* 22 (1992): 111–56. See also Karlsson, *Face to Face with the Absent Buddha,* 48–52.

86. Dehejia, "Aniconism and the Multivalence of Emblems," 45.

87. S. Huntington, "Aniconism and the Multivalence of Emblems."

88. For an analysis of relics and pilgrimage, especially the notion of *pradakṣiṇā,* see Nancy Auer Falk, "To Gaze on the Sacred Traces," *History of Religions* 16, no. 4 (May 1977): 281–93.

89. Robert L. Brown considers that "presence" refers, in particular, to the events of the Buddha's life, such as the iconographic depiction of the Buddha's enlightenment as "a divine and miraculous event." For comments on the Huntington/Dehejia debates, see Brown, "The Miraculous Buddha Image," 44.

90. S. Huntington, "Early Buddhist Art and the Theory of Aniconism," 405. For an analysis of venerated objects and symbols in terms of these three classifications, see Peter Harvey, "Venerated Objects and Symbols of Early Buddhism," in *Symbols in Art and Religions: The Indian and the Comparative Perspectives,* ed. Karel Werner (London: Curzon, 1970).

## CHAPTER 2. MEETING THE BUDDHA

1. Jonathan Z. Smith, *To Take Place: Toward Theory in Ritual* (Chicago: University of Chicago Press, 1987), 103–4.

2. I translate the Thai term *wat* as temple-monastery because most *wats* in Thailand serve as places for monastic practice and public rituals, ceremonies, and festivals.

3. See K. I. Matics, *Introduction to the Thai Temple* (Bangkok: White Lotus, 1992).

4. Luang Boribal Buribhand and A. B. Griswold, *The Royal Monasteries and Their Significance* (Bangkok: Fine Arts Department, 2501 B.E./1958 C.E.). For a listing of all of the *wats* in Thailand with brief descriptions of major sites, see *Thamnīam Wat Hāeng Prathet Thai* [*Directory of all Monasteries in Thailand*] (Bangkok: Wacharinthakān, 2519 B.E./1976 C.E.); *Prawat Wat Thua Rāchānāchak Lem 1* [The History of Wats in Thailand. vol. 1] (Bangkok: Ministry of Education, 2525 B.E./1982 C.E.) For a discussion of *wat* plans, see Hiram W. Woodward Jr., "Monastery, Palace, and City Plans," *Crossroads: An Interdisciplinary Journal of Southeast Asian Studies* 2, no. 2 (1985): 23–60.

5. For a discussion of the development of the physical characteristics of Buddhist monasteries in India, see Sukumar Dutt, *Buddhist Monks and Monasteries of India: Their History and Their Contribution* (London: George Allen and Unwin, 1962), especially pt. 1, chaps. 4–6. For Sri Lankan monasteries, see Senake Bandaranayake, *Sinhalese Monastic Architecture: The Vihāras of Anurādhapura* (Leiden: E. J. Brill, 1974); H. T. Basnayake, *Sri Lankan Monastic Architecture* (Delhi: Sri Satguru, 1986); Walpola Rahula, *History of Buddhism in Ceylon* (Colombo: M. D. Gunasena, 1956), chap. 8. Bandaranayake argues that the *stūpa* was ritually preeminent in Anurādhapura monastic architecture from the first century B.C.E. to the fourth century C.E., but that from the third century the prominence of the image hall reflected the increasing importance of the cult of the Buddha image.

6. In central Thailand the *uposatha* hall often stands within the *buddhavāsa.*

7. For a more detailed discussion, see Swearer, *Wat Haripuñjaya.*

8. Robert L. Brown, "Recent Stupa Literature: A Review Article," *Journal of Asian History* 20 (1986): 219.

9. Trainor, *Relics, Ritual, and Representation in Buddhism,* 97.

10. For information relevant to the architecture of Buddhist sites in Sukhōthai, Lamphūn, and Chiang Mai, see Alexander B. Griswold, *Towards a History of Sukhodaya Art* (Bangkok: The National Museum, 1967); Betty Gosling, *Sukhothai: Its History, Culture, and Art* (Singapore: Oxford University Press, 1991); Alexander B. Griswold, *Wat Pra Yün Reconsidered* (Bangkok: The Siam Society, 1975); E. W. Hutchinson, "The Seven Spires: A Sanctuary of the Sacred Fig Tree at Chiengmai," *Journal of the Siam Society* 39, pt. 1 (June 1951).

11. Brown, "Recent Stupa Literature," 219. For a concise, critical discussion of relic veneration in India and Sri Lanka, see Trainor, *Relics, Ritual, and Representation in Buddhism,* especially, 100–107. See also Adrian Snodgrass, *The Symbolism of the Stupa* (Ithaca, N.Y.: Southeast Asian Program, 1988); H. Kottkamp, *Der Stupa als Repräsentation des buddhistischen Heilsweges: Unter-*

*suchungen zur Entstehung und Entwicklung architektonischer Symbolik* (Wiesbaden: Otto Harrassowitz, 1992); Anna Libera Dallapiccola, ed., *The Stūpa: Its Religious, Historical and Architectural Significance* (Wiesbaden: Franz Steiner Verlag, 1980); Mireille Bénisti, "Étude sur le *stūpa* dans l'Inde ancienne," *BEFEO* 50, no. 1 (1960): 37–88; André Bareau, "La construction et le culte des *stūpa* d'après les *Vinayapiṭaka*," *BEFEO* 50, no. 2 (1962).

12. A. M. Hocart, "The Origin of the Stūpa," *Ceylon Journal of Science* 1, no. 1 (1924); A. K. Coomaraswamy, *History of Indian and Indonesian Art* (New York: Dover, 1965).

13. John Irwin, "The Stūpa and the Cosmic Axis—The Archaeological Evidence," *South Asian Archaeology 1977,* ed. Maurizio Taddei (Naples: Instituto Universitario Orientale, 1979), 799–845.

14. Gérard Fussman, "Symbolisms of the Buddhist Stūpa," *Journal of the International Association of Buddhist Studies* 9, no. 2 (1986): 40.

15. Ibid., 44.

16. Trainor, *Relics, Ritual, and Representation in Buddhism,* 44.

17. Fussman, "Symbolisms of the Buddhist Stūpa," 48.

18. Peter Harvey, "The Symbolism of the Early Stūpa," *Journal of the International Association of Buddhist Studies* 7, no. 2 (1984): 80.

19. Ibid., 69.

20. Ibid., 82.

21. Ibid., 84.

22. Trainor, *Relics, Ritual, and Representation in Buddhism,* 110–14.

23. Ibid., 114. Trainor acknowledges his debt to Jonathan Z. Smith's critique of Mircea Eliade: "Where Eliade has seen cosmological patterns, Smith identifies a vocabulary rooted in ideologies of kingship and political organization," 106.

24. Bandaranayake, *Sinhalese Monastic Architecture,* chap. 3.

25. Hiram W. Woodward Jr., "The Thai *Čhēdī* and the Problem of Stūpa Interpretation," *History of Religions* 33, no. 1 (August 1993): 71–91.

26. Ibid., 90.

27. For this practice in another context, see Schopen, "The Buddha as an Owner of Property and Permanent Resident in Medieval Indian Monasteries," *Journal of Indian Philosophy* 18 (1990): 181–217.

28. See Brian D. Ruppert, *Jewel in the Ashes: Buddha Relics and Power in Early Medieval Japan* (Cambridge, Mass.: Harvard University Press, 2000) for a detailed study of the relationship between relic veneration and political power in medieval Japan.

29. See Ratanapañña Thera, *The Sheaf of Garlands of the Epochs of the Conqueror (Jinakālamālīpakaraṇaṃ)*, trans. N. A. Jayawickrama (London: Luzac, 1968), 114–20.

30. See, for example, *Milindapañho* III. 177–79, *Kāliṅgabodhi Jātaka* (Ja. 4:228). Kevin Trainor notes that the threefold classification of memorials—corporeal relics, relics of use, and commemorative relics (e.g., Buddha images)—was well established by the fifth century in Sri Lanka (*Relics, Ritual, and Representation in Buddhism,* 89).

31. For the role of faith (*saddhā*) in relationship to relic veneration, see Trainor, *Relics, Ritual, and Representation,* chap. 3.

32. For Thai mural depictions of the life of the Buddha, see *Phra Phuttha Prawat Chitarakam Fāphanang Phra Thī Nang Phutthaisawan Phiphithaphanthasathān Hāeng Chāt Phranakorn* [The Life of the Buddha: Murals in the Buddhaisawan Chapel, National Museum] (Bangkok: Department of Fine Arts, 2515 B.E./1972 C.E.); *Phāp Phuttha Prawat Wat Thongnopakhun* [Painted Sculpture on the Life of the Buddha] (Bangkok: Matichon, 1983). For a Burmese illustrated life of the Buddha based on the *Mālālaṅkara Vatthu* written in 1798 by Dutiya Medi Hsayadaw (1747–1834), see Patricia M. Herbert, *The Life of the Buddha* (London: The British Library, 1992). For a discussion of Thai manuscript painting, see Henry Ginsburg, *Thai Manuscript Painting* (Honolulu: University of Hawai'i Press, 1989), especially chap. 4.

33. With minor changes my translation follows N. A. Jayawickrama. See Ratanapañña Thera, *The Sheaf of Garlands of the Epochs of the Conqueror,* 120. For the Pāli version, see *Jinakālamālī,* ed. A. P. Buddhadatta (London: Luzac, 1962), 86–91.

34. In the *Mahāvagga* I.6.6. Upaka, an Ājīvaka ascetic and the first to encounter the Buddha after his enlightenment, comments specifically on the radiance of his physical appearance and purity of his sense organs (*indriyāni parisuddho chavivaṇṇo*). It seems likely that Buddhological debates regarding the form body of the Buddha (*rūpakāya*) and the Buddha's body beyond form (*dhammakāya*) were influenced by devotional practices that included Buddha images.

35. Bandaranayake observes that in Sinhalese archaeological terminology the image house was generally referred to as *gandhakuṭī paṭimāghara,* which suggests that in ritual terms image shrine rooms commemorated or reproduced in architectural and iconographic symbolism the original perfumed chamber in which the Buddha resided in the Jetavana Monastery (*Sinhalese Monastic Architecture,* 190).

36. Kenneth E. Wells, *Thai Buddhism: Its Rites and Activities,* rev. ed. (Bangkok: Suriyabun, 1975), 119–20.

37. These ceremonies are described in Sommai Premchit and Amphay Doré, *The Lan Na Twelve-Month Traditions* (Chiang Mai: So Sap Kanpim, 1992), 141–46; Sanguan Chōtisukharat, *Praphēnī Thai Phāk Nū'a* [The Customs of Northern Thailand] (Bangkok: Odian Store, 2512 B.E./1969 C.E.), 286–90; Manī Phayomyong, *Praphenī Sipsong Du'an Lānnā Thai* [The Twelve Month Customs of Northern Thailand] 2 vols. (Chiang Mai: Chiang Mai University, 2529 B.E./1986 C.E.), 119–32. See also Wells, *Thai Buddhism,* 115–35.

38. According to a traditional northern Thai account of the *arahant,* Upagutta, the holy saint protected Asoka's 84,000 newly built *stūpa*s from the threat of Māra's destructive power. Consequently, he is invoked to protect new *wat* structures when they are dedicated. According to John S. Strong, the source for this tradition is the *Lokapaññatti* compiled in Burma in the eleventh or twelfth century. See Strong, *The Legend and Cult of Upagupta,* 12–13, and chaps. 5 and 6.

39. At major ceremonies involving the dedication of donatory gifts to the *wat,* a lay leader called the *āchān wat* acts on behalf of the assembled congregation. Examples of dedicatory sermons can be found in Thawī Khū'ankāew, *Praphenī Doem* [Customs of the Past] (Chiang Mai: Phra Sing, 2518 B.E./1975 C.E., pt. 2). For

the role of the teacher of the *wat,* see Donald K. Swearer, "The Layman Extraordinaire in Northern Thai Buddhism," *Journal of the Siam Society* 64, no. 1 (January 1976): 151–68.

40. For the following description I am indebted to Wells, *Thai Buddhism,* and Plāek Santhirak, *Lathi Praphenī lae Phithīkam* [Beliefs, Customs, and Ceremonies] (Bangkok: Panākān, 2515 B.E./1972 C.E.), 397–405. For the *sīmā* ritual in Cambodia, see Madeleine Giteau, "Le bornage rituel des temples bouddhiques au Cambodge," *BEFEO* 68 (Paris: École française d'Extrême-Orient, 1969), 31–41. For a discussion of the *sīmā* ritual with special reference to Nan, northern Thailand, see Gehan Wijeyewardene, *Place and Emotion in Northern Thai Ritual Behaviour* (Bangkok: Pandora, 1986), 91–117.

41. Wells, *Thai Buddhism,* 113.

42. Matics, *Introduction to the Thai Temple,* 29–30.

43. There is disagreement over the symbolism of the *cho fā.* It may represent a swan (*haṃsa*) or a water fowl popular in Mon motifs. See Matics, *Introduction to the Thai Temple,* 49–56; H. G. Quartich Wales, *Siamese State Ceremonies* (London: Bernard Quartich, 1931), 114–15.

## CHAPTER 3. CONSTRUCTING A BUDDHA IMAGE

1. The Buddha image construction text, the image construction blessing text, and the text of the Buddha image *yantra* are translations of undated manuscripts on microfilm in the archives of northern Thai texts at the Social Research Institute, Chiang Mai University. The catalogue numbers are 86.150.01L.004-004 and 80.049.09.009-009.

2. Bronze manufacture lineages are patrilineal, although I observed women helping in aspects of the manufacturing process that did not involve direct contact with the image.

3. The following description is based on my observations of the Chiang Mai artisan, Mr. Insorn Kaewduangsaeng.

4. The donor may contribute personal valuables such as a gold ring or other precious metals to the mix of molten bronze poured into the head, because it is regarded as the most sacred part of the image. Devotees may purchase and contribute strips of metal to the bronze melt as an act of merit making.

5. For another description of the casting of bronze Buddha images in Thailand, see Donna K. Strahan, "Bronze Casting in Thailand," in *The Sacred Sculpture of Thailand,* ed. Hiram W. Woodward Jr. (Baltimore: The Walters Art Gallery, 1997), 27–40.

6. Alexander B. Griswold, "Bronze-Casting in Siam," *BEFEO* 46, no. 2 (1954): 635–47.

7. Ibid., 637–39.

8. Translated in collaboration with Sommai Premchit with assistance from Punchi Megaskumbhara, Department of Sinhala, University of Peradeniya, Sri Lanka. This is an anthology of texts relative to the construction and consecration of Buddha images and sacred monastery structures such as a *chedī.*

9. See Hans Penth, *A Brief History of Lān Nā: Civilizations of North Thailand* (Chiang Mai: Sikworm Books, 1994). Penth periodizes the history of northern Thailand as follows:

The arrival of the Thais, ca. 1200–ca. 1300
The making of Lān Nā, ca. 1300–ca. 1400
The Golden Age of Lān Nā, ca. 1400–ca. 1525
Decline and loss of independence to Burma, ca. 1526–ca. 1775
Fragmentation, 1558–ca. 1775
Renaissance and integration as a part of Siam, ca. 1775–present

10. In premodern Thailand it was customary for a *wat* to be served by *khā* (slaves, servants), village or towns folk whose corvée obligation to an overlord included serving the *wat.*

11. I discern no pattern of auspicious and inauspicious days for constructing the Buddha image as outlined in this text other than the fact that the image should be completed during the period of the waxing moon, and that six of these days appear to be auspicious and nine inauspicious.

12. *Gāthā* is used here in the sense of *mantra,* that is, a word or words that denote magical potency and sacred power. A conventional designation of *paritta* chanting in Thai Buddhism is *suat mon kāthā* in which *mantra* and *gāthā* are virtually synonymous, an association not confined to Thai Buddhism.

13. This refers to the chant that appears below, "*itipi so* . . . ; *svākkhāto* . . . ; *supaṭipanno* . . ."

14. *Buddhassa* (I pay homage to the Buddha) is the same case (dative) as *Buddhāya.*

15. Taken from the final paragraph of the *Ahirāja Sutta,* which concludes, "The power of the Buddha is limitless, the power of the Dhamma is limitless, the power of the Saṅgha is limitless. By the power of the Buddha, the Dhamma, and the Saṅgha protection has been made against reptiles, snakes, scorpions, centipedes, spiders, lizards, mice. May these creatures be dispelled. I pay homage to the Exalted One (*bhagavato*), and to the seven fully enlightened ones (*sammāsambuddhaṃ*)."

16. The text is ambiguous regarding the exact placement of the six clay tiles. I have made minor changes to indicate more clearly that the clay tile with the silver plate is placed at the center of the image or *chedī,* that four with copper plates are placed at the cardinal directions, and that the sixth is used as the reliquary cover or put into the reliquary casket with other sacred objects.

17. This recitation is called "The *Guṇa* (Virtue/Power) of the Three Gems." The first fifty-six syllables beginning with "*itipi so bhagavā*" represent the fifty-six *guṇa*s (qualities/virtues/power valencies) of the Buddha; the following thirty-eight syllables beginning with "*savakkhato bhagavatā dhammo,*" the thirty-eight *guṇa* of the *dhamma;* and the final fourteen syllables, "*supaṭipanno bhagavato sāvakasaṅgho,*" the fourteen *guṇa* of the *saṅgha.* This recitation follows the chanting of the *namo tassa* at auspicious (*maṅgala*) rituals. See Bunkhit Wajarasāt, *Suat Mon Mū'ang Nū'a* [Northern Thai Chants] (Chiang Mai: Thārāthong, n.d.), 40–41. See also François Bizot and Oskar von Hinüber, *La guirlande de Joyaux* (Paris: EFEO, 1994).

18. This stanza is called *Aṭṭhavīsati Buddha Paritta,* which begins by paying homage to the twenty-eight Buddhas, namely, Taṇhaṅkara, Medhaṅkara, Saraṇaṅkara, Dīpaṅkara until Gotama Buddha. The *paritta* speaks of the power and compassion of the Buddhas who were worshiped in "all of the worlds." Those who take refuge in these Buddhas will not fall into the state of unhappiness (*duggati*) for 100,000 eons.

19. This *sutta* refers to forest-dwelling monks who were so haunted by evil spirits that they were forced to leave the forest, whereupon they sought the counsel of the Buddha, who advised them to return. The Buddha taught them to chant the *Karaṇīyamettā Sutta* when they lived in the forest. This *sutta* outlines the ideal life that should be lived by a monk. It states that *bhikkhu*s should extend their compassion (*mettā*) toward all living beings, including evil spirits. In Thailand this *sutta* is recited at all auspicious ceremonies (Thai, *phithī mongkhon;* Pāli, *maṅgala vidhi*).

20. *Parāyano* (dependent upon) . . . the Buddha, the Dhamma, the Saṅgha.

21. Buddho me nātho: *"The Buddha is my Lord."*

22. *Hiriottappa* is a stanza from a story in the *Dhammapada* commentary that tells of a demon who devoured the people who came to drink water from his pond unless they knew the following verse: "Those who are ashamed and afraid of evil, endowed with meritorious deeds, peacefulness, and righteousness are called people who possess the *devadhamma.*" The verse is considered by believers to be a *mantra* against evil spirits. The verse is followed by a stanza from the *Vattaka Paritta* that relates the story of a covey of quail chicks who make a vow to stop a forest fire that was advancing toward them. The chicks pray, "We have wings but no feathers; we have legs but are unable to move about; and, our parents have gone out to gather food. May the fire turn away." This *paritta* is believed to protect houses and other property from fire and is usually chanted at the blessing ceremony for a new house.

23. This stanza is found in a story in the *Dhammapada* commentary that instructs people how to act when threatened by danger. Under such a threat, most take refuge in mountains, forests, temples, trees, or *cetiya*s. These are ignoble refuges. Those who seek such refuge will not be free from suffering. Only those who take refuge in the Buddha, the *dhamma,* and the *saṅgha,* and who have realized the four noble truths will transcend suffering. This is the most noble, supreme refuge; the person who takes such refuge will be free from all suffering.

24. The *Jayapañjara* or *Jinapañjara* (The Victor's Cage) may have been composed in Sri Lanka and introduced into Siam with the *Catubhāṇavarapāli,* a Siṅhala *paritta* collection, during the Sukhōthai or early Ayutthaya period. It was known in Chiang Mai as well. The chant became especially popular after it was rediscovered and modified by Somdet Phuthāchān Tō during the reign of King Mongkut. The *Jayapañjara* refers to the twenty-eight Buddhas, beginning with Taṇhaṅkara, and the eighty *arahant*s, and mentions the *Ratana Sutta, Mettā Sutta, Khandha Paritta, Mora Paritta,* and *Āṭānāṭiya Paritta.* Of special interest is the invocation for various elements to reside in parts of the body—the Buddhas in the head, the *dhamma* in the ears, the *saṅgha* in the chest, Anuruddha in the heart, Sāriputta to the right, Moggallāna to the left, Koṇḍañña in the back. The text concludes by requesting protection by the power of the Triple Gem.

25. Because the *Uṇhassavijaya* (The Joy of Victory) is not found in the central Thai collection of *paritta,* it could be of northern Thai origin. The first verse urges people to observe the *dhamma* for the benefit and happiness of all living beings. By virtue of the *dhamma* people will be spared an untimely death. The second stanza praises the Triple Gem as an effective antidote against suffering. The third verse lauds nonkilling (i.e., granting the power of life by not taking life) and merit making. This short *sutta* is often chanted at life extension rituals (Thai, *phithī kān sū'pchātā.*)

26. *"Sukho buddhānaṃ uppādo/sukho saddhamma desanā/sukho saṅghassa sāmaggī/nibbānaṃ paramaṃ sukhaṃ"* (Joyous is the birth of the Buddha; joyous is the proclamation of the *dhamma;* joyous is the fellowship of the *saṅgha*; the greatest joy is *nibbāna*).

27. *"Ārogyā paramā labhā/santuṭṭhi paramaṃ dhanaṃ/vissāso paramo mitto/ nibbānaṃ paramaṃ sukhaṃ."* (The supreme benefit is health; the greatest wealth is contentment; confidence is the best friend; *nibbāna* is the highest happiness).

28. Before the restoration of Sukhōthai and other ancient sites, it was common to see derelict brick and stucco Buddha images with a hole in the chest gouged by robbers in search of relics and valuables put there to represent the image's heart. The custom of installing "hearts" in images is widespread throughout Buddhist Asia. See Henderson and Hurvitz, "The Buddha of Seiryōji," 5–55; François Bizot, "La consécration des statues et le culte des morts," in *Recherches nouvelles sur le Cambodge,* ed. François Bizot (Paris: EFEO, 1994), 101–39. In Chiang Mai silver replicas of the heart and other organs continue to be made, sold, and donated for placement inside an image as an act of merit making.

29. Both the *chedī* and the image (*buddharūpa*) are reminders of the Buddha. This text harmonizes the reliquary and the image by its yantric construction.

30. With some variation in the materials prepared for the offerings to the image, this practice still pertains today. This description links the Buddha image consecration ritual to two northern Thai ceremonies: life extension rituals (*phithī kān sū'pchātā*) and the Brahmanical custom of offerings honoring a teacher.

31. *Dīgha Nikāya,* no. 20.

32. The *Maṅgala Sutta* is one of the most important *paritta* because it is chanted at all auspicious ceremonies that require holy water.

33. A possible allusion to Ja. I.264 or II.104.

34. For a translation of a *Dhammakāya* text, see François Bizot, *Le Chemin de Laṅkā* (Paris: EFEO, 1992), 293–99. See F. L. Woodward, *Manual of a Mystic: The Yogāvachara's Manual,* ed. Caroline Rhys Davids (London: Pali Text Society, 1916), and George Coedès, "Dhammakāya," *Adyar Library Bulletin* 20 (1956): 239–86.

35. Here I follow Coedès rather than the northern Thai *tamrā,* which reads *catuhattha* (four measures).

36. The northern Thai *tamrā* omits the fifth eye, *samantacakkhu,* which is included in the Coedès text.

37. I follow Coedès instead of the northern Thai *tamrā.*

38. The *Bhavatu Sabbamaṅgalaṃ* comes at the conclusion of all ceremonial chanting, and as a blessing following a meal given as *dāna:* "May all auspiciousness (*sabbamaṅgala*) be yours; may all the *devatā* protect you; may you always be

happy by the power of the Buddha. May all auspiciousness be yours; may all the *devatā* protect you; may you always be happy by the power of the *dhamma;* may all auspiciousness be yours; may you always be happy by the power of the *saṅgha.*"

39. In addition to the *cho fā* or sky tassel (see chap. 2) at the end of the ridge pole, an umbrella or series of umbrellas called *pān lom* is situated at the center. The emplacement of these two decorative elements signals the completion of the building.

40. See Strong, *The Legend and Cult of Upagupta;* Olivier De Bernon, "Le rituel de la 'grande probation annuelle' (*mahāparivāsakamma*) des religieux du Cambodge," *BEFEO* 87, no. 2 (2000): 473–510.

41. For a discussion of the historical significance of the iron walking stick in northern Thailand and Laos and its connection to the Mūlasarvāstivāda tradition, see François Bizot, "La place des communautés du Nord-Laos dans l'histoire du bouddhisme d'Asie du Sud-Est," *BEFEO* 87, no. 2 (2000): 521 ff.

42. The palm leaf manuscript on microfilm at the Social Research Institute, Chiang Mai University, was copied in 1841 C.E. but its date of origin is unknown. Translated in collaboration with Sommai Premchit.

43. My teacher of northern Thai, the late Āchān Singkha Wannasai, presented me with a pair of crudely made Buddha images fashioned from food masticated by a holy monk in Nān Province and cured over a charcoal fire. Such a fabricated relic points to a material relationship between holy monk and Buddha image, a matter especially germane to the Buddha image consecration ritual.

44. For the story of Phra Mālai, see Bonnie Pacala Brereton, *Thai Tellings of Phra Mālai: Texts and Rituals Concerning a Popular Buddhist Saint* (Tempe: Arizona State University Program for Southeast Asian Studies, 1995); and Steven Collins, "The Story of the Elder Māleyyadeva," *Journal of the Pali Text Society,* edited by R. Norman, 18 (1993): 65–96.

45. From the microfilm collection of northern Thai manuscripts, Social Research Institute, Chiang Mai University, #80.049.09.008-009. Phaitun Dokbuakaew redrew the Buddha image *yantra* from the text.

46. See François Bizot, *Le Figuier à cinq branches: Recherche sur le bouddhisme khmer I,* Publications de l'école française di Extrême-Orient, 107 (Paris: EFEO, 1976); Bizot, "La grotte de la naissance," in *Recherches sur le bouddhisme khmer II BEFEO* 67 (1980): 222–71; Bizot, *Les traditions de la pabbajjā en Asie du Sud-Est. Recherches sur la bouddhisme khmer IV* (Göttingen: Vandenhoeck and Ruprecht, 1988); Bizot, *Le Chemin de Laṅkā*; Bizot and von Hinüber, *La guirlande de Joyaux*; Bizot and François Lagirarde, *La pureté par les mots* (Paris: EFEO, 1996); L. S. Cousins, "Aspects of Esoteric Southern Buddhism," in *Indian Insights: Buddhism, Brahmanism and Bhakti,* ed. Peter Connolly and Sue Hamilton (London: Luzac Oriental, 1997), 185–207; Peter Skilling, "The Rakṣā Literature of the Śrāvakayāna," *Journal of the Pali Text Society* 16 (1992): 109–82.

47. For an introduction to the use of *yantra*s in the Buddhism of mainland Southeast Asia, see Catherine Becchetti, *Le mystère dans les lettres* (Bangkok: Éditions des Cahiers de France, 1991).

48. One of the acknowledged authorities on northern Thai *yantra* was the late Āchān Insom Chaiyachomphū of Chiang Rai. See his *Yan lae Kāthā Khong Dī*

*Mū'ang Nū'a* [*Yantra* and *Gāthā* of Northern Thailand] (Chiang Rai: The Bunphadung Store, n.d.). Āchān Insom edited the Buddha image *yantra.* Translation mine.

49. Ibid., 3–4. For a study of the yantric practice of the application of the 108-syllable *gāthā, iti pi so—svākkhāto—supaṭipanno,* from the Khmer and northern Thai Yogāvacara tradition, see Bizot and von Hinüber, *La guirlande de Joyaux,* 35–84.

50. Iconometry is well known throughout the Indic world. In the case of the manual included in part III, the breadth of the lap is most often the generative measurement. The distance between the knees "is the traditional reference point for any image." Hiram A. Woodward Jr., "The Buddha Image in Thailand," in *The Sacred Sculpture of Thailand* (Baltimore: The Walters Gallery of Art, 1997), 19–25.

51. *Tamrā Kān Kosāng Phraphuttharūp* [Manual for Making a Buddha Image] (Bangkok: Vajirañāṇa Library, 1920), 2.

52. See Melford E. Spiro, *Buddhism and Society: A Great Tradition and Its Burmese Vicissitudes,* 2d ed. (Berkeley: University of California Press, 1982). For an early and still useful study of magical, apotropaic Buddhist beliefs and practices in Thailand, see Phya Anuman Rajadhon, "Thai Charms and Amulets," in *Essays on Thai Folklore* (Bangkok: Social Science Association Press of Thailand, 1968), 268–95.

53. Nicola Tannenbaum, "Tattoos: Invulnerability and Power in Shan Cosmology," *American Anthropologist* 14, no. 4 (November 1987): 694.

54. Ibid., 695.

55. Ibid., 696.

56. Ibid., 697. This use of tattoos is analogous to the homologic assimilation between parts of the body, Buddhas, *arahant*s, and *paritta*s recited in the *Jinapañjara* (The Victor's Cage) chanted during the *buddhābhiseka.*

57. François Bizot, "Notes sur les *yantra* bouddhiques d'Indochine," *Mélanges chinois et bouddhiques* 20–21, no. 1 (1981): 155–91.

58. Ibid., 157.

59. Ibid.

60. Peter Skilling, personal communication, September 11, 2001.

61. Bizot, "Notes," 162. Bizot cites a book on the *Vedaśāstra* printed in Bangkok in 1973.

62. Bizot's example of this *yantra* and its decoding is taken from the *Vedaśāstra* (163–64).

63. Coedès, "Dhammakāya," 248.

64. F. L. Woodward, *Manual of a Mystic,* vi.

65. Bizot, *Le Chemin de Laṅkā,* 30.

66. Coedès, "Dhammakāya," 248–51. Strong, *The Legend of King Aśoka,* 109–18.

67. Bizot, *Le Chemin de Laṅkā,* 293.

68. Ibid., 294.

## CHAPTER 4. THE RITUAL

1. Michael B. Aune and Valerie DeMarinis, eds., *Religious and Social Ritual: Interdisciplinary Explorations* (Albany: State University of New York Press, 1996), 1.

2. Michael Ondaatje, *Anil's Ghost* (New York: Alfred A. Knopf, 2000), 97 and 99.

3. *Buddhābhisekagāthā,* a palm leaf manuscript copied in 1671 C.E. ascribed to the Venerable Sirisadhammaraṃsi of Jayasenapura (Chiang Saen, northern Thailand), written in 1591. I am indebted to Elizabeth Guthrie, Christchurch, New Zealand, for providing Bumphen Rawin's translation of the manuscript.

4. The description of the *buddhābhiseka* ritual in this chapter is based on my field notes from four image consecrations in northern Thailand in 1989–90: Wat Pā Pāeng, Chiang Mai, October 14, 1989; Wat Chāng Sī, Lamphūn, October 22, 1989; Wat Chet Yot, Chiang Mai, December 28, 1989; Wat Phra Kāew, Chiang Rai, March 22, 1990.

5. The Buddha image consecration ritual in Thailand has received scant scholarly attention. Stanley J. Tambiah discusses the subject in *The Buddhist Saints of the Forest and the Cult of Amulets,* 243–57. Wells includes a brief description in *Thai Buddhism: Its Rites and Activities,* 126–31. See also Donald K. Swearer, "Hypostasizing the Buddha: Buddha Image Consecration in Northern Thailand," *History of Religions* 34, no. 3 (February 1995): 263–80.

6. The *Buddhābhisekagāthā* describes the setting and proceedings of the image consecration ritual in terms similar to the ceremonies I observed. The description includes the *bodhimaṇḍa,* reciting the *paritta* "beginning with *paṭidhānato* [*Ratana Sutta*] to the end," the *Mahāsamaya Sutta, Dhammacakkappavattana Sutta,* and the *Buddhābhisekagāthā.* The monks chant throughout the night, concluding with the "twelvefold interdependent co-arising beginning with *avijjāpaccayā* up to *upādāya nirodha,* and the other verses beginning with *yadā have.*" The description includes offering milk rice to the image and placing twenty *paccayākāra gāthā* on it. Sirisadhammaraṃsi observes that the ritual may have originated in Sri Lanka. The text provides historical evidence that the northern Thai *buddhābhiseka* ritual as currently celebrated has at least a 500-year history.

7. In the *Mahāparinibbāna Sutta* (D II.164) when the Mallas honored the relics of the Buddha in their assembly hall the relics were protected by a latticework of spears and an encircling wall of bows. In *wats* located in the Tai area of China's Yunnan Province (Sipsongpanna) wooden spears and symbols of royal power are used in consecration rituals in the manner of the *rājawat* in northern Thailand.

8. One hundred and eight squares is the traditional number, although they vary depending on the size of the space to be covered. The *sāi siñcana* is comprised of nine threads, an auspicious number with cosmological significance. The *Thūpavaṃsa* describes a relic enshrinement ceremony in which the Elder Indagutta constructs a metal canopy (*lohachattaṃ*) over the reliquary pavilion to protect the relics from Māra. N. A. Jayawickrama, *The Chronicle of the Thūpa and the Thūpavaṃsa* (London: Luzac, 1971), 131 and 245.

9. The use of thread and water in *paritta* rituals is mentioned in the *Samantapāsādikā,* Buddhaghosa's fifth-century commentary on the *Vinaya* and in the

*Vinayavinicchaya*, Buddhadatta's *Vinaya* summary. See Skilling, "The Rakṣā Literature of the Śrāvakayāna," 166.

10. For a discussion of the five royal emblems and the "three-eyed" mirror stand, see Manī Phayomyong, *Khrū'ang Sakkāra Nai Lānnā Thai* [Sacred Implements in Northern Thailand] (Chiang Mai: Thai Dhanu Bank, 2538 B.E./1995 C.E.), 54–55.

11. Ja. I.70. This episode also appears in the *Pathom Somphōt.*

12. Phra Thepwisutthāchān, *Phithī Opromsomphōt Phraphuttharūp lae Phithī Sū'pchātā, Sadonophkhro Chiang Mai* [The Ceremonies of Buddha Image Consecration, Life Extension, and Dispelling Misfortune in Chiang Mai] (Chiang Mai: Wat Phrathāt Doi Suthep, 2518 B.E./1975 C.E.), 5–6. The *Dhammakāya* text stipulates four eyes (divine, wisdom, Buddha, Dhamma). The orthodox Theravāda position set forth in the *Kathāvatthu* is three eyes (physical, divine, Dhamma), although *Cullanidessa* 235 refers to five eyes (physical, divine, wisdom, Buddha, and the all-round eye or all-seeing eye [*samanta*] or the eye of the *tathāgata*.) Rājavaramunī (P. A. Payutto), *Phachanānukrom Phutthasāsāt* [Dictionary of Buddhism] (Bangkok: Mahāchulālongkorn Buddhist University, 1985), 190–91. The *Mahāprajñāpāramitā Śāstra* stipulates five eyes (flesh, divine, wisdom, Buddha, Dharma) as does the *Mahāvastu* (J. J. Jones, *The Mahāvastu,* vol. 1 [London: Luzac, 1949], 125.

13. Some informants report that the mirrors symbolize the knowledge of past (*atītaṃsa*), future (*anāgataṃsa*), and present (*paccupannaṃsa*), an interpretation consistent with the Pāli *Apadāna.*

14. In my view the *buddhābhiseka* supports Tambiah's observation that rituals enact and incarnate cosmological "conceptions that enumerate and classify the phenomena that compose the universe as an ordered whole and the norms and processes that govern it." Stanley J. Tambiah, "A Performative Approach to Ritual," *Proceedings of the British Academy* 65 (1979): 121.

15. See Robert H. Sharf, "The Idolization of Enlightenment: On the Mummification of Ch'an Masters in Medieval China," *History of Religions* 32, no. 1 (August 1992): 1–31.

16. See Faure, *The Rhetoric of Immediacy,* especially chap. 8. Also, Robert H. Sharf, "On the Ritual Use of Ch'an Portraiture in Medieval China," *Cahiers d'Extrême-Asie,* no. 7 (1993–94): 149–219.

17. Sharf, "The Idolization of Enlightenment," 13. Sharf notes that the reason given for this practice in the *Pao-p'u tzu* is to prevent bodily decay.

18. J. Prien, *Praphenī lae Mongkhon Khong Thai* [Customs and Auspicious Ceremonies of the Thai] (Bangkok: Thammabanākhān, 2514 B.E./1971 C.E.), 351. Parallels can also be found in Indian funerary rites, where bodily orifices may be filled with clarified butter and sandalwood paste. See Veena Das, *Structure and Cognition: Aspects of Hindu Caste and Ritual,* 2d ed. (Delhi: Oxford University Press, 1982), 121. Since death is regarded as inauspicious, R. Pandey interprets the underlying intention of Hindu funerary rites as an attempt to dispel the inauspicious. See Rajbali Pandey, *Hindu Saṃskāras: Socio-Religious Study of the Hindu Sacraments,* 2d ed. (Delhi: Motilal Banarsidass, 1969), 121.

19. See J. P. Parry, "Death and Cosmogony in Kashi," in *Way of Life: King, Householder, Renouncer: Essays in Honour of Louis Dumont,* ed. T. N. Madan

(Paris: La Maison des sciences de l'homme, 1982), 356ff. Parry understands cremation rites to be the microcosmic equivalent to the macrocosmic pattern of destruction and creation.

20. See Faure, *The Rhetoric of Immediacy,* chaps. 8 and 9; Sharf, "The Idolization of Enlightenment"; Ray, *Buddhist Saints in India,* chaps. 10 and 11; Gregory Schopen, "Burial '*ad sanctos*' and the Physical Presence of the Buddha in Early Indian Buddhism: A Study in the Archaeology of Religions," *Religion* 17 (1987): 193–225. In Schopen's "The Buddha as an Owner of Property," he observes, "It would seem, then, again in the 'medieval age,' that the remains of dead 'images' were ritually treated and permanently housed exactly like the mortuary remains of dead Buddhas, that—in fact—the equivalence of 'image' and 'actual person' . . . held not just during the life of the 'image', but in its death, as well" (203).

21. For a description of the traditions of honoring the teacher in northern Thailand, see Manī, *Praphenī Sipsong Du'an Lānnā Thai,* 241–64.

22. Jan Gonda, "À propos d'un sens magico-religieux de skt. *guru-,*" *Selected Studies,* vol. 2 (Leiden: E. J. Brill, 1975), 295–302. "Le mot *tejas-* exprime l'essence divine qui habite dans un roi, un brahmane ou dans une autre personne importante (le Bouddha p.e.), il exprime les concepts que nous désignons par les mots 'energie'" (295–96).

23. Thai ethnographic sources provide few descriptions of the northern Thai Buddha image consecration. The most recent contributions are Manī, *Praphenī Sipsong Du'an;* and Phra Khrū Siriratanasunthorn, *Pap Suat Mon Tan* [The Complete Folio of Chants] (Chiang Mai, 2533 B.E./1990 C.E.). I have complied the list of *khan wai khrū* objects from these two sources together with my own observations. Manī's list includes a shirt and fan, but they were not present on the *khan wai khrū* table at consecration ceremonies I observed. Neither have I seen as many small figurines as inventoried by Phra Khrū Siriratanasunthorn.

24. Ja. I.70ff. This episode also appears in *Sitthāt Ōk Buat.*

25. Mhv 5.87–94. Adapted from Wilhelm Geiger, trans., *The Mahāvaṃsa or The Great Chronicle of Ceylon* (1912; reprint, Colombo: Ceylon Government Information Department, 1960), 33–34.

26. Manī considers *sado khro* or *song khro* rituals to be magical and Brahmanistic (Thai, *saiyasāt*) for the purpose of preventing bad luck. They are customarily performed at times of illness, danger, or the potential threat posed by transitions such as entering the New Year. The ritual is performed by an older layman who has usually been a monk for several years. See Manī Phayomyong, *Wathanatham Lānnā Thai* [Northern Thai Culture] (Bangkok: Thaiwathanāphānit, 2529 B.E./1986 C.E.), 42–43, 55. In 1969 Sanguan Chōtisukharat commented that the observance was dying out in northern Thailand. See his *Praphenī Thai Phāk Nū'a,* 251–57.

27. The Indra pillar (*Sao Inthakin*) protecting the city is propitiated during the annual *sū'pchātā* ceremony held in May at Wat Chedī Luang in Chiang Mai. This ceremony follows the April celebration of the Thai New Year (*songkrān*) during which the major event is the procession of the Lion Buddha image (Phra Buddha Sihing) through the city of Chiang Mai in an act of sympathetic magic to ensure the arrival of the monsoon rains. After the *sū'pchātā* and Sao Inthakin rites, a buffalo sacrifice conducted by a shaman is held in the forest at the base of Suthep

Mountain to propitiate the indigenous guardian spirits of the Lawa who inhabited the Chiang Mai valley prior to Tai dominance. Within a period of approximately one month, annual Buddhist, Brahmanical, and animistic events are held to usher in the new year. The *sū'pchātā* rite is discussed in Sanguan, *Praphenī Thai Phāk Nū'a,* 53–61; Manī, *Praphenī Sipsong Du'an,* vol. 1, 89–101. For a study of the Indra pillar in Sri Lanka, see Lily de Silva, "The Symbolism of the Indrakīla in the Parittamaṇḍapa," in *Senarat Paranavitana Commemoration Volume,* ed. L. Prematilleke et al. (Leiden: E. J. Brill, 1978), 234–50.

28. At the Buddhist Studies Workshop, Princeton University, November 12, 2001, Charles Hallisey suggested that in the light of the ritual's apparent "internal logic," namely, the metamorphization of a material object into the person of the Buddha, unhusked and husked rice and white and red cloth could be interpreted as reinforcing the theme of transformation from incomplete or unformed to formed and complete.

29. For example, Brenda E. F. Beck, "Colour and Heat in South Indian Ritual," *Man* 4, no. 4 (1969): 553–72; E. Valentine Daniel, *Fluid Signs: Being a Person the Tamil Way* (Berkeley: University of California Press, 1988), 191–202.

30. Beck, "Colour and Heat in South Indian Ritual," 553.

31. Ibid., 553–54.

32. Two Chiang Mai abbots, Phra Khrū Prachak of Wat Sāen Fāng Monastery and Phra Khrū Anuson of Wat Mū'n Lān graciously shared with me their extensive knowledge of the Buddha image consecration ceremony in several extended interviews in 1990.

33. *Pūjā Phraratanatrai* (Paying Respects to the Triple Gem): "He is the Blessed One, the All-Enlightened One. I pay respects to Him, the Blessed One, with these offerings; I pay respects to the Dhamma well-preached by the Blessed One with these offerings; I pay respects to the well-ordered Sangha of the Blessed One with these offerings."

34. Swearer, "The Layman Extraordinaire."

35. Robert C. Childers, *A Dictionary of the Pāli Language* (Rangoon: Buddha Sāsana Council Press, 1974), 179–80: "*kammaṭṭhānaṃ* is a term of wide significance, embracing a succession of rites and exercise, which form the basis or frame-work of all those modes of mystic meditation by means of which sanctification is attained."

36. Lighting the *thīan chai* also opens the ceremony marking the beginning of the Buddhist rains retreat (*phithī khaw pansā*).

37. The critical text is the *Mahāpadāna Sutta* (D II.2ff.). Vipassī is the nineteenth Buddha in the *Buddhavaṃsa,* and in other texts appears as the teacher of *dhamma* every seven years (AA I.165) and the leader of an every seventh year *uposatha* (DhA III.236).

38. See Richard Gombrich, "The Significance of Former Buddhas in the Theravādin Tradition," in *Buddhist Studies in Honour of Walpola Rahula,* ed. Somaratna Balasooriya et al. (London: Gordon Fraser, 1980), 62–72; Frank E. Reynolds, "Rebirth Traditions and the Lineages of Gotama: A Study in Theravāda Buddhology," in *Sacred Biography in the Buddhist Traditions of South and Southeast Asia,* ed. Juliane Schober (Honolulu: University of Hawai'i Press, 1997).

39. The central Thai term is *makhanayok* (Pāli, *mahānāyaka*).

40. Thanissaro Bhikkhu observes that architectural metaphors are frequently applied to this kind of chanting—laying a foundation, building a surrounding wall, constructing a tower. Personal communication, December 27, 2000.

41. For a discussion of the major *paritta* collections in Thailand, see Wells, *Thai Buddhism,* 276–82. Even though monastic ritual in Thailand was standardized in the late nineteenth and early twentieth centuries during the reigns of Kings Mongkut and Chulalongkorn, regional variation persists. See *Phra Rājā Phithī Sipsong Dū'an* [Royal Twelve Month Ceremonies] (Bangkok: Department of Fine Arts, 2511 B.E./1968 C.E.).

42. In Chiang Mai the most readily available book is *Suat Mon Mū'ang Nū'a* [Northern Thai Chants], compiled by Bunkhit Wacharasāt, an editor, publisher, and former monk, whose teacher Thawī Khū'ankāew compiled the first collection of chants specifically for northern or Tai Yüan traditions.

43. My principal informant for this list was Phra Khrū Anusorn, abbot of Wat Mū'n Lān, Chiang Mai. I corroborated his list with *Suat Mon Mū'ang Nū'a* and with Phra Khrū Phrachak, abbot of Wat Sāen Fāng, Chiang Mai.

44. Better known as the *Jinapañjara Gāthā* (The Victor's Cage) attributed to the noted late-nineteenth/early-twentieth-century central Thai monk, Somdet Phraphutthāchān Tō, also known as Brahmaraṃsī. An almost identical text, the *Mahājinapañjara,* is included in the *Pirit-pota.* Lily de Silva observes: "The . . . sutta is quite alien to canonical literature and it seems to have been influenced by Tantric literature." See Lily de Silva, *Paritta: A Historical and Religious Study of the Buddhist Ceremony for Peace and Prosperity in Sri Lanka* (Colombo: National Museums of Sri Lanka, 1981), 9. For a discussion of the *Jinapañjara* and possible Tantric influences, see Roger R. Jackson, "A Tantric Echo in Sinhalese Theravāda: *Pirit* Ritual, the Book of *Paritta* and the *Jinapañjaraya,*" *Journal of the Rare Buddhist Texts Research Project* 18 (1994): 121–40. John S. Strong includes it in *The Experience of Buddhism: Sources and Interpretations,* 2d ed. (Belmont, Calif.: Wadsworth, 2001), 241–43.

45. For a discussion of *paritta* in a northeast Thai village, see Tambiah, *Buddhism and the Spirit Cults in North-east Thailand* (Cambridge: Cambridge University Press, 1970).

46. Bunkhit, *Suat Mon Mū'ang Nū'a,* 107–8.

47. Ibid., 179–80.

48. Ibid., 219.

49. *Yot Phrakantraipitok* [The Pinnacle of the *Tipiṭaka*] (Bangkok, n.d.), 48–51. Slightly modified from a translation by Thanissaro Bhikkhu. The booklet is a widely distributed collection of apotropaic *gāthā* believed to protect from misfortune and bring good luck if distributed free for seven days or given away on one's birthday.

50. *khīṇaṃ purāṇaṃ navaṃ n'atthi sambhavaṃ/viratta-cittāyatike bhavasmiṃ/te khīṇa-bījā avirulhi-chandā/nibbanti dhirā yathā'yam-padīpo* (ended the old, there is no new birth/their minds without passion toward further becoming/they, devoid of seeds, without desire for growth/the wise go out like this flame). The candle may also be lighted by the *āchān wat.*

51. Jackson, "A Tantric Echo in Sinhalese Theravāda," 129.

52. Donald K. Swearer, *The Buddhist World of Southeast Asia* (Albany: State University of New York Press, 1995), 32–35.

53. In Central and East Asian Buddhist traditions, drums, gongs, and bells are commonly used to maintain cadence and punctuate chanting but such ritual instruments are uncommon in Theravāda chant recitation.

54. Stanley Tambiah links preaching and chanting via the mechanism of merit transference. Tambiah, *Buddhism and the Spirit Cults,* 209.

55. For a discussion of "calling the spirits" in Thai religious practice, see Anuman, *Essays on Thai Folklore,* 202–45; Ruth-Inge Heinze, *Tham Khwan: How to Contain the Essence of Life* (Singapore: Singapore University Press, 1982); Tambiah, *Buddhism and the Spirit Cults,* chap. 13. See also Swearer, "The Layman Extraordinaire," 151–68.

56. For a detailed description of a village *buat nāk* ceremony, see Tambiah, *Buddhism and the Spirit Cults,* chap. 7. For a description of novitiate ordination in Burma, see Shway Yoe [Sir James George Scott], *The Burman: His Life and Notions* (1882; reprint, New York: W. W. Norton, 1963), chap. 3.

57. See Anuman, *Essays on Thai Folklore.* For the relationship between calling the spirits and novitiate ordination, see Phya Anuman Rajadhon, *Popular Buddhism in Siam and Other Essays on Thai Studies* (Bangkok: Thai Interreligious Committee on Development and the Santhirakoses Nagapradipa Foundation, 1986), 33–43; Heinze, *Tham Khwan*; Donald K. Swearer, "A New Look at Prince Vessantara," *Research Bulletin* (National Research Council of Thailand) 10, no. 1 (1978): 1–9; Swearer, *The Buddhist World of Southeast Asia,* 46–52; Tambiah, *Buddhism and the Spirit Cults,* chaps. 13 and 14.

58. Anuman, *Popular Buddhism in Siam,* 38.

59. Tambiah is indebted to his mentor, Edmund R. Leach, "Magical Hair," *Journal of the Royal Anthropological Institute* 88 (1958): 147–64.

60. *Mahāvagga* I.86. See I. B. Horner, trans., *The Book of Discipline* (*Vinaya Pitaka*) 4 (London: Luzac, 1962), 110.

61. Several Pāli terms appropriated into Thai are translated by the word *meditation.* They include *bhāvanā, bhāvanā citta, adhiṭṭhāna citta, vipassanā, vipassanā-kammaṭṭhāna, kammaṭṭhāna, samatha.* Although technical distinctions pertain among them, Thai Buddhists tend to use the terms interchangeably. In consecration rituals two other terms signifying meditation are widely used, *plūk sek* and *nang prok. Plūk sek* literally means to arouse or awaken the power of the image, while *nang prok* refers to the monks sitting (*nang*) in meditation during a period of intense training (Pāli, *paṭivasa*). The Thai term, *prok,* is written *paraka* and may be derived from the Pāli, *parakkaṃ,* meaning strenuous exertion. *Nang prok* may refer either to the intense monastic practice sustained during a *paṭivasa* or monks meditating during the Buddha image consecration ritual.

62. This practice may reflect the association of special qualities of practice and attainment with particular disciples of the Buddha, e.g., Sāriputta—wisdom, Moggallāna—supernormal powers (A I.23), and also the cult of saints (*arahants*) as fields of merit. See John S. Strong, "The Legend of the Lion-Roarer: A Study of the Buddhist Arhat Piṇḍola Bhāradvāja," *Numen* 26 (1979): 50–88.

63. While observing holy monks at an image consecration ceremony, I am reminded of devotees seeking *darśan* from Hindu holy men, or the ecstatic response of Burmese Buddhists upon receiving a towel used in the daily morning face washing of the great Buddha image at the Mahāmuni temple near Mandalay.

64. See Appendix 4.2 for abbreviated biographies of three recently deceased, highly revered northern Thai monks who were invited to participate in several of the *buddhābhiseka* rituals I observed. For a study of sacred biography, see Frank E. Reynolds and Donald Capps, eds., *The Biographical Process: Studies in the History and Psychology of Religion* (The Hague: Mouton, 1976); and Charles F. Keyes, "Introduction: Charisma: From Social Life to Sacred Biography," and "Death of Two Buddhist Saints," in *Charisma and Sacred Biography,* ed. Michael A. Williams (Chambersburg, Pa.: American Academy of Religion, 1982), 1–22 and 149–80, respectively.

65. See Manī, *Khrū'ang Sakkāra Nai Lānnā Thai,* 57–58. In Myanmar Sujātā's offering is memorialized in the Sondawgyi feast celebrated on the full moon day of Ta'saung-mon in November. Shway Yoe, *The Burman: His Life and Notions,* 334–40.

66. Pandey, *Hindu Saṃskāras,* 92.

67. *Nidāna-Kathā,* 70. N. A. Jayawickrama, trans. *The Story of Gotama Buddha: Nidāna-kathā of the Jātakaṭṭhakathā* (Oxford: Pali Text Society, 1990), 90–91.

68. Western scholars have emphasized the efficacious power of merit-making rituals in terms of the ideology of *kamma* and rebirth. For understanding giving as a bond-creating mechanism, in this case between laity and *saṅgha,* see Lewis Hyde, *The Gift: Imagination and the Erotic Life of Property* (New York: Vintage Books, 1979), chap. 5. John S. Strong proposes that *dāna* has both rūpalogical and dharmalogical significance. Strong's enlargement of the conventional, functionalist interpretation of merit making is especially relevant to the *dhammakāya/rūpakāya* Buddhological underpinnings of the *buddhābhiseka* ritual. Strong, "The Transforming Gift," 221–37.

69. Found in the *Mahāvagga, Udāna, Jātaka,* and *Dhammapada* 153.

70. Bunkhit, *Suat Mon Mū'ang Nū'a,* 221.

71. Ibid., 183. In the *buddhānussati* section of the Vism VII.2–67, Buddhaghosa defines the special qualities of the Buddha as fully accomplished, fully enlightened, endowed with [clear] vision and [virtuous] conduct, sublime, the knower of worlds, the incomparable leader of men to be tamed, the teacher of gods and men, enlightened and blessed (M I.37; A II.285). Buddhaghosa's exegesis of these terms is nothing other than an exposition of the *dhamma.* In other words, to contemplate the person of the Buddha is, in effect, to contemplate the *dhamma.* Bhadantācariya Buddhaghosa, *The Path of Purification* (*Visuddhimagga*), trans. Bhikkhu Ñāṇamoli (Seattle: BPS Pariyatti Editions, 1999), 192–209.

72. Bizot, "La Consécration des statues et le culte des morts," 108. Italics mine.

73. Trainor, *Relics, Ritual, and Representation in Buddhism,* 166.

74. For example, see Ray, *Buddhist Saints in India;* Gustav Roth, "The Physical Presence of the Buddha and Its Representation in Buddhist Literature," in

*Investigating Indian Art* 8, ed. Marianne Yaldiz and Wibke Lobo (Berlin: Museum für indischekunst, 1987), 291–312; Schopen, "Burial '*ad sanctos*,'" 193–225; Trainor, *Relics, Ritual, and Representation in Buddhism,* especially chap. 4; Sharf, "The Idolization of Enlightenment," 1–31; Faure, *The Rhetoric of Immediacy,* especially chaps. 7, 8, and 9.

75. See Schopen, "Burial '*ad sanctos*'"; "On Monks, Nuns and 'Vulgar' Practices"; and "The Buddha as an Owner of Property."

76. Ray, *Buddhist Saints in India,* 377.

77. Faure points out the blurred distinction between the relics of the Buddha and those of saints in *The Rhetoric of Immediacy,* 148. In the opinion of both Faure and Sharf the *śarīra* cult in China was pre-Buddhistic, a view compatible with Ray's position that early Indian Buddhism was associated with a cult of saints.

78. See Robert H. Sharf, "On the Allure of Buddhist Relics," *Representations* 66 (spring 1999): 75–99.

79. See the *Kāliṅgabodhi Jātaka* (Ja IV.228) and the *Milindapañho, 95–96.*

80. Gombrich, *Precept and Practice,* chap. 3.

81. Tambiah, *The Buddhist Saints of the Forest,* 203–5. Borrowing from Charles Peirce, Tambiah refers to the Buddha as being "indexically present" in relics, images, and other signs.

82. Jacob N. Kinnard, *Imaging Wisdom: Seeing and Knowing in the Art of Indian Buddhism* (London: Curzon, 1999), 43.

83. Ibid., 34–35.

84. Ibid., 42. Kinnard acknowledges his debt to Hans-Georg Gadamer's discussion of visual images in *Truth and Method.*

85. Ibid., 42.

86. Eckel, *To See the Buddha.*

87. Malcolm David Eckel, "The Power of the Buddha's Absence: On the Foundations of Mahāyāna Buddhist Ritual," *Journal of Ritual Studies* 4, no. 2 (summer 1990): 61–95.

88. Eckel, *To See the Buddha,* 58.

89. Eckel, "The Power of the Buddha's Absence," 77.

90. Ibid., 66ff. Eckel's discussion of the Buddha's material traces borrows Charles Peirce's distinction between symbol and index, and Stanley Tambiah's development of the notion of "sedimentation" in his study of the cult of relics in Thai Buddhism.

91. Strong, *The Legend of King Aśoka,* 101.

92. Ibid., 116–17.

93. Ibid., 108.

94. In particular, John S. Strong, "Buddha Bhakti and the Absence of the Blessed One," in *Colloque Étienne Lamotte in Brussels and Liège, Belgium* (Louvain: Université Catholique de Louvain, 1989), 131–40. See also Strong, *The Legend of Upagupta,* 104–17. Strong justifies Sarvāstivāda interpretation of Buddha images on the historical grounds that Buddha images may have developed first in a Sarvāstivāda milieu, the Mathurā area of northwest India in the first century C.E. The *avadāna* texts he cites are also linked with the Sarvāstivāda tradition. He correctly points out that Western scholars have focused their

attention on the Sarvāstvāda *abhidharma* and *vinaya* rather than devotional literature.

95. Strong, "Buddha Bhakti," 133–34.

96. Strong's interpretation can be applied to the northern Thai Buddha image consecration ritual where the image is programmed with the story of the Buddha, that is, the Buddha is made present via his story or history (*phutthaphrawat*).

97. Strong, "Buddha Bhakti," 134.

98. Strong, *The Legend of Upagupta,* 112.

99. Strong, "Buddha Bhakti," 137.

100. John S. Strong, "*Gandhakuṭī:* The Perfumed Chamber of the Buddha," *History of Religions* 16, no. 4 (May 1977): 390–406. "What this effects ritually is the construction in the image hall itself of a floral perfumed chamber in which the presence of the Buddha can be realized here and now, even though he is in Nirvāṇa" (398).

101. Trainor, *Relics, Ritual, and Representation in Buddhism,* 142–44.

102. Ibid., 144.

103. Ibid.

104. Kinnard, *Imaging Wisdom,* 39. Kinnard cites Thomas Kasulis, "Philosophy as Metapraxis," in *Discourse and Practice,* ed. Frank E. Reynolds and David Tracy (Albany: State University of New York Press, 1992), 169–95.

105. Ibid. For a discussion of the relationship between meditation and Buddhist art, both iconic and aniconic, see Karlsson, *Face to Face with the Absent Buddha,* chap. 3.

106. Schopen, "The Buddha as an Owner of Property," 181–217.

107. Ibid., 185. Italics mine.

108. Ibid., 186. Italics mine.

109. Ibid., 193.

110. Ibid., 197. Italics mine.

111. Ibid., 205.

112. Strong, "*Gandhakuṭī:* The Perfumed Chamber of the Buddha," 394. Strong argues that in the Sanskrit *avadāna* literature whether or not the Buddha is depicted in a pre- or post-*nibbāna* absence, the *gandhakuṭī* provides a space in which the absent Buddha can be present in the here and now (395).

113. For a description of Buddhist chant, see Paul Demieville, "Notes on Buddhist Hymnology in the Far East," in *Buddhist Studies in Honour of Walpola Rahula,* ed. Somaratna Balasooriya et al. (London: Gordon Fraser, 1980), 44–61. For chant in Cambodia and Laos, see Alain Daniélou, *La musique du Cambodge et du Laos* (Pondicherry: Publication de l'Institute française d'indologie, 1957).

114. Piyadassi Thera, trans., *The Book of Protection: Paritta* (Kandy: The Buddhist Publication Society, 1975), 5. For a detailed description and analysis, see Lily de Silva, *Paritta,* and Peter Harvey, "The Dynamics of *Paritta* Chanting in Southern Buddhism," in *Love Divine: Studies in Bhakti and Devotional Mysticism* (London: Curzon, 1993), 53–84; Hammalawa Saddhatissa, "The Significance of Paritta and Its Application in the Theravāda Tradition," in *Buddhist Thought and Ritual,* ed. David Kalupahana (New York: Paragon House, 1991), and in the same volume, Lily de Silva, "The Paritta Ceremony of Sri Lanka: Its Antiquity and Symbolism."

115. Lily de Silva, *Paritta,* 5.

116. For a detailed comparative study of protection literature (*rakṣā*), see Peter Skilling, "The Rakṣā Literature of the Śrāvakayāna," 109–82. Skilling contends that the chanting of certain auspicious texts to protect against disease and malignant spirits and promote welfare was a "pan-nikāya" practice common to all branches of the *saṅgha* prior to the early schisms, and that the *paritta* of the Theravādins are related to other forms of protection texts and verses, e.g., mantras in both Śrāvakayāna and Mahāyāna traditions (168). This view challenges rigid distinctions between Indian Buddhist traditions based primarily on doctrinal constructions.

117. Vin II.110; A II.72. See Lynn de Silva, *Buddhism: Beliefs and Practices in Sri Lanka,* 2d ed. (Colombo: Wesley, 1980), 111–22.

118. Mhv, xxxvii, 55, 189–98. Quoted in G. P. Malalasekera, *The Pāli Literature of Ceylon* (Colombo: M. D. Gunasena, Ltd., 1958), 75. According to the commentary, at the Buddha's request Ānanda chants the *sutta* to end a cholera epidemic.

119. Mabel Haynes Bode, *The Pāli Literature of Burma* (1909; reprint, Rangoon: Burma Research Society, 1965), 3.

120. Ritual manuals are available at religious paraphernalia stores in cities and at pilgrimage centers in Thailand and Myanmar. For example, see U Thin Win, *Phaya She Kho An Myo Myo* [Various Kinds of Devotional Chants] (Rangoon, 1987); Bunkhit, *Suat Mon Mū'ang Nū'a;* Phra Sāsanasōphon, *Suat Mon Plāe* [Chants in Translation] (Bangkok: Mahāmakut, 1970). For an English translation of the *paritta,* see Piyadassi Thera, *The Book of Protection;* Sao Hutn Hmat Win, *Eleven Holy Discourses of Protection: Mahāparitta* (Rangoon: Department of Religious Affairs, 1981).

121. See Lily de Silva, *Paritta,* 5–6, for a canonical identification of the *sutta*s in the *Pirit-pota.*

122. The story of Aṅgulimāla is found in Sutta 86 in the *Majjhima Nikāya.* Aṅgulimāla Cora (the robber with a garland of fingers) was converted by the Buddha from a life of violence, became a monk, and soon realized arahantship. One day after seeing a pregnant woman in difficult labor he reported the situation to the Buddha. The Blessed One advised Aṅgulimāla to perform an act of truth by declaring that he had never intentionally taken life from the time he became an Aryan monk. He did so and the lives of mother and child were saved: "Since I was born of Aryan birth, O sister, I am not aware of having intentionally deprived any living being of life. By this assertion of Truth may you be well! May thy unborn child be well!" (*The Book of Protection,* 116).

123. Saddhatissa, "The Significance of Paritta," 125–35.

124. Lynn de Silva, *Buddhism: Beliefs and Practices in Sri Lanka,* 119.

125. Saddhatissa, "The Significance of Paritta," 126–27.

126. Phra Khrū Sitthiwarawet, *Sāsana Phithī Phū'an Mū'ang* [Northern Thai Religious Ceremonies] (Chiang Mai: S. Sapakan, 1989), 5.

127. Manī Phayomyong, "Kānsuat lae Khamsuatphithīsamkhan" [Chanting and Ritual Chants], in *Phithī Kam Lānnā Thai* [Northern Thai Rituals], ed. Phrakhrū Sittithep-chedīyārak et al. (Chiang Mai: Thārāthong, 1989): 28–55.

128. Ibid.

129. Manī, "Kānsuat lae Khamsuatphithīsamkhan."

130. Kenneth E. Wells lists seven principal modes of chanting in Thailand. To the five mentioned above he adds Indhravijien, a simple style of chanting used by school children as well as monks, and a style distinctive to chanting the *Buddha Abhiseka* in Pāli while monks sit in meditation around the *rājawat,* a practice called *nang prok (*to sit with a concentrated mind). Wells, *Thai Buddhism,* 130. He makes no mention of the *phāneyak* style of highly emphatic, rhythmic chant used in exorcist rites.

131. *Sarapanya* (Pāli, *sarabhañña*) literally means "to recite (*bhāṇa*) melodically (*sara*)."

132. For a study of the Thai forest monk tradition based largely on popular biographical and hagiographic accounts that includes Wāen, see Kamala Tiyavanich, *Forest Recollections: Wandering Monks in Twentieth-Century Thailand* (Honolulu: University of Hawai'i Press, 1997). See also Thanissaro Bhikkhu, "The Home Culture of the Dharma," *Tricycle* 8, no. 2 (1998): 59–62. His translations from the Thai forest tradition are found on the website, www.accesstoin sight.

133. Cakraphan Wongburanawat, *Kham Son Khong Luang Pū Lā* [The Teachings of Luang Pū Lā] (Chiang Mai, 2532 B.E./1989 C.E.), 38.

134. Ibid., 40.

135. Ibid.

136. Ibid.

137. Ibid., 45.

138. Sittha Chetawan and Nirōt Kasetsiri, *Luang Pū Wāen Sucinnō: Phra Arahant Yuk Paccupan* [Luang Pū Wāen Sucinnō: Contemporary Arahant] (Bangkok: Nangu' Thip, n.d.), 23. This hagiographic sacred biography of Luang Pū Wāen contrasts with a more straightforward historical life by Niyom Nikrotha, *Luang Pū Wāen Sucinnō, Wat Doi Māe Ping, Phrao, Chiang Mai Province* (Chiang Mai: Chiang Mai University, n.d.).

139. Niyom, *Luang Pū Wāen Sucinnō,* 46.

140. Ibid., 123.

141. Ibid., 51.

142. Ibid., 64.

143. Ibid., 152.

144. Thera Prawat: *Phra Khrū Phrohmcakkasanworn* [A Monk's Story] (Bangkok: Thai Kasem, 2519 B.E./1976 C.E.), 11.

145. Ibid., 31–32. This is a typical blessing that extends lovingkindness to all living beings.

146. Ibid., 21.

## CHAPTER 5. INSTRUCTING THE IMAGE

1. Bumphen Rawin, *Pathom Somphōt Samnuan Lānnā* [The Northern Thai Version of the *Pathama Sambodhi*] (Bangkok: Odian Store, 2535 B.E./1992 C.E.).

2. Manī Phayomyong, professor emeritus, Chiang Mai University, and an authority on northern Thai religion and culture, suggested that *Siddhattha's Re-*

*nunciation* be included in this study of the *buddhābhiseka* ritual and assisted in the translation.

3. See *Buddhism in Practice,* ed. Donald S. Lopez Jr. (Princeton, N.J.: Princeton University Press, 1995), 541–52, for my translation of *Bimbā's Lament.* This episode in the Buddha's legendary life appears in other Pāli, Sanskrit, Prakrit, and vernacular biographies of the Buddha. See John S. Strong, "A Family Quest: The Buddha, Yaśodharā, and Rāhula in the *Mūlasarvāstivāda Vinaya,*" in *Sacred Biography in the Buddhist Traditions of South and Southeast Asia,* ed. Juliane Schober (Honolulu: University of Hawai'i Press, 1997), 113–27. *Bimbā's Lament* may echo the version of the Great Departure found in the *Saṅghabhedavastu* (*Mūlasarvāstivāda Vinaya*).

4. Étienne Lamotte, *History of Indian Buddhism: From the Origins to the Śakya Era,* trans. Sara Webb-Boin (Louvain-La-Neuve: Université Catholique de Louvain, 1988), 644.

5. Frank E. Reynolds, "The Many Lives of the Buddha," in *The Biographical Process: Studies in the History and Psychology of Religion,* ed. Frank E. Reynolds and Donald Capps (The Hague: Mouton, 1976), 37–62.

6. George Coedès, "Une vie indochinoise du Buddha: la Paṭhamasambodhi," in *Mélanges d'indianisme à la mémoire de Louis Renou* (Paris: Éditions E. de Boccard, 1968), 217.

7. Bumphen, *Pathom Somphōt Samnuan Lānnā,* iii–v.

8. Ibid., 7.

9. Hammalawa Saddhatissa, "Pāli Literature from Laos," in *Buddhist Studies in Honour of I. B. Horner,* ed. L. S. Cousins et al. (Dordrecht: D. Reidel, 1974), 340, n. 56.

10. Somdet Krom Phra Paramānuchit-chinōrot, *Phra Pathomsomphōt Kathā* (Bangkok: Amnuaysān, 2530 B.E./1987 C.E.).

11. For English translations of the MLV, see Chester Bennett, "Life of Gaudama," *Journal of the American Oriental Society* 3 (1852–53): 1–163, and Paul Bigandet, *The Life or Legend of Gaudama: The Buddha of the Burmese,* 2 vols. (1858; reprint, 3d ed., Varanasi: Bharatiya, 1979). Bennett only translates the *Mālālaṅkāravatthu* whereas Bigandet augments his translation with material from the *Tathāgata Udāna* and other Burmese Buddha biographical texts, accounts of the three councils, and the spread of Buddhism in Burma.

12. Craig James Reynolds, *The Buddhist Monkhood in Nineteenth-Century Thailand* (Ann Arbor: University Microfilms, 1973), 136.

13. Coedès, "Une vie indochinoise du Buddha," 226.

14. For a discussion of Māra, see Trevor O. Ling, *Buddhism and the Mythology of Evil: A Study in Theravāda Buddhism* (London: George Allen and Unwin, 1962), especially chap. 4; James W. Boyd, *Satan and Māra: Christian and Buddhist Symbols of Evil* (Leiden: E. J. Brill, 1975), 2.

15. AA I. 397–98. Edmund Hardy, "Māra in the Guise of Buddha," *Journal of the Royal Asiatic Society* (1902): 951–55.

16. The Bv begins with a section on the jewel walk prior to the account of Sumedha in the story of the Buddha Dīpaṅkara. This episode receives extensive elaboration in the BvA and is also mentioned in the DhpA.

17. This translation is based on two texts, one in northern Thai script on palm leaves (*pai lān*) inscribed by a novice monk, Philawong Suandok in Culasakarāja 1225 (1842 C.E.) at Wat Bān Nōi in Chiang Mai Province, and the other printed in central Thai script redacted by Bunkhit Wacharasāt, owner of the Thārāthong Press. This publishing firm and similar ones in Lampāng and Chiang Rai edit and publish many texts on heavy brown paper folded accordion style. Since most of the texts now presented to monasteries on special merit-making occasions are the printed paper editions, Bunkhit and his fellow editors wield a significant unofficial influence over what is preached. In the case of the *Pathom Somphōt,* even though Bunkhit has edited out many details, the two texts are substantially the same.

18. In this context, the term *guṇa* refers to those qualities the Buddha achieved on the night of his enlightenment, in particular, his victory over Māra, the attainment of extraordinary states of consciousness, and his comprehension of the *dhamma.*

19. Variant reading: "On him the three worlds depend."

20. Of the thirty perfections (*pāramī*) the ten most prominent are: charity (*dāna*), good conduct (*sīla*), renunciation (*nekkhamma*), wisdom (*paññā*), endeavor (*viriya*), forbearance (*khanti*), truthfulness (*sacca*), determination (*adhiṭṭhāna*), lovingkindness (*mettā*), and equanimity (*upekkhā*). The ten perfections are found in the Bv and the Cp, two Pāli texts central to the popular understanding of the nature of the Buddha. These virtues are also illustrated in the final ten *bodhisatta* lives of the Buddha (*dasajātaka*).

21. In the Pāli tradition the standard five conditions are: time (*kāla*), country (*desa*), continent (*dīpa*), family (*kula*), mother (*matara*).

22. The text incorporates the two Theravāda etymologies given for Rāhula: binding in the sense that a son binds a father to the world; the lunar calendar designation of Rāhu as the midpoint of the week and, hence, by analogy the sign that marks the turning point in the future Buddha's life. Rāhu can also refer to a lunar eclipse.

23. The seven jewels of the *cakkavattin* are: disc or wheel (*cakka*), elephant, horse, jewel, queen, attendants, military leader.

24. See Edward J. Thomas, *The Life of the Buddha as Legend and History* (London: Routledge and Kegan Paul, 1956), 70, n. 4. Thomas lists the standard five dreams as: (1) the Buddha reclines on the world as a great couch with the Himālaya mountains as a pillow; his hands and feet stretch into the oceans, signifying that the *tathāgata* attained complete enlightenment; (2) a *tiriyā* plant that grew from the Buddha's hand touches the sky, signifying the noble eightfold path; (3) white worms with black heads creep up to his knees and cover them, representing white-robed householders who come to the *tathāgata* for refuge; (4) four birds of different colors come from the four quarters, fall at his feet, and change to white, symbolizing the four castes who, upon leaving the householder life for the doctrine taught by the *tathāgata,* realize the highest release; (5) the Buddha walks undefiled on a mountain of dung, signifying that the *tathāgata* is unattached to the monastic requisites (A III.240; *Mahāvastu* II.136).

25. Variant reading, 8 cubits.

26. A distance that can be traveled with one yoke of oxen, about 7 miles.

27. Variant reading: "had the length and width of one *yojana.*"

28. The variant reading contains a more detailed description of the weapons of Māra's army.

29. The Buddha sitting in the middle of a lotus surrounded by a wheel (*cakka*) describes the *bodhimaṇḍala* referred to in the text.

30. The Thai term, *winyān,* from the Pāli, *viññāṇa,* refers to a disembodied spirit rather than consciousness, one of the five aggregates.

31. In the Sanskrit *Lalitavistara,* her name is Sthavara.

32. The miraculous floodwaters that symbolize the future Buddha's collective merit provides a mythic parallel to the water of lustration (*abhiseka*) created by the power of the Buddha image consecration ritual.

33. The five Māras appear in the commentaries (ThagA ii.46) and the Vism 211, although elsewhere Māra is spoken of as one, three, or four. "Where Māra is one, the reference is generally either to the *kilesa*s or death," according to G. P. Malalasekera, *Dictionary of Pāli Proper Names,* vol. 2 (London: Pali Text Society, 1974), 611.

34. The scene illustrates a cosmic version of the *bodhimaṇḍa,* a golden Buddha sitting on a diamond throne under a silver *bodhi* tree within a radiant, multicolored wheel joining heaven and earth.

35. In the *Mahāvagga* account, after hearing the Buddha's first teaching, Koṇḍañña requests ordination.

36. The five extinctions of defilements are: suppression (*vikkhambana-nirodha*); substitution of opposites (*tadaṅga-*); cutting off (*sammuccheda-*); tranquilization (*paṭipassaddhi-*); escape or getting freed from (*nissaraṇa-*). Paṭis I.27, 220–21, Vism 410.

37. Gotamī's presence at the birth at Lumbinī is omitted from both the Ja-nidāna and the northern and central Thai versions of the PS. It does appear, however, in the MLV.

38. Literally, "what will be the balance of suffering (*dukkha*) and happiness (*sukha*)."

39. In the standard Pāli account in the Ja-nidāna eight Brahmans make the prediction. Seven raise two fingers, indicating that Siddhattha will become either a *cakkavattin* or a *sammāsambuddha,* while the eighth holds up only one finger, predicting that he will become a fully enlightened Buddha.

40. In the *Lalitavistara* the number is given as 20,000.

41. In the *Sutta Nipāta* and the *Lalitavistara,* the name of the sage is Asita. In the Ja-nidāna he is called Kāladevala, or Devala the Black. This text follows the Ja-nidāna but uses the variant, Devala.

42. In the Pāli tradition Suddhodana pays homage to his son Siddhattha on three occasions: the visit by the sage, Devala; the plowing ceremony and the miracle of the roseapple tree; the miracle of the jewel walk when the Buddha returns to Kapilavatthu after his enlightenment. This text omits the third and reverses the order of the first two.

43. In the standard lives of the Buddha, Siddhattha's wife is called Yasodharā, although in some popular Pāli texts she is known as Bimbā.

44. In the Ja-nidāna the Sakyans' criticism of Siddhattha applies only to his archery prowess, not his proposed marriage to Bimbā. The episode in SB may reflect the account in the commentary to A I.145 or other traditional lives of the Buddha. Details of the archery feat vary greatly among the accounts. For example, it is highly elaborated in the *Lalitavistara* but receives only a brief mention in the Ja-nidāna.

45. The standard account in the Ja-nidāna, *Mahāvastu,* and *Lalitavistara* includes the encounter with a renunciant as the fourth of four sights preceded by old age, sickness, and death.

46. The etymology of Rāhula differs from the *Pathom Somphōt.*

47. Thai, *khwām rak,* love in the sense of attachment.

48. The jewel wheel is the symbol of the *cakkavattin* world ruler. See *Cakkavatti Sīhanāda Sutta* (D III), *Mahāsuddassana Sutta* (D II), and also, Strong, *The Legend of King Aśoka,* 49–56.

49. The eight monastic requisites are: three robes, belt, bowl, razor, needle, water strainer. Another list includes the basic requisites as food, clothing, lodging, and medicine.

50. An elaboration on *Sutta Nipāta* iii.1.

51. In the Ja-nidāna the five ascetics leave Siddhattha after he ends his ascetic fast (Ja. I.67).

52. The passage describing the creation of what can be regarded as the essence of milk from 1,000 cows (i.e., the one underlying the many) is corrupt in the text. I have adapted the description from Paramānuchit-chinōrot, *Phra Pathomsomphōt Kathā,* 115–16. This passage does not appear in the northern Thai version of the *Pathomsomphōt.*

53. In the text there is a long, hyperbolic description of the construction of a 90 meter, elaborately carved *pāsāda* decorated with jewels, bronze, and gold. In northern Thailand such elaborate, expensive preparations characterize the cremations of revered monks.

54. This episode is absent from the *Mahāparinibbāna Sutta,* which the SB otherwise follows quite closely in the narrative of the Buddha's last days. The story of Mālikā does occur in the *Mālālaṅkāravatthu,* where she is identified as the wife of a Malla general. Mālikā also appears in the *Candagādha Jātaka* included in the *Paññāsajātaka* collection compiled in Chiang Mai in the sixteenth century.

55. DhA I.392.

56. An *ājīvaka* ascetic. Thomas, *The Life of the Buddha,* 155.

57. A *kannika* tree appears when the Buddha is born, reaches enlightenment, and dies.

58. The miraculous extension of the Buddha's feet from the funeral pyre is found in the Pāli commentary on the *Mahāparinibbāna Sutta.*

## CHAPTER 6. EMPOWERING THE IMAGE

1. The title of the image consecration text appears as *Buddha Abhiseka* (BA) but when referring just to the ritual it is written as *buddhābhiseka.* The BA trans-

lated in this chapter is the shorter preached text. An abbreviated version of this translation appears in *Buddhism in Practice,* ed. Donald S. Lopez Jr. (Princeton, N.J.: Princeton University Press, 1995), 50–58.

2. Redundancy and repetition have been removed wherever possible without compromising the sense of the text.

3. For a discussion of mindful awareness, see Nyanaponika Thera, *The Heart of Buddhist Meditation* (London: Rider, 1962); Soma Thera, *The Way of Mindfulness: The Satipaṭṭhāna Sutta and Commentary,* 3d ed. (Kandy: The Buddhist Publication Society, 1967); Thanissaro Bhikkhu (Geoffrey DeGraff), *The Wings to Awakening* (Barre, Mass.: Dharma Dana, 1996), especially 72–104, 154–72. See also Winston L. King, *Theravāda Meditation: The Buddhist Transformation of Yoga* (Delhi: Motilal Banarsidass, 1992).

4. For recent studies on the *jhāna*s, see Roderick S. Bucknell, "Reinterpreting the *Jhānas,*" *Journal of the International Association of Buddhist Studies* 16, no. 2 (winter 1993): 375–401; Martin Stuart-Fox, "Jhāna and Buddhist Scholasticism," *Journal of the International Association of Buddhist Studies* 12, no. 2 (1989): 79–110; Paul Griffiths, "Buddhist Jhāna: A Form-Critical Study," *Religion* 13 (1983): 55–68. Bucknell cites the increasing complexity of the jhānic scheme in late canonical and postcanonical texts as evidence of an early split in the *saṅgha* between meditator and scholar monks.

5. The *Mahāsaccaka Sutta* (M I.36) describes the Buddha's enlightenment in a manner similar to the BA and the SBN.

6. Another autobiographical *sutta* in the *Majjhima Nikāya,* the *Ariyapariyesanā Sutta,* adds four additional *jhāna*s to the Buddha's realization: the plane of infinite ether, the plane of infinite consciousness, the plane of nothingness, the plane of neither perception nor nonperception.

7. T. W. Rhys Davids and William Stede, eds., *The Pali Text Society's Pali-English Dictionary* (London: Luzac,1959), 64.

8. See Alfred Foucher, *The Life of the Buddha According to the Ancient Texts and Monuments of India,* trans. Simone Brangier Boas (Middletown, Conn.: Wesleyan University Press, 1963), chap. 6.

9. Louis de LaVallée Poussin, "Le Bouddha et les Abhijñas," *Le Muséon* 32 (1931): 335–42.

10. *Thus Have I Heard: The Long Discourses of the Buddha,* trans. Maurice Walshe (London: Wisdom, 1987), 105.

11. La Vallée Poussin, "Le Bouddha et les Abhijñas," 337.

12. For a summary discussion of the appearance of *paṭicca samuppāda* with regard to the Buddha's enlightenment, see Étienne Lamotte, "Conditioned Coproduction and Supreme Enlightenment," in *Buddhist Studies in Honour of Walpola Rahula,* ed. S. Balasooriya, et al. (London: Gordon Fraser, 1980).

13. Nalinaksha Dutt, *Early Monastic Buddhism* (Calcutta: Calcutta Oriental Book Agency, 1960), chap. 10. See also David J. Kalupahana, *Causality: The Central Philosophy of Buddhism* (Honolulu: University of Hawai'i Press, 1975).

14. Thanissaro, *The Wings to Awakening,* 302.

15. Ibid.

16. In the Vism the steps are *vipassanā, magga, phala, paccavekkhaṇa.*

17. See Vism 630–71, Paṭis I.1.

18. Translated in collaboration with Sommai Premchit, Social Research Institute, Chiang Mai University. Subject headings have been inserted to clarify the organization of the text. The translation is based on a version of the BA redacted by Bunkhit Wacharasāt. A palm leaf manuscript from the Duang Dī Monastery in Chiang Mai, copied in 1576 C.E. in Chiang Saen, was also consulted. The text is of the *vohara* genre, in Tai Yüan (northern Thai) vernacular and Pāli. Pāli manuscripts of the BA appear in northern Thai monastery catalogues. Saddhatissa refers to the *Dasavarañāṇabuddhābhiseka,* a Pāli text in Laos and describes it as "a compilation of verses in praise of the Buddha, designed to procure happiness and to invite the power of the Buddha to enter the image. Likewise, it is particularly recited at the time of the making of images of the Buddha" (Saddhatissa, "Pāli Literature from Laos," 334).

19. The fourth level of the heavenly realm (*devaloka*).

20. The classic interdependent co-arising formula is twelve stages: ignorance, mental formations, consciousness, name and form, the sense spheres, contact, feeling, craving, clinging, becoming, birth, old age.

21. The standard pattern is craving->clinging->becoming->birth.

22. The four *apāya* are *niraya* (hell), *tiracchānayoni* (realm of beasts), *pittivisaya* (realm of the hungry ghosts), and *asurakayā* (realm of the demons). See It 50–99.

23. Sirisadhammaraṃsi's *Buddhābhisekagāthā* (1591 C.E.) also concludes with verses that implant into the image the powers of the Buddha's *nibbāna,* although the lists differ. Sirisadhammaraṃsi's text includes the Five Wisdom Eyes.

24. This translation is based on a Pāli manuscript at Lai Hin Monastery, Lampāng, Thailand. Also consulted was a manuscript from Wat Pākkong, Chiang Mai, Thailand. Translated in collaboration with Sommai Premchit. Subject topics have been inserted to clarify the organization of the text. See Louis Finot, *Liste Gènérale des Manuscrits Laotien, BEFEO* 7 (1917): 197.

25. See *Udāna* I.1–3, *Mahāvagga* I.1–7.

26. The *gāthā* was reconstructed by Punchi Megaskumbhara, Department of Sinhala, University of Peradeniya, Peradeniya, Sri Lanka.

## CHAPTER 7. THE BODY OF THE BUDDHA

1. Schopen, "The Buddha as an Owner of Property," 181–217. See also Gregory Schopen, *Bones, Stones, and Buddhist Monks: Collected Papers on the Archaeology, Epigraphy, and Texts of Monastic Buddhism in India* (Honolulu: University of Hawai'i Press, 1997), 258–89.

2. J.A.B. Van Buitenen considers that the term *tathāgata* was derived from the sentence construction *yathāgata . . . tathāgata,* meaning, "just as [the Buddhas of the past] came, so too [did Gotama]." Personal communication, John S. Strong, June 20, 1999.

3. Malalasekera, *Dictionary of Pāli Proper Names,* vol. 2, 886.

4. Richard Gombrich points out that the pattern of Vipassī's life and the other Buddhas of this eon follows that of Siddhattha Gotama rather than the reverse,

in "The Significance of Former Buddhas in the Theravāda Tradition," 65. This shared life pattern gives a timeless dimension to the story of Siddhattha Gotama's realization of Buddhahood. When referring to the expansion of the Buddha story in Bv and Cp, Jonathan S. Walters uses the terms *universal soteriology* and *cosmic Buddha biography* in "Stūpa, Story, and Empire," 166.

5. T. W. Rhys Davids and C.A.F. Rhys Davids, trans., *Dialogues of the Buddha,* 4th ed., pt. 2 (London: Pali Text Society, 1959), 1.

6. Steven Collins demonstrates that the idea of multiple Buddhas is acknowledged by the earliest Pāli texts and is intrinsic to the logic of Buddhism in *Nirvana and Other Buddhist Felicities: Utopias of the Pali Imaginaire* (Cambridge: Cambridge University Press, 1998), 347–55.

7. See Alan Sponberg and Helen Hardacre, eds., *Maitreya, the Future Buddha* (Cambridge: Cambridge University Press, 1988). For two important Metteyya texts in northern Thailand, see Bumphen Rawin, *Lānnā Anāgatavaṃsa and Metteyyavaṃsa* (Chiang Mai: Mahāchulalongkorn Buddhist University, 2535 B.E./1992 C.E.). See also Udaya Meddagama, trans., *Anāgatavaṃsa Desanā: The Sermon of the Chronicle-To-Be,* ed. John C. Holt (Delhi: Motilal Banarsidass, 1993).

8. For references to the eonic Buddhas in Pagan's architecture and iconography, see Paul Strachan, *Pagan: Art and Architecture of Old Burma* (Whiting Bay: Kiscadale, 1989), especially chaps. 2 and 3; Gordon Luce, *Old Burma-Early Pagan,* 3 vols. (Locust Valley, N.Y.: J. J. Augustin, 1969–70).

9. Mireille Bénisti, "Les *stūpa* aux cinq piliers," *BEFEO* 58 (1971): 131–62; Bizot, *Le figuier à cinq branches: Recherche sur le bouddhisme khmer I.*

10. Gombrich, "The Significance of Former Buddhas," 64. The names of twenty-eight Buddhas are also mentioned in the Bv, and there is a Southeast Asian tradition of the veneration of twenty-eight Buddhas. See *The Minor Anthologies of the Pali Canon: Chronicle of the Buddhas (Buddhavaṃsa) and Basket of Conduct (Cariyāpiṭaka),* trans. I. B. Horner (London: Pali Text Society, 1975), xl–xlii.

11. Walshe, trans., *Thus Have I Heard,* 215–16.

12. Reynolds, "Rebirth Traditions," 28.

13. Gombrich, "The Significance of Former Buddhas," 64.

14. D II.10.

15. D II.12–15.

16. Reynolds, "Rebirth Traditions," 28.

17. The seven perfections are selfless giving, moral rectitude, renunciation, resolute determination, truthfulness, lovingkindness, and equanimity. Wisdom, energy, and patience are omitted from the traditional list of ten *pāramī* but they are mentioned in a concluding envoi verse.

18. Reynolds, "Rebirth Traditions," 22–24.

19. Horner, *The Minor Anthologies of the Pali Canon,* 9.

20. Gombrich, "The Significance of Former Buddhas," 68.

21. Horner, *The Minor Anthologies of the Pali Canon,* 10.

22. Ibid., 15.

23. Punchi B. Megaskumbhara and Udaya Meddegama, University of Peradeniya, Sri Lanka, provided information regarding the Suvisi Vivaraṇa Pūjā.

24. Gombrich, *Precept and Practice,* 217–25. See also Richard Gombrich, "Feminine Elements in Sinhalese Buddhism," *Wiener Zeitschrift für die Kunde Südasiens und Archiv für Indische Philosophie* 16 (1972): 67–93.

25. Bénisti, "Les stūpa aux cinq piliers," especially 145–58. Also Bénisti, "Étude sur le *stūpa,*" especially 70–72, 81–85.

26. Frank E. Reynolds and Charles Hallisey, "Buddha," in *Encyclopedia of Religion,* 1–2, ed. Mircea Eliade (New York: Macmillan, 1989), 327.

27. Ibid., 149.

28. Luce, *Old Burma-Early Pagan,* vol. 1, 244. Also Strachan, *Pagan: Art and Architecture of Old Burma,* 70.

29. Ginette Martini, "Pañcabuddhabyākaraṇa," *BEFEO* 55 (1969): 127.

30. Adhémard Leclère, *Cambodge, fêtes civiles et religieuses* (Paris: Imprimerie Nationale, 1916), 143.

31. Peter Skilling, "Five Bodhisattvas," in *Fragile Palm Leaves: For the Preservation of Buddhist Literature,* no. 5 (2542 B.E./1999 C.E.) 10.

32. Bruce Evans, trans., "The Blessings of the Five Buddhas," in *Fragile Palm Leaves: For the Preservation of Buddhist Literature,* no. 4 (2541 B.E./1998 C.E.) 10–12.

33. *Paññāsachādok* [The Fifty Jātakas], 2 vols. (Bangkok: National Library, 1956). See I. B. Horner and Padmanabh S. Jaini, trans., *Apocryphal Birth-Stories* (*Paññāsa Jātaka*), 2 vols. (London: Pali Text Society, 1985–86).

34. *Tamnān Kā Phū'ak: Thammathesanā Phū'anmū'angnū'a* [The White Crow: A Sermon in Northern Thai] (Chiang Mai: Thārāthong Press, n.d.).

35. Strong, *The Legend and Cult of Upagupta,* 202–4.

36. In Tai traditions becoming a monk earns special merit for one's mother. See Charles F. Keyes, "Mother, Mistress, But Never a Monk: Buddhist Notions of Female Gender in Rural Thailand," *American Ethnologist* 11, no. 2 (May 1984): 223–41.

37. Summarized from Gombrich, "The Significance of Former Buddhas."

38. Horner, "Introduction," in *The Minor Anthologies of the Pali Canon, Part III,* xxx.

39. In the *Buddhāpadāna* (*Khuddaka Nikāya*) the Buddha Gotama conjures a Buddha field with all the past Buddhas and their *saṅghas*. The *apadāna* collection is one of the last books added to the Pāli canon. Oskar von Hinüber, *A Handbook of Pāli Literature* (Berlin: Walter de Gruyter, 1996), 61.

40. Jinak 3. Like the Legend of the White Crow, the narrative centers on the mutual caring between mother and son.

41. Gombrich, "The Significance of Former Buddhas," 70.

42. Ibid., 71.

43. André Bareau, "The Notion of Time in Early Buddhism," *East and West* 7, no. 4 (January 1957): 353–64.

44. Prince Damrong Rājānubhāb, *Monuments of the Buddha in Siam,* 2d ed., trans. Sulak Sivaraksa and A. B. Griswold (Bangkok: The Siam Society, 1973), 38. See also Carol Stratton and Miriam McNair Scott, *The Buddhist Sculpture of Northern Thailand* (Chiang Mai: Silkworm Books, 1999).

45. K. I. Matics, *Gestures of the Buddha* (Bangkok: Chulalongkorn University Press, 1998), 169–93; Manī Phayomyong, *Wathanatham Lānnā* [Northern Thai

Culture] (Bangkok: Thaiwathanāphānit, 2529 B.E./1986 C.E.), 34–36. For an association between previous Buddhas and pre-Buddhist divinities, see Georg von Simson, "Die Buddhas der Vorzeit: Versuch einer astralmythologischen Deutung," *Studien zur Indologie und Iranistik* 7 (1981): 77–91.

46. Hutchinson, "The Seven Spires," 1–68.

47. "It is taught that one should build a Buddha image appropriate to the day, month, and year of one's birth in order to ensure happiness and prosperity. These images will usually be made out of brass, bronze, or a mixture of metals. Wealthy people may have them made from gold or silver. Or, sometimes images may be chisled from stone, wood, or according to the means of the sponsor." Sanguan Chōtisukharat, *Praphenī Thai Phāk Nū'a* [The Customs of Northern Thailand] (Bangkok: Odian Store, 2512 B.E./1969 C.E.), 187 (translation mine). In Burma, the addition of an eighth day to the week (Wednesday P.M.) allows a correlation between the birthday Buddhas and the eight directions, a tradition also followed in northern Thailand.

48. Votive candle instructions purchased at Wat Phra Kāew, Lampāng, Thailand. Translation mine.

49. For descriptions of amulets and votive tablets, see Pattaratorn Chirapravati, *Votive Tablets in Thailand: Origin, Styles, and Uses* (Kuala Lumpur: Oxford University Press, 1997; Chit Buwabut, *Prawat Yo Phraphim Nai Prathet Thai* [A Short History of Votive Tablets in Thailand] (Bangkok: Umphornphitaya, 2514 B.E./1971 C.E.); Songchai Chetbut et. al., *Phra Khrū'ang Mū'ang Nū'a: 15 Changwat* [Northern Thai Amulets in Fifteen Provinces] (Chiang Mai: Changphū'ak, 2503 B.E./1960 C.E.).

50. Herman Oldenberg and Richard Pischel, *Therā- and Therīgāthā,* 2d ed. (London: Luzac, 1966), 51.

51. Akanuma Chizen, "Triple Body of the Buddha," *The Eastern Buddhist* 1 (May–August 1922): 9.

52. *Mahāpadāna Sutta,* D II.32–35. See Mark R. Woodward, "The Biographical Imperative in Theravāda Buddhism," in *Sacred Biography in the Buddhist Traditions of South and Southeast Asia,* ed. Juliane Schober (Honolulu: University of Hawai'i Press, 1997), 42.

53. Nalinaksha Dutt, *Mahayana Buddhism* (Calcutta: Firma K. L. Mukhopadhyay, 1973), 141.

54. For a general study of Mantrayānic elements in Theravāda, see L. S. Cousins, "Aspects of Esoteric Southern Buddhism," in *Indian Insights: Buddhism, Brahmanism and Bhakti,* ed. Peter Connolly and Sue Hamilton (London: Luzac Oriental, 1997), 185–207.

55. Italics mine.

56. Lamotte, *History of Indian Buddhism,* 622.

57. Frank E. Reynolds, "The Several Bodies of the Buddha: Reflections on a Neglected Aspect of the Theravāda Tradition," *History of Religions* 16, no. 4 (May 1977): 374.

58. Ibid, 375.

59. Ibid., 383–87.

60. See Anne M. Blackburn, *Buddhist Learning and Textual Practice in Eighteenth-Century Lankan Monastic Culture* (Princeton, N.J.: Princeton University Press, 2001).

61. Reynolds, "The Several Bodies of the Buddha," 386. For an examination of the Yogāvacara tradition in Southeast Asia, see the work of François Bizot, especially *Le Chemin de Laṅkā.*

62. Strong, "The Transforming Gift," 222. See also Nagao, "On the Theory of Buddha-Body (*Buddha-kāya*)," 26.

63. See Louis de La Vallée Poussin, "Note sur les corps du Bouddha," *Le Muséon* 14 (1913): 257–90, especially 260–62; Sukumar Dutt, *The Buddha and Five After-Centuries* (London: Luzac, 1957), chap. 7.

64. Reynolds, "The Several Bodies of the Buddha," and Strong, "The Transforming Gift."

65. A II.38. The Brahman, Droṇa, noticing the sign of the wheel on the feet of the Buddha, asked whether he was a *deva, gandhabba, yakkha,* or human being. The Buddha replied that having eliminated all impurities (*āsava*s) he had attained Buddhahood and should be considered a fully enlightened Buddha (*sammāsambuddha*).

66. Strong, *The Legend of King Aśoka,* 109–19.

67. Reynolds, "The Several Bodies of the Buddha," 376.

68. For example, see Schopen, "Monks and the Relic Cult," and "On Monks, Nuns, and 'Vulgar' Practices," 153–68.

69. Strong, "The Transforming Gift," 227–37.

70. Ibid., 224. Quoting the *Aṣṭasāhasrikāprajñāpāramitā.*

71. Ibid., 225.

72. André Bareau, "The Superhuman Personality of the Buddha and Its Symbolism in the Mahāparinirvāṇasūtra of the Dharmaguptaka," in *Myths and Symbols in Honor of Mircea Eliade,* ed. Joseph M. Kitagawa and Charles H. Long (Chicago: University of Chicago Press, 1969), 11.

73. D I. 77. Otto Stein proposes that the mind-created body is connected with the Mahāyāna *sambhogakāya.* O. Stein, "Notes on the Trikāya-Doctrine," in *Jhā Commemoration Volume: Essays on Oriental Subjects,* Poona Oriental Series, no. 39 (Poona: Oriental Book Agency, 1937), 395.

74. N. Dutt, *Mahayana Buddhism,* 147, referring to Buddhagosha's commentary on the *Dhammasaṅgaṇī.*

75. A V.355.

76. M I.190–91; S III.120.

77. N. Dutt, *Mahayana Buddhism,* 141. For example, *dharmakāya* becomes an expression of *tathāgatagarbha.* D. Seyfort Ruegg, *La Théorie du Tathāgatagarbha et du Gotra* (Paris: Publications de l'École française d'Extrême-Orient 70, 1969), 509.

78. Paul Harrison, "Is the *Dharma-kāya* the Real 'Phantom Body' of the Buddha?"*Journal of the International Association of Buddhist Studies* 15 (1992): 50.

79. Strong, *The Legend of King Aśoka,* 116–17.

80. Bizot, *Le Chemin de Laṅkā,* 293.

81. Ibid., 30.

82. Ibid., 299. There are several divergences among the *dhammakāya* texts included in chap. 3 and those studied by Bizot, Coedès, and Finot. For example, the enumerated bodily parts and corresponding doctrinal teachings vary from twenty-six or twenty-seven to thirty-two. On the basis of the tradition of the thirty-two

rūpic marks of the great person (D I.30), it is reasonable to assume there would be a corresponding number of dhammic marks.

83. Ibid., 294.

84. Bizot, "La Consécration des Statues et le Culte des Morts," 113.

85. Ibid.

86. Below is a comparison of the *rūpakāya* elements in three *dhammakāya* formula from Bizot, *Le Chemin de Laṅkā,* 295–300; Coedès, "Dhammakāya," 248–86; and the northern Thai text included in chap. 3.

| *Bizot* | *Coedès* | *Swearer* |
|---|---|---|
| 1. head | head | head |
| 2. aura of flame | hair | hair |
| | | [body?] |
| 3. forehead | forehead | forehead |
| 4. forehead mark | forehead mark | forehead mark |
| 5. eyebrows | eyebrows | eyebrows |
| 6. eyes | eyes | eyes |
| 7. ears | ears | ears |
| 8. nose | nose | nose |
| 9. cheeks | cheeks | earlobes |
| 10. teeth | teeth | lips |
| 11. lips | lips | teeth |
| 12. eyeteeth | eyeteeth | eyeteeth |
| 13. tongue | tongue | tongue |
| 14. jaw | jaw | jaw |
| 15. neck | neck | neck |
| 16. throat | throat | throat |
| 17. arms | arms | arms |
| 18. fingers | fingers | fingers |
| 19. palms of hands | chest | chest |
| 20. breasts | breasts | breasts |
| 21. abdomen | abdomen | calves |
| 22. thighs | navel | feet |
| 23. calves | buttocks | *saṅghāṭī* robe |
| 24. feet | thighs | *cīvara* robe |
| 25. *cīvara* robe | calves | outer robe |
| 26. outer robe | feet | belt |
| 27. belt | *saṅghāṭī* robe | |
| 28. | *cīvara* robe | |
| 29. | outer robe | |
| 30. | belt | |

87. For purposes of simplicity and because it is the most complete, I follow the sequence in the Coedès version of the text.

88. See Maryla Falk, *Nāma-Rūpa, Dharma-Rūpa: Origin and Aspects of an Ancient Indian Conception* (Calcutta: University of Calcutta Press, 1943).

89. *Ñāṇa* in this context conveys a state of knowing rather than a knowledge of a particular subject or object.

90. See D. Seyfort Ruegg, "Pāli *gotta/gotra* and the Term *gotrabhū* in Pāli and Buddhist Sanskrit," in *Buddhist Studies in Honour of I. B. Horner,* ed. L. Cousins, A. Kunst, and K. R. Norman (Dordrecht: D. Reidel, 1974), 199–210.

91. See M I.71; A II.8.

92. Recollection of the Buddha, the *dhamma,* the *saṅgha,* moral virtue, generosity, the deities, death, the body, breathing, quietude (A I.30; Vism 197).

93. The seven factors of enlightenment are mindfulness, truth-investigation, effort, joy, tranquillity, concentration, equanimity (D III.251, 282).

94. Coedès, "Dhammakāya," 28.

95. I adopted these terms from M. Woodward, "The Biographical Imperative in Theravāda Buddhism," 40–63; Robert L. Brown, "Narrative as Icon: The Jātaka Stories in Ancient Indian and Southeast Asian Architecture," in *Sacred Biography in the Buddhist Traditions of South and Southeast Asia,* ed. Juliane Schober (Honolulu: University of Hawai'i Press, 1997), 64–109. Brown uses the term *icon* in the Peircean sense of shared characteristics as, for example, a cloth sample signifies similarity with other pieces of that cloth not based on conventional or causal connections but because they are actually alike.

96. Jerome Bruner, *Actual Minds, Possible Worlds* (Cambridge, Mass.: Harvard University Press, 1986), 12–13.

97. Ibid., 13.

98. Brown, "Narrative as Icon," 65. Brown develops his position in contrast to Vidya Dehejia's view that bas-reliefs at early Buddhist sites in India are "visual narratives" of the life of the Buddha.

99. S. Dutt, *The Buddha and Five After-Centuries,* 234.

100. Bareau, "The Superhuman Personality of the Buddha," 9–21. Bareau connects the Buddha as supreme conqueror to the myth of royalty.

101. Reynolds, "Rebirth Traditions," 31.

102. David L. Snellgrove, ed., *The Image of the Buddha* (Tokyo: Kodansha International, 1978), 53.

103. Robert L. Brown, "God on Earth: The Walking Buddha in the Art of South and Southeast Asia," *Artibus Asiae* 50 (1990): 73–107.

104. For a general discussion of Buddha images in royal attire and the debates regarding their origin and meaning, see Dorothy H. Fickle, "Crowned Buddha Images in Southeast Asia," in *Silapa lae Bōrānakhadī nai Prathet Thai* [Art and Archaeology in Thailand] (Bangkok: Fine Arts Department, 1974), 85–119. For the association between Buddha images in royal regalia and the Buddha *cakkavatti,* see Paul Mus, "Le Buddha paré," *BEFEO* 28 (1928): 153–278.

105. Fickle, "Crowned Buddha Images in Southeast Asia," 115.

106. Ibid., 85.

107. For photographs of the image in its three season attires, see *Phra Phutthamahāmanīratanapatimākan* [Images of the Emerald Buddha] (Bangkok: Wat Phra Srīratanasāsadārām and the Thai Military Bank, 2525 B.E./1982 C.E.), 164–91. Two sets of regalia were donated by King Rama I (1782–1809), who brought the image from Vientiane following a military victory over the Lao. The third set was given by King Rama III (1824–51).

108. For accounts of the Emerald Buddha, see Ratanapañña Thera, *The Sheaf of Garlands of the Epochs of the Conqueror,* 120–26, 139–45; Camille Notton, *The*

*Chronicle of the Emerald Buddha* (Bangkok: Bangkok Times Press, 1932); Hiram W. Woodward Jr., "The Emerald and Sihing Buddhas: Interpretations of Their Significance," in *Living a Life in Accord with Dhamma: Papers in Honor of Professor Jean Boisselier on his Eightieth Birthday,* ed. Natasha Eilenberg, M. C. Subhadradis Diskul, and Robert L. Brown (Bangkok: Silapakorn University, 1997), 502–13; Reynolds, "The Holy Emerald Jewel," 175–93; Karen Schur Narula, *The Voyage of the Emerald Buddha* (Kuala Lumpur: Oxford University Press, 1994).

109. Jinak 99.

110. In constructing an image of Upagutta known as Phra Bua Khem, five to nine small cylinders (*khem*) are inserted into the small figure. The *khem* are thought to impart magical powers to the image, not unlike the miraculous insertion of the seven bodily relics of the Buddha in the Stone Image. Strong, *The Legend and Cult of Upagupta,* 282.

111. Reynolds, "The Holy Emerald Jewel," 180.

112. For an account of the Lion Buddha image, see Camille Notton, *P'ra Buddha Sihiṅga* (Bangkok: Bangkok Times Press, 1933); Hutchinson, "Sacred Images in Chiengmai," *Journal of the Siam Society* 28 (1935): 115–42; H. Woodward, "The Emerald and Sihing Buddhas"; Tambiah, *The Buddhist Saints of the Forest and the Cult of Amulets,* 230–42; Bodhiraṃsi, *Nithān Phraphuttha Sihing* [The Legend of the Sihing Buddha Image], trans. into Thai by Sāeng Manawithun (Bangkok: Fine Arts Department, 2506 B.E./1963 C.E.).

113. The Jinak Pāli text records that because the king of the Siṅhalese wished to see the form or body of the Buddha (*buddharūpa*), the *nāga* made a likeness of the Buddha (*buddhavesaṃ*) from which the sculptors then made an image (*buddhapaṭima*).

114. Notton, *P'ra Buddha Sihiṅga,* 43–44, with minor modifications.

115. Hutchinson, "The Seven Spires."

116. Alexander B. Griswold, *Dated Buddha Images of Northern Siam* (Ascona: Artibus Asiae, 1957), 36–37.

117. Ibid., 33.

118. Ibid.

119. The White Crystal Buddha image (Phra Setaṅgamaṇī), enshrined at Wat Chiang Man in Chiang Mai, is also believed to have the power to ensure the onset of the monsoon rains and thus guarantee the prosperity of the region. It, too, is given a place of honor in the New Year procession.

120. For an account of the Stone and White Crystal Buddha images, see Camille Notton, *P'ra Setaṁgamaṇī* (Bangkok: Bangkok Times Press, 1936); Hutchinson, "Sacred Images in Chiengmai"; J. E. van Lohuizen-de Leeuw, "The Stone Buddha of Chiengmai and Its Inscription," *Artibus Asiae* 24 (1961): 324–29.

121. Hutchinson, "Sacred Images in Chiengmai," 116.

122. *Tamnān Phra Kāewkhāw (Setaṅgamaṇī) kap Phrasilā (Phrahinōn)* [The Chronicle of the White Crystal Buddha Image and the Stone Buddha Image] (Chiang Mai: Wat Chiang Man, 2515 B.E./1975 C.E.).

123. Hutchinson, "Sacred Images in Chiengmai," 117.

124. The translation of *Tamnān Kā Phū'ak* is based on a palm leaf manuscript from Wat Tung Yū, Chiang Mai, Thailand, from the microfilm archive of the Social Research Institute, Chiang Mai University (no. 7800501D127129). Phaitun

Dokbuakaew of the SRI assisted in the translation. Also consulted was the printed sermon version of the text, *Kā Pū'ak: Thammadesanā Phū'anmū'angnu'a* [The White Crow: A Sermon in Northern Thai]. Topic headings added for clarity.

125. Peter Skilling, "Five Bodhisatttvas," introduction to the translation of "The Blessings of the Five Buddhas," in *Fragile Palm Leaves for the Preservation of Buddhist Literature,* no. 4 (September 2541 B.E./1998 C.E.): 10. The etymology of the names is corrupted in the Wat Tung Yū manuscript.

126. Ibid.

127. See Steven Collins, "Braḥ Māleyyadevattheravatthuṃ" and "The Story of the Elder Māleyyadeva," *Journal of the Pali Text Society* 18, ed. K. R. Norman (Oxford: Pali Text Society, 1993): 1-17; 65–96, and in the same volume the Pāli text edited by Eugène Denis S.J., 19–74. For a discussion of two Thai versions of the story of Phra Malāi and their ritual contexts, see Brereton, *Thai Tellings of Phra Malāi.*

128. John S. Strong suggests that a ritual progression of the texts may parallel the three watches of the night. The White Crow Chronicle—past lives in review; Phra Mālai—realms of rebirth in review; Vessantara and the story of enlightenment—dharmic realization in review (personal communication, June 20, 1999).

129. In the northern Thai version of the Chronicle of the White Crow, Strong sees elements that may have come from the Mon story of the Buddha's hair relics and their enshrinement in the Shwe Dagon pagoda, especially the connection to Tapussa and Bhallika. In that story Mount Siṅgakutta is identified with the Shwe Dagon. See John S. Strong, "Les reliques des cheveux du Bouddha au Shwe Dagon de Rangoon," *Aséanie* 2 (November 1998): 79–107.

130. Ghaṭīkāra appears in the *Majjhima Nikāya* as a devout follower of Kassapa Buddha and a devoted son who cares for his blind, aged parents. Although a layman, he lived as a monk, and was reborn a Mahābrahmā in the Avihā Brahma realm of Suddhāvāsā Heaven. Later in the story the mother crow takes the name Ghaṭīkāramahābrahma. The *Ghaṭīkāra Sutta* (M #81) and the *Tamnān Kā Phū'ak* celebrate the mutual devotion of parents and children.

131. Here I follow the text of *Sadāeng Ānisaṁsa Phra Chao 5 Phra Ong* rather than the Wat Tung Yū palm leaf text of the *Kā Phū'ak Jātaka* in which the fifth *bodhisatta* is discovered by a washer woman.

132. These *dāna* gifts are associated with each of the *bodhisatta* sons of the white crow. The objects double as monastic requisites (e.g., walking stick, drinking cup, monastic robe) and signs of the five Buddhas, and are associated with the *nigrodha* tree and Siṅgkuttara Mountain. The *dāna* gifts connect the story of the merchants with the story of the white crow and her *bodhisatta* progeny, and also link the pentadic Buddhology of the text with the cult of relics.

133. *Tamnān Phra Kāewkhāw* (*Setaṅgamaṇī*), 12–24. In "Sacred Images in Chiengmai," E. W. Hutchinson includes a Thai and English translation of the Stone Buddha Chronicle based on a 1758 Pāli text; my translation is based on the Thai-language booklet, *Tamnān Phra Kāewkhāw (Setaṅgamaṇī) kap Phrasilā (Phrahinōn)* (The Chronicle of the White Crystal Buddha Image and the Stone Buddha Image) (Chiang Mai: Wat Chiang Man, 2515 B.E./1975 C.E.).

134. Hutchinson, "Sacred Images in Chiengmai," 118. Also Lohuizen-de Leeuw, "The Stone Buddha of Chiengmai and its Inscription," 324.

135. The nine supramundane *dhamma*s are the four paths, the four fruits, and *nibbāna*. The five Māras are: defilement (*kilesa*), the five aggregates of grasping (*khandha*), *kamma*-formations, Māra as a deity (*devaputta*), and Māra as death (*maccumāra*).

136. *Vinaya* II.94ff., Ja. V.333ff. The story of Devadatta's evil plot to have the elephant Nālāgiri kill the Buddha appears in the *Dhammapada* commentary. There is a bas-relief of Nālāgiri bowing before the Buddha at Amarāvatī (second century C.E.).

137. The dimensions of the Phra Silā image are 14 inches high by 10 inches wide.

138. According to the Jinak the kingdom of Haripuñjaya was founded in 662 C.E.

139. This passage may relate to a common northern Thai practice of putting small Buddha images and amulets in a monk's alms bowl during an ordination ceremony. The auspiciousness of the ordination ritual charges the Buddha images with power as it does in the case of the *buddhābhiseka* rite.

140. Monks' robes are signs of sacred power. In this case, as in a similar use of monks' robes in this text, they serve as a sacred altar for the image and protect the image from a defiling contact with the earth.

141. Wat Pā Dāeng was the major monastic center of the Sīhaḷa Nikāya in Chiang Mai in the fifteenth and sixteenth centuries. See Donald K. Swearer and Sommai Premchit, "The Relation Between the Religious and Political Orders in Northern Thailand (14th–16th Centuries)," in *Religion and Legitimation of Power in Thailand, Laos, and Burma*, ed. Bardwell Smith (Chambersburg, Pa.: Anima Books, 1978), 20–33. For a translation of the Wat Pā Daeng Chronicle, see Donald K. Swearer and Sommai Premchit, trans., "Mūlasāsanā Wat Pā Dāeng: The Chronicle of the Founding of Buddhism of the Wat Pā Dāeng Tradition," *Journal of the Siam Society* 65, no. 2 (July 1977): 73–110.

142. Currently the image resides at Wat Chiang Man. Wat Suan Dok became the major royal monastery of the princes of Chiang Mai, and the site for the reliquary remains of Chiang Mai's royal family.

## CHAPTER 8. CONSECRATION TRADITIONS IN OTHER BUDDHIST CULTURES

1. Giuseppe Tucci, *Tibetan Painted Scrolls*, vol. 1 (Kyoto: Rinsen Books, 1980), 309.

2. Robert Knox, *An Historical Relation of Ceylon*, 2d ed. (Dehiwala: Tisara Prakasakayo, 1966), 135.

3. Richard Gombrich, "The Consecration of a Buddha Image," *Journal of Asian Studies* 26, no. 1 (November 1966): 23–36. According to G. P. Malalasekera and N. A. Jayawickrama, *akkhipūjā* may refer to a ceremony in which the king gazed on a Buddha image for seven days, recalling the seven days the Buddha spent at Bodhgayā staring with unblinking eyes seated under the *bodhi* tree, where he attained enlightenment. Malalasekera, *Dictionary of Pāli Proper Names*, vol. 1, 5; N. A. Jayawickrama, ed. and trans., *The Inception of Discipline and the*

*Vinaya Nidāna* (London: Luzac, 1962), 105. *Akkhipūjā* is similar to the Thai *tham thawāi netra* (literally, to make an offering of one's eyes), meaning, in this context, to remain awake all night as an act of homage.

4. *Cūlavaṃsa* 73, 78. See Gombrich, "The Consecration of a Buddha Image," 26. This practice emphasizes both the privilege accorded royal patronage and the symbolic power of the king to perform such an auspicious and potentially dangerous ritual act.

5. Descriptions of deity *pūjā* by Coomaraswamy, Gombrich, and Ruelius differ. Ruelius notes that while it is said to consist of six elements (*sadaṅga*), those elements are ambiguous. Hans Ruelius, "Netrapratiṣṭhāpana—eine singhalesische Zeremonie zur Weihe von Kultbildern," in *Buddhism in Ceylon and Studies on Religious Syncretism in Buddhist Countries,* ed. Heinz Bechert (Göttingen: Vandenhoeck and Ruprecht, 1978), 320–21.

6. The ceremony witnessed by Gombrich contained thirteen squares. In Coomaraswamy's account there are eighty.

7. Gombrich, "The Consecration of a Buddha Image," 35.

8. See Lily de Silva, "The Symbolism of the Indrakīla in the Parittamaṇḍapa," 234–50.

9. Following Coomaraswamy, Gombrich describes a more elaborate ceremony in which the ritualist takes 108 steps, walks on 108 balls of milk rice placed on betel leaves, and ends the ceremony by slashing a tree that exudes a milky sap. Gombrich, "The Consecration of a Buddha Image," 35.

10. Reulius, "Netrapratiṣṭhāpana," 321. See also Paul Wirz, *Exorcism and the Art of Healing in Ceylon* (Leiden: E. J. Brill, 1954). Tucci notes the similarity between the Tibetan rite of consecration and the Hindu *kumbhaṣṭhāpana* in *Tibetan Painted Scrolls,* vol. 1, 310.

11. Gombrich, "The Consecration of a Buddha Image," 25–26.

12. Also hidden from human view, the Mahābodhi image at Bodhgayā fabricates itself inside the *gandhakuṭī* in a miracle of auto-genesis. See John S. Strong's discussion of Dharmasvāmin's account of this strange legend in "Gandhakuṭī: The Perfumed Chamber of the Buddha," *History of Religions* 16, no. 4 (May 1977): 405–6.

13. Ruelius, Netrapratiṣṭhāpana, 325. In Gombrich's view the cutting of the tree is a substitute for killing the bull because killing offends Buddhist moral sensibilities.

14. Ananda K. Coomaraswamy, *Medieval Sinhalese Art,* 2d ed. (1908; reprint, New York: Pantheon Books, 1956), 74.

15. Gombrich, "The Consecration of a Buddha Image," 24.

16. Ruelius, "Netrapratiṣṭhāpana," 324.

17. Ibid.

18. Schopen, "Burial '*ad sanctos,*'" 216.

19. Marcel Zago, *Rites et Cérémonies en Milieu Bouddhiste Lao* (Roma: University Gregoriana Editrice, 1972), 103–4, n. 44.

20. Leclère, *Cambodge, fêtes civiles et religieuses* (Paris: Imprimerie Nationale, 1916), 147.

21. See Faure, *The Rhetoric of Immediacy,* 170–71, especially the distinction between *ri kaigen* and *ji tengen.* Today, Japanese politicians celebrate election

victories by painting the eyes on large Daruma dolls, an act reminiscent of the eye-opening ritual of images of the Buddha.

22. Lawrence G. Thompson, "Consecration Magic in Chinese Religion," *Journal of Chinese Religions* 15 (1991): 3.

23. Bernard Frank, "Vacuité et corps actualisé: Le problème de la présence des 'Personnages Vénérés' dans leurs images selon la tradition du bouddhisme japonais," *Journal of the International Association for Buddhist Studies* 11, no. 2 (1988): 70.

24. For example, see Faure, *The Rhetoric of Immediacy,* chap. 7; Bernard Faure, *Visions of Power: Imagining Medieval Japanese Buddhism,* trans. Phyllis Brooks (Princeton, N.J.: Princeton University Press,1996), chaps. 10 and 11.

25. Takahashi Chikumei, *Ingen, Mokuan, Sokuhi* (1916: reprint, Tokyo: Kokushori Kōkai, 1978), 197–98. Passage translated by Helen Bondi.

26. Yael Bentor, *Consecration of Images and Stūpas in Indo-Tibetan Tantric Buddhism* (Leiden: E. J. Brill, 1996), 34.

27. Quoted in Bentor, *Consecration of Images and Stūpas,* 38.

28. *Sŏk mun wibŏm* [The Buddhist Ritual], ed. Chin-ho Ahn (Seoul: Pômrunsa, 1983). Translated by Mei-huang Lee.

29. Alex Wayman, "The Buddhist Theory of Vision," in *Buddhist Insight: Essays by Alex Wayman,* ed. George Elder (Delhi: Motilal Banarsidass, 1990), 151.

30. Ibid., 155. Wayman cites M. Falk, *Nāma-Rūpa and Dharma-Rūpa.* The eye of flesh, divine eye, and wisdom eye are mentioned in It. III.ii.ii, and in the *Kathāvatthu* the Theravāda position of three eyes is argued over against the Andhakas and Sammitiyas, who uphold only the flesh and divine eyes.

31. In the *Mahāprajñāpāramitā Śāstra* the five eyes are the flesh eye, divine eye, Dharma eye, Buddha eye, and wisdom eye.

32. Wayman, "The Buddhist Theory of Vision," 161.

33. M I.169. Emphasis mine.

34. M I.251.

35. M II.92. *The Middle Length Discourses of the Buddha,* trans. Bhikkhu Ñāṇamoli and Bhikkhu Bodhi (Boston: Wisdom, 1995), 705. Emphasis mine.

36. The commentary explains that the childless Prince Bodhi believed that if the Buddha stepped on the white cloth he would be granted a son. This episode led to a disciplinary rule prohibiting monks from stepping on a white cloth but was modified later to allow *bhikkhu*s to do so as a blessing for householders.

37. Jan Gonda, *Eye and Gaze in the Veda* (Amsterdam: North-Holland, 1969), 4.

38. Diana Eck, *Darśan: Seeing the Divine Image in India,* 2d ed. (New York: Columbia University Press, 1996), 6–7.

39. Tucci, *Tibetan Painted Scrolls,* vol. 1, 312.

40. Hwangsoo Kim, personal communication, August 5, 2001.

41. James J. Preston, "Creation of a Sacred Image: Apotheosis and Destruction in Hinduism," in *Gods of Flesh, Gods of Stone: The Embodiment of Divinity in India,* ed. Joanne Punzo Waghorne and Norman Cutler (New York: Columbia University Press, 1996), 18.

42. Ibid.

43. Freedberg, *The Power of Images,* 83, quoting S. Smith, "The Babylonian Ritual for the Consecration and Induction of a Divine Image," *Journal of the Royal Asiatic Society* (1925): 37–60.

44. Field notes, Myanmar, January 1990.

45. See Daniel Boucher, "The *Pratītyasamutpādagāthā* and Its Role in the Medieval Cult of the Relics," *Journal of the International Association of Buddhist Studies* 14, no.1 (1991): 4–6.

46. Bentor, *Consecration of Images and Stūpas,* 42, 114, 217. In Korean practice, red beans are cast on the images several times during the ritual by the chief ritualist referred to as the "Witness Dharma Master." Hwangsoo Kim, personal communication, August 5, 2001.

47. Bentor, *Consecration of Images and Stūpas,* 115.

48. See Gregory Henderson and Leon Hurvitz, "The Buddha of Seiryōji: New Finds and New Theory," *Artibus Asiae* 19, no. 1 (1956): 5–55; Donald F. McCallum, "The Replication of Miraculous Images: Zenkōji Amida and Seiryōji Shaka," in *Images, Miracles, and Authority in Asian Religious Traditions,* ed. Richard H. Davis (Boulder, Colo.: Westview, 1998), 207–26.

49. Based on the Inaugural Ceremony Program of the Tian Tan Buddha Statue, Po Lin Monastery, Hong Kong, December 29, 1993, and personal communication from Mei-huang Lee.

50. Alex Wayman, "The Mirror as a Pan-Buddhist Metaphor-Simile," *History of Religions* 13, no. 4 (May 1974): 252.

51. Ibid., 255.

52. Khin Myo Chit, "Maha Myat Muni Buddha Image: The Arakan Pagoda," in *A Wonderland of Burmese Legends* (Bangkok: Tamarind, 1984), 77. See also Schober, "In the Presence of the Buddha," 259–88; McCallum, "The Replication of Miraculous Images: 207–26.

53. Yael Bentor, "Downpour of Virtue and Goodness: The Consecration Ritual based on the *Dge-legs Char-'bebs* composed by the First Panchen Lama," *A Turning of The Wheel* (New Delhi: Tibet House, 1993), 21.

54. *Sŏk mun wibŏm* [The Buddhist Ritual], ed. Chin-ho Ahn, trans. Mei-huang Lee.

55. Yael Bentor, "On the Symbolism of the Mirror in Indo-Tibetan Consecration Rituals," *Journal of Indian Philosophy* 23 (1995): 63.

56. Wayman, "The Mirror," 263.

57. T. Griffith Foulk and Robert H. Sharf, "On the Ritual Use of Ch'an Portraiture in Medieval China," *Cahiers d'Extrême-Asie* 7 (1993–94): 160.

58. Manī, *Khrū'ang Sakkāra Nai Lānnā Thai,* 55–56.

59. This discussion is taken from Yael Bentor's study of the *rab gnas* ritual based on Khri-byang's text and her observation of the reconsecration of the Bodhath *stūpa* in 1988. See *Consecration of Images and Stūpas in Indo-Tibetan Tantric Buddhism.* For an outline of the eight-day Guhyasamāja Anuttarayogatantra ritual of consecration, see Sharpa Tulku and Michael Perrott, "The Ritual of Consecration," *The Tibet Journal* 10, no. 2 (1985): 35–49.

60. Thompson, "Consecration Magic in Chinese Religion," 6–7.

61. Yael Bentor, "The Literature on Consecration (*Rab gnas*)," in *Tibetan Literature: Studies in Genre,* ed. José Ignacio Cabezón and Roger Jackson (Ithaca, N.Y.: Snow Lion, 1996), 292.

62. Ibid. For a brief discussion of *sādhana* practice based on the Kālacakra, see Daniel Cozort, "Sādhana (*sGrub thabs*): Means of Achievement for Deity Yoga," in *Tibetan Literature: Studies in Genre,* ed. José Ignacio Cabezón and Roger Jackson (Ithaca: Snow Lion, 1996): 331–43.

63. Tucci, *Tibetan Painted Scrolls,* vol. 1, 309.

64. Richard K. Payne, "Realizing Inherent Enlightenment: Ritual and Self-Transformation in Shingon Buddhism," in *Religious and Social Ritual: Interdisciplinary Explorations,* ed. Michael B. Aune and Valerie DeMarinis (Albany: State University of New York Press, 1996), 71–104.

65. Ibid., 89.

66. Ruelius, "Netrapratiṣṭhāpana," 319.

67. See Phra Khrū Phrachak, "Kham Sangwoey Pūjā Thewadā Ārak lae Phrawiññān nai Kāntham Mahākan Tāng Tāng" [Words of Propitiatory Offering to the Protective Gods and Spirits on Various Important Occasions], in *Phrawat Wat Sænfāng* [History of Wat Saeng Fāng] (Chiang Mai, 1994), 19–25

68. Strong, *The Legend and Cult of Upagupta,* especially chap. 5.

69. For a brief description of the Buddha image consecration ritual in nineteenth-century Cambodia, see Leclére, *Cambodge, fêtes civiles et religieuses,* 139–44. See also Giteau, "Le bornage rituel des temple bouddhiques au Cambodge," 31–41.

70. Bizot, "La consécration," 108.

71. Tucci, *Tibetan Painted Scrolls,* vol. 1, 313.

72. Jan Gonda, "Pratiṣṭha," in *Selected Studies* 2 (Leiden: E. J. Brill, 1975), 338–74.

73. Bizot, "La consécration," 102.

74. Ibid.

75. Ibid., 108. Here Bizot cites George Coedès, "Le culte de la royauté divinisée, source d'inspiration des grands monuments du Cambodge ancien," *Serie Orientale Roma* V, I (Roma: Instituto Italiano per il Medio ed Estremo Oriente, 1941), 1–23.

76. Ibid.

77. According to Bizot, in Cambodia it is Visākhā not Sujātā who is honored by this act.

78. Bizot, "La consécration," 109–10. Using the Cambodian ritual as a case in point, one could hypothesize that in the premodern period the *buddhābhiseka* in northern Thailand and Laos included a more extensive mimetic performance of the future Buddha's enlightenment journey.

79. Bizot, *Le Chemin Laṅkā,* chap. 11.

80. Bizot, "La consécration," 110.

81. This gathering of the relics into the Buddha image points to the image as the body (*rūpa*) of the Buddha, and it resonates with the millennial notion of the coming together of the 84,000 relics at the end of the present era.

82. Bizot, "La consécration," 112–14.

83. Ibid., 114–15.

84. Ibid., 117.

85. Ibid., 127.

86. Coomaraswamy, *Medieval Sinhalese Art,* 71.

87. For a critique of Coomaraswamy, see Davis, "Enlivening Images, 351–59.

88. The Cambodian ritual also emphasizes the story of the Buddha's enlightenment through recitation, mime, and reenactment, a feature of the Tai consecration tradition in the Shan States of Myanmar and the Sipsongpanna region of Yunnan, China.

89. Swearer, "Signs of the Buddha in the Northern Thai Chronicles," 278–92.

90. Schober, "In the Presence of the Buddha," 259–60.

91. Ibid., 260.

92. Brown, "Narrative as Icon," 73.

93. Gudrun Bühnemann, "The Ritual for Infusing Life (*prāṇapratiṣṭhā*) and the Goddess Prāṇaśakti," *Zeitschrift der Deutsche Morgenländische Gesellschaft* 141 (1991): 353.

94. G. R. Welbon, "Mahāsaṃprokṣaṇa 1981: Āgama and Actuality in a Contemporary Temple Renovation," in *Āgama and Silpa,* ed. K.K.A. Venkatachari (Bombay: Ananthacharya Indological Research Institute, 1984), 80. See also Hélèn Brunner, "L'image Divine dans le Culte Āgamique de Śiva: Rapport entre image mental et le support concret du culte," in *L'image Divine Culte et Méditation dans L'Hindouisme* (Paris: Centre National de la Recherche Scientifique, 1990), 9–29.

95. H. Daniel Smith, "Pratiṣṭha," in *Āgama and Silpa,* ed. K.K.A. Venkatachari (Bombay: Ananthacharya Indological Research Institute, 1984), 52.

96. Ibid.

97. Preston, "Creation of a Sacred Image," 9.

98. Vasudha Narayan, "Arcāvatāra: On Earth as He Is in Heaven," in *Gods of Flesh, Gods of Stone: The Embodiment of Divinity in India,* ed. Joanne Punzo Waghorne and Norman Cutler (New York: Columbia University Press, 1996), 54.

99. Gonda, "Pratiṣṭha," 371. Italics mine.

100. Welbon, "Mahāsaṃprokṣaṇa 1981," 75–76.

101. Smith, "Pratiṣṭha," 54.

102. Richard H. Davis, *Lives of Indian Images* (Princeton, N.J.: Princeton University Press, 1997), 34.

103. Ibid., 34–36.

104. Smith, "Pratiṣṭha," 57–62.

105. Welbon, "Mahāsaṃprokṣaṇa," 77.

106. Ibid., 80

107. Waghorne, "Introduction," in *Gods of Flesh,* 7.

## EPILOGUE

1. Ian Reader and George J. Tanabe Jr., *Practically Religious: Worldly Benefits and the Common Religion of Japan* (Honolulu: University of Hawai'i Press, 1998), 262. Some material in this chapter appears in "Aniconism and Iconism in Thai Buddhism," in *Buddhism and Modernity,* ed. Steven Heine and Charles Prebish (Oxford University Press, 2003).

2. Thai, "Kring Phrachao Tāksin Kū Cāt." The *phra kring* is a small Buddha image worn or carried as an amulet with a *yantra* or *gāthā* written on a small piece of gold leaf, rolled into a ball, and inserted into the image so that when shaken it rings or tinkles (*kring*). Although called "King Taksin," after the Thai ruler (r. 1767–82) who drove out the Burmese following their sack of Ayutthaya and who established a new capital in Thonburi, the amulet is a small Buddha image measuring approximately an inch in height.

3. Luang Pho (Venerable Father) is an informal title often used for older, charismatic monks who are reputed to possess magical powers associated with meditation.

4. Translation mine.

5. Adapted with permission from Sanitsuda Ekachai, "Sale of Amulets Is Not So Charming," *Bangkok Post,* November 26, 1997.

6. For a discussion of the cult of amulets, see Tambiah, *The Buddhist Saints of the Forest and the Cult of Amulets,* pt. 3.

7. Interview with Chiang Mai amulet vendor, Somchāt Nawalanon on February 26, 1999. Somchāt's interest in amulets developed after two near-death experiences. His mother attributed his survival of a serious motorcycle accident when he was a teenager to the Phra Rod amulet she had given him. In his mid-thirties, having become a "hippie musician," while he was playing in a Bangkok bar a drunken patron pulled out a gun, pointed it at him, and pulled the trigger, but it failed to fire. Once again, Somchāt attributed his good fortune to his amulets. This led to a sideline business of "renting" amulets. For a description of Thai amulets, see Srisakara Vallibhotama, *Phra Kru'ang nai Mū'ang Siam* [Amulets in Thailand] (Bangkok: Matichon, 1994).

8. Peter A. Jackson, "The Enchanting Spirit of Thai Capitalism: The Cult of Luang Phor Khoon and the Post-modernization of Thai Buddhism," *South East Asian Research Journal* 7, no. 1 (March 1999): 5–60; Peter A. Jackson, "Royal Spirits, Chinese Gods, and Magic Monks: Thailand's Boom Time Religious Prosperity," *South East Asian Research Journal* 7, no. 3 (November 1999): 245–320.

9. ML Pattaratorn Chirapravati, *Votive Tablets in Thailand: Origin, Styles, and Uses* (Kuala Lumpur: Oxford University Press, 1997), 5.

10. Ibid., 54.

11. The critics of the cult of charismatic monks, relics, and material icons make a sharp distinction between religion and magic, a distinction increasingly called into question by anthropologists, historians of religion, and art historians. See, for example, David Freedberg, *The Power of Images.*

12. In his long and distinguished monastic career, P. A. Payutto (Phra Dhammapiṭaka) has held several different titles indicative of advancement in ecclesiastical rank in the Thai *saṅgha.* His current title, Phra Dhammapiṭaka, was formally conferred by the king of Thailand in 1993. His many publications have appeared under his various monastic names, which can be confusing to Western readers unfamiliar with Payutto's career. Grant A. Olson, the translator of the first edition of P. A. Payutto's magnum opus, *Buddhadhamma,* uses the designation Phra Prayudh Payutto, Phra being the Thai honorific for monk from the Pāli, *vara,* Prayudh being his given name, and Payutto being his early monastic title, Phra Mahā Payutto. Recent English translations of Payutto's writings published in

Thailand by the Buddhadhamma Foundation use P. A. Payutto as his *nom de plume* (P. A. stands for his given and family names, Prayudh Arayangkun). I have chosen to follow this convention.

13. Phra Prayudh Payutto, *Buddhadhamma: Natural Laws and Values for Life,* trans. Grant A. Olson (Albany: State University of New York Press, 1995), 12.

14. For a discussion of *yoniso manasikāra,* see Bruce Evans, "Contributions of Venerable Prayudh to Buddhism and Society," in *Socially Engaged Buddhism for the New Millennium: Essays in Honor of the Ven. Phra Dhammapiṭaka (Bhikkhu P. A. Payutto)* (Bangkok: Sathirakoses-Nagapradipa Foundation and the Foundation for Children, 2542 B.E./1999 C.E.), 3–14.

15. Phra Dhammapiṭaka (P. A. Payutto), *Thāyākphonwikru't Tong L'uk Khit Saiyasāt* [To Be Free from Supernatural Powers, Give Up Thinking in Terms of Magic] (Bangkok: Thammasān, 2540 B.E./1997 C.E.), 9.

16. Phra Dhammapiṭaka (P. A. Payutto), *Sing Saksit, Devakru't, Pāthihān* [Sacred Objects, Efficacious Deities, and Miracles ] (Bangkok: The Buddhadhamma Foundation, 2536 B.E./1995 C.E.); Phra Dhammapiṭaka, *Thāyākphonwikru't Tong L'uk Khit Saiyasāt.*

17. Phra Dhammapiṭaka (P. A. Payutto), *Sing Saksit, Devakru't, Pāthihān,* 1.

18. See Buddhadāsa Bhikkhu, *Me and Mine: Selected Essays of Bhikkhu Buddhadāsa,* ed. and with an introduction by Donald K. Swearer, trans., et al. (Albany: State University of New York Press, 1989). The following discussion of Buddhadāsa's Buddhology is revised from Donald K. Swearer, "Bhikkhu Buddhadāsa's Interpretation of the Buddha," *Journal of the American Academy of Religion* 64, no. 2 (summer, 1996): 313–36.

19. Buddhadāsa's critics, uneasy with his unorthodox Buddhology and epistemology, charge that his views tend to be Mahāyanistic rather than strictly Theravādin.

20. Buddhadāsa Bhikkhu, *Phra Phuttha Chao Thī Yū Kap Raw Dai Talot Welā* [The Buddha Is with Us All the Time] (Bangkok: Healthy Mind, 1990), 8.

21. Ibid., 8–9.

22. Ibid., 10.

23. Ibid., 13.

24. Ibid., 14.

25. Ibid., 15.

26. Ibid., 25.

27. Buddhadāsa's distinction between ordinary language and *dhamma* language is close to the Pāli commentarial distinction between *puggalādhiṭṭhana* and *dhammādhiṭṭhana,* and correlates with the Mādhyamika epistemological distinction between two levels of truth.

28. Buddhadāsa Bhikkhu, "Everyday Language and Truth Language," in *Me and Mine,* 127–28.

29. Buddhadāsa Bhikkhu, *Phra Phuttha Chao Thī Yū Kap Raw,* 37.

30. Ibid., 63. For a discussion of Buddhadāsa and Zen, see Louis Gabaude, "Bouddhismes en contact un zeste de Zen dans le bouddhisme thaï," *BEFEO* 87, no. 2 (2000): 389–442.

31. Buddhadāsa Bhikkhu, *Phra Phuttha Chao Thī Yū Kap Raw,* 20–21.

32. Ibid., 21.

33. Phra Bodhirak, *Sacca Hāeng Chīwit* [The Truth of My Life] (Bangkok: Dhammasanti Foundation, 2530 B.E./1987 C.E.), 180.

34. Ibid., 186.

35. For a more extensive discussion of Santi Asok, see Donald K. Swearer, "Fundamentalistic Movements in Theravāda Buddhism," in *Fundamentalisms Observed,* ed. Martin E. Marty and R. Scott Appleby (Chicago: University of Chicago Press, 1991), 628–90. See also Marja-Leena Heikkilä-Horn, *Buddhism With Open Eyes: Belief and Practice of Santi Asoke* (Bangkok: Fah Apai, 1997).

36. "Phraphuttharūp Pen Hed Rū" [Is the Buddha Image the Cause?], *Saengsūn* [The Light of the Void] 10, nos. 37–38 (2532 B.E./1989 C.E.): 69–76. The discussion that follows is based primarily on this article, author anonymous.

37. "Plūksek Phrathāe Khong Phuttha Khrang Thī 13" [The Thirteenth Authentic Buddhist Consecration Retreat], *Sānasok* 9, nos. 7–8 (1989): 19.

38. Ibid., 27.

# GLOSSARY OF SELECTED PĀLI AND THAI TERMS

All Pāli and Thai words are glossed in the text and many are referenced in the index. Terms are listed in either Pāli or Thai but are only so designated in the body of the text and the glossary when both forms appear together.

*abhiññā*—Higher knowledges; supernatural faculties achieved through higher states of consciousness.

*abhiseka*—To consecrate; sprinkle with sacred water.

*āchān* (Pāli, *ācariya*)—Teacher; *āchān wat* (temple teacher).

*anāgāmī*—Never-returner; third stage on the path to *nibbāna*.

*ānisaṃsa* (Thai, *ānisong*)—Merit, blessing, reward, benefit.

*anussati*—To recall, remember; recalling the Buddha (*buddhānussati*) as a means of being in the presence of the Buddha.

*arahant*—Worthy one; highest of the four stages of the path to *nibbāna*.

*bhagavā*—Blessed one; an epithet for the Buddha.

*bhāvanā citta*—To train the mind; meditation.

*bodhi*—Supreme knowledge; *bodhi* tree under which the Buddha achieved *nibbāna*.

*bodhimaṇḍa*—The throne of enlightenment.

*bodhisatta*—Buddha to be; in Theravāda especially in reference to the previous lives of the Buddha Gotama.

*bōek phranet*—Opening the eyes of the Buddha.

*buddhakhetta*—Buddha-field; a Buddha as a field of merit.

*buddharūpa*—An image of the Buddha.

*cakkavāḷa* (Thai, *cakkawān*)—Circle; a ring of mountains encircling the world; cosmos.

*cakkavattin*—World ruler; a wheel-turning monarch who rules according to the *dhamma*.

*chedī* (Pāli, *cetiya*)—A monument, usually a reliquary, as a reminder of the presence of the Buddha or Buddhist saint.

*cho fā*—Decorative extension at the finial of a Thai temple ridge pole.

*dāna*—Charity, generosity; material gifts offered to the *saṅgha*.

*dhammakāya*—The Dhamma-body (of the Buddha).

*dukkha*—Life in the mundane world experienced as unsatisfactory; suffering.

*gandhakuṭī*—Perfumed chamber; a room set aside in the monastery for the parinibbāned Buddha that served as his functional surrogate.

*gāthā* (Thai, *kāthā*)—A verse or stanza.

*gotrabhū*—Noble lineage; lineage of the *ariya*.

*guṇa*—Virtue, quality, especially denoting powers of the Buddha.

*iddhi*—Miraculous powers associated with the higher knowledges (*abhiñña*).

*jhāna*—Mental absorptions; higher states of consciousness associated with the attainment of supermundane powers.

*kammaṭṭhāna*—Meditation subjects; forty are enumerated in the *Visuddhimagga*.

*karuṇā*—Compassion; the second of the four sublime states of mental attainment (*brahmavihāra*).

*lokapāla*—World guardians; the rulers of the four quarters.

*lokiya*—Mundane, worldly.

*lokuttara*—Transmundane.

*magga/phala*—Path and fruit; referring especially to stream-enterer, once-returner, never-returner, and *arahant.*

*mahāpurisa*—Great person; an epithet for the Buddha, especially in reference to his auspicious bodily signs.

*māravijaya*—Victory over Māra; the most frequent Buddha image posture in Thailand.

*mettā*—Lovingkindness;—*bhāvanā,* lovingkindness meditation, extending lovingkindness.

*muni*—Sage; an epithet for the Buddha.

*nām mon*—Water consecrated by chanting *paritta* or *mantra*s.

*ñāṇa*—Knowledge; in particular, the knowledge that defines the Buddha's enlightenment: *pubbenivāsānussati-* (knowledge of the Buddha's past lives), *cutūpapāta-* (knowledge of the coming into being and passing away of all beings), *āsavakkhaya-* (knowledge of the destruction of the mental intoxicants).

*nātha*—Protector, mainstay, lord; a frequent epithet for the Buddha.

*ngan poy luang*—A major *wat* festival.

*nibbāna*—Soteriological goal of Buddhist practice.

*paccavekkhaṇa*—Contemplation; contemplative reflection associated especially with the Ariyan path and its fruit.

*pān lom*—A set of umbrellas installed at the center of a temple ridge pole in northern Thailand and Laos.

*pāpa* (Thai, *bāp*)—Evil; demeritorious deeds.

*pāramī*—Perfections; the ten principal virtues of the *bodhisatta.*

*parinibbāna*—The final *nibbāna* of the Buddha occurring at his death, or the death of a fully enlightened being after which there is no rebirth.

*paritta*—Protection, and to ward off danger; especially in relationship to the chanting of Pāli texts that bear this designation.

*paṭicca-samuppāda*—The interdependent and co-arising nature of things; the conditionality of all physical and psychical phenomena.

*paṭimā*—Image, counterpart, representation.

*phithī sado khro*—A ritual performed at Thai New Year (*songkhrān*) or at other times to avert misfortune.

*phutthawāt* (Pāli, *buddhavāsa*)—The "buddha's place"; the section of a *wat* containing reliquary and image hall.

*pūjā*—Offerings, veneration.

*puñña* (Thai, *bun*)—Good; meritorious deeds; to make merit (*tham bun*).

*rājawat* (Pāli, *rājavati*)—The boundary protecting a sacred space where auspicious rituals such as the Buddha image consecration are conducted.

*riak khwan*—To call the spirits at a spirit calling ritual; also as in implanting (*plūk*) or making (*tham*) the spirits (*khwan*).

*rūpakāya*—The form or visible body of the Buddha.

*sabbaññutā*—Omniscience (in reference to the Buddha).
*sacca(dhamma)*—The truth; the true nature of things (*dhamma*).
*saccakiriyā*—Act of truth; vow.
*sādhana*—Accomplishment, means of achievement, transformation.
*sāi siñcana*—Sacred cord; the string used in rituals to transfer power from Buddha images and monks to material objects; used especially in making holy water (Thai, *nām mon*).
*sakadāgāmī*—Once-returner; second stage on the path to *nibbāna.*
*saksit* (Pāli, *satti-siddha*)—Sacred power associated with persons or objects such as the relics and images of the Buddha and saints.
*samatha*—Tranquillity, calm, stilling of the senses through meditation.
*saṃsāra*—Rebirth; the flow of death and rebirth.
*saṅgha*—Buddhist monastic order; *saṅghawāt* (Thai), the "monk's place"; that section of the *wat* where monastic activities are conducted.
*saṅghathān* (Pāli, *saṅghadāna*)—Offerings to the monastic order.
*sarīradhātu*—Bodily relic of a Buddha.
*sāsana*—The Buddhist religious tradition.
*satthā*—Teacher; an epithet for the Buddha.
*sīmā*—Boundary, limit; boundary stones demarcating the *ubōsot.*
*sotāpanna*—Stream-enterer; the first stage of the path to *nibbāna.*
*suat mon* (Pāli, *manta*; Sanskrit, *mantra*)—Chanting the *paritta.*
*sugato*—One who goes well, blessed, noble; a common epithet for the Buddha.
*supaṭipanno*—Well-disciplined, well-practiced with reference to the *saṅgha.*
*sū'pchātā* (*phithī-*)—Life extension rituals performed at life crisis or life transition occasions.
*svākkhāto*—Well-proclaimed, well-preached in reference to the *dhamma.*
*tamnān*—Chronicle; similar in meaning to Pāli *vaṃsa.*
*tathāgata*—Perfect one; thus-gone-one; an epithet used for a Buddha.
*teja*—Flame, fire, brilliant.
*thewadā* (Pāli, *devatā*)—Deity, celestial being.
*thīan*—Candle; as present in the Buddha image consecration ritual: *thīan chai* (victory candle), *thīan mongkhon* (auspicious candle), *thīan Wipassī,* the first Buddha of this age.
*ubōsot* (*bōt*)—The *uposatha* (Pāli) hall sanctified by boundary stones in which monastic activities such at the fortnightly recitation of the *pātimokkha* are held.
*vihāra* (Thai, *wihān*)—Dwelling; a Buddhist monastery; in northern Thailand usually refers to the image hall at a *wat.*
*vimutti-sukha*—The joy of liberation.
*vipassanā* (*-ñāṇa*)—Insight meditation; knowledge derived from insight.
*wat*—Buddhist monastery-temple.
*yan* (Pāli, *yanta;* Sanskrit, *yantra*)—A diagram of magical letters.

# SELECTED BIBLIOGRAPHY

Thai names are alphabetized by the first name following Thai convention.


*Anāgatavaṃsa Desanā: The Sermon of the Chronicle-To-Be.* Edited by John Clifford Holt and translated by Udaya Meddegama. Delhi: Motilal Banarsidass, 1993.

*Ānisong Kān Kosāng Phraphutthарūp* [The Meritorious Blessing of Making a Buddha Image]. Chiang Mai: Thārāthong, n.d.

Anuman Rajadhon, Phya. *Essays on Thai Folklore.* Bangkok: Social Science Association Press of Thailand, 1968.

———. *Popular Buddhism in Siam and Other Essays on Thai Studies.* Bangkok: Thai Interreligious Committee on Development and the Santhirakoses Nagapradipa Foundation, 1986.

———. "Thai Charms and Amulets." In *Essays on Thai Folklore.* Bangkok: Social Science Association Press of Thailand, 1968.

Bandaranayake, Senake. *Sinhalese Monastic Architecture: The Vihāras of Anurādhapura.* Leiden: E. J. Brill, 1974.

Bareau, André. "La composition et les étapes de la formation progressive du Mahāparinirvāṇasūtra ancien." *BEFEO* 66 (1979): 45–103.

———. "The Notion of Time in Early Buddhism." *East and West* 7, no. 4 (January 1957): 353–64.

———. *Recherches sur la biographie du Buddha dans les sūtrapiṭaka et les vinayapiṭaka anciens* II, 53. Paris: Publications de l'École française d'Extrême-Orient, 1963.

———. "The Superhuman Personality of the Buddha and Its Symbolism in the Mahāparinirvāṇasūtra of the Dharmaguptaka." In *Myths and Symbols in Honor of Mircea Eliade,* edited by Joseph M. Kitagawa and Charles H. Long. Chicago: University of Chicago Press, 1969.

Basnayake, H. T. *Sri Lankan Monastic Architecture.* Delhi: Sri Satguru, 1986.

Beal, Samuel, trans. *Si-Yu-Ki: Buddhist Records of the Western World* by Hiuen Tsiang [Hsuang-tsang/Xuanzang]. 2 vols. 1884. Reprint, Delhi: Oriental Books Reprint Corporation, 1969.

Becchetti, Catherine. *La mystère dans les lettres.* Bangkok: Éditions des Cahiers de France, 1991.

Bechert, Heinz. "On the Popular Religion of the Sinhalese." In *Buddhism in Ceylon and Studies on the Religious Syncretism in Buddhist Countries,* edited by Heniz Bechert. Göttingen: Vandenhoeck and Ruprecht, 1978.

———. *When Did the Buddha Live? The Controversy on the Dating of the Historical Buddha.* Delhi: Sri Satguru, 1995.

Beck, Brenda E. F. "Colour and Heat in South Indian Ritual." *Man* 4, no. 4 (1969): 553–72.

Bénisti, Mireille. "Étude sur le *stūpa* dan l'Inde ancienne." *BEFEO* 50 (1960): 37–88.

———. "Les stūpa aux cinq piliers." *BEFEO* 58 (1971): 131–62.

Bennett, Chester. "Life of Gaudama." *Journal of the American Oriental Society* 3 (1852–53): 1–163.

Bentor, Yael. "Consecration." In *Tibetan Literature: Studies in Genre,* edited by José Ignacio Cabezón and Roger R. Jackson. Ithaca, N.Y.: Snow Lion, 1996.

———. *Consecration of Images and Stūpas in Indo-Tibetan Tantric Buddhism.* Leiden: E. J. Brill, 1996.

———. "Downpour of Virtue and Goodness: The Consecration Ritual Based on the *Dge-legs Char-'bebs* Composed by the First Panchen Lama." In *A Turning of the Wheel.* New Delhi: Tibet House, 1993.

———. "The Literature on Consecration (*Rab gnas*)." In *Tibetan Literature: Studies in Genre,* edited by José Ignacio Cabezón and Roger Jackson. Ithaca, N.Y.: Snow Lion, 1996.

———. "On the Symbolism of the Mirror in Indo-Tibetan Consecration Rituals." *Journal of Indian Philosophy* 23 (1995): 57–71.

———. "Sūtra-style Consecration in Tibet and Its Importance for Understanding the Historical Development of the Indo-Tibetan Consecration Ritual for Stūpas and Images." *Tibetan Studies* (1989): 1–12.

Bigandet, Paul. *The Life or Legend of Gaudama: The Buddha of the Burmese.* 2 vols. 1858. Reprint, 3d ed. Varanasi: Bharatiya, 1979.

Bizot, François. "La consécration des statues et le culte des morts." In *Recherches nouvelles sur le Cambodge,* edited by François Bizot. Paris: EFEO, 1994.

———. "La grotte de la naissance." In *Recherches sur le bouddhisme khmer II, BEFEO* 67. Paris: EFEO, 1980: 221–73.

———. "La place des communautés du Nord-Laos dans l'histoire du bouddhisme d'Asie du Sud-Est." *BEFEO* 87, vol. 2 (2000): 511–28.

———. *Le Chemin de Laṅkā.* Paris: EFEO, 1992.

———. "Le Don De Soi-Même." *Recherches sur le bouddhisme khmer III. BEFEO* 130. Paris: EFEO, 1981.

———. "Le figuier à cinq branches." In *Recherche sur le bouddhisme khmer I.* Publications de l'École française d'Extrême-Orient 107. Paris: EFEO, 1976.

———. *Les traditions de la pabbajjā en Asie du Sud-Est. Recherches sur le bouddhisme khmer IV.* Göttingen: Vanderhoeck and Ruprecht, 1988.

———. "Notes sur les *yantra* bouddhiques d'Indochine." *Mélanges chinois et Bouddhiques* 20–21, no. 1 (1981): 155–91.

Bizot, François, and François Lagirarde. *La pureté par les mots.* Paris: EFEO, 1996.

Bizot, François, and Oskar von Hinüber. *La guirlande de Joyaux.* Paris: EFEO, 1994.

Blackburn, Anne M. *Buddhist Learning and Textual Practice in Eighteenth-Century Lankan Monastic Culture.* Princeton: Princeton University Press, 2001.

Bode, Mabel Haynes. *The Pāli Literature of Burma.* 1909. Reprint, Rangoon: Burma Research Society, 1965.

Bodhirak, Phra. *Sacca Hāeng Chīwit* [The Truth of My Life]. Bangkok: Dhammasanti Foundation, 2530 B.E./1987 C.E.

Bodhiraṃsi, Phra. *Nithān Phraphuttha Sihing* [The Legend of the Sihing Buddha Image]. Translated into Thai by Sāeng Manawithun. Bangkok: Fine Arts Department, 2506 B.E./1963 C.E.

Boribal Buribhand, Luang, and Alexander B. Griswold. *The Royal Monasteries and Their Significance.* Bangkok: Fine Arts Department, 2501 B.E./1958 C.E.

———. *Thai Images of the Buddha.* 4th ed. Thai Culture, New Series, no. 18. Bangkok: Fine Arts Department, 2514 B.E./1971 C.E.

Boucher, Daniel. "The *Pratītyasamutpādagāthā* and Its Role in the Medieval Cult of the Relics." *Journal of the International Association of Buddhist Studies* 14, no. 1 (1991): 1–27.

Brereton, Bonnie Pacala. *Thai Tellings of Phra Malai: Texts and Rituals Concerning a Popular Buddhist Saint.* Tempe: Arizona State University Program for Southeast Asian Studies, 1995.

Brown, Robert L. "God on Earth: The Walking Buddha in the Art of South and Southeast Asia." *Artibus Asiae* 50 (1990): 73–107.

———. "The Miraculous Buddha Image: Portrait, God, or Object?" In *Images, Miracles, and Authority in Asian Religious Traditions,* edited by Richard H. Davis. Boulder, Colo.: Westview, 1998.

———. "Narrative as Icon: The Jātaka Stories in Ancient Indian and Southeast Asian Architecture." In *Sacred Biography in the Buddhist Traditions of South and Southeast Asia,* edited by Juliane Schober. Honolulu: University of Hawai'i Press, 1997.

———. "Recent Stupa Literature: A Review Article." *Journal of Asian History* 20 (1986): 215–32.

Brunner, Hélèn. "L'image Divine dans le Culte Āgamique de Śiva: Rapport entre image mental et le support concret du culte." In *L'image Divine Culte et Méditation dans L'Hindouisme.* Paris: Centre National de la Recherche Scientifique, 1990.

Brunner, Jerome. *Actual Minds, Possible Worlds.* Cambridge, Mass.: Harvard University Press, 1986.

Bucknell, Roderick S. "Reinterpreting the *Jhānas.*" *Journal of the International Association of Buddhist Studies* 16, no. 2 (winter 1993): 375–401.

Buddhadāsa Bhikkhu. *Me and Mine: Selected Essays of Bhikkhu Buddhadāsa.* Edited and with an introduction by Donald K. Swearer, trans., et al. Albany: State University of New York Press, 1989.

———. *Phra Phuttha Chao Thī Yū Kap Raw Dai Talot Welā* [The Buddha is with Us All the Time]. Bangkok: Healthy Mind, 1990.

———. *The Prison of Life (Khuk Khong Chīwit).* Translated by Santikaro Bhikkhu. Bangkok: The Dhamma Study and Practice Group, 1988.

Buddhadatta, A. P., ed. *Jinakālamālī.* London: Luzac, 1962.

Bhadantācariya Buddhaghosa. *The Path of Purification (Visuddhimagga).* Translated by Bhikkhu Ñāṇamoli. Seattle: Buddhist Publication Society, Pariyatti Editions, 1999.

Bühnemann, Gudrun. "The Ritual for Infusing Life (*prāṇapratiṣṭhā*) and the Goddess Prāṇaśakti." *Zeitschrift der Deutsche Morgenländische Gesellschaft* 141 (1991): 353–65.

Bumphen Rawin. *Lānnā Anāgatavaṃsa and Metteyyavaṃsa.* Chiang Mai: Mahāchulālongkorn Buddhist University, 2535 B.E./1992 C.E.

———. *Pathom Somphōt Samnuan Lānnā* [The Northern Thai Version of the *Pathama Sambodhi*]. Bangkok: Odian Store, 2535 B.E./1992 C.E.

Bunkhit Wacharasāt. *Suat Mon Mū'ang Nū'a* [Northern Thai Chants]. Chiang Mai: Thārāthong, n.d.

Burlingame, E. W., trans. *Buddhist Legends.* 3 vols. Harvard Oriental Series 30. Cambridge, Mass.: Harvard University Press, 1921.

Cakraphan Wongburanawat. *Kham Son Khong Luang Pū Lā* [The Teachings of Luang Pū Lā]. Chiang Mai, 2532 B.E./1989 C.E.

Carter, Martha L. *The Mystery of the Udayana Buddha.* Supplemento n. 64 agli Annali, vol. 50, fasc. 3. Napoli: Instituto Universitario Orientale, 1990.

Chit Buwabut. *Prawat Yo Phraphim Nai Prathet Thai* [A Short History of Votive Tablets in Thailand]. Bangkok: Umphornphitaya, 2514 B.E./1971 C.E.

Chizen, Akanuma. "Triple Body of the Buddha." *The Eastern Buddhist* 1 (May–August 1992): 1–29.

Coedès, George. "Dhammakāya." *Adyar Library Bulletin* 20 (1956): 239–86.

———. "Le culte de la royauté divinsée, source d'inspiration des grands monuments du Cambodge ancien." *Seire Orientale Roma* V, I (Roma: Instituto Italiano peril Medio ed Estremo Oriente, 1941): 1–23.

———. *The Indianized States of Southeast Asia.* Edited by Walter F. Vella and translated by Susan Brown Cowing. Honolulu: East-West Center Press, 1968.

———. "Une vie indochinoise du Buddha: la Paṭhamasambodhi." *Mélanges d'indianisme à la mémoire de Louis Renou.* Paris: Éditions E. de Boccard, 1968.

Collins, Steven. "Braḥ Māleyyadevattheravattuṃ." *Journal of the Pali Text Society* 18, edited by K. R. Norman (1993): 1–17.

———. "The Story of the Elder Māleyyadeva." *Journal of the Pali Text Society* 18, edited by K. R. Norman (1993): 65–96.

———. *Nirvana and other Buddhist felicities: Utopias of the Pali imaginaire.* Cambridge: Cambridge University Press, 1998.

Coomaraswamy, Ananda K. *History of Indian and Indonesian Art.* New York: Dover, 1965.

———. *Medieval Sinhalese Art.* 2d ed. 1908. Reprint, New York: Pantheon Books, 1956.

———. *The Origin of the Buddha Image.* 1927. Reprint, New Delhi: Munishiram Manoharlal, 1972.

Cort, John E. "Bhakti in the Early Jain Tradition: Understanding Devotional Religion in South Asia." *History of Religions* 42, no. 1 (August 2002): 59–86.

Cousins, L. S. "Aspects of Esoteric Southern Buddhism." In *Indian Insights: Buddhism, Brahmanism and Bhakti.* Papers from the Annual Spalding Symposium on Indian religion, edited by Peter Connolly and Sue Hamilton. London: Luzac Oriental, 1997.

———. "Samatha-Yāna and Vipassanā-Yāna." In *Buddhist Studies in Honour of Hammalawa Saddhātissa,* edited by Gatara Dhammapāla, Richard Gombrich, and K. R. Norman. Nugegoda: University of Jayewardenepura, 1984.

Cozort, Daniel. "Sādhana (*sGrub thabs*): Means of Achievement for Deity Yoga." In *Tibetan Literature: Studies in Genre,* edited by José Ignacio Cabezón and Roger Jackson. Ithaca, N.Y.: Snow Lion, 1996.

Crosby, Kate. "Tantric Theravāda: A Bibliographic Essay on the Writings of François Bizot and others on the Yogāvacara Tradition." *Contemporary Buddhism An Interdisciplinary Journal* 1, no. 2 (November 2000): 141–98.

Dallapiccola, Anna Libera, ed. *The Stūpa: Its Religious, Historical and Architectural Significance.* Wiesbaden: Franz Steiner Verlag, 1980.

Damrong Rājānubhāb, Prince. *Monuments of the Buddha in Siam.* 2d ed. Translated by Sulak Sivaraksa and A. B. Griswold. Bangkok: The Siam Society, 1973.

Daniel, E. Valentine. *Fluid Signs: Being a Person the Tamil Way.* Berkeley: University of California Press, 1988.

Das, Veena. *Structure and Cognition: Aspects of Hindu Caste and Ritual.* 2d ed. Delhi: Oxford University Press, 1982.

Davids, T. W. Rhys. *Manual of a Mystic: The Yogāvachara's Manual.* London: Pali Text Society, 1916.

Davids, T. W. Rhys and C.A.F. Rhys Davids, trans. *Dialogues of the Buddha.* 4th ed. London: Pali Text Society, 1959.

Davis, Richard H. "Enlivening Images: The Śaiva Rite of Invocation." In *Shastric Traditions in Indian Arts,* edited by Anna Libera Dallapiccola. Stuttgart: Steiner Verlag Wiesbaden, 1989.

———. *Lives of Indian Images.* Princeton, N.J.: Princeton University Press, 1997.

de Bernon, Olivier. "Le rituel de la 'grande probation annuelle' (*mahāparivāsakamma*) des religieux du Cambodge." *BEFEO* 87, vol. 2 (2000): 473–510.

Dehejia, Vidya. "Aniconism and the Multivalence of Emblems." *Ars Orientalis* 21 (1991): 45–66.

Demieville, Paul. "Notes on Buddhist Hymnology in the Far East." In *Buddhist Studies in Honour of Walpola Rahula,* edited by Somaratna Balasooriya, et al. London: Gordon Fraser, 1980.

de Silva, Lily. *Paritta: A Historical and Religious Study of the Buddhist Ceremony for Peace and Prosperity in Sri Lanka.* Colombo: National Museums of Sri Lanka, 1981.

———. "The Paritta Ceremony of Sri Lanka: Its Antiquity and Symbolism." In *Buddhist Thought and Ritual,* edited by David Kalupahana. New York: Paragon House, 1991.

———. "The Symbolism of the Indrakīla in the Parittamaṇḍapa." In *Senarat Paranavitana Commemoration Volume,* edited by Leelananda Prematilleke et al. Leiden: E. J. Brill, 1978.

de Silva, Lynn. *Buddhism: Beliefs and Practices in Sri Lanka.* 2d ed. Colombo: Wesley, 1980.

Dhammapiṭaka, Phra (P. A. Payutto). *Sing Saksit, Devakru't, Pāthihān* [Sacred Objects, Efficacious Deities, and Miracles]. Bangkok: The Buddhadhamma Foundation, 2538 B.E./1995 C.E.

———. *Thāyākphonwikru't Tong L'uk Khit Saiyasāt* [To Be Free from Supernatural Powers, Give Up Thinking in Terms of Magic]. Bangkok: Thammasān, 2540 B.E./1997 C.E.

Dutt, Nalinaksha. *Early Monastic Buddhism.* Calcutta: Calcutta Oriental Book Agency, 1960.

———. *Mahayana Buddhism.* Calcutta: Firma K. L. Mukhopadhyay, 1973.

Dutt, Sukumar. *The Buddha and Five After-Centuries.* London: Luzac, 1957.

———. *Buddhist Monks and Monasteries of India: Their History and Their Contribution.* London: George Allen and Unwin, 1962.

Eck, Diana. *Darśan: Seeing the Divine Image in India.* 2d ed. New York: Columbia University Press, 1996.

Eckel, Malcolm David. "The Power of the Buddha's Absence: On the Foundations of Mahāyāna Buddhist Ritual." *Journal of Ritual Studies* 4, no. 2 (summer 1990): 61–95.

———. *To See the Buddha: A Philosopher's Quest for the Meaning of Emptiness.* San Francisco: HarperCollins, 1992.

Evans, Bruce, trans. "The Blessings of the Five Buddhas." *Fragile Palm Leaves: For the Preservation of Buddhist Literature,* no. 4 (September 2541 B.E./1998 C.E.): 10–12.

———. "Contributions of Venerable Prayudh to Buddhism and Society." In *Socially Engaged Buddhism for the New Millennium: Essays in Honor of the Ven. Phra Dhammapitaka (Bhikkhu P. A. Payutto).* Bangkok: Santirakoses-Nagapradīpa Foundation and the Foundation for Children, 2542 B.E./1999 C.E.: 3–14.

Falk, Maryla. *Nāma-Rūpa, Dharma-Rūpa: Origin and Aspects of an Ancient Indian Conception.* Calcutta: University of Calcutta Press, 1943.

Falk, Nancy Auer. "To Gaze on the Sacred Traces." *History of Religions* 16, no. 4 (May 1977): 281–93.

Faure, Bernard. "The Buddhist Icon and the Modern Gaze." *Critical Inquiry* 24, no. 3 (spring 1998): 768–814.

———. *The Rhetoric of Immediacy: A Cultural Critique of Chan/Zen Buddhism.* Princeton, N.J.: Princeton University Press, 1991.

———. *Visions of Power: Imagining Medieval Japanese Buddhism.* Translated by Phyllis Brooks. Princeton, N.J.: Princeton University Press, 1996.

Fickle, Dorothy H. "Crowned Buddha Images in Southeast Asia." In *Silapa lae Bōrānakhadī nai Prathet Thai* [Art and Archeology in Thailand]. Bangkok: Fine Arts Department, 1974.

———. *Images of the Buddha in Thailand.* Singapore: Oxford University Press, 1989.

Finot, Louis. "List gènérale des manuscrits laotien." *BEFEO* 7 (1917): 1–218.

Foucher, Alfred. "The Beginnings of Buddhist Art." In *The Beginnings of Buddhist Art and Other Essays in Indian and Central-Asian Archaeology,* edited by Alfred Foucher and translated by L. A. Thomas. Varanasi: Indological Book House, 1972.

———. "L'Origine grecque de l'image du Bouddha." *Annales du Musée Guimet* 38 (1913): 231–72.

———. *The Life of the Buddha According to the Ancient Texts and Monuments of India.* Translated by Simone Braniger Boas. Middletown, Conn.: Wesleyan University Press, 1963.

Foulk, T. Griffith, and Robert H. Sharf. "On the Ritual Use of Ch'an Portraiture in Medieval China." *Cahiers d'Extrême-Asie* 7 (1993–94): 156–219.

Frank, Bernard. "Vacuité et corps actualisé: Le problème de la présence des 'Personnages Vénérés' dans leurs images selon la tradition du bouddhisme japonais." *Journal of the International Association for Buddhist Studies* 11, no. 2 (1988): 53–86.

Freedberg, David. *The Power of Images: Studies in the History and Theory of Response.* Chicago: University of Chicago Press, 1989.

Fussman, Gérard. "Symbolisms of the Buddhist Stūpa." *Journal of the International Association of Buddhist Studies* 9, no. 2 (1986): 37–58.

Gabaude, Louis. "Bouddhismes en contact un zeste de Zen dans le bouddhisme thai." *BEFEO* 87, no. 2 (2000): 389–442.

Gangoly, O. C. *The Antiquity of the Buddha-Image: The Cult of the Buddha.* 1938. Reprint, Calcutta: Bani, 1965.

Geiger, Wilhelm, trans. *The Mahāvaṃsa or the Great Chronicle of Ceylon.* 1912. Reprint, Colombo: Ceylon Government Information Department, 1960.

Gerini, G. E. *A Retrospective View and Account of the Origin of the Thet Mahā Ch'at Ceremony (Mahā Jāti Desanā) or Exposition of the Tale of the Great Birth as Performed in Siam.* 2d ed. Bangkok: Sathirakoses-Nagapradipa Foundation, 1976.

Giles, H. A., trans. *The Travels of Fa-Hsien.* Cambridge: At the University Press, 1923.

Ginsburg, Henry. *Thai Manuscript Painting.* Honolulu: University of Hawai'i Press, 1989.

Giteau, Madeleine. "Le bornage rituel des temple bouddhiques au Cambodge." *BEFEO* 68 (1969): 3–41.

Gombrich, Richard F. "The Consecration of a Buddha Image." *Journal of Asian Studies* 26, no. 1 (November 1966): 23–36.

———. "Feminine Elements in Sinhalese Buddhism." *Wiener Zeitschrift für die Kunde Südasiens und Archiv für Indische Philosophie* 16 (1972): 67–93.

———. "Kosala-Bimba-Vaṇṇanā." In *Buddhism in Ceylon and Studies on Religious Syncretism in Buddhist Countries.* Symposium zur Buddhismusforschung I, edited by Heinz Bechert. Göttingen: Abhandlungen der Akademie der Wissenschaften, 1978.

———. *Precept and Practice: Traditional Buddhism in the Rural Highlands of Ceylon.* Oxford: Clarendon, 1971.

———. "The Significance of Former Buddhas in the Theravādin Tradition." In *Buddhist Studies in Honour of Walpola Rahula,* edited by Somaratna Balasooriya et al. London: Gordon Fraser, 1980.

Gonda, Jan. "À propos d'un sens magico-religieux de skt. *guru-*." In *Selected Studies,* vol. 2. Sanskrit Word Studies. Leiden: E. J. Brill, 1975.

———. *Eye and Gaze in the Veda.* Amsterdam: North-Holland, 1969.

———. "Pratiṣṭha." In *Selected Studies,* vol. 2. Sanskrit Word Studies. Leiden: E. J. Brill, 1975.

Gosling, Betty. *Sukhothai: Its History, Culture, and Art.* Singapore: Oxford University Press, 1991.

Griffiths, Paul J. "Buddhist Jhāna: A Form-Critical Study." *Religion* 13 (1983): 55–68.

Griswold, Alexander B. "Bronze-Casting in Siam." *BEFEO* 46 (1954): 635–47.

———. *Dated Buddha Images of Northern Siam.* Ascona: Artibus Asiae, 1957.

———. *Towards a History of Sukhodaya Art.* Bangkok: The National Museum, 1967.

———. *Wat Pra Yün Reconsidered.* Bangkok: The Siam Society, 1975.

———. *What Is a Buddha Image?* 2d ed. Thai Culture, New Series, no. 19. Bangkok: Fine Arts Department, 2511 B.E./1968 C.E.

Hallisey, Charles. "Roads Taken and Not Taken in the Study of Theravāda Buddhism." In *Curators of the Buddha: The Study of Buddhism Under Colonialism,* edited by Donald S. Lopez Jr. Chicago: University of Chicago Press, 1995.

Hardy, Edmund. "Māra in the Guise of Buddha." *Journal of the Royal Asiatic Society* (1902): 951–55.

Harrison, Paul. "Is the *Dharma-kāya* the Real 'Phantom Body' of the Buddha?" *Journal of the International Association of Buddhist Studies* 15 (1992): 44–94.

Harvey, Peter. "The Dynamics of *Paritta* Chanting in Southern Buddhism." In *Love Divine: Studies in Bhakti and Devotional Mysticism.* London: Curzon, 1993.

———. "The Nature of the Tathāgata." In *Buddhist Studies: Ancient and Modern,* edited by Philip Denwood and Alexander Piatagorsky. London: Curzon, 1983.

———. "The Symbolism of the Early Stūpa." *Journal of the International Association of Buddhist Studies* 7, no. 2 (1984): 67–93.

———. "Venerated Objects and Symbols of Early Buddhism." In *Symbols in Art and Religions: The Indian and the Comparative Perspectives,* edited by Karel Werner. London: Curzon, 1990.

Heikkilä-Horn, Marja-Leena. *Buddhism with Open Eyes: Belief and Practice of Santi Asoke.* Bangkok: Fah Apai, Ltd., 1997.

Heinze, Ruth-Inge. *Tham Khwan: How to Contain the Essence of Life.* Singapore: Singapore University Press, 1982.

Henderson, Gregory, and Leon Hurvitz. "The Buddha of Seiryōji: New Finds and New Theory." *Artibus Asiae* 19, no. 1 (1956): 5–55.

Herbert, Patricia. *The Life of the Buddha.* London: The British Library, 1992.

Hocart, A. M. "The Origin of the Stūpa." *Ceylon Journal of Science* 1, no. 1 (1924).

Horner, I. B., trans. *The Book of Discipline (Vinaya Pitaka)* 4. London: Luzac, 1962.

———, trans. *The Minor Anthologies of the Pali Canon.* London: Pali Text Society, 1975.

Horner, I. B., and Padmanabh S. Jaini, trans. *Apocryphal Birth-Stories* (*Paññāsa Jātaka*). 2 vols. London: Pali Text Society, 1985–86.

Huntington, John C. "The Origin of the Buddha Image: Early Image Traditions and the Concept of Buddhadar Śanapunyā." In *Studies in Buddhist Art of South Asia,* edited by A. K. Narain. New Delhi: Kanak, 1985.

Huntington, Susan L. "Aniconism and the Multivalence of Emblems: Another Look." *Ars Orientalis* 22 (1992): 111–56.

———. *The Art of Ancient India: Buddhist, Hindu, Jain.* New York: John Weatherill, 1985.

———. "Early Buddhist Art and the Theory of Aniconism." *Art Journal* 49, no. 4 (winter 1990): 401–8.

Hutchinson, E. W. "Sacred Images in Chiengmai." *Journal of the Siam Society* 28 (1935): 115–42.

———. "The Seven Spires: A Sanctuary of the Sacred Fig Tree at Chiengmai." *Journal of the Siam Society* 39 (June 1951): 1–68.

Hutn Hmat Win, Sao. *Eleven Holy Discourses of Protection (Mahāparitta)*. Rangoon: Department of Religious Affairs, 1981.

Hyde, Lewis. *The Gift: Imagination and the Erotic Life of Property.* New York: Vintage Books, 1979.

Insom Chaiyachomphū. *Yan lae Kāthā Khong Dī Mū'ang Nū'a* [*Yantra* and *Gāthā* of Northern Thailand]. Chiang Rai: The Bunphadung Store, n.d.

Irwin, John. "The Stūpa and the Cosmic Axis—The Archaeological Evidence." *South Asian Archaeology 1977,* ed. Maurizio Taddei (Naples: Instituto Universitario Orientale, 1979): 799–845.

Jackson, Peter A. "The Enchanting Spirit of Thai Capitalism: The Cult of Luang Phor Khoon and the Post-modernization of Thai Buddhism." *South East Asian Research Journal* 7, no. 1 (March 1999): 5–60.

———. "Royal spirits, Chinese gods, and magic monks: Thailand's boom time religious prosperity." *South East Asian Research Journal* 7, no. 3 (November 1999): 245–320.

Jackson, Roger R. "A Tantric Echo in Sinhalese Theravāda: *Pirit* Ritual, the Book of *Paritta* and the *Jinapañjaraya*." *Journal of the Rare Buddhist Texts Research Project* 18 (1994): 121–40.

Jaini, Padmanabh S. "On the Buddha Image." In *Studies in Pāli Buddhism,* edited by A. K. Narain. Delhi: B. R. Publishing Corp., 1979.

———, ed. *Paññāsa-Jātaka*. 2 vols. London: Pali Text Society, 1982–83.

Jayawickrama, N. A. *The Chronicle of the Thūpa and Thūpavaṃsa*. London: Luzac, 1971.

———, ed. and trans. *The Inception of Discipline and the Vinaya Nidāna*. London: Luzac, 1962.

———, trans. *The Story of Gotama Buddha: The Nidāna-kathā of the Jātakaṭṭhakathā*. Oxford: Pali Text Society, 1990.

Johnston, E. H. *The Buddhacarita or Acts of the Buddha*. 1936. 2d ed., Delhi: Motilal Barnasidass, 1984.

Jones, J. J. *The Mahāvastu*. Vol. 1. London: Luzac, 1949.

Kamala Tiyavanich. *Forest Recollections: Wandering Monks in Twentieth-Century Thailand*. Honolulu: University of Hawai'i Press, 1997.

Karlsson, Klemens. *Face to Face with the Absent Buddha: The Formation of Buddhist Aniconic Art*. Uppsala: Uppsala University, 1999.

Keyes, Charles F. "Buddhist Pilgrimage Centers and the Twelve-Year Cycle: Northern Thai Moral Orders in Space and Time." *History of Religions* 15, no. 1 (1975): 71–89.

———. "Death of Two Buddhist Saints." In *Charisma and Sacred Biography,* edited by Michael A. Williams. Chambersburg, Pa.: American Academy of Religion, 1982.

———. "Introduction: Charisma: From Social Life to Sacred Biography." In *Charisma and Sacred Biography,* edited by Michael A. Williams. Chambersburg, Pa.: American Academy of Religion, 1982.

———. "Mother, Mistress, but Never a Monk: Buddhist Notions of Female Gender in Rural Thailand." *American Ethnologist* 11, no. 2 (May 1984): 223–41.

Khin Myo Chit. "Maha Myat Muni Buddha Image: The Arakan Pagoda." In *A Wonderland of Burmese Legends*. Bangkok: Tamarind, 1984.

King, Winston L. *Theravāda Meditation: The Buddhist Transformation of Yoga*. Delhi: Motilal Banarsidass, 1992.

Kinnard, Jacob N. *Imaging Wisdom: Seeing and Knowing in the Art of Indian Buddhism*. London: Curzon, 1999.

Knox, Robert. *An Historical Relation of Ceylon*. 2d ed. Dehiwala: Tisara Prakasakayo, 1966.

Lamotte, Étienne. "Conditioned Co-production and Supreme Enlightenment." In *Buddhist Studies in Honour of Walpola Rahula*, edited by Somaratna Balasooriya et al. London: Gordon Fraser, 1980.

———. *History of Indian Buddhism: From the Origins to the Śakya Era*. Translated by Sara Webb-Boin. Louvain-La-Neuve: Université Catholique de Louvain, 1988.

Lancaster, Lewis R. "An Early Mahāyāna Sermon about the Body of the Buddha and the Making of Images." *Artibus Asiae* 36 (1974): 287–91.

La Vallee Poussin, Louis de. "Le Bouddha et les Abhijñas." *Le Muséon* 32 (1931): 335–42.

———. "Note sur les corps du Bouddha." *Le Muséon* 14 (1913): 257–90.

Leclère, Adhémard. *Cambodge, fêtes civiles et religieuses*. Paris: Imprimerie Nationale, 1916.

Lefferts, H. Leedom, Jr. "Clothing the Serpent: Transformations of the *Naak* in Thai-Lao Theravada Buddhism." In *Transformative Power of Cloth in Southeast Asia*, edited by Lynne Milgram and Penny van Esterik. Montreal: Canadian Council for Southeast Asian Studies, 1994.

Ling, Trevor O. *Buddhism and the Mythology of Evil: A Study in Theravāda Buddhism*. London: George Allen and Unwin, 1962.

Lohuizen-de-Leeuw, J. E. van. "New Evidence with Regard to the Origin of the Buddha Image." In *South Asian Archaeology 1979*, edited by Hebert Härtel. Berlin: Dietrich Reimer Verlag, 1981.

———. "The Stone Buddha of Chiengmai and Its Inscription." *Artibus Asiae* 24 (1961): 324–29.

Lopez, Donald S., Jr., ed. *Buddhism in Practice*. Princeton, N.J.: Princeton University Press, 1995.

Luce, Gordon. *Old Burma—Early Pagan*. 3 vols. Locust Valley, N.Y.: J. J. Augustin, 1969–70.

McCallum, Donald F. "The Replication of Miraculous Images: The Zenkōji Amida and Seiryōji Shaka." In *Images, Miracles, and Authority in Asian Religious Traditions*, edited by Richard H. Davis. Boulder, Colo.: Westview, 1998.

———. "The Saidaiji Lineage of the Seriyōji Shaka Tradition." *Archives of Asian Art* 41 (1996): 51–67.

———. *Zenkōji and Its Icon: A Study in Japanese Religious Art*. Princeton, N.J.: Princeton University Press, 1994.

Malalasekera, G. P. *Dictionary of Pāli Proper Names.* 2 vols. London: Pali Text Society, 1974.

———. *The Pāli Literature of Ceylon.* Colombo: M. D. Gunasena, 1958.

Manī Phayomyong. "Kānsuat lae Khamsuatphithīsamkhan" [Chanting and Ritual Chants]. In *Phithī Kam Lānnā Thai* [Northern Thai Rituals], edited by Phrakhrū Sittithep-chedīyārak et al. Chiang Mai: Thārāthong, 1989.

———. "Kān Thawāi lae Ōkadwāenthān." In *Phithī Kam Lānnā Thai* [Northern Thai Rituals], edited by Phrakhrū Sittithep-chedīyārak et al. Chiang Mai: Tharathong, 1989.

———. *Khrū'ang Sakkāra Nai Lānnā Thai* [Sacred Implements in Northern Thailand]. Chiang Mai: Thai Dhanu Bank, 2538 B.E./1995 C.E.

———. *Praphenī Sipsong Du'an Lānnā Thai* [The Twelve Month Customs of Northern Thailand]. 2 vols. Chiang Mai: Chiang Mai University, 2529 B.E./ 1986 C.E.

———. *Wathanatham Lānnā* [Northern Thai Culture]. Bangkok: Thaiwathanāphānit, 2529 B.E./1986 C.E.

Martini, Ginette. "Pañcabuddhabyākaraṇa." *BEFEO* 55 (1969): 123–47.

Matics, K. I. *Gestures of the Buddha.* Bangkok: Chulalongkorn University Press, 1998.

———. *Introduction to the Thai Temple.* Bangkok: White Lotus, 1992.

Morris, Charles. *Signification and Significance: A Study of the Relations of Signs and Values.* Cambridge, Mass.: The MIT Press, 1964.

Mus, Paul. "Le Buddha paré." *BEFEO* 28 (1928): 153–278.

Nagao, Gadjin M. "On the Theory of Buddha-Body (*Buddha-kāya*)." *Eastern Buddhist,* n.s., 6, no. 1 (May 1973): 25–53.

Ñāṇamoli, Bhikkhu, and Bhikkhu Bodhi, trans. *The Middle Length Discourses of the Buddha.* Boston: Wisdom, 1995.

Narayan, Vasudha. "Arcāvatāra: On Earth as He Is in Heaven." In *Gods of Flesh, Gods of Stone: The Embodiment of Divinity in India,* edited by Joanne Punzo Waghorne and Norman Cutler. New York: Columbia University Press, 1996.

Narula, Karen Schur. *The Voyage of the Emerald Buddha.* Kuala Lumpur: Oxford University Press, 1994.

Niyom Nikrotha. *Luang Pū Wāen Succinō, Wat Doi Māe Ping, Phrao, Chiang Mai Province.* Chiang Mai: Chiang Mai University, n.d.

Norman, K. R. *Pāli Literature.* Wiesbaden: Otto Harrassowitz, 1983.

Notton, Camille. *The Chronicle of the Emerald Buddha.* Bangkok: Bangkok Times Press, 1932.

———. *P'ra Buddha Sihiṅga.* Bangkok: Bangkok Times Press, 1933.

———. *P'ra Setaṃgamaṇī.* Bangkok: Bangkok Times Press, 1936.

Nyanaponika, Thera. *The Heart of Buddhist Meditation.* London: Rider, 1962.

Oldenberg, Herman, and Richard Pischel. *Therā- and Therīgathā.* 2d ed. London: Luzac, 1966.

Pandey, Rajbali. *Hindu Saṃskāras: Socio-Religious Study of the Hindu Sacraments.* 2d ed. Delhi: Motilal Banarsidass, 1969.

*Paññāsachādok* [The Fifty Jātakas]. 2 vols. Bangkok: National Library, 1956.

Paramānuchit-chinōrot, Somdet Krom Phra. *Phra Pathomsomphōt Kathā* [The Buddha's Supreme Enlightenment]. Bangkok: Amnuaysān, 2530 B.E./1987 C.E.

Parry, J. P. "Death and Cosmogony in Kashi." In *Way of Life: King, Householder, Renouncer: Essays in Honour of Louis Dumont,* edited by T. N. Madan. Paris: La Maison des sciences de l'homme, 1982.

Pattaratorn Chirapravati, ML. *Votive Tablets in Thailand: Origin, Styles, and Uses.* Kuala Lumpur: Oxford University Press, 1997.

Payne, Richard D. "Realizing Inherent Enlightenment: Ritual and Self-Transformation in Shingon Buddhism." In *Religious and Social Ritual: Interdisciplinary Explorations,* edited by Michael B. Aune and Valerie DeMarinis. Albany: State University of New York Press, 1996.

Payutto, Phra Prayudh (P. A. Payutto). *Buddhadhamma: Natural Laws and Values for Life.* Translated by Grant A. Olson. Albany: State University of New York Press, 1995.

Penth, Hans. *A Brief History of Lān Nā: Civilizations of North Thailand.* Chiang Mai: Silkworm Books, 1994.

*Phāp Phuttha Prawat Wat Thongnopakhun* [Painted Sculpture on the Life of the Buddha]. Bangkok: Matichon, 1983.

Phrachak, Phra Khrū. "Kham Sangwoey Pūjā Thewadā Ārak lae Phrawiññān nai Kāntham Mahākan Tāng Tāng" [Words of Propitiatory Offering to the Protective Gods and Spirits on Various Important Occasions]. In *Phrawat Wat Sāenfāng* [History of Wat Sāeng Fāng]. Chiang Mai, 1994.

*Phra Phuttha Prawat Chitarakam Fāphanang Phra Thī Nang Phutthaisawan Phiphithaphanthasathān Hāeng Chāt Phranakorn* [The Life of the Buddha: Murals in the Buddhaisawan Chapel, National Museum]. Bangkok: Department of Fine Arts, 2515 B.E./1972 C.E.

*Phra Rājā Phithī Sipsong Dū'an* [Royal Twelve Month Ceremonies]. Bangkok: Department of Fine Arts, 2511 B.E./1968 C.E.

*Phutthamahāmanīratanapatimākan* [Images of the Emerald Buddha]. Bangkok: Wat Phra Srīratanasāsadārām and the Thai Military Bank, 2525 B.E./1982 C.E.

Piyadassi Thera, trans. *The Book of Protection: Paritta.* Kandy: The Buddhist Publication Society, 1975.

Plāek Santhirak. *Lathi Praphenī lae Phithīkam* [Beliefs, Customs, and Ceremonies]. Bangkok: Panākān, 2515 B.E./1972 C.E.

*Prawat Wat Thua Rāchānāchak Lem 1* [The History of Wats in Thailand, vol. 1]. Bangkok: Ministry of Education, 2525 B.E./1982 C.E.

Preston, James J. "Creation of a Sacred Image: Apotheosis and Destruction in Hinduism." In *Gods of Flesh, Gods of Stone: The Embodiment of Divinity in India,* edited by Joanne Punzo Waghorne and Norman Culter. New York: Columbia University Press, 1996.

Prien, J. *Praphenī lae Mongkhon Khong Thai* [Customs and Auspicious Ceremonies of the Thai]. Bangkok: Thammabanākhān, 2514 B.E./1971 C.E.

Rahula, Walpola. *History of Buddhism in Ceylon.* Colombo: M. D. Gunasena, 1956.

Rājavaramunī (P. A. Payutto). *Phachanānukrom Phutthasāsāt* (Dictionary of Buddhism). Bangkok: Mahāchulālongkorn Buddhist University, 1985.

Ratanapañña Thera. *The Sheaf of Garlands of the Epochs of the Conqueror (Jinakālamālīpakaraṇaṃ),* translated by N. A. Jayawickrama. Pali Text Society Translation Series no. 36. London: Luzac, 1968.

Ray, Reginald. *Buddhist Saints in India: A Study in Buddhist Values and Orientations.* New York: Oxford University Press, 1994.

Reynolds, Frank E. "The Holy Emerald Jewel: Some Aspects of Buddhist Symbolism and Political Legitimation in Thailand and Laos." In *Religion and Legitimation of Power in Thailand, Laos, and Burma,* edited by Bardwell L. Smith. Chambersburg, Pa.: Anima Books, 1978.

———. "The Many Lives of the Buddha." In *The Biographical Process: Studies in the History and Psychology of Religion,* edited by Frank E. Reynolds and Donald Capps. The Hague: Mouton, 1976.

———. "Rebirth Traditions and the Lineages of Gotama: A Study in Theravāda Buddhology." In *Sacred Biography in the Buddhist Traditions of South and Southeast Asia,* edited by Juliane Schober. Honolulu: University of Hawai'i Press, 1997.

———. "The Several Bodies of the Buddha: Reflections on a Neglected Aspect of the Theravāda Tradition." *History of Religions* 16, no. 4 (May 1977): 374–89.

Reynolds, Frank E., and Donald Capps, eds. *The Biographical Process: Studies in the History and Psychology of Religion.* The Hague: Mouton, 1976.

Reynolds, Frank E., and Charles Hallisey. "Buddha." In *Encyclopedia of Religion,* 1–2, edited by Mircea Eliade. New York: Macmillan, 1989: 319–32.

Reynolds, Frank E., and Mani B. Reynolds. *The Three Worlds According to King Ruang: A Thai Buddhist Cosmology.* Berkeley: Asian Humanities Press, 1982.

Roth, Gustav. "The Physical Presence of the Buddha and Its Representation in Buddhist Literature." In *Investigating Indian Art* 8, edited by Marianne Yaldiz and Wibke Lobo. Berlin: Museum für indischekunst, 1987.

Ruegg, D. Seyfort. *La Théorie du Tathāgatagarbha et du Gotra.* Paris: Publications de l'École française d'Extrême-Orient 70, 1969.

———. "Pāli *gotta/gotra* and the Term *gotrabhū* in Pāli and Buddhist Sanskrit." In *Buddhist Studies in Honour of I. B. Horner,* edited by L. Cousins, A. Kunst, and K. R. Norman. Dordrecht: D. Reidel, 1974.

Ruelius, Hans. "Netrapratiṣṭhāpana—eine singhalesische Zeremonie zur Weihe von Kultbildern." In *Buddhism in Ceylon and Studies on Religious Syncretism in Buddhist Countries,* edited by Heinz Bechert. Göttingen: Vandenhoeck and Ruprecht, 1978.

Ruppert, Brian D. *Jewel in the Ashes: Buddha Relics and Power in Early Medieval Japan.* Cambridge, Mass.: Harvard University Press, 2000.

Saddhatissa, Hammalawa. "Pāli Literature from Laos." In *Buddhist Studies in Honour of I. B. Horner,* edited by L. S. Cousins et al. Dordrecht: D. Reidel, 1974.

———. "The Significance of Paritta and Its Application in the Theravāda Tradition." In *Buddhist Thought and Ritual,* edited by David Kalupahana. New York: Paragon House, 1991.

Sanguan Chōtisukharat. *Praphenī Thai Phāk Nū'a* [The Customs of Northern Thailand]. Bangkok: Odian Store, 2512 B.E./1969 C.E.

Sāsanasōphon, Phra. *Suat Mon Plāe* [Chants in Translation]. Bangkok: Mahamakut, 1970.

Schober, Juliane. "In the Presence of the Buddha: Ritual Veneration of the Burmese Mahāmuni Image." In *Sacred Biography in the Buddhist Traditions of South and Southeast Asia,* edited by Juliane Schober. Honolulu: University of Hawai'i Press, 1997.

Schopen, Gregory. "Archaeology and Protestant Presuppositions in the Study of Indian Buddhism." *History of Religions* 31, no. 1 (August 1991): 1–23.

———. *Bones, Stones, and Buddhist Monks: Collected Papers on the Archaeology, Epigraphy, and Texts of Monastic Buddhism in India.* Honolulu: University of Hawai'i Press, 1997.

———. "The Buddha as an Owner of Property and Permanent Resident in Medieval Indian Monasteries." *Journal of Indian Philosophy* 18 (1990): 181–217.

———. "Burial *'ad santos'* and the Physical Presence of the Buddha in Early Indian Buddhism: A Study in the Archaeology of Religions." *Religion* 17 (1987): 193–225.

———. "Monks and the Relic Cult in the *Mahāparinibbānasutta*: An Old Misunderstanding in Regard to Monastic Buddhism." In *From Benares to Beijing: Essays on Buddhism and Chinese Religions in Honour of Prof. Jan Yün-Hua,* edited by Koichi Shinohara and Gregory Schopen. Oakville, Ont.: Mosaic, 1991.

———. "On Monks, Nuns, and 'Vulgar' Practices: The Introduction of the Image Cult into Indian Buddhism." *Artibus Asiae* 49, nos. 1–2 (1988–89): 153–68.

Shah, U. P. "A Unique Jaina Image of Jīvantasvāmi." *Journal of the Oriental Institute* 1, no. 1 (1951): 71–79.

Sharf, Robert H. "On the Allure of Buddhist Relics." *Representations* 66 (spring 1999): 75–99.

———. "On the Ritual Use of Ch'an Portraiture in Medieval China." *Cahiers d'Extrême-Asie,* no. 7 (1993–94): 149–219.

———. "The Idolization of Enlightenment: On the Mummification of Ch'an Masters in Medieval China." *History of Religions* 32, no. 1 (August 1992): 1–31.

———. "The Scripture on the Production of Buddha Images." In *Religions of China in Practice,* edited by Donald S. Lopez Jr. Princeton, N.J.: Princeton University Press, 1996.

Sharpa, Tulku, and Michael Perrott. "The Ritual of Consecration." *Tibet Journal* 10, no. 2 (1985): 35–49.

Shway Yoe [Sir James George Scott]. *The Burman: His Life and Notions.* 1882. Reprint, New York: W. W. Norton, 1963.

Siriratanasunthorn, Phra Khrū. *Pap Suat Mon Tan* [The Complete Folio of Chants]. Chiang Mai, 2533 B.E./1990 C.E.

Sittha Chetawan and Nirōt Kasetsiri. *Luang Pū Wāen Sucinnō: Phra Arahant Yuk Paccupan* [Luang Pū Wāen Sucinnō: Contemporary Arahant]. Bangkok: Nangu' Thip, n.d.

Sitthiwarawet, Phra Khrū. *Sāsana Phithī Phū'an Mū'ang* [Northern Thai Religious Ceremonies]. Chiang Mai: S. Sapakan, 1989.

*Sŏk mun wibŏm* [The Buddhist Ritual], edited by Chin-ho Ahn. Seoul: Pomrunsa, 1983.

Skilling, Peter. "Five Bodhisattvas." *Fragile Palm Leaves: For the Preservation of Buddhist Literature* no. 5 (2542 B.E./1999 C.E.): 8–12.

———. "Introduction to 'The Blessings of the Five Buddhas.'" *Fragile Palm Leaves,* no. 4 (2541 B.E./1998 C.E.): 10.

———. "The Rakṣā Literature of the Śrāvakayāna." *Journal of the Pali Text Society* 16 (1992): 109–82.

Smith, H. Daniel. "Pratiṣṭha." In *Āgama and Silpa,* edited by K.K.A. Venkatachari. Bombay: Ananthacharya Indological Research Institute, 1984.

Smith, Jonathan Z. *To Take Place: Toward Theory in Ritual.* Chicago: University of Chicago Press, 1987.

Snellgrove, David L., ed. *The Image of the Buddha.* Tokyo: Kodansha International, 1978.

Snodgrass, Adrian. *The Symbolism of the Stupa.* Ithaca, N.Y.: Southeast Asian Program, 1988.

Soma Thera. *The Way of Mindfulness: The Satipaṭṭhāna Sutta and Commentary.* 3d ed. Kandy: The Buddhist Publication Society, 1967.

Sommai Premchit, and Amphay Doré. *The Lan Na Twelve-Month Traditions.* Chiang Mai: So Sap Kanpim, 1992.

Soper, Alexander Coburn. *Literary Evidence for Early Buddhist Art in China.* Ascona: Artibus Asiae, 1959.

Sponberg, Alan, and Helen Hardacre, eds. *Maitreya, the Future Buddha.* Cambridge: Cambridge University Press, 1988.

Srisakara Vallibhotama. *Phra Kru'ang nai Mū'ang Siam* [Amulets in Thailand]. Bangkok: Matichon, 1994.

Stein, Otto. "Notes on the Trikāya-Doctrine." In *Jhā Commemoration Volume: Essays on Oriental Subjects.* Poona Oriental Series, no. 39. Poona: Oriental Book Agency, 1937.

Strachan, Paul. *Pagan: Art and Architecture of Old Burma.* Whiting Bay: Kiscadale, 1989.

Strahan, Donna K. "Bronze Casting in Thailand." In *The Sacred Sculpture of Thailand,* edited by Hiram W. Woodward Jr. Baltimore: The Walters Art Gallery, 1997.

Stratton, Carol, and Miriam McNair Scott. *The Buddhist Sculpture of Northern Thailand.* Chiang Mai: Silkworm Books, 1999.

Strong, John S. "Buddha Bhakti and the Absence of the Blessed One." In *Colloque Étienne Lamotte in Brussels and Liège, Belgium.* Louvain: Université Catholique de Louvain, 1989.

———. *The Experience of Buddhism: Sources and Interpretations.* 2d ed. Belmont, Calif.: Wadsworth, 2001.

———. "A Family Quest: The Buddha, Yaśodharā, and Rāhula in the *Mūlasarvāstivāda Vinaya.*" In *Sacred Biography in the Buddhist Traditions of South and Southeast Asia,* edited by Juliane Schober. Honolulu: University of Hawai'i Press, 1997.

———. "*Gandhakuṭī:* The Perfumed Chamber of the Buddha." *History of Religions* 16, no. 4 (May 1977): 390–406.

———. "Images." *Encyclopedia of Religion,* 5. New York: Macmillan, 1987: 97–104.

———. *The Legend of King Aśoka: A Study and Translation of the Aśokāvadāna.* Princeton, N.J.: Princeton University Press, 1983.

———. "The Legend of the Lion-Roarer: A Study of the Buddhist Arhat Piṇḍola Bhāradvāja." *Numen* 26 (1979): 50–88.

———. *The Legend and Cult of Upagupta: Sanskrit Buddhism in North India and Southeast Asia.* Princeton, N.J.: Princeton University Press, 1992.

———. "Les reliques des cheveux du Bouddha au Shwe Dagon de Rangoon." *Aséanie* 2 (November 1998): 79–107.

———. "The Transforming Gift: An Analysis of Devotional Acts of Offering in Buddhist *Avadāna* Literature." *History of Religions* 18, no. 3 (February 1979): 221–37.

Stuart-Fox, Martin. "Jhāna and Buddhist Scholasticism." *Journal of the International Association of Buddhist Studies* 12, no. 2 (1989): 79–110.

Swearer, Donald K. "Bhikkhu Buddhadāsa's Interpretation of the Buddha." *Journal of the American Academy of Religion* 64, no. 2 (summer 1996): 313–36.

———. *The Buddhist World of Southeast Asia.* Albany: State University of New York Press, 1995.

———. "Fundamentalistic Movements in Theravāda Buddhism." In *Fundamentalisms Observed,* edited by Martin E. Marty and R. Scott Appleby. Chicago: University of Chicago Press, 1991.

———. "Hypostasizing the Buddha: Buddha Image Consecration in Northern Thailand." *History of Religions* 34, no. 3 (February 1995): 263–80.

———. "The Layman Extraordinaire in Northern Thai Buddhism." *Journal of the Siam Society* 64, no. 1 (January 1976): 151–68.

———. "A New Look at Prince Vessantara." *Research Bulletin* (National Research Council of Thailand) 10, no. 1 (1978): 1–9.

———. "Signs of the Buddha in the Northern Thai Chronicles." In *Wannakam Phutthasāsanā Nai Lānnā* [Buddhist Literature in Northern Thailand], edited by Phanphen Khrū'ngthai. Chiang Mai: Silkworm Books, 2540 B.E./ 1997 C.E.

———. *Wat Haripuñjaya: A Study of the Royal Temple of the Buddha's Relic, Lamphūn, Thailand.* AAR Studies in Religion, no. 10. Missoula, Mont.: Scholars, 1976.

Swearer, Donald K., and Sommai Premchit. *The Legend of Queen Cāma.* Albany: State University of New York Press, 1998.

———. "Mūlasāsanā Wat Pā Daeng: The Chronicle of the Founding of Buddhism of the Wat Pā Daeng Tradition." *Journal of the Siam Society* 65, no. 2 (July 1977): 73–110.

———. "The Relation Between the Religious and Political Orders in Northern Thailand (14th–16th Centuries)." In *Religion and Legitimation of Power in Thailand, Laos, and Burma,* edited by Bardwell L. Smith. Chambersburg, Pa.: Anima Books, 1978.

Tambiah, Stanley J. *Buddhism and the Spirit Cults in North-east Thailand.* Cambridge: Cambridge University Press, 1970.

———. *The Buddhist Saints of the Forest and the Cult of Amulets.* Cambridge: Cambridge University Press, 1984.

———. "The Magical Power of Words." *Man,* n.s. 3, no. 2 (1968): 175–208.

———. "A Performative Approach to Ritual." *Proceedings of the British Academy* 65 (1979): 113–69.

*Tamnān Phra Kāewkhāw (Setaṅgamaṇī) kap Phrasilā (Phrahinōn)* [The Chronicle of the White Crystal Buddha Image and the Stone Buddha Image]. Chiang Mai: Wat Chiang Man, 2515 B.E./1975 C.E.

*Tamnān Kā Phū'ak: Thammadesanā Phū'anmū'angnu'a* [The Chronicle of the White Crow: A Sermon in Northern Thai]. Chiang Mai: Thārāthong, n.d.

*Tamnān Wat Phrathāt Doi Suthep* [The Chronicle of the Temple of the Buddha's Relic on Suthep Mountain]. Chiang Mai: 2526 B.E./1969 C.E.

*Tamrā Kān Kosāng Phraphuttharūp* [Manual for Making a Buddha Image]. Bangkok: Vajirañāṇa Library, 1920.

Tannenbaum, Nicola. "Tattoos: Invulnerability and Power in Shan Cosmology." *American Anthropologist* 14, no. 4 (November 1987): 693–711.

Thanissaro Bhikkhu. "The Home Culture of the Dharma: The Story of the Thai Forest Tradition." *Tricycle* 8, no. 2 (1998): 59–62.

———. *The Wings to Awakening.* Barre, Mass.: Dharma Dana, 1996.

Thawī Khū'ankāew. *Praphenī Doem* [Customs of the Past]. Chiang Mai: Phra Sing, 2518 B.E./1975 C.E.

Thepwisutthāchān, Phra. *Phithī Opromsomphōt Phraphuttharūp lae Phithī Sū'pchātā Sadonophkhro Chiang Mai* [The Ceremonies of Buddha Image Consecration, Life Extension, and Dispelling Misfortune in Chiang Mai]. Chiang Mai: Wat Phrathāt Doi Suthep, 2518 B.E./1975 C.E.

Thera Prawat: *Phra Khrū Phrohmcakkasanworn* [A Monk's Story]. Bangkok: Thai Kasem, 2519 B.E./1976 C.E.

Thin Win, U. *Phaya She Kho An Myo Myo* [Various Kinds of Devotional Chants]. Rangoon, 1987.

Thomas, Edward J. *The Life of the Buddha as Legend and History.* London: Routledge and Kegan Paul, 1956.

Thompson, Lawrence G. "Consecration Magic in Chinese Religion." *Journal of Chinese Religions* 15 (1991): 1–9.

Trainor, Kevin. *Relics, Ritual, and Representation in Buddhism: Rematerializing the Sri Lankan Theravāda Tradition.* Cambridge: Cambridge University Press, 1997.

Tucci, Giuseppe. *Tibetan Painted Scrolls.* Vol. 1. Kyoto: Rinsen Books, 1980.

von Hinüber, Oskar. *A Handbook of Pāli Literature.* Berlin: Walter de Gruyter, 1996.

von Simson, Georg. "Die Buddhas der Vorzeit: Versuch einer astralmythologischen Deutung." *Studien zur Indologie und Iranistik* 7 (1981): 77–91.

Waghorne, Joanne Punzo. "Introduction." In *Gods of Flesh, Gods of Stone: The Embodiment of Divinity in India,* edited by Joanne Punzo Waghorne and Norman Cutler. New York: Columbia University Press, 1996.

Wales, H. G. Quartich. *Siamese State Ceremonies.* London: Bernard Quartich, 1931.

Walshe, Maurice, trans. *Thus Have I Heard: The Long Discourses of the Buddha. Dīgha Nikāya.* London: Wisdom, 1987.

Walters, Jonathan S. "Stūpa, Story, and Empire: Constructions of the Buddha Biography in Early Post-Aśokan India." In *Sacred Biography in the Buddhist Traditions of South and Southeast Asia,* edited by Juliane Schober. Honolulu: University of Hawai'i Press, 1997.

Wayman, Alex. "The Buddhist Theory of Vision." In *Buddhist Insight: Essays by Alex Wayman,* edited by George Elder. Delhi: Motilal Banarsidass, 1990.

———. "The Mirror as a Pan-Buddhist Metaphor-Simile." *History of Religions* 13, no. 4 (May 1974): 251–69.

Welbon, Guy R. "Mahāsaṃprokṣaṇa 1981: Āgama and Actuality in a Contemporary Temple Renovation." In *Āgama and Silpa,* edited by K.K.A. Venkatachari. Bombay: Ananthacharya Indological Research Institute, 1984.

Wells, Kenneth E. *Thai Buddhism: Its Rites and Activities.* Rev. ed. Bangkok: Suriyabun, 1975.

Wijeyewardene, Gehan. *Place and Emotion in Northern Thai Ritual Behaviour.* Bangkok: Pandora, 1986.

Woodward, F. L. *Manual of a Mystic: The Yogāvachara's Manual.* Edited by Caroline Rhys Davids. London: Pali Text Society, 1916.

Woodward, Hiram W., Jr. "The Buddha Image in Thailand." In *Sacred Sculpture of Thailand.* Baltimore: The Walters Gallery of Art, 1997.

———. "The Emerald and Sihing Buddhas: Interpretations of Their Significance." In *Living a Life in Accord with Dhamma: Papers in Honor of Professor Jean Boisselier on His Eightieth Birthday,* edited by Natasha Eilenberg, M. C. Subhadradis Diskul, and Robert L. Brown. Bangkok: Silapakorn University, 1997.

———. "Monastery, Palace, and City Plans." *Crossroads: An Interdisciplinary Journal of Southeast Asian Studies* 2, no. 2 (1985): 23–60.

———. "The Thai *čhēdī* and the Problem of Stūpa Interpretation." *History of Religions* 33, no. 1 (August 1993): 71–91.

Woodward, Mark R. "The Biographical Imperative in Theravāda Buddhism." In *Sacred Biography in the Buddhist Traditions of South and Southeast Asia,* edited by Juliane Schober. Honolulu: University of Hawai'i Press, 1997.

Zago, Marcel. *Rites and Ceremonies en Milieu Bouddhiste Lao.* Roma: University Gregoriana Editrice, 1972.

# INDEX

Page references to figures are in bold.


*Abhidhamma,* 117, 155, 163, 188
*Abhidhammatthasaṅgaha,* 71
*abhiññā* (higher knowledges), 153, 154, 156, 158, 169. *See also* knowledge
*abhiseka* ritual, 5–6, 42–43, 70, 72, 77, 82, 83, 85, 106; in Cambodia, 189–90, 215; climax of, 102–104; commencement of, 86–88; conclusion of, 104, **105, 106,** 107; in Korea, 218; in Myanmar, 218–19; and *paritta,* 93–94; in Sri Lanka, 213–14; in Tibet, 219–20
absence and presence, 16, 72, 108–15; Eckel on, 110–11; Gombrich on, 110; Kinnard on, 110; mirror as symbol of, 214, 222; Ruelius on, 214; Tambiah on, 110; Strong on, 111–12. *See also* polarities
Āchān Mun, 119, 120, 121
*āchān wat* (monastery teacher), 48, 86, 88, 96, 104, 258n.39, 269n.50
act of truth (*saccakiriya*), 66, 116–17, 202, 274n.122
Ajaṇṭā, 181, 231
Ajapāla [banyan] Tree, 135, 179
Ajātasattu, King, 187, 197, 205, 206, 207
alchemy, 82, 214
Amarāvatī, 176, 179, 181
Amida Buddha, 18; in Amida Buddha Triad, 18–19; Amitābha, 176
Amoghasiddhi, 221
amulets, 12, 119, 284n.49, 296n.7; cult of, 238; of King Taksin, 235; types of, 237
*anāgāmī.* See never–returner
Ānanda, 3, 92, 107, 147, 187, 205, 206
*ānāpānasati kammaṭṭhāna* (mindfulness of breathing). *See* meditation
Anāthapiṇḍika, 60, 123, 124, 163, 177
ancestors, 226
Angkor, 226
Aṅgulimāla, 92, 163, 274n.122. See *paritta*
aniconic/iconic debate, 24, 25, 29–30, 251n.30, 255n.85
*ānisaṃsa* (meritorious blessing), 16, 19, 20, 22, 60–63
*Ānisong Kān Kosāng Phraphuttharūp* [The Meritorious Blessing for Making Buddha Images] 46, 60–63
*Ānisong Pathom Somphōt* [The Meritorious Blessing for Copying or Listening to the Pathom Somphōt], 137
Anuman Rajadhon, Phya, 270n.57
Anuruddha, 92, 149, 150
Anuson, Phra Khrū, 268n.32, 269n.43
*anussati* (remember), 41, 68, 107, 108, 122, 133
*apadāna,* 20, 252n.44; *Buddhāpadāna,* 283n.39
apotropaism, 68–69, 101; and *paritta* 117; in Sri Lanka, 213, 214
*arahant*(s), 137, 155, 160, 188; in the *Jinapañjara Gāthā,* 92. *See also* Buddha, disciples of
Ariya, lineage of, 153, 155, 159–60, 168, 188
*āsava* (mental intoxicants), 155, 160, 161, 164
Asoka, King, 16, 111, 123, 193; and 84,000 *stūpas,* 72, 111, 187, 258n.38; and Mahākāḷa, 85; and redistribution of relics, 124, 127, 187, 189
Assaji, 136, 137
Atiśa, 220
*avadāna,* 24, 111; 272n.94; *Aśoksāvadāna,* 16, 111, 112
Avalokiteśvara, 221
awareness, 153
Ayutthaya, 194

Bandaranayake, Senake, 37, 256n.5, 258n.35
Bareau, André, 109
Becchetti, Catherine, 263n.47
Bechert, Heinz, 255n.78
Benares. *See* Vārāṇasī
Bentor, Yael, 215–16, 219, 220, 223, 293n.59
Bhaddiya, 136, 137
*bhakti,* 25–26, 27, 28,192, 227. *See also* devotion
Bhallika, 127, 135, 199
Bhārhut, 26, 29, 176, 231
*Bhavatu Sabbamaṅgala,* 262n.38

Bhāvaviveka, 110
Bimbā, 140, 141, 142, 143, 144; *Bimbā Philāp,* 123, 129, 276n.3. *See also* Yasodharā
Bimbisāra, King, 23, 126, 144, 145, 193
Bizot, François, 70, 71, 72, 225, 226, 229, 260n.17, 262n.32, 263n.41, 285n.61, 286n.86, 294n.77
Bodhgayā, 27, 28, 193, 195, 192n.12
*bodhi* tree, 12, 16, 29, 31, 53, 62, 87, 91, 111, 112, 114, 127, 134, 162, 180, 290n.3; at *bodhimaṇḍa,* 81; at enlightenment, 157, 160, 164, 167, 169
*bodhimaṇḍa,* 79, **80,** 80–83, **82,** 87, 90, 99, 152, 224, 265n.6, 278n.29. *See also* sacred space
Bodhirak, Phra, 238, 247, 248; mystical experience of, 246
*bodhisatta*(s), 16, 26, 31, 102; five, 197, 200, 201, 202
*bōek phranet, phithī. See* eye-opening ritual
Boribal Buribhand, Luang, 12
Borobudur, 35; as mesocosm, 111
*bōt* (*uposatha* hall), 33, 45, 58, 77; consecration of, 43, 58
Brahman/Brahmanism, 61, 92, 117, 138, 140, 157, 164, 169, 179, 180, 212, 225. *See also* Sottiya; Sumedha
Brown, Robert L., 16, 191, 193, 231–32, 255n.89, 287n.95
Bruner, Jerome, 191
Bucknell, Roderick, S., 280n.4
Buddha: biography of, 4, 5, 29, 123, 124; compassion of, 162; cult of, 109; dates of, 255n.78; disciples of 92, 116, 136, 137, 149, 150, 270n.62; enlightenment of, 79, 81, 129–137, 157; footprint of, 16, 31, 33, 87, 114; kingship and, 15–17; merit of, 20, 133; miracles by, 157, 163; presence of, 20, 35, 109; signs of, 30, 33; as thaumaturge, 154; visions of, 217
*Buddha Abhiseka* [Buddha Image Consecration Sutta], xv, 44, 95, 96, 97, 99, 152, 153, 154, 155, 156, 157, 198, 224, 279n.1; structure of, 152
Buddha bodies (*kāya*), 20, 36, 71; Buddhadāsa on, 243; *nirmanakāya,* 223; *sambhogakāya,* 221, 285n.73; three, 186, 219, 221, 223; two, theory of, 185. *See also* dhammakāya; rūpakāya
Buddha image(s), 5; of birth day, 184; as Buddha's double, 18, 29, 79; as Buddha's surrogate, 28, 29, 124; construction of, 46, 51–55, 56–7; cult of, 18, 183, 213, 238; dhammacization of, 218, 230; empowerment of, 162; enlivening of, 230; first, 14–25, 26, 27, 28, 78, 180, 192; Gandhāra, 25, 26; as indexical sign, 38; and kingship, 15–16; Mahābodhi, 27, 291n.12; Mathurā, 25–26; origin of, 17, 25–28, 78, 192; *pāramī* of, 155, 172; Phra Bua Khem, 288n.110; postures of, 27, 183, 192, 195; Tian Tan Buddha, 220; transformation of, 222–24, 230; Udayana, 21, 188, 253n.59; *yantra* of, 46, 70. *See also* Emerald Buddha Image; Lion Buddha Image; Mahāmūni image; Sandalwood Buddha Image; Stone Buddha Image; White Crystal Buddha Image
Buddha nature, 219, 221
Buddha relics, 35, 87, 114; and Buddha image, 35–39; classification of, 30, 247; cult of, 112, 197. *See also* relics
*Buddha Sihing, Phra:* chronicle of, 194. *See also* Lion Buddha Image
Buddhabhadra, 21
*Buddhābhisekagāthā,* 77, 265n.3
*Buddhacarita,* 127
Buddhadāsa Bhikkhu, 6, 238, 242–45, 248, 297n.27; Māgha Pūjā talk by, 243; Visākha Pūjā talk by, 245
Buddhaghosa, 125, 188, 212, 271n.71
*Buddhajayamaṅgala Aṭṭhagāthā,* 90
*buddhānussati* (remembering the Buddha), 41, 107–08, 271n.71
Buddhas, birth day, 184
Buddhas, cosmic (maṇḍalic), 221; Akṣobhya, 221; Amoghasiddhi, 221; Ratnasambhava, 221; Vairocana, 176, 221, 224
Buddhas, eonic (past), 5, 261n.8, 282n.8; Dipaṅkara, 5, 127, 128, 176, 177, 179, 182, 183, 261n.18; 276n.16; five, 69, 176, 181, 182, 197, 198–204; Kakusandha, 146, 177, 181, 184, 197, 199, 200, 203; Kassapa, 5, 92, 146, 177, 181, 184, 197, 199, 200, 204; Koṇāgamana, 146, 177, 181, 184, 197, 199, 200, 204; Koṇḍañña, 92, 116,136, 137; Med-

haṅkara, 261n.18; Saraṇaṅkara, 261n.18; Sikhī, 177, 184; Taṇhaṅkara, 92, 261n.8; twenty-four, 175, 179; Vessabhū, 177, 184; Vipassī, 87, 127, 175, 177, 178, 180, 183, 184, 185, 281n.4
*Buddha's Supreme Enlightenment, The.* See *Pathom Somphōt*
*Buddhavaṃsa* (Bv), 125, 126, 129, 175, 178, 179, 180, 182, 183, 197, 268n.37, 276n.16, 281n.4; commentary on, 154; twenty-eight Buddhas in, 282n.10
Bumphen Rawin, xv, 124
Bunkhit Wacharasāt, 268n.36, 269n.42, 277n.l7
Burma, 121. *See also* Myanmar

*cakkavattin,* 16, 36, 61, 126, 148, 187, 192, 193; seven jewels of, 277n.23
Cāma, Queen, 196, 237
Cambodia, 70, 71, 72, 181, 186; eye-opening ritual in, 72; image consecration in, 189, 191, 215, 225, 226–30
candles: at image consecration, 87–88; *thīan chai* (victory candle), 87, 88, 175; Vipassī, 87, 175, 185
*Cariyāpiṭaka* (Cp), 155, 163, 178, 277n.20, 281n.4, 282n.10
*cetiya,* 38, 87, 162; analysis of, 249n.2; Cūḷmāṇī, 129, 144, 151, 196. See also *chedī*
Ch'an, 83
Channa, 126, 131, 143
chant: styles of, 94; *suat bōek,* 94, **95,** 96; *suat mon,* 42, 63, 88, 93, 100, 102
charismatic monks, 118–121, 197. *See also* Āchān Mun; Khrūbā Phrohm; Khrūbā Pinta; Luang Pho Sawat; Luang Pū Lā; Luang Pū Wāen
*chedī,* 11, 31–38, **39,** 45, 50–53, 72, 121; and Buddha image, 37, 38, 40, 262n.29; consecration of, 44, 57–58, 72; at Wat Phrathāt Haripuñjaya, 39. See also *cetiya, stūpa*
Chiang Mai: Jinak written in, 182; and Lion Buddha Image, 194, 195, 196; and Stone Buddha Image, 196, 205, 209
Chiang Rai, 194
Chiang Saen, 35
China, 110, 111, 182, 211, 215; consecration ritual in, 222, 223; cult of saints' bodies in, 109
chronicle. *See* tamnān
Chulalongkorn, King, 125, 236–37; cult of, 237
Coedès, Georges, 71, 125, 186, 262n.34, 286n.86
Collins, Steven, 282n.6
compassion (*karuṇā*), 162, 202, 217; Buddha's, 147, 156, 162, 207; Gotamī's, 139; white crow mother's, 202
consecrated water. See *nām mon*
Coomaraswamy, Ananda K., 25, 26, 214, 230, 250n.19, 291n.5
cosmology, 36, 44, 82, 148
Cousins, L. S., 284n.54
crow, the white, 197–205
Cūḷamāṇī. See *cetiya*
*Cūlavaṃsa,* 212, 291n.4
*Cullanidessa,* 266n.12
*Cullavagga,* 116

*dāna* (giving), 63, 72, 73, 91, **101,** 104, 149, 289n.132; at funerals, 117; and the Sandalwood Image, 15; by Siddhattha, 133, 139; by Vessantara 130, 133, 157, 170, 178, 198
*Dao-xing bo-re jing,* 22, 23
*darśan,* 11, 24, 29, 217, 218
Davids, Caroline Rhys, 71
Davids, T. W. Rhys, 71
Davis, Richard H., 233, 295n.87
de Silva, Lily,115, 267n.27, 273n.114; on *Jinapañjara Gāthā,* 269n.44
de Silva, Lynn, 116
Deer Park, 136, 137, 169
Dehejia, Vidya, 29–30
deity yoga, 223
Demieville, Paul, 273n.113
Devadatta, 64, 205, 290n.136
Devala, 139, 140
*devatā,* 88, 121, 145, 146, 226. See also *thewadā*
devotion, 25, 26, 31, 37; Hindu, 232–33; practice of, 35; rituals of, 29. See also *bhakti*
*Dhammacakkappavattana Sutta,* 16, 35, 54, 104, 116, 127, 135, 136, 140, 155, 163, 185. See also *Sutta*

Dhammakosāchān, Phra. *See* Buddhadāsa Bhikkhu
*dhammakāya,* 71, 108, 156, 186, 197, 215; 251n.30, 285 nn. 77 and 78; analysis of, 185, 189; and Buddha image, 124, 191; formulas of, 190; and *mahāpurisa,* 72; in *Manual for Making a Buddha Image,* 55–56; and *rūpakāya,* 17, 64, 68, 96, 111, 186, 187, 214, 251n.30, 258n.34, 286n.86; *stūpa* as, 37
*Dhammapada,* 63, 219; commentary on, 154, 250n.21; 261 nn. 22 and 23, 276n.16
Dhammapiṭaka, Phra, 6. *See also* Payutto, P. A.
*dhāraṇī,* 64, 117, 156, 170, 220, 237
Dharaṇī. *See* Thoranī, Nang
*dharmakāya,* 221, 223, 224
Dharmakīrti, 183
Dharmasvāmi, 27
Dīpaṅkara. *See* Buddhas, eonic
divination, 82, 222
*Divyāvādāna,* 24
Duangchan Chantharat, 46
Dutt, Nalinaksha, 188
Dutt, Sukumar, 192, 256n.5

Eck, Diana, 217
Eckel, Malcolm, David, 110–11, 112, 113, 251n.28, 254n.70, 272n.90
eightfold noble path, 136, 185
Emerald Buddha Image, 38, 194, 196, 251n.26, 287n.108, 288n.112; in Bangkok, 5, 16, 287n.107; in Chiang Mai, 251n.26; in Chiang Rai, 78, 194, 251n.26; and Tilokarāja, 205. *See also* Buddha image
emptiness. See *śunyatā*
equanimity (*uppekkhā*), 153, 158
exorcism, 213–14
eye(s), 24, 104, 190, 265n.12, 291n.30; all-seeing, 81, 190; Buddha, 81, 103, 190, 216; of compassion, 217; *dharma,* 81, 190, 216, 220; diamond, 216; divine, 100, 104, 119, 158, 161, 166, 168, 190, 199, 204, 216; evil, 214; and gaze, 214, 217; five, 216, 281n.23, 292n.31; flesh, 216; of insight, 216; *nibbāna,* 81; *samantacakkhu,* 262n.36; *saṅgha,* 81; Indra of the thousand, 104; wisdom, 81, 190, 216, 218
eye opening ritual, 5, 88, 94–107; *akkhipūjā,* 290n.3; Brahmanical elements in, 213; in Cambodia, 72, 189; in Sri Lanka, 212–14, 230

Faulk, Maryla, 186
Faulk, Nancy Auer, 255n.88
Faure, Bernard, 109, 272n.77, 291n.21
Faxian, 19, 20, 22, 176, 221
festival of the floating boats, 182, 198
Fickle, Dorothy H., 12, 249n.12, 287n.104
Finot, Louis, 186
five aggregates, 128–29, 134, 160
five ascetics, the (*pañcavaggiya*), 88, 126, 127, 145, 169
five elders, the, 92
forest lineage monks, 38
Foucher, Alfred, 25, 26, 29
four noble truths, 155, 156, 158, 159, 160, 161, 166, 167, 168, 177, 185, 206, 216, 244
four sights, the, 126, 131, 157, 164, 177
Freedberg, David, 249n.3, 296n.11
Fussman, Gérard, 36

Gabaude, Louis, 297n.30
*gandhakuṭī,* (perfumed chamber), 23, 27, 41, 87, 112–14, 258n.35, 273n.100, 291n.12
Gandhāra, 25, 26, 27, 182, 227
Gangoly, O. C., 24, 254n.65
*gāthā:* as apotropaic, 269n.49; *Maṅgala Jaya,* 134; *Maṅgala Udāna,*104, 107; of 108 syllables, 264n.49
Ghaṭīkāra, 289n.130
Ghatīkāramahābrahma, 202, 203, 204. *See also* crow, the white
Girimekhalā, 133
Giteau, Madeleine, 259n.40
gods, 212, 226, 234; Agni, 212; Brahmā, 49, 61, 69, 130, 132, 133, 134, 136, 137, 138, 144, 148, 149, 150, 151, 160, 163, 164, 167, 168, 169, 170, 182, 213, 227, 241; Indra, 36, 44, 61, 130, 132, 133, 134, 135, 136, 144, 145, 148, 149, 150, 151, 164, 170, 172, 194, 196, 212, 229, 241; Payutto's critique of, 241; protective power of, 229; Sakka/Śakra, 194, 213; Sahaṃpatimahābrahmā, 136; Śiva, 65, 134, 148, 149, 150, 213, 241; Viṣṇu, 26, 44, 49, 69, 213, 234, 241;

Vissakamma, 194, 196; Yama, 132, 134, 148, 149, 150, 212
Gombrich, Richard, 110,212, 213, 214, 250n.15, 250n.29, 281n.4, 282n.10, 291n.9
Gonda, Jan, 225, 233, 267n.22
Gosling, Betty, 56n.10
Gotama Buddha, 5, 14, 85, 122, 124, 127, 136, 171, 178, 179, 180, 181, 183, 193, 261n.18; as cow, 197; as son of white crow, 204
Gotamī, 126, 138, 139, 278n.37
*gotrabhū* (lineage of the Ariya), 153, 159, 166, 190, 287n.90
great person. See *mahāpuriṣa*
Griffiths, Paul, 280n.4
Griswold, Alexander B., 49, 195; 256n.10
guardians: Khmer cult of, 225–26; *loka-pāla,* 134, 135, 138, 144
*guṇa* (qualities), 87, 117, 260n.17; of the Buddha, 87, 121, 129, 134; of the *dhamma,* 87, 129; of the *saṅgha,* 87, 129; of the three gems, 100
*guru,* offerings to, 83, **84**

Hallisey, Charles, 268n.28
Haripuñjaya, 35, 196, 208, 290n.138. *See also* Phrathāt Haripuñjaya, Wat
Harrison, Paul, 188
Harvey, Peter, 36, 37, 255n.90, 273n.114
heaven(s): Brahma, 134, 136, 138, 148, 149, 151, 200, 202; Paranimitta, 172; Tāvatiṃsa, 20, 21, 22, 27, 126, 144, 145, 151, 171, 196; Tusita, 122, 125, 128, 130, 138, 139, 157, 164, 170, 177, 188, 203
hell(s), 159, 161, 166, 168; Apāya, 149; Avīci, 148; *nirāya,* 159, 161, 166
Hinayāna, 13, 29, 195
Hinduism, 217; consecration rituals in, 218, 225, 232–35; sectarian traditions in, 233
Hocart, A. M., 35
Huntington, John, 26, 27, 28, 253n.53, 255n.82
Huntington, Susan L., 29
Hutchinson, E. W., 256n.10

icon, 9, 18, 19, 28, 37, 42, 110,191, 215, 287 nn. 95 and 98; cult image as, 218, 230, 233; and *darśan,* 218; mirror as, 222; Zenkōji Āmida image as, 18
*iddhi,* 154; Buddha's 197; Payutto on, 240; Stone Buddha Image's, 297; as thaumaturgical, 154
Indra. *See* gods, Indra
Indra Pillar (Indakīla/Indrakīla), 213, 214, 229, 267n.27
Insom Chaiyachomphū, 64, 259n.3.
Insorn Kaewduangsaeng, **48,** 259n.3
intention (*adhiṭṭāna*), 112–13
interdependent co–arising (*paṭicca samuppāda*), 135, 156, 161, 167, 168, 169, 190, 218, 219, 221
Irwin, John, 35, 36, 37
Isipatāna Forest, 136, 137

Jackson, Peter A., 237
Jackson, Roger, R., 93, 269n.44
Jaini, Padmanabh, S., 250n.19
Jambudīpa, 21, 138, 140, 141, 147, 187, 195, 203, 227
Japan, 109, 211, 215; cult of saints' bodies in, 109; Obaku school in, 215; Vajrayāna tradition (Shingon) in, 224
Jātaka, 15, 20, 22, 60, 116, 122, 123, 178, 179, 182, 197, 231–232; *Chandagādha,* 279n.54; *Gāmaṇicaṇḍa,* 221; *Kāliṅga-bodhi,* 83, 257n.30; 272n.79; *Vaka,* 23; *Vaṭṭaṅgulirāja,* 15, 19–20, 221. See also *Paññāsajātaka; Vessantara Jātaka*
*Jayapañjara Gāthā.* See *paritta*
Jetavana Monastery, 15, 22, 123, 124, 155, 163, 177
jewel walk, 129, 135
*jhānas* (meditative absorptions), 150, 156, 164, 190, 217, 228, 280n.4; Buddha body and, 188; components of, 153; four stages of, 158, 165; and meditation, 164–65; powers of, 115
*Jinakālāmālīpakaraṇaṃ* (Jinak), 193, 258n.33, 283n.40, 288 nn. 109 and 113; and Buddhism in Thailand, 193–94, 211; eonic Buddhas in, 183, and the Lion Buddha, 40, 194
*jñānasattvas* (enlightened beings), 221, 223

Kāladevala, 126
Kamala Tiyvanich, 275n.132
*kamma,* law of, 241, 242
*Kā Phū'ak, Tamnān.* See *tamnān*

Kaniṣka, King, 26
Kanthaka, 126, 131, 143, 144
Kapilavatthu, 126, 128, 129, 144, 155, 163, 179, 226, 278n.42
Karlsson, Klemens, 273n.105
*karuṇā. See* compassion
*Katthāvatthu,* 180, 292n.30
Keyes, Charles, F., 271n.64, 283n.36
Khrūbā Phrohm, 100, 120–21
Khrūbā Pinta, 119
Khrūbā Sīwichāi, 44
*Khuddakapāṭha,* 115, 116
*khwan. See* spirits; spirit calling
*kilesa,* 201, 218, 241, 244
Kinnard, Jacob, 110, 113, 272n.84
knowledge(s): three, 81, 134, 153, 166, 216; insight, 155, 159, 160, 161–67, 168. See also *abhiññā*
Knox, Robert, 212
Koṇḍañña. *See* Buddhas, eonic
Korea, 211; eye opening in, 216, 221; image consecration in, 218
Kosala, 15, 16, 17, 21
*Kosala-Bimba-Vaṇṇanā* (KBV), 11, 15, 16, 17, 21, 22, 23, 24, 29, 30, 41, 72, 114, 115, 129, 180, 187, 221, 252n.33
Kosambī, 20, 21, 22, 253 nn. 50 and 59
Kraisī Nimmānhemin, 96
Kū'nā, King, 38, 196
Kuṣāna, 26, 29, 192
Kusināra, 147, 148

*Lalitavistara,* 124, 127, 278 nn. 31, 40, 41, 279 nn. 44 and 45
Lamotte, Étienne, 280n.12
Lampāng, 124, 205, 208
Lamphūn, 33, 34, 35, 44, 120, 196, 198; Queen Cāma of, 237
Lancaster, Lewis, 28
Laos, 70, 121, 181, 186, 194, 215
Lawa, 267n.27; and buffalo sacrifice, 267n.27
Leclère, Adhémard, 181
life-extension rite, 49, 78, 85, 117. See also *sū'pchātā*
Lion Buddha Image, 5, 48, 55, 194, 195, 196, 267n.27, 288n.112; legend of, 40–41. *See also* Buddha image
Lohuizen-de-leeuw, J. E. van, 206, 254n.73; 288n.120
*lokapāla. See* guardians
lovingkindness. See *mettā*
Luang Pho Sawat, 235
Luang Prabang, 252n.33
Luang Pū Lā, 100, **101, 106,** 118–19
Luang Pū Wāen, 119; relics of, 119–20; 275n.138.
Lumbinī, 130, 138

McCallum, Donald, 18–19
*madhupāyāsa* (sweetened milk rice), 82, 102, 104, 107, 199; offered to Buddha images, **103,** 226; preparation of, **103**; as symbol of first feeding, 82, 102; Sujātā's offering of, 102, 104, 132, 146, 164, 179
Mādhyamika, 112–13
Magadha, 193, 205
Māgha Pūjā, 49
Mahākassapa, Thera, 150, 163, 206
Mahāmāya, 130, 138, 139, 145
Mahāmūni image, 221, 231, 271n.63. *See also* Buddha image
*Mahāparinibbāna Sutta,* 3–4, 23, 36, 107, 114, 123, 128, 129, 187, 193, 221, 237, 247, 251n.30, 265n.7, 279n.54. See also *Sutta*
*mahāpuriṣa* (great person), 15, 37, 130, 139; eighty marks of, 72, 188; thirty-two marks of, 189, 190, 192
*Mahāvagga,* 99, 122, 258n.34; 278n.35
*Mahāvaṃsa,* 23, 116, 192, 212, 267n.25
*Mahāvastu,* 124, 127, 277n.24
Mahāvihāra, 70, 116
Mahāyāna, 13, 21, 25, 112, 117, 176, 186, 188, 193, 216, 219, 221, 223, 231
*Mālālaṅkāravatthu,* 124, 127, 258n.32, 276n.11, 279n.54
Malalasekera, G. P., 274n.118, 290n.3
Mālikā, 149, 150, 151, 279n.54
Mallas, 147, 148, 149, 150
*maṇḍala,* 36, **82,** 176, 218, 221, 222, 223
Mangrai, King, 196, 237
*Maṅgala Udāna Gāthā.* See *gāthā*
Manī Phayomyong, xv, 117; 258n.37, 267 nn. 21, 23, 26; on *sū'pchātā,* 267n.27, 275n.2
*mantra,* 63, 70, 93, 94, 117, 121, 138, 185, 189, 213, 220, 233, 261n.22, 274n.116; and *gāthā,* 260n.12; and image consecration, 69, 80

*Manual for Making a Buddha Image,* 46, 50, 69, 70, 71, 72, 185
Māra, 5, 81, 136, 139, 156, 160, 164, 167, 171, 206, 226, 276n.15; attack on Buddha by, 126, 133, 176, 278n.28; Buddha's victory over, 42, 65, 91, 127, 147, 163, 169, 172, 175, 199, 204; daughters of, 126; five forms of, 134, 207, 278n.33, 290n.135; temptation of Buddha by, 131, 143, 144; and Upagutta, 24, 59, 60, 69, 111, 124, 258n.38
Mathurā, 25, 26, 27, 192, 253 nn. 50 and 59
Matics, K. I., 259n.43
Mauss, Marcel, 111
meditation, 73, 99, **100,** 115, 117, 157, 159; *bhāvanā,* 100; Buddha's achievement of, 216; insight, 152, 153, 155, 156; *kammaṭṭhāna,* 189, 268n.35; *mettābhāvāna,* 63, 73; and mindfulness of breathing, 152, 156, 157, 164, 165; and monks, 119, 120, 121; performative power of, 99, 100; *plūk sek,* 119, 248; *samādhi,* 72, 81, 120, 155, 214, 242; *samatha kammaṭṭhāna,* 165; terms for, 270n.61; *vipassanāñāṇa,* 142, 153, 155, 159, 166; visualization, 223, 224; in Yogāvacara tradition, 72. See also *jhānas*
mental intoxicants. See *āsava*
merit and merit making (*tham phun*), 17, 20, 23, 24, 27, 28, 46, 60, 61, 68, 72, 104, 147, 180, 243; in blessing texts, 72; and demerit, 161, 162; of five *bodhisatta*s, 202; rituals of, 42, 181, 271n.68; and the white crow, 200, 201, 202, 203
meritorious blessing. See *ānisaṃsa*
Meru, Mount, 15, 170. *See also* Sumeru, Mount
*mettā,* 91, 116, 117, 119, 120, 121; of Buddha, 128; of Luang Pū Lā, 119; of Luang Pū Wāen, 120; of Khrūbā Phrohm, 121; *-bhāvana,* 63, 73; and *paritta,* 117
Metteyya Buddha, 5, 124, 137, 176, 181, 197, 201, 204
microcosm/macrocosm. *See* polarities
*Milindapañho,* 83, 187, 257n.30, 272n.79
mimetic reenactment, 191, 224, 230; of Buddha's enlightenment, 79, 152, 185, 214, 294n.78; of ordination, 97, 98; of Sujātā's offering, 82, 102, **103,** 104
mirror, 54, 81, 82, 104, 213, 214, 220; in consecration ritual, 221; and divination, 221–22; as symbol of knowledge, 81, 266n.13; and Tibetan ritual, 220
Moggallāna, 92, 261, 270n.62
Mongkut, King, 237
monk(s), 10, 92–100, 211, 232; Buddha surrogates, as, 102, 152; charismatic, 100–101, **101,** 118–121, 152, 156, 197, 232, 235; *dhutaṅga,* 120, 121; relics of, 119–20; Sinhala order of, 38
Mucalinda. See *nāga*
Mūlasārvāstivāda, 263n.41, 276n.3
Mus, Paul, 35, 37, 111, 225, 287n.104
mutual gaze, 16, 18, 22, 24
Myanmar (Burma), 70, 181, 205; image consecration in, 218–19

*nāga* (*nāk*), 26, 41, 99, 136, 146, 227; as image maker, 194; Kalana, 126, 132, 134; Mahākāḷa, 84, 85, 98; Mucalinda, 44, 98, 135; as ordinand, 97–98; transformation of, 98–99
Nāgasena, 194
Nālandā, 237
*nām mon* (consecrated water), 49, 80, 93, 94, 99, 107, 119, 120
*ñāṇa* (knowledge, mental powers), 97, 155
Narayan, Vasudha, 233
narrative and Buddha image, 38, 230–31
never-returner, 137, 155, 160, 167, 188
*nibbāna,* 82, 127, 142, 153, 203, 205; Buddhadāsa on, 245; as Emerald City, 136, 137, 147, 148; and image and relic, 20, 22, 129, 190; and meditation 152; and *nāga,* 84; seekers of, 28, 108
*Nidānakathā,* 122, 123–124, 127, 129, 177, 178, 197, 278 nn. 37 and 38, 279 nn. 44, 45, 51
Norman, K. R, 252n.44
Nyanaponika Thera, 280n.3

omniscience. See *sabbaññutāñāṇa*
once-returner, 137, 155, 160, 167, 168, 188
ordination, 78, 97, 127; 270n.56, 290n.139; and image consecration, 97, 122–23, as interpreted by Tambiah, 99; as reenactment of Siddhattha's renunciation, 97–98; and spirit calling, 98; as transformation, 98

Pagan, 70, 176, 282n.8
Pandey, Rajbali, 266n.18
*Paññāsajātaka,* 182, 279n.54; 283n.33
Paramānuchit–chinōrot, Somdet Krom Phra, 124, 183, 279n.52
*pāramī,* 79, 97, 102, 125, 131, 156, 164, 178, 190; and Buddha image, 190; and Buddhahood, 224; of generosity, 164; power of, 226, 229; seven, 282n.17; ten, 16, 91, 225, 228, 277n.20; thirty, 130, 133, 138, 139, 156–57, 277n.20
*parinibbāna,* 13, 23, 26, 28, 30, 124,127, 129, 148, 229, 247; and relics, 123, 125, 186; and the Buddha's absence, 187
*paritta,* 42, 48, 49, 50, 63, 70, 80, 88–90, 114–118, 265n.9, 273n.114, 274n.120; *Aṅgulimāla,* 90, 116; *Āṭānāṭiya,* 90, 261n.24; *Aṭṭhavīsati Buddha,* 90; *Catubhāṇavārapāli,* 115, 261n.24; *Dhajagga,* 90, 92, 116; and *gāthā;* 260n.12; *Jinapañjara Gāthā,* 90, 92, 261n.24, 269n.44; *Khanda,* 89, 90, 92, 116; *Mora,* 90, 92, 116, 261n.24; *Pirit-pota,* 115, 116; as prelude to image consecration, 90–92; Thai collections of, 89; *Unhassavijaya* 262n.25; *Vattaka,* 261n.22. See also *Sutta*
*paritta* cord. See *sāi siñcana*
Pasenadi, King, 11, 15, 16, 17, 18, 19, 20, 21, 22, 29, 30
path and fruit (*magga/phala*), 136, 137
*Paṭhama Sambodhi.* See *Pathom Somphōt*
*Pathom Somphōt* (PS) [The Buddha's Supreme Enlightenment], 4, 96, 97, 122, 123, 124, 125, 126, 127, 146, 266n.11, 277n.17; analysis of, 125–27; Buddha's enlightenment in, 129–37
*Pathom Somphōt Lānnā* (PSL), 125, 126, 127
*Pathom Somphōt Thet* (PST), 125, 126, 127
*paṭicca samuppāda* (interdependent co-arising), 14, 135, 153, 154, 159, 161, 166, 218, 280n.12, 281n.20
*paṭimokkha,* 32, 33, 25
Payne, Richard, 224
Payutto, P. A., 238, 247, 248, 266n.12, 296n.12; career of, 238–39; lecture by, 239–42.
Peirce, Charles, 19, 191, 252n.39
Penth, Hans, 260n.9
perfections. See *pāramī*
perfumed chamber. See *gandhakuṭī*
Phaitun Dokbuakaew, xv, 263n.45
Phra Buddha Sihiṅg. *See* Lion Buddha Image
Phra Mālai, 5, 63, 198, 263n.44, 289n.127
Phra Setaṅgamaṇī. *See* White Crystal Buddha Image
Phrathāt Doi Suthep, Wat, **32,** 33, 38, **39,** 40, 266n.12; Buddha mural at, **32;** *chedī* at, 33, 44; pilgrimage at, 33
Phrathāt Haripuñjaya, Wat, 33, **34,** 35, 40, 41, 196, 198; diagram of, 34; structure of, 32
*phutthawāt* (*buddhavāsa*), 32, 33, 35, 40
pilgrimage, 25, 29, 30, 31, 33, 114–15, 123; Bodhgayā, 27, 28, 193, 195; Śrāvastī, 27–28, Sāṅkāśya, 27–28, 253n.53
polarities, 9, 16, 85–86, 112, 194, 214; birth/death, 82–83; conventional language/*dhamma* language, 244, 245; mundane/transmundane, 4, 85, 87, 101, 190, 201; microcosmic/macrocosmic, 35, 266n.19. *See also* absence and presence
Prachak, Phra Khrū, 268n.32, 269n.43
Premchit, Sommai, 251n.25, 258n.37
*puñña. See* merit and merit making

Rāhula, 126, 131, 142, 143, 277n.22
rains retreat, 122, 127, 137, 182
Rājagaha, 27, 144, 145; council of, 187; Stone Buddha Image and, 206, 207
*rājawat,* 50, 79, 80–83, 99, 152, 265n.7
*Ratanamālā,* 70
Ratanapaññana Thera, 40, 182, 258n.33, 287n.108
Ray, Reginald, 109
relics, 16, 20, 25, 113, 119, 123, 203; bodily, of Buddha, 23, 30, 38, 83, 87, 114, 127, 128, 129, 135, 151, 197, 204, 205; classification of, 30, 109; cult of, 23, 24, 36, 37, 112, 123; distribution of, 122, 129; as indexical sign, 38; *pāramī* of, 227; of saints, 87; and Stone Buddha, 206–7; Sumana Thera and, 38
Reynolds, Frank, E., 178, 186, 271n.64
*riak khwan. See* spirit calling
rite of passage, 102, 127

ritual: as performative, 85, 94, 104, 123, 152; as rite of passage, 102, 127; as shamanistic, 221. *See also* eye-opening ritual
ritualization, 69
rivers: Anomā, 131, 144, 157, 164; Ganges, 172, 199, 200, 202; Nerañjarā, 84, 132, 146, 157, 164, 179
Ruelius, Hans, 214, 291n.5
*rūpakāya,* 17, 64, 68, 96, 111, 112, 187, 214, 215, 226, 251n.30, 258n.34, 286n.86; analysis of, 185, 186; Ruelius on, 214; in Sarvāstivāda, 112; *yantra* and, 64
Ruppert, Brian, D., 257n.28

Sā, Supreme Patriarch, 124–25
*sabbaññutāñāṇa* (omniscience), 135, 137, 155, 156, 202
sacred cord. See *sāi siñcana*
sacred numbers: "56," 83, 84, 87; "108," 80, 82, 84, 100, 138, 139, 235, 265n.8, 291n.9; "84,000," 72, 87, 89, 111, 155, 177, 187, 189, 258n.38
sacred space: *wat* as, 31–45. See also *bodhimaṇḍa*; *rājawat*
Saddhatissa, Hammalawa, 116, 117, 273n.114
*sādhana,* 215, 222, 223, 294n.62
*sāi siñcana* (sacred cord, *paritta* cord), 42, 44, 49, 80, 90, 93, 99, 107, 119, 265 nn. 8 and 9
*sakadāgāmī. See* once-returner
Sakyamuni Buddha, 21, 46, 85, 109. *See also* Buddha
*samādhi. See* meditation
*Samantapāsādika,* 212, 265n.9
Sāñcī, 26, 176, 231
Sandalwood Buddha Image, 15, 16–22, 23 24, 62, 188, 253n.59. *See also* Buddha image
*saṅgkhawāt* (*saṅgkhavāsa*), 32, 33
Sanguan Chōtisukharat, 258n.37, 267n.26; on birth day Buddha images, 284n47; on *sū'pchātā,* 267n.27
Sanitsuda Ekachai, 235
Sāṅkāśya. *See* pilgrimage
Santi Asok, 6, 238, 246–48, 298n.35; and icon veneration, 247; and Phalang Dhamma Party, 246
Saraṇaṃkara, 71, 186
Sarvāstivāda, 21, 111, 112, 113, 115, 188, 272n.94
*Sāsanavaṃsa,* 116
scapegoat, 213–14, 218
Schober, Juliane, 231
Schopen, Gregory, 28, 108, 113–14, 215, 250n.14, 252n.32, 257n.27, 267n.2
Seriyōjī temple, 253n. 59
sermons (*desanā*), 96, 125, 137; at image consecration, 96, **97**
Setaṅgamaṇī, Phra. *See* White Crystal Buddha Image
Shan, 63, 69–70
Sharf, Robert, 109, 253n.57, 272n.77
Sheaf of Garlands of Epochs of the Conqueror. See *Jinakālāmālīpakaraṇaṃ*
Siddhattha, Prince: birth of 130; awakening of, 81, 216; marriage of, 131, 140, 142; miracles by 141–42, 157; *nāga* king and, 84; monastic ordination and, 98; renunciation of, 122, 128, 138–39, 144, 193, 226; temptation of, 145; testing of, 141–42; in Theravāda, 13–14
Siddhattha's Renunciation. See *Sitthāt Õk Buat*
sign: image as, 109; material; 16, 23, 33, 72, 109, 128; representational, 30, 35
sign, indexical, 19, 20; Buddha image as, 24, 38; relic as, 24, 38
*sīla* (ethical precepts), 73, 240, 241, 242, 247
sīmā (boundary stones), 33, 87; consecration of, 43
Singkha Wannasai, xv
Siṅgkuttara, Mount, 199, 201
Sirisadhammaraṃsi, 265n.3, 281n.23
*Sitthāt Õk Buat,* xv, 97, 122, 123, 124, 127, 128, 129, 138–51
Skilling, Peter, 197, 274n.116
Sommai Premchit, xv
*songkrān* (Thai New Year), 85, 176, 194, 195, 196, 198, 267n.27
*sotāpanna. See* stream-enterer
Sottiya, 81, 126, 132, 146, 157, 164
spirits (*khwan*), 98, 117, 240
spirit calling (*riak khwan*), 96, 97, 98, 270n.55
Śrāvastī, 27, 28, 253 nn. 50 and 59
Sri Lanka, 13, 16, 24, 32, 35, 110–11, 115–116, 183; eye opening ceremony in, 212–14, 218; Lion Buddha Image, and,

Sri Lanka (*continued*)
40–41; *pirit* in, 93, 115, 116; Stone Buddha Image, and, 205, 207; *stūpa* and relic cult in, 37, 38, 112; twenty-four Buddhas in, 180; Yogāvacara tradition in, 71, 186
Stein, Otto, 285n.73
Stone Buddha Image, 38, 194, 196, 197, 205–10; worship of, 207–8
Strahan, Donna K., 259n.5
stream-enterer (*sotāpanna*), 63, 116, 137, 155, 159, 166, 168, 188, 205
Strong, John, 111, 112, 113, 114; 258n.38, 271n.68, 272n.94, 273n.100; 289 nn. 128 and 129, 291n.12
Stuart-Fox, Martin, 280n.4
*stūpa,* 35, 72, 108, 112, 191; at Anurādhapura, 37; at Bodnath, 220; as Buddha body, 36, 37; and cosmology, 36; as *dhamma* body, 36, 37; "84,000," 72, 111, 187, 189; as icon, 191; as reliquary, 36; as world mountain, 36. *See also* Bhārhut; *cetiya*; *chedī*; Sāñcī
Suan Mokkhabalārāma (Suan Mokkha), Wat, 242, 243, 245
*suat bōek. See* chant
*Suat Bōek Phranet* (SBN), xv, 94, 95, 96, 152, 155, 156, 164, 171
*suat mon. See* chant
Suddhodana, King, 129, 130, 138, 139, 140, 141, 145, 278n.42
Sujātā, 5, 82, 102, **103,** 104, 126, 131–32, 146, 157, 164, 179, 271n.65; *dāna* by, **32,** 102
Sukhōthai 35, 38,194, 237, 262n.28
Sumana Thera, 33, 38
Sumedha, 126, 178, 179, 180
Sumeru, Mount, 137, 148. *See also* Meru, Mount
*śunyatā* (emptiness), 219, 221, 222, 223
*sū'pchātā,* 49, 85, 117, 262n.25. *See also* life-extension rite
Suthep, Mount, 33, 38, 44, 196
*Sutta*(s): *Aggañña,* 188, 192; *Ahirāja,* 260n.15; *Ariyapariyesanā,* 217, 280n.6; *Bhayabherava,* 153; *Cakkavatti Sīhanāda,* 279n.48; *Ghaṭīkāra,* 289n.130; *Karaṇīyamettā,* 89, 90, 116; 261n.19; *Lakkhaṇa,* 72; 176, 177, 178, 183, 197; *Mahāsaccaka,* 122, 217, 280n.5; *Mahāsamaya,* 54, 90; *Mahāsuddassana,* 279n48; *Maṅgala,* 54, 89, 90, 93, 116, 219, 262n.32; *Mettā,* 92, 219, 261n.24; *Ratana,* 89, 90, 92, 93, 116, 219, 261n.24; *Samaññaphala,* 154; *Sutta Nipāta,* 24, 279n.50. See also *Dhammacakkappavattana Sutta*; *Mahāparinibbāna Sutta*; *paritta*
Suvaṇṇabhūmi, 198, 199
Swearer, Donald K., 249n. 13, 251n.25, 254n.65, 259n.39, 265n.5, 286n.86, 298n.35
syncretization, 224, 230; in Khmer image consecration 225–26

Tambiah, Stanley J., 99, 110, 265n.5, 266n.14, 270n.59, 296n.6; on indexical icon, 252n.42; on *paritta,* 269n.45
*tamnān* (chronicle), 38, 60, 123, 231; *Doi Ang Salūng* 254n.65; *Kā Phū'ak,* xv, 176, 182, 197, 198; 288n.124, 289 nn. 128 and 129; *Phra Kāewkhāw* (*Setaṅgamaṇī*), 289n.133; *Phra Silā,* 176, 205–10, 289 nn. 128 and 129
*Tamrā Kān Kosāng Phraphuttharūp.* See *Manual for Making a Buddha Image*
Tannenbaum, Nicola, 69, 70
Tantrayāna, 70, 93, 219–20, 225, 231; deity yoga in, 22–24; Dge-lugs-pa tradition and, 222; eye opening ritual in, 215–16, 218; *maṇḍala* visualization in, 224; *rab gnas,* 222; *stūpa* consecration in, 219, 220–21
Tapussa, 127, 135, 199
Tāranātha, 27
*tathāgata,* 83, 128
tattoos, 70; Five Buddhas type of, 69
Tāvatiṃsa Heaven, 20, 21, 22, 27, 144, 145, 151, 171, 196, 253 nn. 47 and 53
temple-monastery. See *wat*
Thanissaro Bhikkhu, 20, 252n.45, 269n.40, 275n.132, 280n.3
*Theragāthā,* 184, 252n. 44
Theravāda, 13, 14, 16, 32, 38, 115, 123, 183, 188, 225, 231; chant in, 270n.53; eonic Buddhas in, 176, 179, 180, 181, 182, 183; five Buddhas in, 197–205; Mahāvihāra in, 70, 116; *paritta* texts in, 89, 115–16, 219; view of time in, 183
*thewadā* (*devatā*), 44, 49, 88, 157; and Buddha image cult, 226; at the Buddha's

birth, 130; at the Buddha's death, 148; at the Buddha's enlightenment, 132, 134, 135, 172; at the Buddha's renunciation, 143, 144; and image maker, 69; as tree deity, 56, 121, 145, 146
Thomas, Edward, J., 277n.24
Thompson, Lawrence G., 223
Thoranī, Nang, 126, 133, 146, 172
three characteristics of existence, 155, 156, 159, 160, 161, 166, 167, 168
three knowledges, 81, 134
Tilokarāja, King, 194, 195, 196, 205, 209
Tō, Somdet Phuthāchān, 261n.24, 269n.44
Trainor, Kevin, 19, 23, 36, 37, 38, 112–13, 256n.11, 257 nn. 23, 30, 31
*trikāya*. *See* Buddha bodies
Triple Gem, 68, 69, 71, 86–87, 116, 182, 241, 260n.17
Tucci, Giuseppe, 211, 218, 224, 225, 291n.10
two truths, 219, 223

Udayana, King, 20, 21, 22, 253n.59
Upagutta, Phra (Upagupta, Upakut), 50; and Buddha, 111, 112; in *Divyāvadāna*, 24; and Māra, 124, 125; offerings to, 225; as Phra Bua Khem, 288n.110; as protector, 42, 58–61, 69, 258n.38
*upekkhā* (equanimity), 153, 158
Uruvela Kassapa, 155, 163

Vaiśālī, 36. *See also* Vesali
Van Buitenen, J.A.B., 281n.2
Vajrayāna, 69, 224, 225; *dhyāni* Buddhas in, 176
Vārāṇasī, 27, 28, 123, 124, 127, 136, 163, 169
Veda/Vedism, 36, 70, 225; *Puruṣa Sukta*, 71–72
Vesali, 60, 116. *See also* Vaiśālī
Vessantara, Prince, 5, 122, 125, 130, 133, 138, 163, 164, 170, 177, 178; *dāna* given by, 157, 198
*Vessantara Jātaka*, 94, 155, 163, 198
Victor's Cage (*Jinapañjara*). See *paritta*
*Vinaya*, 3, 116
Vipassī. *See* Buddhas, eonic
Visākha Pūjā, 45, 77
*Visuddhimagga*, 71, 188, 192, 271n.71, 278n.36

von Hinüber, Oskar, 260n.17; 283n.39

Waghorne, Joanne Punzo, 234
Walters, Jonathan, S., 251n.44, 281n.4
Wannasi, Singkha, xv, 263n.43
*wat*(s) (temple-monastery) 12, 31–45, 260n.10; Ban Nōi 137; Benchamabophit, 78; Chedī Luang, 119, 194, 196, 251n.26; Chet Yot, 100, 183, 194, 195, 265n.4; Chetuphon, 118; Chiang Man, 176, 196, 288n.119; 290n.142; Chiang Thong, 252n.33; Doi Māepang, 120; Duang Dī, 281n.18; Lai Hin, 124, 169, 281n.24; Māe Takhrai, 49; Mū'ang Man, xv, **2, 80, 84, 97, 103, 105, 106**; Mū'n Lān, 268n.32, 269n.43; Nanthārām, 89; Pā Daeng, 209, 290n.141; Pā Pāeng, **100, 101,** 265n.4; Pā Sao, 44; Pā Tu'ng , 118, 119; Pākkong, 281n.24; Phra Kāew, **78, 95,** 251n.26, 265n.4; Phra Phirain, 238; Phra Singh, 195; Phraphutthabāttākphā,**10,** 11, 120, 225n.1; *poy luang* festival at, 42, 43, 46, 50, 60, 78; Sāen Fāng, 268n.32, 269n.43; Sangtho, 119; Suan Dok, 38, 209, 290n.142; translation of the term, 256n.2; Tung Yū, 288n.124, 289 nn. 125 and 131. *See also* Phrathāt Doi Suthep, Wat; Phrathāt Haripuñjaya, Wat; Suan Mokkhabalārāma, Wat
water lustration. See *nām mon*
water pouring ritual, **106,** 107
Wayman, Alex, 220, 221
Wells, Kenneth E., 259n.40, 265n.5; on Thai chant, 275n.130; on Thai *paritta*, 269n.41
White Crow, Chronicle of. See *tamnān, Kā Phū'ak*
White Crystal Buddha Image, 196, 288 nn. 119 and 120; chronicle of, 289n.133
*wihān* (*vihāra*/image hall), 45, 49, 50, 72; atmosphere of during image consecration, 90; consecration of, 43, 44, 58; as site of image consecration, 79
Woodward, Hiram, W., 37, 256n.4, 264n.50
Woodward, Mark R., 191, 287n.95

Xuanzang (Hsüan-tsang), 20, 22, 110–11, 112, 176, 193, 221, 254n.65

*yakkha/yakṣa,* 25, 26, 134, 192, 227
*yantra,* **51,** 52, 69, 70, 71, 185, 212–13, 235, 263n.47, 263n.48, 264n.62; and *bodhimaṇḍa,* 80; diagrams of, 65–66; "skip" type of, 64; in *Yan Phraphuttharūp,* 63–68
Yasa, 155, 163
Yasodharā, 123, 131, 140, 142, 143, 278n.43. *See also* Bimbā
*ye dharmā* formula, 197, 206, 219–20
*yi-dam* (chosen Buddha), 222, 223
Yogācāra, 71, 72, 186, 220
Yogāvacara, 71, 264n.49, 285n.61

Zen, 83, 215
Zenkōji Temple, 18

## BUDDHISMS:

## A PRINCETON UNIVERSITY PRESS SERIES

*Becoming the Buddha: The Ritual of Image Consecration in Thailand*,
by Donald K. Swearer

*The Impact of Buddhism on Chinese Material Culture*,
by John Kieschnick

*The Power of Denial: Buddhism, Purity, and Gender*,
by Bernard Faure

*Neither Monk nor Layman: Clerical Marriage in Modern Japanese Buddhism*,
by Richard M. Jaffe

*Buddhist Learning and Textual Practice in Eighteenth-Century Lankan Monastic Culture*,
by Anne M. Blackburn

*The Red Thread: Buddhist Approaches to Sexuality*,
by Bernard Faure